INTRODUCTION TO INTERACTIVE PROGRAMMING ON THE INTERNET
Using HTML & JavaScript

KU-586-975

INTRODUCTION TO INTERACTIVE PROGRAMMING ON THE INTERNET
Using HTML & JavaScript

DR. CRAIG D. KNUCKLES
Lake Forest College, IL

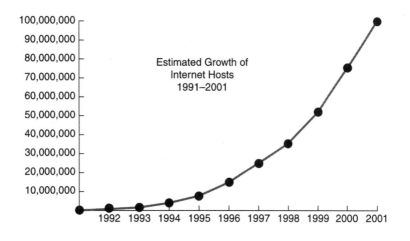

Estimated Growth of
Internet Hosts
1991–2001

JOHN WILEY & SONS, INC.

Acquisitions Editor	*Paul Crockett*
Marketing Manager	*Katherine Hepburn*
Senior Production Editor	*Petrina Kulek*
Illustration Coordinator	*Anna Melhorn*
Cover Illustrator	*Jane Marinsky/SIS*

This book was set in *Times Roman* by *Bi-Comp Inc.* and printed and bound by *Malloy Lithographing.* The cover was printed by *Lehigh Press.*

The book is printed on acid-free paper. ∞

Copyright © 2001 John Wiley & Sons, Inc. All rights reserved.

No part of this publication may be reproduced, stored in a retrieval system or transmitted in any form or by any means, electronic, mechanical, photocopying, recording, scanning or otherwise, except as permitted under Sections 107 or 108 of the 1976 United States Copyright Act, without either the prior written permission of the Publisher, or authorization through payment of the appropriate per-copy fee to the Copyright Clearance Center, 222 Rosewood Drive, Danvers, MA 01923, (978) 750-8400, fax (978) 750-4470. Requests to the Publisher for permission should be addressed to the Permissions Department, John Wiley & Sons, Inc., 111 River Street, Hoboken, NJ 07030, (201) 748-6011, fax (201) 748-6008, E-Mail: PERMREQ@WILEY.COM.

To order books or for customer service please, call 1(800)-CALL-WILEY (225-5945).

Library of Congress Cataloging in Publication Data:
Knuckles, Craig D.
    Introduction to interactive programming on the internet : using HTML & Javascript / Craig D. Knuckles.
        p.   cm.
    ISBN 0-471-38366-X (pbk. : alk. paper)
    1. Internet programming.   2. HTML (Document markup language)   3. JavaScript (Computer program language) I. Title.
    QA76.625 .K58   2000
    005.7′2—dc21   00-043555

Printed in the United States of America

10   9   8   7   6   5   4

This book is dedicated to my wife, Hope, and my new daughter, Katy,
without whom I would have slept more, but written less.

It is also dedicated to my parents, Otis and Rossie Knuckles,
whose encouragement and support enabled my 23 years of formal education and
continuing academic career.

PREFACE

Origins

Prior to the summer of 1998, the Academic Innovations Group at Lake Forest College called for proposals for new and innovative courses. My proposal called for a "from the ground up" introduction to programming using the Internet. Perhaps the most significant of the proposed features was that the course was to be accessible to a general audience, including students majoring in the Arts, Humanities, and Social Sciences. While general audience computer science courses exist, they are primarily geared toward computer literacy, rather than toward fostering any significant programming skills.

The proposal being accepted, I set out to find a suitable text from which to base the course. On the lower end, I found "Internet literacy" texts. These texts spend whole chapters on topics such as e-mail, news groups, and searching the Internet. But these are the skills that more and more students emerging from high school already possess. On the upper end, programming texts in languages like C++ and Java abound, but these are geared toward computer science majors. Indeed, such courses often turn unsuspecting general audience students off from computer science, rather than providing a gateway. In reality, students often find such courses more difficult than calculus.

Fitting into the middle, and suited perfectly toward the general audience, is HTML and JavaScript. All the publications I found relating to these topics were reference-type books, not constructed in such a manner to support a college course. So, during the summer of 1998, I wrote a 250-page manuscript from which to base the new course. While teaching from the manuscript during both semesters of the '98–'99 academic year, I developed a final vision for the book based upon what worked and what didn't. Student input was instrumental in formulating the final plan.

Upon the strength of the course-tested proposal, I secured a contract with John Wiley & Sons, Inc. in the summer of 1999. The text you now see was written during the '99–'00 academic year, again while refining it in the classroom setting both semesters. Thus, this book is the culmination of two full years of classroom testing. The course has gained significant popularity on campus among both the general audience and the science majors. In fact, large waiting lists have resulted in additional sections being opened. Popularity has even grown beyond the student base, with other professors and secretaries taking the course. I have even received comments from my students' parents who like the book, and have found its contents valuable.

Who Should Read this Book?

The answer is simple. Anyone who wishes to arm themselves for the 21st century with substantive Internet programming skills. In short, this book covers the "nuts and bolts" of programming on the Internet. To skillfully publish information on the Internet, one must gain a proficiency with HTML and web page construction. To process information one must learn programming fundamentals. This book provides the fundamentals that one must learn in order to pursue virtually any other programming endeavor on the Internet. It is important to learn the fundamentals now so that one has the tools necessary to learn newer, emerging technologies as they become more commonplace. Simply put, this book contains those core fundamentals.

The book assumes no prior knowledge of HTML or a programming language. The prerequisite skills can be summed up succinctly. As far as the computer goes, the reader should be familiar with word processing, creating, and organizing documents. On the Internet side, the reader should be familiar with surfing the Internet with a browser.

That gives considerable latitude. Advanced high school students would be equipping themselves well by arming themselves with the skills presented in this book. Anyone in a general collegiate audience would be remiss if he or she were to graduate without possessing these skills. Anyone in the professional setting wishing to be better equipped for the Internet revolution will find the skills fostered in this book indispensable. In short, if you know how to use a computer, and wish to develop your skills further in the Internet environment, you should read this book.

The reader who has some knowledge of programming will certainly find the HTML skills useful. Moreover, the reader with some knowledge of a compiled language like C++ will find the portable, interpreted JavaScript language a refreshing change, especially given the natural graphic user interface that HTML forms provide for user input. The only audience to which we would not recommend this book, is that of the professional programmer. Indeed, the highly skilled programmer may be better suited reading a professional reference book on HTML, and one on JavaScript.

Outstanding Features

- The book is designed to be platform independent. This means that the reader can use virtually any type of personal computer. All that is required is a basic text editor, which any computer provides, and a relatively current web browser, which can be downloaded for free. Thus, it is not required that the reader purchase any software. The HTML and JavaScript coverage sticks to a subset of the languages which will work on any version 3 or higher of the Netscape or Internet Explorer browsers. Moreover, other emerging browser types also support this common subset of HTML and JavaScript, and on virtually any computer type.

- The book introduces programming with objects. The Document Object Model and HTML form objects provide a perfect setting for using objects. So, not only does this book foster a proficiency for using conventional programming structures (variables, decisions, functions, arrays, and loops), but also provides a gentle introduction to objects. The book is, thus, a perfect introduction for anyone wishing to learn an object oriented programming language such as Java.

- The book covers the basics of web server accounts and transferring documents web servers. It also covers strategies for maintaining and updating a web site on the server. However, if a web server account is not available to the reader, those topics can be omitted with no difficulties whatsoever.

- Each of the 18 lessons features a summary, review questions, and exercises. The exercises feature both stand alone exercises, and two project threads that run throughout the book. The project threads guide the reader through the construction of a structured web site—a site that eventually evidences all of those skills acquired through reading this book. The first project thread, which features development of a personal web site, is also ideal for someone who wishes to read this book, but is not formally enrolled in a course.

- The book contains several optional sections that may be used to provide an extra challenge for the more advanced reader. Often, a general audience contains a variety of backgrounds. The optional material provides extra latitude for confronting that challenge.

- The book is fully supported by a web site.

The Web Site

- The web site contains all of the examples and figures of the book for use in classroom demonstration. Moreover, the interactive nature of many of the examples warrants such on-line access so that a true feel for the examples can be realized. The web site also features reference to many on-line materials, such as freeware and shareware applications, that can be used as valuable tools while developing the material of this book.

- Some of the exercises are inextricably bound to the web site. For example, the reader may be asked to incorporate downloadable materials from the web site into the pages they construct, or may be asked to approximately duplicate a page pictured on the site. For another example, some exercises in Lesson 18, require the reader to submit HTML form data to a CGI program on the web site. The web site also provides a perfect place to provide newly designed and updated exercises, making the text a continually evolving instructional resource.

- The book contains reference appendices for both of HTML elements, and JavaScript objects. These are valuable in a reference capacity after the course is completed. Moreover, HTML and JavaScript are constantly evolving. So, as new features become uniformly supported on all web browsers, the web site will be updated with supplements to the reference appendices. In this way, the text will remain current in a reference capacity.

- The solutions to the exercises are available to instructors via a password protected web site.

Coverage Overview

Lesson 1 gives a brief history of the Internet, and covers the fundamentals about how the Internet and World Wide Web work. The Internet is explained in terms of IP addresses, servers, routers, and packets. The World Wide Web is explained in terms of the URL, Web protocols, and domain names. In the process, a basic foundation of Internet vocabulary is developed.

Lesson 2 begins to explore the various types of transactions on the Internet. This includes transfering web pages to browsers for viewing (http), transferring web pages to web servers so that they are available on the Internet (ftp), and talking to web servers to set passwords (telnet). Lesson 2 also explores the nature of web server accounts and public directories. Much of this lesson may be omitted if web server accounts are not available.

Lessons 3 through 8 provide a conceptual introduction to HTML and web page construction. The coverage of HTML is not exhaustive, but sticks to a subset of HTML that works in virtually any browser. Moreover, topics such as audio and video are omitted in favor of the fundamental concepts. These core concepts are the syntax of tags and attributes, linking and site structure, various uses of images, and page formatting with tables and frames. Mastery of these concepts provides a perfect graphical user interface for the last ten lessons of the book in which JavaScript programming is used to support HTML forms and web pages. While Lesson 7 mentions the virtues of HTML editors, use of an editor remains optional throughout the remainder of the book. But when an editor is adopted, the core concepts presented in Lessons 3 through 8 are precisely those needed to skillfully use it.

Lesson 3 explores construction of web pages using basic HTML tags. The basic syntax of HTML is introduced.

Lesson 4 explores use of attributes in HTML tags to more precisely control HTML markup instructions. In the process, pixels, hexadecimal colors, and fonts are discussed. (Appendix C provides full detail on hexadecimal color representations.) Lesson 4 also includes an optional section which introduces style sheets.

Lesson 5 explores hypertext links in web pages. Hierarchal and linear linking strategies for web collections are explored. With potentially larger collections of documents to deal with, Lesson 5 also introduces strategies updating a web site on a web server. Named anchors are also covered in detail.

Lesson 6 explores the nature of images, and their inclusion in web pages. In the process, different types of images are explored as well as different ways images can provide extra functionality in a web page. Lesson 6 concludes with an optional section which covers image maps.

Lesson 7 first covers lists, and then turns to the more important notion of HTML tables. In particular, tables are used to provide entire layout structures for web pages.

Lesson 8 covers HTML frames as an alternative page layout mechanism. Here the differing functionalities of tables and frames are compared and contrasted.

The remainder of the book is dedicated to JavaScript. Again, to ensure full browser support, the book adheres to a standardized subset of JavaScript (and JScript). The goal is a marriage of programming theory and application. Indeed, the need for variables, decisions, functions, objects, loops, and arrays is motivated in a natural way using the graphical user interface that web pages and HTML forms provide. Throughout Lessons 9–18, the virtues of knowing HTML fundamentals are overtly manifested. Moreover, with the introduction to syntax and coding provided in Lessons 3–8 by HTML already in place, the transition to the rigors of actual programming is not overly arduous.

Lesson 9 provides an overview of HTML forms, and their role in obtaining input from the user. Moreover, Lesson 9 explores the nature of JavaScript and its roll in processing form data in the client-server model. This lesson also points out that JavaScript is not Java.

Lesson 10 formally introduces JavaScript and the use of variables to store user input. The complex HTML form object structure is not yet introduced, in favor of using the prompt box to obtain user input. The nature of writing programs and the types of potential programming errors are explored.

Lesson 11 explores the ability of JavaScript to make decisions based on user input, again obtained with prompt boxes. The decision-making capabilities are employed both to process information based on user input and to alert the user if improper information is supplied.

Lesson 12 introduces the nature and syntax of using objects in programming. This discussion has proven both valuable and necessary in the transition to using HTML forms to obtain user input. Several hands-on objects are introduced with the Document Object Model.

Lesson 13 turns to the use of HTML forms for obtaining user input. This lesson introduces the HTML input elements used for obtaining textual input, and using HTML form buttons for calling JavaScript functions to process the input. In the process, the concept of local vs. global variables is introduced. The theme of verifying that the user has entered proper input is further emphasized.

Lesson 14 augments the input capabilities of HTML forms by exploring checkboxes, radio buttons, and pull-down menus. These option-creating form elements further emphasize the decision-making capabilities of JavaScript. Moreover, Lesson 14 introduces the necessity for using arrays.

Lesson 15 explores repetition in programming using loops. The utility of looping is emphasized by the need to process larger HTML forms, but without undue redundant code. Looping over arrays of HTML form elements further explores using arrays—arrays of objects.

Lesson 16 covers the manual creation of arrays, and their utility. The arrays used prior to this lesson are created automatically when a browser loads an HTML form. One of the main applications of self-defined arrays presented in Lesson 16 involves pre-loading images from the server. The pre-loaded arrays of images are used for purposes such as cycling image displays in web pages.

Lesson 17 explores creating self-defined functions that use parameters. The reader will have been creating self-defined functions since Lesson 13, but ones without formal parameters. Applications of the detailed discussion on functions include creating image rollovers in web pages, and creating functions to aid in verification of the validity of user input into HTML forms. To augment form verification, the String object is also introduced.

Lesson 18, the final Lesson of the book, introduces the security capabilities of JavaScript and the password form element. JavaScript's security weaknesses are discussed, together with the associated necessity for submitting HTML form data to the server. The submit button is explored, and hidden form elements are employed to facilitate the submission of "cleaned up" form data to the server. No server-side programming is introduced. Rather, the existence of server-side programs is assumed, and the nature of the client-server model (as introduced in Lesson 9) is further explored. Several examples and exercises feature the submission of form data to server-side Perl programs on the web site for this book.

For the Instructor: Dependency and Organization

The following diagram indicates how the Lessons depend upon previous ones in terms of necessity of coverage.

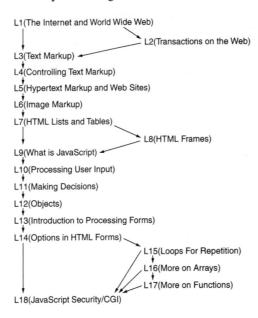

```
L1(The Internet and World Wide Web)
    |                              L2(Transactions on the Web)
    ↓
L3(Text Markup)
    ↕
L4(Controlling Text Markup)
    ↕
L5(Hypertext Markup and Web Sites)
    ↕
L6(Image Markup)
    ↕
L7(HTML Lists and Tables)
    |                              L8(HTML Frames)
    ↓
L9(What is JavaScript)
    ↕
L10(Processing User Input)
    ↕
L11(Making Decisions)
    ↕
L12(Objects)
    ↕
L13(Introduction to Processing Forms)
    ↕
L14(Options in HTML Forms)
    |                              L15(Loops For Repetition)
    |                                   ↕
    |                              L16(More on Arrays)
    |                                   ↕
    |                              L17(More on Functions)
    ↓
L18(JavaScript Security/CGI)
```

The book has been designed for flexibility of coverage. A course for the most general of audiences requires significant time and detail in Lessons 1 through 8, perhaps half a semester. Such general audiences are not only learning HTML, but bolstering their general computer skills. The goal is then to cover Lessons 9 through 14, and Lesson 18 if time permits. This provides a gentle introduction to programming and using objects. The end product is a feel for programming and an understanding of the nature and capabilities of HTML forms.

If it is desirable to cover programming in more detail, the HTML lessons can be covered more quickly, perhaps in a third of a semester. This level of coverage is appropriate for a more advanced audience or one with some prior knowledge of constructing web pages.

At any point after Lesson 14, Lesson 18 can be covered as a fitting capstone for the course. In this way, as many (or all) of the desired programming concepts can be covered. The end product is a proficiency with programming fundamentals and a comprehensive grasp of the capabilities of JavaScript as used to support web pages and HTML forms.

Upon a cursory inspection, it might appear that the book jumps around a bit in terms of covering programming fundamentals. The first draft of this book did, in fact, feature a more detailed coverage of structures such as loops and arrays, before objects and HTML forms were introduced. Several reviewers commented that this approach failed to let the true flavor of JavaScript come through until very late in the text. The JavaScript presentation was analogous to that of a Pascal text, for example. With the added burden of early presentation of more programming structures, it was difficult to do justice to HTML forms in the allocated time of one semester. Indeed, that approach didn't work as well with the most general audience. The students left with a feel for programming, but little feel for objects, HTML forms, and the practical capabilities of JavaScript.

The organization of the current text, as seen above, has proven highly successful. Not only does the approach offer significantly more latitude in terms of structuring courses for varying audiences, but it ensures coverage of HTML forms and the flavor of JavaScript. A surprising by-product of this organization is that the concepts of functions, local variables, and arrays are covered in Lessons 10 through 14, but in a non-rigorous way. For example, it is necessary to handle user events by calling self-defined JavaScript functions, and to access HTML form elements using the elements[] array, which is created automatically by the browser. Lessons 15 through 17 then add rigor to these concepts in a natural way, and with practical applications. Finally, regardless of the extent of coverage, Lesson 18 provides a natural closure for the course.

Craig D. Knuckles

ACKNOWLEDGMENTS

First, I would like to thank professors Michael Ebner, Richard Mallette, and Carolyn Tuttle for their work on the academic innovations committee. Without that spark, my idea would likely not have kindled. Second, thanks go to professor David Yuen, who encouraged my ideas from the onset. Coming from someone with knowledge so pervasive that I consider him a mentor of sorts, the encouragement was particularly motivating. Professor Edward Packel also proved to have a valuable ear when I began musing about designing the course. Of course, I also extend thanks to professors Lowell Carmony, Robert Holliday, DeJuran Richardson, and Jill Van Newenhizen for their moral support along the way.

My sincerest gratitude goes to Bill Zobrist at Wiley for believing in this project and getting it off the ground. The fact that he got a promotion shortly after signing my book makes me aspire to deem myself partly responsible, although I'm sure it was merely a coincidence. In relief, Paul Crockett has been most helpful and proficient. I particularly appreciate his diplomacy in my attempt to put an Ozzy T-shirt on the guy on the cover of the book. Also, throughout the writing period and review stages, Jenny Welter was extremely helpful.

Instrumental in the reality that you are now reading a polished manuscript was Petrina Kulek. Coordinating the transformation of a rough work, replete with some hand drawn diagrams and myriad split verb infinitives just to name two shortcomings, is no small undertaking. Responsible for extricating the hapless adverbs from the aforementioned verb infinitives, and generally whipping my English into shape, was Katuna Avery. Her meticulousness is highly appreciated. Thanks is also extended to Anna Melhorn and the artists for rescuing my figures from the obscurity of being somewhat amorphis.

My professional peers at various universities, who reviewed the manuscript at several stages, are thanked profusely for their valuable suggestions and comments. Many of them will find evidence of their suggestions incorporated into this text.

My best buds, Steve Grodrian and Bryan Moore, are to be applauded for their long term fortitude in friendship. One of the few things you can count on in life is a true friend. Open palm on top of closed fist.

CONTENTS

LESSON 1   *THE INTERNET AND WORLD WIDE WEB*   **1**

1.1   The Internet   **1**
1.2   A Brief History of the Internet   **3**
1.3   Intranets   **4**
1.4   Controlling Traffic on the Internet (TCP/IP)   **5**
1.5   IP Addresses   **5**
1.6   Routers and Packets   **6**
1.7   The World Wide Web   **7**
1.8   The Internet vs. the World Wide Web   **10**
1.9   Named Addresses and Domains   **11**
1.10   Domain Name Servers   **12**
1.11   Domains and Web Servers   **12**
1.12   Web Server Accounts   **14**
1.13   Domain Suffixes   **15**
1.14   Summary   **16**
1.15   Review Questions   **17**
1.16   Exercises   **17**
1.17   Project Threads   **18**

LESSON 2   *TRANSACTIONS ON THE WEB*   **20**

2.1   Platform Independence   **20**
2.2   The HTML Document   **22**
2.3   The file Protocol   **23**
2.4   The http Protocol   **25**
2.5   The ftp Protocol vs. http   **28**
2.6   Public Directories on Web Servers   **31**
2.7   Web Servers and ftp   **33**
2.8   Hiding Directories on Web Servers   **37**
2.9   The telnet Protocol   **41**
2.10   Summary   **42**
2.11   Review Questions   **43**
2.12   Exercises   **44**
2.13   Project Threads   **44**

LESSON 3   *TEXT MARKUP*   **45**

3.1   HTML Tags and Document Structure   **46**
3.2   Container Elements   **49**
3.3   Formatting Text   **50**

3.4   Horizontal and Vertical Space   **52**
3.5   Header Elements   **54**
3.6   Preformatted Text and Quoted Material   **56**
3.7   Summary   **58**
3.8   Review Questions   **59**
3.9   Exercises   **59**
3.10   Project Threads   **60**

LESSON 4   *CONTROLLING TEXT MARKUP*   **61**

4.1   Default Settings   **61**
4.2   The HR Element and HTML Attributes   **62**
4.3   HTML Attributes in General   **66**
4.4   Paragraph Alignment   **68**
4.5   Attributes of the BODY Element   **69**
4.6   The FONT Element (Depreciated)   **71**
4.7   Putting It All Together: A Practical Example   **73**
4.8   Style Sheets (Optional)   **76**
4.9   Summary   **84**
4.10   Review Questions   **86**
4.11   Exercises   **87**
4.12   Project Threads   **87**

LESSON 5   *HYPERTEXT MARKUP AND WEB SITES*   **88**

5.1   HREF Anchors (Links)   **88**
5.2   Absolute and Relative URLs   **90**
5.3   Site Portability   **96**
5.4   Web Site Design Strategies   **97**
5.5   Named Anchors   **100**
5.6   Links to Named Anchors in Other Documents   **104**
5.7   The Mailto Link   **105**
5.8   Summary   **106**
5.9   Review Questions   **108**
5.10   Exercises   **108**
5.11   Project Threads   **109**

LESSON 6   *IMAGE MARKUP*   **111**

6.1   Image Files   **111**
6.2   Image Markup   **114**

xvi CONTENTS

6.3 Creating Space: The Width and Height Attributes **116**
6.4 Positioning Images with Text **118**
6.5 Images as Links **121**
6.6 Organizing Image Files **123**
6.7 Putting Images on a Web Server **124**
6.8 Transparent GIFs and Animated GIFs **124**
6.9 Background Images **125**
6.10 Image Maps (Optional) **126**
6.11 Summary **131**
6.12 Review Questions **134**
6.13 Exercises **134**
6.14 Project Threads **135**

LESSON 7 *HTML LISTS AND TABLES* **136**

7.1 HTML Editors **136**
7.2 Unordered Lists **137**
7.3 Ordered Lists **139**
7.4 HTML Tables **141**
7.5 Controlling TABLE Properties **142**
7.6 Controlling Row Properties **144**
7.7 Controlling Properties of Individual Cells **144**
7.8 HTML Tables as Page Organizers **146**
7.9 Spanning Rows and Columns **149**
7.10 Advanced Page Layout **151**
7.10 Summary **153**
7.11 Review Questions **155**
7.12 Exercises **155**
7.13 Project Threads **156**

LESSON 8 *HTML FRAMES* **158**

8.1 Framed Web Pages **158**
8.2 Attributes of the FRAMESET Element **160**
8.3 Attributes of the FRAME Element **161**
8.4 Targeting Links to Frames **163**
8.5 Nested Frames **165**
8.6 The Pros and Cons of Frames **168**
8.7 Summary **169**
8.8 Review Questions **171**
8.9 Exercises **171**
8.10 Project Threads **172**

LESSON 9 *WHAT IS JAVASCRIPT?* **174**

9.1 Overview of HTML Forms **175**
9.2 The Client-Server Model **178**
9.3 Interpreted Programming Languages **180**
9.4 JavaScript is Not Java **181**

9.5 Why Learn JavaScript? **182**
9.6 Related Technologies **183**
9.7 Summary **184**
9.8 Review Questions **185**
9.9 Exercises **185**
9.10 Project Threads **185**

LESSON 10 *PROCESSING USER INPUT* **186**

10.1 Using JavaScript to Generate HTML **186**
10.2 Interpreting JavaScript and HTML **189**
10.3 Where Can JavaScript Be Located? **189**
10.4 Prompting for and Storing User Input **191**
10.5 Using Variables to Process Information **193**
10.6 Variables Names **195**
10.7 Variable Types **196**
10.8 Concatenation of Strings **198**
10.9 Variable Assignment **199**
10.10 Parsing User Input **200**
10.11 Statements and Punctuation **203**
10.12 Errors **205**
10.13 Flexibility **206**
10.14 Summary **210**
10.15 Review Questions **211**
10.16 Exercises **212**
10.17 Project Threads **212**

LESSON 11 *MAKING DECISIONS* **213**

11.1 Boolean Variables **213**
11.2 The "if" Statement: Making Decisions **216**
11.3 A Concatenation Shortcut **220**
11.4 The "if … else" Structure **221**
11.5 Basic Input Verification **225**
11.6 Writing Programs **227**
11.7 An Advanced Example (Optional) **227**
11.8 Summary **234**
11.9 Review Questions **236**
11.10 Exercises **237**
11.11 Project Threads **238**

LESSON 12 *OBJECTS* **239**

12.1 The Nature of Objects **239**
12.2 JavaScript Objects **240**
12.3 Objects and Primitives **241**
12.4 A Simple Program Using Objects **242**
12.5 Compound Objects **244**
12.6 The Object Model for the Browser Window **245**
12.7 Using Window and Document Properties **247**

12.8   Object Methods   **249**
12.9   Methods of the Window Object   **250**
12.10 The *Math* Object   **252**
12.11 Summary   **253**
12.12 Review Questions   **254**
12.13 Exercises   **255**
12.14 Project Threads   **255**

LESSON 13   *INTRODUCTION TO PROCESSING HTML FORMS*   **256**

13.1   User Events   **256**
13.2   The *Form* Object   **258**
13.3   Using Local Variables in Functions   **260**
13.4   The *With* Statement   **264**
13.5   Organizing Forms with HTML Tables   **264**
13.6   Verification of Text Input   **265**
13.7   An Advanced Example (Optional)   **267**
13.8   Summary   **270**
13.9   Review Questions   **271**
13.10 Exercises   **272**
13.11 Project Threads   **272**

LESSON 14   *OPTIONS IN HTML FORMS*   **273**

14.1   The Checkbox   **273**
14.2   Using Hidden Values for Checkboxes   **276**
14.3   Radio Buttons and the *elements[]* Array   **278**
14.4   Using Radio Buttons and the *elements[]* Array   **280**
14.5   The Pull-Down Menu   **283**
14.6   The *onchange* Event Handler   **286**
14.7   Verification of User Choices   **287**
14.8   An Advanced Example (Optional)   **288**
14.9   Summary   **291**
14.10 Review Questions   **292**
14.11 Exercises   **292**
14.12 Project Threads   **293**

LESSON 15   *LOOPS FOR REPETITION*   **294**

15.1   The *for* Loop   **294**
15.2   Counters in Loops   **297**
15.3   Using Loops to Process Forms   **299**
15.4   The *while* Loop   **304**
15.5   Indefinite Verification of Prompt Input   **307**
15.6   Nested Loops (Optional)   **309**
15.7   An Example Using Nested Loops (Optional)   **311**
15.8   Summary   **315**

15.9   Review Questions   **315**
15.10 Exercises   **316**
15.11 Project Threads   **317**

LESSON 16   *MORE ON ARRAYS*   **318**

16.1   Parallel Arrays   **318**
16.2   The *Array* Object   **321**
16.3   The *Image* Object and *Images[]* Array   **323**
16.4   Preloading Images into Arrays   **325**
16.5   The *Onload* Event Handler   **326**
16.6   Displaying a Randomly Selected Image   **328**
16.7   Cycling Image Displays   **329**
16.8   Searching Arrays (Optional)   **331**
16.9   Summary   **336**
16.10 Review Questions   **337**
16.11 Exercises   **338**
16.12 Project Threads   **339**

LESSON 17   *MORE ON FUNCTIONS*   **340**

17.1   Calling Self-Defined Procedure Functions Without Event Handlers   **340**
17.2   Using Parameters in Procedure Functions   **342**
17.3   Opening New Windows With Form Buttons   **345**
17.4   Image Rollovers   **347**
17.5   Self-Defined Value Functions   **349**
17.6   Using Boolean Return Functions to Verify Form Input   **354**
17.7   The *String* Object and Verification   **356**
17.8   Advanced Form Verification Using the *String* Object (Optional)   **358**
17.9   Summary   **361**
17.10 Review Questions   **362**
17.11 Exercises   **363**
17.12 Project Threads   **364**

LESSON 18   *JAVASCRIPT SECURITY AND SUBMITTING FORM DATA*   **365**

18.1   The Password Input Element   **366**
18.2   Importing External Scripts   **368**
18.3   Other Security Tricks on the Client   **369**
18.4   CGI Programs   **370**
18.5   The Submit Button   **372**
18.6   Using Hidden Form Elements   **374**
18.7   Summary   **379**

18.8   Review Questions **380**
18.9   Exercises **381**
18.10   Project Threads **382**

APPENDIX A   *HTML QUICK REFERENCE* **383**

APPENDIX B   *JAVASCRIPT OBJECTS* **399**

JavaScript Reserved Words **405**

APPENDIX C   *HEXADECIMAL COLOR REPRESENTATIONS* **406**

APPENDIX D   *ANSWERS TO SELECTED REVIEW QUESTIONS* **409**

INDEX **419**

LESSON *1*

THE INTERNET AND WORLD WIDE WEB

BEFORE EMBARKING upon this journey into programming on the Internet, it is appropriate to gain some insight into the nature of the Internet and World Wide Web. Many people, in fact, view the two as synonymous. But that is definitely not the case. The Internet was born in the 1960s, while the World Wide Web, which lives on the Internet, was not born until the early 1990s. The World Wide Web was able to make many of the Internet's resources available to the average person. Prior to the World Wide Web, the Internet was primarily only available to government agencies and to the scientific communities at colleges and universities. The World Wide Web and its ability to make the Internet publicly accessible has taken the world by storm. It is amazing, in fact, how rapidly and successfully the World Wide Web has infiltrated our daily lives. One can scarcely watch a television commercial these days without a "www.something.com" staring out at you from the bottom of the screen.

The goal of this first lesson is not to make you an expert on all the technical details surrounding the Internet and World Wide Web, but to set in place a general understanding of the history and nature of these two beasts. To this end, we present for a general audience an intuitive, informal discussion aimed at fostering an understanding of some underlying principles and, in the process, lay down a foundation of Internet vocabulary we will use throughout this book.

1.1 THE INTERNET

With the proliferation of the telephone throughout this century, came an ever-increasing amount of telephone wires and cables. In fact, today the planet is fairly strangled with them. Cables span the ocean floors linking continents, cross continents linking countries and states, and criss-cross our neighborhoods like gigantic spider webs.

How do they transmit information? In the conventional copper phone cable, information is transmitted by streams of unimaginable numbers of electrons. The electrons are whizzing through these cables at very high speeds. When one speaks into a phone, a stream

1

of electrons, with patterns and frequencies unique to what was said, zips through these wires to deliver the message, perhaps across the world.

Fairly recently in the scheme of things, many fiber optic cables have been added to this global network. These fiber optic wires carry information as streams of visible light and other frequencies of electromagnetic radiation, rather than as streams of electrons. The particles (well, kind of like particles) comprising the light, called photons, move through fiber optic cables at the speed of light (186,000 miles per second—that's fast!). Although the speed of light is substantially faster than the speed at which electrons move through conventional copper wires and cables, that is not where the main advantage comes into play. Even with conventional copper phone cables, information transmission is very fast. One can speak on the phone to someone in Asia, for example, with little perceived delay.

The biggest advantage of the fiber optic cable is that little or no energy is dissipated through transmission. With conventional copper wires, the clumsy electrons are always slamming into the atoms and molecules that comprise the metal core of the wire. A substantial amount of energy is dissipated in this way. But through fiber optic cables, photons move with little or no resistance. Huge amounts of information can thus be transmitted through fiber optic cables with virtually no loss of energy or degradation of signal.

Satellites have even come into the picture. They can bounce information all over the world without cables of any sort. Few would dispute that satellites will play a big part in the future of global communications. Of course, satellites are already in wide use for spying, scientific research, and even TV signal transmission. But satellite transmission may eventually be as common as the conventional phone cable. In fact, a company called Teledesic° has made plans for a network of 841 low-orbit satellites that will transmit information to virtually everywhere on the planet, to be operational by 2004.

Internet traffic is digital. It is comprised of strings of 0s and 1s. One term you have probably heard in conjunction with the amount of digital information that a given medium can transport is **bandwidth.** A higher-bandwidth communications medium can transport more information at once than a lower-bandwidth medium. In light of the previous discussion, fiber optic cable has a much higher bandwidth than copper cable. As we shall see later in this lesson, there is somewhat more to bandwidth considerations than just types of cable or satellites, but transmission medium is certainly a major factor.

Whatever the means, information can be sent around the world practically instantaneously. That is the foundation of the Internet—a world in which information can be globally passed around. Of course, in this context, we are not focusing on passing around TV signals or telephone dialogue, but on information usable by computers—digital information. There are huge numbers of computers hooked up to this global network of information transmission possibilities. That is the essence of the Internet. It is a global network of computers together with the resources that they can share. The computers range from personal computers to larger computers used by industry and academia. Many of the computers are used only for accessing information, but many of them are used exclusively for making information available. The computers responsible for making information available on the Internet are commonly called **servers**—they serve up information.

Figure 1.1 shows a graphical depiction of the modern Internet. Of course, many computers both serve and receive resources on the Internet, but Figure 1.1 is nonetheless a good visualization of the modern Internet. One curiosity you might be pondering is the term **backbone** appearing in the middle of all the world's criss-crossed cables. This term is often used to describe the Internet's infrastructure, which makes global sharing of resources possible.

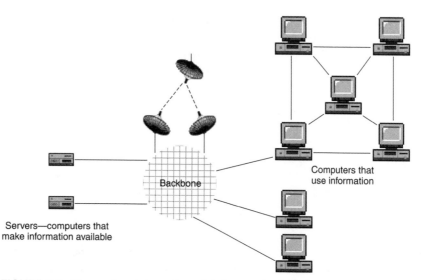

FIGURE 1.1 The modern Internet is a global network of computers that share various resources via a world of cables.

1.2 A BRIEF HISTORY OF THE INTERNET

In the mid-1940s, the computer was a behemoth, containing thousands of vacuum tubes and weighing many tons. In fact, the ENIAC (Electronic Numerical Integrator And Calculator), which was developed at the University of Pennsylvania around 1946, contained 18,000 vacuum tubes, weighed 60,000 pounds (30 tons), and occupied as much floor space (1,600 square feet) as a moderately sized house.

By the 1960s, computers had gotten somewhat less massive, although not by today's standards. Throughout that decade, nearly all computers were maintained by universities. However, many U.S. government agencies, such as the Department of Defense, were using these computers on a regular basis. In fact, the Department of Defense created the first functioning Internet in 1969.

This first Internet backbone had only four networked computers. They were at UCLA, UC Santa Barbara, the University of Utah, and the Stanford Research Institute. At that time, these networked computers were called the Advanced Research Projects Agency Network (ARPANET). Figure 1.2 depicts the first version of what grew into the Internet as we know it today.

It is widely rumored that the ARPANET was developed by the Department of Defense so that key government agencies could maintain communication in the event of a nuclear war. Original plans called for 256 host computers at various sites. By 1971, there were 26 computers hooked up to the ARPANET. Throughout the 1970s the number of computers hooked up to the ARPANET tended to double each year. Also, throughout that decade, use of the ARPANET was restricted to the military, universities, and a few large companies. By 1984, ARPANET had far exceeded the original plans and linked around 1000 hosts.

In 1986, the federal government took a larger role in Internet development, creating NSFNET through funding from the National Science Foundation. The goal of NSFNET was to connect all computer and engineering researchers to the Internet. As a result, throughout

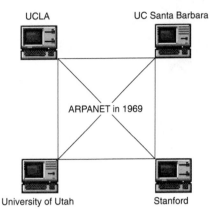

UCLA   UC Santa Barbara

ARPANET in 1969

University of Utah   Stanford   **FIGURE 1.2** The first version of the Internet.

the late eighties, there were two viable Internet backbones, ARPANET and NSFNET. By 1987, there were over 10,000 Internet hosts. But in short order (and with lots of government money), NSFNET was more extensive and had much greater bandwidth than ARPANET. The fact that there were already around 100,000 hosts by 1989 attests to the rapid expansion of NSFNET. In fact, in 1990 NSFNET took over center stage, replacing ARPANET as the Internet backbone. Also, 1990 marked the first year that Internet access could be obtained without formal permission or sponsorship from a government agency.

In short order, virtually every college and university was hooked up to what was becoming widely termed the Internet. Many businesses now owned computers and found the Internet useful for coordinating national or global efforts. In the 1990s computers became very small, fast, and relatively inexpensive. They were, in fact, available to the average household. By 1992, there were over 1,000,000 hosts on the Internet. It was becoming too expensive for the government to control the NSFNET backbone so, in 1992, control of the Internet was transferred to a non-profit corporation, partially created by IBM and MCI.

It was also around this time that the World Wide Web architecture appeared, providing an organized way to make the vast resources of the Internet easily portable to any computer on the Internet. Now, not only could scientists use the Internet, but so could the average person with a personal computer. With this newfound ease of Internet use, its popularity grew like wildfire. Today, the number of computers with Internet access tallies in the tens of millions. At the time of the printing of this book, most estimates put the number at over 100,000,000.

1.3 INTRANETS

One often hears the term **intranet** bantered around in computer lingo. We choose here to give a brief discourse in order to differentiate between the terms intranet and Internet.

Figure 1.1 suggests that, aside from this sprawling network of computers, there are smaller, self-contained networks of computers. The five computers on the right not only are tied into the backbone, but are linked together. Such a linked group of computers is often called an intranet. Another common term synonymous with intranet is **local network,** or simply **network.** If the connection to the Internet backbone is removed, the linked group of computers is still a viable network of computers, but is accessible only to those on the "inside." Hence the term intranet (the prefix "intra" is Latin for "within" or "inside of"). The computer systems of large companies and universities are good examples of intranets.

With the connection to the Internet removed, an intranet can function in much the same capacity, just in a local setting. Most all of the stuff that can be done in the global setting can be done locally. Students at a large university can send e-mail, view web pages, transfer files, and search databases such as libraries, all without leaving the confines of the university's network. However, once the network is linked to the Internet backbone, each computer in the network can explore the virtually endless resources of the Internet.

So, in reality, the Internet is basically a huge network of networks. Local networks at colleges, businesses, libraries, and so forth can function as independent networks but, when hooked up to the Internet backbone, contribute to what we know as the Internet today.

1.4 CONTROLLING TRAFFIC ON THE INTERNET (TCP/IP)

What we have not mentioned is how the passing of information on the Internet is coordinated. In light of the current size of the Internet, this could be a huge problem. Luckily, in the early stages of Internet development this problem was addressed. In 1982, a **protocol** set, which standardized how information was passed around the Internet, was adopted to help unify ARPANET. These protocols were actually first proposed in 1974, but were not adopted as a formal standard until 1982.

Loosely speaking, a protocol is an established and adhered-to way of doing things, a set of rules that everyone obeys. So, all of the computers on the Internet must obey an established protocol; otherwise, it would be very difficult for all of the different types of computers to communicate and pass information. This group of protocols is termed Transmission Control Protocol/Internet Protocol (**TCP/IP**). These are fancy terms, but they simply coordinate the addresses of all the computers on the Internet and the way resources are passed around.

Most formal definitions of the Internet not only include talk of the global network as shown in Figure 1.1, but also the governing TCP/IP protocols. The term "information superhighway" is often associated with the Internet. The highways are the physical means of transmitting information, and these protocols are kind of like the rules of the road. Imagine the chaos of a modern system of roads without any formal rules controlling traffic! The Internet protocols serve to make traffic on the Internet uniform and organized.

1.5 IP ADDRESSES

Each computer on the Internet has to have an address. There is really no other alternative. It would simply be impossible to locate a specific resource on the Internet if you couldn't find the server on which it is stored. Imagine a city in which none of the houses have addresses!

The TCP/IP protocol gives a standard with which computers are addressed. These addresses are called **IP addresses** and are of the form

204.202.129.230

consisting of four numbers separated by periods. In general, each of the four numbers in an IP address has to be in the range 0–255. That gives 256 to the fourth power different possible Internet computer addresses. For the inquisitive, that's over four billion possible addresses.

The term **Internet host** is often used to describe any computer that has access to the Internet. But actually, in the strict sense of the term, an Internet host is a computer with a fixed IP address. But, if every computer in the Internet has to have an IP address, isn't that the same thing? Well, not exactly. Unless you are getting Internet access from a college, business, or other large organization, you are probably getting access from an Internet service provider. The most common means of access is via a phone modem. You pay ten or twenty dollars a month so that you can dial up an Internet connection through your phone modem from your home. In most cases, what this means is that you actually don't have your own IP address. Here's how that works.

A service provider is allocated roughly one IP address for every eight or ten of its customers. So, for example, a large service provider with 100,000 customers has roughly 10,000 to 12,500 IP addresses. Each one of these IP addresses is associated with a phone line. When you dial up and make a connection, your computer is associated with the IP address allocated to the particular phone line with which you have connected. The next time you call in, you will most likely get a different phone line and, hence, a different IP address for that session of Internet access.

When the number of Internet hosts is estimated, it's actually just an estimate of the number of IP addresses that have been given out. So, in reality, the 100,000,000 estimate we mentioned above for the number of computers on the internet only estimates IP addresses. If we were to use "Internet host" in the loose sense, and estimate the number of computers that have access to the Internet, the number would be much larger.

NOTE

Some means of Internet access other than the phone modem are becoming viable for the masses, two of which are digital subscriber lines (DSL) and cable modems. With the conventional phone modem, digital computer information is converted into analog so that the information can travel across the phone line to your service provider, just like an ordinary phone message. It then is converted back into digital form for travel on the Internet backbone. This process is cumbersome and slow, even with a 56K modem.

With DSL or cable access, the information is never converted into analog. In other words, your computer sends digital information straight to the service provider. So the Internet connection is basically straight onto the backbone. With DSL this is done with a special phone line for carrying digital information. In fact, you can't even use a conventional telephone on a DSL line. With cable modems, the digital information is sent through the cable television line.

One advantage of these service types, which is relevant to the discussion in this section, is the fact that you can get your own IP address. Another advantage is that these service types offer much higher bandwidth than the conventional phone modem. But they are more expensive, perhaps around $50 per month.

1.6 ROUTERS AND PACKETS

Another interesting feature of the TCP/IP protocols is the way that information is actually passed from one IP address to another. Suppose that a lengthy MS Word document, for example, is to be passed from one computer in Chicago to another in Dallas. The document is first divided up into small **packets** of digital information, each about 1.5K or less in size. To put that in perspective, if a digital copy of this book, graphics and all, were broken into packets, more than 10,000 small packets of information would likely result. Each packet is labeled with the IP addresses of both the sending computer in Chicago and the receiving computer in Dallas, as well as some other information about how to order the packets when reassembling the document in Dallas. Along the journey, there are computers called **routers** that steer the packets toward their goal. Routers are kind of like post offices in the sense that they receive a packet and then decide where the packet should be sent next in order to reach its destination. Just as post offices are all over the place, almost one in each small town and many in large cities, there are numerous routers on the Internet backbone sending off packets in all directions.

When a router receives a packet, it sends it off to another router, based upon current traffic, in an effort to optimize both its trip and the general traffic situation on the Internet at that time. Thus, a particular packet may travel not the shortest path to its destination, but one which is best for the Internet traffic situation as a whole. A good analogy here is rush-hour traffic. You might not take the shortest route home at 5:00 pm on a given day, but might take a longer, circuitous route to avoid congestion and headaches (at least packets don't get angry with one another!). The longer route might be greater in distance, but might take the same amount of time, or even less.

Perhaps the most interesting feature here is the fact that all the packets from a given file, say the MS Word file traveling from Chicago to Dallas, don't necessarily travel together on the journey. They might get split up at various routers and end up traveling many different paths. It is concievable that one of the packets might travel through California on its way to Dallas, while another might go through New York. It's kind of like following a friend to some destination and you get caught at a red light while they cruise right on through. If you have the address you should still make it, but perhaps by a different route. That's why all the packets are labeled with the information we mentioned above, and more. The file certainly can't get reassembled properly if all of its constituent packets don't arrive.

This notion of sending files in small packets is a large contributor to the efficiency of the Internet. Suppose the document arrives in Dallas, but one of the packets has been damaged in some way along its journey through multiple routers. It is not necessary to retransmit the whole document over the Internet, just the damaged packet. This tends to keep traffic down and flowing smoothly.

1.7   THE WORLD WIDE WEB

The world is essentially at one's fingertips on the Internet. Well, not the world, but the resources that this global network of computers brings to bear. The resources available on the Internet are vast. Not only is the amount of stuff on the Internet mind-boggling, but there are many types of stuff available. There are web pages to view, files to download, databases in which to search for information, and people waiting for e-mail, to name only a few. With this multiplicity of types of resources, comes the need for some means to deal with all of these different types. That is where the World Wide Web (WWW) comes in to play. But before discussing the details of what the WWW actually is, we attempt to illustrate the general concept. To accomplish this we offer a metaphor.

When sitting at a computer hooked up to the Internet nowadays, the possibilities seem limitless, almost like the vastness of space. (We're starting to lean toward Star Trek here.) Each computer on the Internet is like a planet out there. Much as we have the Internet to reach this myriad of computers, the crew of the starship USS Enterprise had their starship to reach all of these planets. The key here is what the Enterprise did upon reaching some distant planet. They established a connection to the planet by going into orbit and then communicated with the inhabitants of the planet (when the Prime Directive allowed, that is). Well, the crew of the Enterprise often had marvelous luck in communicating with the different species. The species often spoke English, but when that was not the case, the crew was armed with a universal translator device that could translate between any two languages in the universe. Without such a device, the Enterprise would often have traveled to other planets in vain. They simply would have found nothing intelligible there. The resources and knowledge of these species would have been unattainable.

So, too, reaching a computer on the Internet is only part of the battle; our computer has to communicate with a remote computer. Such communication among computers makes possible the sharing of their resources. But this is not as easy as you might imagine. Just as there were various species with which the Enterprise sought to communicate, there are several varieties of computers on the Internet. By varieties, we mean different operating systems. An operating system is basically a language or system a computer uses internally. PCs use Windows 2000 (or '95 or '98), Macintosh uses Mac OS, and many server-type computers use operating systems like UNIX or LINUX.

Well, there is a universal translating device to make such communications possible. Without this translating device, our travels on the Internet would be as limited as the Enterprise trying to communicate with a variety of aliens without their universal translator device. This device is the Uniform Resource Locator (**URL**). Obviously, a URL locates a resource on the Internet (otherwise, its name would be poorly chosen!). However, URLs do much more than that, as we shall see.

The URL is a device that uses a set of protocols to communicate on the WWW. We have discussed how the TCP/IP protocols direct traffic on the information superhighway, but the URL protocols make the sharing of various resources on the Internet practical. These protocols, which are fundamentally different from TCP/IP, and their implementation in URLs are essentially what defines the WWW aspect of the Internet. It is worth mentioning here that the URL is not a mechanical device, such as the universal translating device of the USS Enterprise, but rather a universally accepted standard of communication. Before the emergence of the URL, communications among computers on the Internet was limited in much the same way as communications among planets would have been without the universal translating device. Whether mechanical or not, the URL together with the accepted protocols does indeed provide a "device" enabling all computers to communicate and share resources on the Internet.

The table in Figure 1.3 lists the WWW protocols in most common use today. By examining the purposes of the respective protocols, one can see that they encompass some of the most common activities occurring on the Web. They might not all seem familiar, but it is likely that most every Web surfer has used most of these protocols, even if unwittingly.

To further illustrate this notion that the Web is an abundance of resources made accessible by URLs and protocols, we offer a simple example with which any casual Web surfer should be somewhat familiar. We mentioned above that the computers responsible

Protocol	Purpose
http	transferring web pages
ftp	transferring files
telnet	remote login
news	requesting news from a news group
mailto	sending e-mail
file	local file access

FIGURE 1.3 The most widely used WWW protocols.

for making information available on the Internet, and hence the Web, are called servers. ESPN, a major sports network, has a Web server with which it serves up the latest sports information to the world. The address of their server is *espn.go.com*. To visit their Web site, specifically their NFL football page, we type the URL *http://espn.go.com/nfl* into the address location of a web browser as depicted in Figure 1.4.

The URL request depicted in Figure 1.4 contains all the instructions required to cause the desired football page to be loaded into our browser. In layman's terms, this URL says "go to the server at *espn.go.com* and initiate a web page transfer of the NFL web page." Notice that the *http* part at the beginning of the URL is the web protocol listed in Figure 1.3, which indicates that a web page is to be transferred. The acronym *http* stands for "hypertext transfer protocol," where "hypertext" refers to a hypertext document (web page).

So, conceptually, URL requests are of the form

how://where/what

where the "how" specifies the protocol (type of transaction), the "where" corresponds to the address of some server, and the "what" specifies the particular resource sought on that server. Current browsers can make URL requests using most of the other protocols listed in Figure 1.3 as well. Although the method of response varies from protocol to protocol, this basic idea is the same: find the server and tell it what is wanted and how to serve it up.

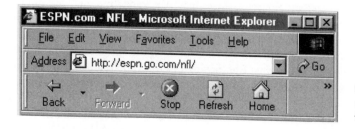

FIGURE 1.4 A browser request for ESPN's NFL football page.

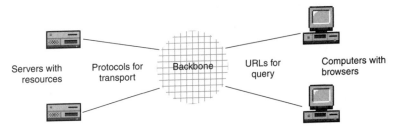

FIGURE 1.5 The essence of the WWW.

N O T E
In practice, URLs get much more complicated than this. For example, when you load the login page at "hotmail.com", a popular e-mail provider at Microsoft, you will see a URL something like

http://www.hotmail.msn.com/cgi-bin/sbox?js=yes

in the address window of your browser. This still adheres to the basic format of a URL, but carries some extra information on the end. For now, you shouldn't concern yourself with this extra information when you see it. We will gradually learn more about URLs as we progress through this text.

Given that there are several protocols available for the "how" part of a URL query, URLs can initiate Internet transactions other than web page transport. However, we defer discussion of the other Web protocols until Lesson 2 where, in particular, we explore the nature of "ftp" in relation to that of "http."

In conclusion, the WWW boils down to a multitude of servers that have resources available and understand the URL and the associated protocols, and myriad computers with browsers hooked up to the Internet that can use these resources by making URL queries. See Figure 1.5.

This idea of an organized web of available resources helps give credence to the name "World Wide Web." It is world wide and the Internet provides the web of connectivity. The URL and the associated protocols are what transform the Internet into a uniformly accessible World Wide Web of information resources. Indeed, the protocols listed in Figure 1.3 provide for worldwide transactions involving several useful resource types.

1.8 THE INTERNET vs. THE WORLD WIDE WEB

In common colloquial jargon, the terms "Web" and "Internet" are often used interchangeably. In fact, in the remainder of this book (after the next discussion) we too tend to disregard the distinction, using the terms interchangeably. Given the increasing dominance of the World Wide Web as the main force on the Internet, the future will probably see a marriage of the two terms. But, having discussed both the TCP/IP protocols in relation to the Internet and then the web protocols, we would be remiss if we were to fail to show how they interact. Intrinsically, the protocols are unlike. The TCP/IP Internet protocols were used as early as the 1970s to direct traffic on the Internet. In contrast, the URL and World Wide Web protocols were not used widely until the 1990s to coordinate the types of resources comprising the internet traffic. But, as we shall shortly see, they do interact together to some extent.

1.9 NAMED ADDRESSES AND DOMAINS

The Web being the user-friendly entity that it is, the long numeric IP address just doesn't seem to fit in. Indeed, imagine ESPN touting its web site on a television commercial with the slogan "just log on to 204.202.129.230 for all the latest sports news." We believe the disadvantages of this are obvious. Maybe the guy from India who memorized and recited the first 40,000 digits of π would thrive under such a convention, but not the average Web surfer.

The convention of using **named addresses** in Web URLs has made Web surfing significantly more pragmatic. The character string *espn.go.com* is an example of a named address. In fact, ESPN's server has at least two addresses, a numeric IP address and the named address above. Their server's numeric address can function in the same capacity as its numeric IP address. The URL

http://204.202.129.230/nfl

brings up the NFL football page just as well as the URL

http://espn.go.com/nfl

which we used as an example above. We have chosen the term "named address" to contrast more definitively with the term "IP address." A more common synonym for named address is **domain name.** So in reality, named address and domain name mean the same thing. This term is not quite as indicative of an actual computer address but lends itself nicely to the concept of a web site. A particular web site can be likened to a domain. For example, all of ESPN's web pages located at *espn.go.com* can be thought of as comprising its web domain.

IP addresses are basically free, whereas domain names have to be purchased. There are numerous companies that will register a domain name for you for a small fee. We did a quick search on the Internet and found several companies more than happy to register your domain name for fees ranging from $25 to $75. After that, a yearly fee of $35 must be paid to InterNIC (INTERnet Network Information Center), the domain-name governing body. The catch here is that many domain names are already taken. For example (to our dismay), "knuckles.com" is registered to a sporting goods store in Canada. In fact, a recent trend has emerged in which opportunistic people (cyber-squatters) are buying up potentially popular domain names, "drugs.com" for example, even though they have no intention of using the domain name for themselves. It is easy to find web sites with potentially coveted domain names for sale. Many domain names are advertised by cyber-squatters for tens of thousands of dollars.

NOTE Named addresses are not case-sensitive. This means that *ESPN.go.com* does just as well as *espn.go.com* in a URL request. This serves a very important purpose. It is not uncommon for businesses to advertise their web sites using capital letters to emphasize their name so that it stands out from the "www." and ".com" parts of the address. It would simply be a nightmare if you had to remember not only the domain name, but also which letters were capitalized. Even if you remembered the characters comprising the domain name, you could waste a lot of time trying to find the web site. The case *in*sensitivity of domain names makes the Web more user-friendly.

1.10 DOMAIN NAME SERVERS

To facilitate this duality of addressing Internet hosts and web servers with both IP addresses and domain names, there is yet another type of server lurking behind the scenes. It is aptly called a **domain name server (DNS).** A simple example suffices to explain a DNS. Suppose you send the URL request

http://espn.go.com/nfl

from your browser by typing it into the address location of your browser or simply by clicking the football link in ESPN's main page. Since all the routing on the Internet backbone is handled with the IP address, the named address must be converted into an IP address before navigating the backbone. This is precisely the job of domain name servers. Figure 1.6 gives you a rough idea of how your request is processed for its trip across the backbone to retrieve the desired web page.

Typically, one thinks of a computer network as a group of linked computers at a college or business. But even if you are at home using an Internet service provider, you are in a network of sorts. All of the computers hooked up to your service provider's local office can be thought of as a network. Even if your URL gets to the provider's local office by going through a modem and then over a phone line, Figure 1.6 still provides a reasonable graphical depiction of what must occur prior to travel on the backbone.

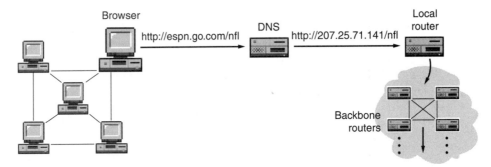

FIGURE 1.6 A URL request is processed so that it can navigate the Internet backbone.

1.11 DOMAINS AND WEB SERVERS

Aside from the obvious advantage of the domain name over the IP address, there is another benefit. A web server can have multiple domain names but only one numerical IP address. That way different web sites can run off the same server, but can have distinguishing named addresses.

For example, consider a hypothetical web server serving up web sites for two different U.S. senators, say SenatorA and SenatorB. Suppose this server has IP address 123.1.2.3. Now each web site is to have its own domain name, say *www.senatorA.gov* and *www.senatorB.gov,* so that the two senators can easily advertise their web sites. Each

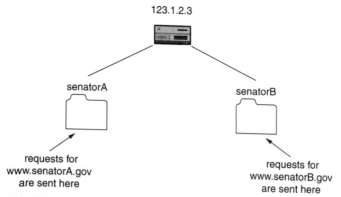

123.1.2.3

senatorA

senatorB

requests for
www.senatorA.gov
are sent here

requests for
www.senatorB.gov
are sent here

FIGURE 1.7 A server with multiple named addresses.

of the two web sites needs to be kept in a separate folder (directory) on the server so that a request for SenatorA's page, for example, pulls up the correct page. Otherwise, if the pages for both senators were kept in the same directory, how would the server know which page to pull up for SenatorA and which to pull up for SenatorB? So, in a loose sense, a domain name corresponds to a directory on a server that contains all the web pages for that domain (web site). Figure 1.7 illustrates this situation. We choose to call such directories the **root directories** of the respective domains. All of SenatorA's web pages are stored within his/her root directory.

As we saw in the discussion pertaining to Figure 1.6, once a URL request gets past your local router, it navigates the Internet backbone using the IP address of the destination server. So, if the DNS translates both of the requests *www.senatorB.gov* and *www.senatorA.gov* only into the IP address 123.1.2.3, how can the appropriate page be pulled up when the request reaches the server? In other words, if the following conversions are enacted by the DNS:

http://www.senatorA.gov ------------> http://123.1.2.3

http://www.senatorB.gov ------------> http://123.1.2.3

the information about which web site or root directory is targeted by the request would be simply lost. Clearly, then, the DNS conversion has to include both the IP address of the server and the particular domain that has been requested. In reality, such domain-name-to-IP conversions are complicated. The details are best left to experts in networking. In the following, we offer a naive (lacking technical detail) explanation of how different domain names can effectively reference different root directories at the same IP address. Moreover, our contrived conceptualization serves further to emphasize the intrinsic nature of URLs.

An easy way to think of such a conversion is to remember that URLs are of the form "how://where/what," but the URL *http://www.senatorA.gov,* for example, seems to carry only two pieces of information, "how://what." It then seems logical that a domain name must somehow contain both the "where" and "what" information. So, before the requests for the respective senator's pages reach the backbone, the DNS performs conversions that can be thought of as

http://www.senatorA.gov	-------------> http://123.1.2.3/senatorA
http://www.senatorB.gov	-------------> http://123.1.2.3/senatorB

In other words, when purchased, each domain name must in some sense be associated with an IP address as well as a root directory. That way, conversions roughly equivalent to the preceding can enable multiple domain names to access one server and find the right root directories.

In a case of multiple domains on one server, as depicted in Figure 1.7, the disadvantage is having to pay for named addresses for all of the senators. But given that domain names are relatively cheap (unless a cyber-squatter beat you to the punch), the simplicity and clarity of having individualized domain names is advantageous when money is not too tight or only a few different domains are required. However, in many (perhaps most) situations, having individualized domain names is simply not practical. Consider a college or university where each student is given some space on a web server for his or her own web site. In this case, each student must have his or her own directory on the server for web pages. Because of the thousands of students and an approximate four-year turnover rate (we hope) of students, it would be simply outrageous to buy each student a domain name.

1.12 WEB SERVER ACCOUNTS

While the above server setup certainly emphasizes the utility of domain names, the most common server setup by far is to have one main domain name for the server and simply to shunt requests for different sites on that server into different directories. A concrete example should adequately illustrate this situation. Suppose Danny Jones is a student at the University of the Web (UWeb). (That's a hypothetical university, in case you are wondering.) In this case, "www.uweb.edu" is the primary domain name registered to the server at UWeb. Of course then, "www.uweb.edu" is virtually just a named alias for the actual IP address of the server. For purposes of this example, we'll simply refer to the server as "www.uweb.edu" rather than its IP address, since no ambiguity arises.

Now each student needs an account on "www.uweb.edu" so that the whole world has access to his or her web site. To this end, each student is given a **user name,** probably some combination of first name and last name, like "djones" for Danny Jones. (There is no widespread convention for constructing user names. For example, "jonesd" would work equally well. So, to avoid this inconsistency, we'll just stick to last names for user names.)

The solution is quite simple. A root directory (folder) is set up somewhere on the server for each student. That directory is accessed by appending the student's user name to the end of a URL. For example, to access Jones' domain on "www.uweb.edu", the URL

http://www.uweb.edu/jones

is required.

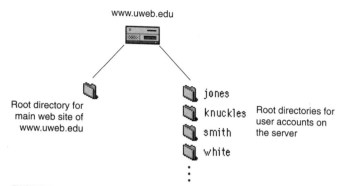

FIGURE 1.8 A common web server setup with multiple accounts.

N O T E

Often, the "~" symbol is required to precede the user name. This symbol is called a "tilde" (pronounced "till-da") is required by many web servers. So, depending on the type of web server, the URL

http://www.uweb.edu/~jones

might be required to access Jones's account.

Note that the URLs above once again adhere to the general concept of "how://where/ what". Here the "whats" are all the different students (and faculty). Other students' web sites can be accessed in similar fashion. The astute reader might be wondering what would happen if we leave off the what and just make the request

http://www.uweb.edu

There is simply another root directory (folder) on the server to which such a request defaults. In this example, it is simply UWeb's main web site. This situation is depicted in Figure 1.8.

Actually putting a web page into such a directory requires further discussion of web protocols, which we defer until Lesson 2. Note also that Internet service providers such as AOL must also give each of their customers some user name and his/her own root directory similar to the depiction in Figure 1.8.

1.13 DOMAIN SUFFIXES

So far we have offered several examples of domain names, but there is something in which they all differ, namely, their suffixes. The three suffixes we have seen are ".com," ".gov," and ".edu." From the contexts of the examples one should be able to deduce the function of these suffixes. ESPN is a commercial organization, the hypothetical senators' pages are government-related, and UWeb is an educational institution. Not only are there suffixes for different types of organizations, there are suffixes for different countries as well. Figure 1.9 gives some of the common organization suffixes and a few country suffixes. The country suffixes are quite numerous so we choose to list only a few large countries to get the idea across. As a simple example, a web site for a restaurant somewhere in India might have the domain name "www.goodcurry.in".

Suffix	Use
com	commercial sites
edu	educational institutions
gov	U.S. government agencies
net	network organizations
org	non-profit organizations

Suffix	Country
ca	Canada
au	Australia
ch	China
gb	Great Britain
in	India

FIGURE 1.9 Some common domain name suffixes.

1.14 SUMMARY

Key Terms

Internet	WWW	intranet	network
bandwidth	server	backbone	protocol
TCP/IP	IP address	packet	router
URL	http	named address	domain name
DNS	root directory	user name	domain suffix
domain	(of domain)		

The Internet is the collection of all the cables (and satellites) and all of the computers that these cables link together in a global network. Many of these computers are also linked together in local networks, often referred to as intranets. An intranet is a local network of computers that can exchange information in much the same way as computers on the Internet. An intranet is often linked to the Internet, giving the computers of the intranet access to the global resources of the Internet.

There are protocols that basically set standardized ways of doing things on the Internet. The TCP/IP protocol sets rules so that traffic on the Internet flows smoothly. One of the features of the TCP/IP protocol is that it sets a standard that Internet hosts should be addressed with IP addresses in a uniform way. That way, when information makes its way onto the Internet backbone (the system of routers and cables that forms the "spine" of the Internet), it can easily find the appropriate destination computer. Another feature of TCP/IP is that digital information is broken up into small packets for its travel on the backbone. Much of the traffic on the backbone is now handled with a high-bandwidth medium, such as fiber optic cable. Bandwidth basically refers to the amount of digital information (number of packets, if you will) that the medium can transport at a given time.

The World Wide Web (WWW) is basically made possible by a different set of protocols. We simply refer to these as WWW protocols. The set of WWW protocols specifies standardized formats for viewing web pages, transferring files, sending e-mail, etc. One of the great facilitators of the WWW and the implementation of these protocols is the Uniform Resource Locator (URL). A URL is a succinct piece of information that finds a server and tells the server what to serve up and how to serve it. Servers, actually web servers in this case, are computers dedicated to making information available on the Internet. A URL that a web browser sends to request a web page from a server specifies the hypertext transfer protocol (http).

In order to make URL requests user-friendly, web servers are given named addresses in addition to the required IP address. Typically a named address, such as "www.uweb.edu", is used to access a given web site. But, since a web server can host more than one web site, named Internet addresses are often called domain names. In other words, one web server can host several web sites (domains), each with its own domain name. To keep track of all this, URL requests are processed before travel on the backbone by domain name servers (DNS). A DNS associates various domain names with the proper IP address so that a request can actually find the right computer, and hence the right domain.

So that individual web sites remain individual, each web site is often given its own root directory on the server. In other words, all of the web pages comprising a web site are kept in a special directory (folder) on the server, namely the root directory for that domain. It is not always the case that every domain has its own named address; after all, that costs money. It is common for several domains to exist on a server, all tied to the same domain name. In this case, each domain has a user name, "jones" for example. In order to access the domain, the user name is appended to the end of the domain name in a URL request, "http://www.uweb.edu/jones" for example.

Finally, as a way to keep domain names categorized to an extent, domain suffixes are used. The domain suffix is the final part of a named address. Different types of organizations are given different suffixes. For example, ".com" is by far the most common. Each country also has its own domain suffix.

1.15   REVIEW QUESTIONS

In most cases, it is not sufficient to answer these from the Lesson Summary.

1. How is digital information transmitted through fiber optic cables? How is information transmitted through conventional copper cables? Give two reasons why fiber optic has higher bandwidth than copper.

2. In what decade were computers first constructed? In what year was the Internet born? How many computers were present in the first Internet version and where were they located geographically? What was it called?

3. When could Internet access first be obtained without sponsorship by a government organization? When was control of the Internet turned over to private business?

4. What is the definition of an Internet host? Why is every computer with Internet access not an official host? What is the difference between a DSL connection and conventional phone modem service providers?

5. Describe two advantages of sending information across the backbone in packets, rather than in one piece.

6. How are the Internet protocols fundamentally different from the Web protocols?

7. Which is free, an IP address or named address? Name an advantage of named addresses over IP addresses. What purpose does it serve for a single computer to have more than one named address?

8. Describe by example the basic structure of a URL.

9. Do URL requests navigate the backbone using named addresses or IP addresses? Explain the function of a DNS.

10. What is a domain? How does this relate to file directories on a computer?

11. Are domain names case-sensitive?

1.16   EXERCISES

1. Inquire about setting up an account on a web server, either from your institution or from your service provider.

2. Go to the Lesson 1 section in the web site for this book and use the resources there to see if your name is already

registered as a domain name. Try your first and last names in the form "www.name.com".

3. Go to the Lesson 1 section in the web site for this book and use the resources there to find the IP addresses for "amazon.com" and "yahoo.com". Type these IP addresses into the address field of your browser to access the two web sites without using their domain names.

4. (a) Access the Major League Baseball site at ESPN by typing the URL "http://espn.go.com/mlb" into the address field of your browser.

(b) Access ESPN's main page by typing the URL "http://espn.go.com" into the address field of your browser.

(c) From their main page you loaded in part (b), click on the link for Major League Baseball. Note the change that this causes in the address field of the browser and how this relates to what you did in part (a).

(d) While viewing the baseball page, go to the address field of your browser and delete everything after the ".com" from the end of the URL. Now hit return on your keyboard.

INTERNET RESEARCH QUESTIONS

If one (or more) of these research questions is assigned, it may be used as subject matter for construction of a web page in the exercises of Lessons 2, 3, and 4. They should be written up using a text editor and saved for later use. The research should be supported by URLs of informational web sites. The research need not be exhaustive (that's what informational sites are for), but it should adequately answer the question in about a page. By "adequately," we mean so that someone with no idea of the answer would get the general idea by reading your work. The gory details can be referenced on the informational sites using the URLs you have gathered.

1. Some URLs contain more information than we outlined in this lesson. Research and discuss the nature of a "query string" and provide a concrete example.

2. Research and discuss various phone modem speeds. How do these compare to DSL modems, cable modems, ISDN, T1, T2, and T3 connections?

3. A converter is referenced in the Lesson 1 section of the web site for this book that converts between IP addresses and domain names. Find the IP address of "www.lfc.edu"

and the IP address of "math.lfc.edu". What are class A, B, and C licenses for IP addresses? Speculate on how this applies to the "lfc.edu" domain.

4. Research and discuss statistics on the growth of Internet hosts and the growth in the number of packets that travel the backbone.

5. Research and discuss the number and types of web servers in use on the Internet. In particular, discuss the estimated proportion of each type of server.

6. Research and discuss statistics on the sizes of packets that travel the backbone.

7. Research and discuss the nature of routers on the backbone. In particular, what types of computers are used and who makes them?

8. Research and discuss what is meant by hierarchical resolution with respect to domain names and routing.

9. Find and index several sites that discuss domain suffixes for countries. List some that are not listed in this lesson. Find the named addresses of 10 sites, each with a different international suffix.

10. Research and discuss issues surrounding taxation of commerce on the Internet. What are current practices and laws?

11. Research and discuss issues surrounding freedom of speech on the Internet.

12. Find at least two products that can be used to block pornographic Internet content on a personal computer. How do they work?

13. Each search engine indexes only a relatively small percentage of the web sites on the Internet. Find statistics indicating which search engines are best and statistics giving the approximate percentages for several leading search engines.

14. Find out what a metasearch engine is and give a few examples. For each example, list the subsidiary search engines.

1.17 PROJECT THREADS

Each of these project threads results in a structured web site whose pages utilize most of the material covered in this book. The two threads merge after Lesson 8, and function on a common level throughout the JavaScript programming lessons. They are especially ideal when accounts on a web

server are available. Otherwise, the sites may become too large to fit on a 1.44 disk. However, if it is practical to use larger disks, such as 100 meg zip disks for example, a web server is not necessary.

THREAD A

This thread begins in Lesson 2. It features development of a home page and a homework page that indexes all exercises worked. The reader is given latitude over the subject matter for the home page. It does include latitude for utilization of one or more of the above research questions, but does not require their use.

THREAD B

This thread unfolds in a manner similar to that of Thread A, but favors specific exercises over a home page.

Assignment

Do one or more of the above research questions.

TRANSACTIONS ON THE WEB

HAVING LEARNED the distinctions between the Internet and the WWW, we must learn some of the fundamentals of how resources are actually located and passed around on the Internet. We all know how to crank up a web browser and start clicking on links. But understanding what is going on is another matter. Moreover, the types of transactions that link clicking can initiate are limited. In order to get web pages onto web servers and to make them accessible to the masses, use of web protocols other than "http" must be explored. In an effort to accomplish this, we begin by discussing computer platforms and some of the associated terminology. Then we present a couple of very simple examples of web pages and explore how they are transported on the Internet with regard to various protocols. By simple web pages, we don't necessarily mean that you will understand all of the symbols required to make the actual pages, but that the web pages are about as basic as can be made. We simply need concrete examples of web pages so that we can explore their travels. We turn to the actual nuts and bolts of making web pages in Lesson 3.

2.1 PLATFORM INDEPENDENCE

By computer **platform** we mean the operating system the computer uses. In particular, we focus on Microsoft's Windows 2000 ('95 or '98) and Apple's Macintosh OS. Many popular brands of computers (Compaq, Dell, and Hewlett Packard, just to name a few) use Microsoft's windows operating system. We refer to these as PCs. Apple computers use the Macintosh (Mac OS) operating system. We simply refer to these as Macs. There are a few other types of operating systems, but the above two are the ones most commonly used in personal computing.

A software program, such as Microsoft Word (MS Word), is often called an **application.** Applications are basically computer programs written to accomplish certain tasks for you. Among common application types are word processors, spread sheets, and web browsers. Software made for PCs won't work on Macs, and vice versa. For example, Microsoft, the software company which makes the MS Word word processor, has to make two different versions, PC and Mac versions. This is true of virtually any software. You simply can't install an application made for one platform on the other. So applications are what are commonly termed **platform-dependent.** Applications merely serve as a handy example; platform dependency goes well beyond just applications. Macs and PCs simply don't share resources very well.

When you open an application on a given platform and wish to do something, you create a new file, work for a while, and then save the file. For example, you might open Word Perfect and create a file named "termpaper.wp" in which you write laboriously in an attempt to appease your English teacher. Files are, for the most part, application-dependent. That is, a file created by one application is often not readable by other applications. For example, if you try to open the Word Perfect file "termpaper.wp" with MS Word, you will either get some sort of incompatibility message or, if MS Word does open the file, you will probably see gibberish rather than the file's intended contents. There are special translators available so that files can be used by different word processors, but that is beside the point. Different applications simply format files differently. Suffixes like ".wp" are appended to the end of file names to help differentiate among files. So, for example, Word Perfect files typically end in ".wp" or ".wpd", whereas MS Word files often end with ".doc". Given such incompatibility among applications, suffixes like ".wp" and ".doc" certainly help one keep track of which types of files are which. It is worth noting, however, that such suffixes aren't as important as they used to be. If you view your file directories as icons rather than mere file names, the application that created the file can often be deduced by the icon's picture. In fact, on PCs running Windows, the file suffix is often suppressed in favor of the icon.

Let's summarize. Files are mostly application-dependent and applications are platform-dependent. Thus, according to syllogistic logic, files are mostly platform-dependent. Indeed, this is true, but only because of the "mostly." There is a very common type of file that transcends computer platforms, namely **ASCII** files. ASCII is an acronym that stands for American Standard Code for Information Interchange. An ASCII file can basically contain only those symbols that you can produce with a standard keyboard, together with a few special characters. ASCII files don't make use of the stuff like boldface, italics, fancy fonts, and other types of word-processing gimmicks. In short, ASCII files basically adhere to a minimal standard necessary to contain information readable by humans.

The most common web browsers, Netscape and Internet Explorer, are applications and are thus platform-dependent. Microsoft, for example, has to make two different versions of Explorer, one for PCs and one for Macs. But the key here is that web browsing is **platform-independent.** No, we didn't just contradict ourselves. We said web browsing is platform-independent, not the browsers themselves. Regardless of whether you are sitting at a Mac or PC, you can visit the same web page, check your e-mail, or bone up on your favorite news group. Indeed, this independence has helped to make the Web as popular as it is. The primary reason for this is that the developers of the browsers have adhered to the basic Web protocols. In particular, focusing on "http" and web pages, this means that all browsers make web pages out of ASCII-type files, which transcend platforms.

Adding yet further to the fact that web pages transcend platforms is that both Macs and PCs have applications that are minimal in the sense that they generate ASCII files. On Macs, one such application is called "Simple Text," and on PCs one such application is called "Notepad." So anyone who knows HTML can sit down at either type of computer and create a file capable of being made into a web page by a browser running on either type of computer. You don't even need to buy any fancy software. Rather than continuing to use the term ACSII to describe this basic file type, we will simply refer to them as text files.

This versatility has helped not only fuel the Web's growth, but helped Macintosh out of some tough times in the early '90s. During that time, most of the software developers were busy developing applications for PCs. Well, to make money that made sense: the vast majority of people were using PCs. Many people were leery of buying Macs because of the very real problem of lack of software development. With the growth of the Web during the mid- and late '90s and the associated decrease in limitations due to the platform issue, Macintosh has rebounded quite nicely. The World Wide Web has largely transcended the platform issue.

2.2 THE HTML DOCUMENT

As we noted above, web pages are generated from ordinary text files. It doesn't take some extravagant type of file created by a fancy application. In fact, we recommend that the reader make use of either "Simple Text" or "Notepad," depending upon whether you are using a Mac or PC, to create web pages. There are special editors available for creating web pages, but only after you learn the basics of HTML should you employ an HTML editor. Certain fundamentals must be put in place before one can adeptly exploit all the features of such editors.

Figure 2.1 shows the most basic HTML file imaginable. It is a text file named "simple.html" and was created with "Simple Text". For now, we won't focus on the contents of the file, but just on the fact that "simple.html" is a very simple HTML file. We will, however, note that the file's contents are easily produced by a standard keyboard, as you would expect from a plain text file. Also, we mention again that HTML stands for "HyperText Markup Language" and that the strange symbols in Figure 2.1 are part of the HTML language. Don't focus on the details of HTML at this point, just on the fact that "simple.html" will create a simple web page.

All "simple.html" needs to become a web page is a browser. This distinction is certainly worth noting. The file "simple.html" is not a web page, merely a "Simple Text"-generated text file whose name has the suffix ".html". Note that this file could just as easily have been created with "Notepad" on a PC. Only when "simple.html" is opened by a browser does it become a web page. An HTML document is really nothing like the web page it creates. As per the discussion above about file suffixes helping to create distinction among files, any file intended to become a web page should have the suffix ".html" (or ".htm"). There are other suffixes in use, but those are for special kinds of HTML documents.

FIGURE 2.1 A simple HTML file.

The files that applications like Word Perfect and MS Word create are not basic text files. They contain formatting features to make fancy text, tables, and lists so that information can be displayed in an organized and aesthetically pleasing fashion. So, if you were to copy the contents of "simple.html", paste them into a Word Perfect or MS Word file, and try to load the resulting file into a web browser, you would most likely have no luck. Such word-processor files simply carry extra formatting baggage with them that web browsers don't want. As we shall see in Lesson 3, formatting issues in web pages are handled with HTML code, some of which appears in "simple.html", rather than with fancy text options. The current word processor versions do, however, have special features with which you can create HTML files, but for purposes of learning we had best stick to "Simple Text" and "Notepad."

2.3   THE file PROTOCOL

Ok, so how does the above file, "simple.html", become a web page? As we have already noted, the answer is easy. Just load it into a browser. Recalling the URL example from Figure 1.4, you might be thinking of some type of "http" transaction. After all, it is an HTML document. That is certainly correct thinking, but the key question here is: "Where is the file 'simple.html' located?" If it were located on a remote web server, say "www.somewebserver.com", an "http"-type URL request of the form "http://www.somewebserver.com/simple.html" from your browser would certainly be in order. However, making "simple.html" into a web page does not require that it be on a web server.

When you create a file like "simple.html", you typically do it on your personal computer. In fact "simple.html" can easily be created on a computer that is not even hooked up to the Internet. It's kind of like when you write a term paper. You sit at a computer, type the darn thing, and then do some editing before you even consider turning it in for the instructor to see. Except it's even worse when you put an HTML document on a web server: the whole world can pull it up and see it. It is, thus, advantageous to create the thing locally and edit it, before you turn it loose. Now, "simple.html" is as basic as it gets and won't require editing, but for more complicated HTML files, that is not the case. There are many small errors that can cause a web page not to be displayed as intended, or even not to be displayed at all.

The protocol that browsers use to deal with loading HTML files locally is the "file" protocol. When we say local, we mean on your personal computer. It need not even be hooked up to the Internet. The "http" protocol is to enable HTML files and other related resources to be transferred over the Internet, whereas the "file" protocol is for loading HTML files locally, straight from your computer's hard-drive memory. The easiest way to illustrate this is by an example. Suppose the HTML document "simple.html" is saved on the hard drive of your personal computer, PC or Mac. You simply load the document into the browser by using the "open file" option in the browser's "file" pull-down menu.

NOTE   There are shortcuts for loading files into your browser locally. For example, on a Mac, you can simply drag the icon for "simple.html" onto the icon for the web browser and the file is loaded into the browser. Thus, if you are developing web pages, it is advantageous to keep an icon for your browser somewhere where you can easily drag files onto it, perhaps in a corner of the screen. On PCs running recent Windows versions, such dragging also suffices to load a web page locally. Even better yet, versions like Windows '98 and 2000 should actually recognize text files appended with the suffix ".html" and create an icon for the file somewhat resembling the Explorer icon. In other words, Windows effectively "ties" the HTML file to explorer by giving it an Explorer icon. If this is the case, you simply have to double-click this icon to load it into Explorer. However, if you wish to view the file in Netscape, you still have to drag the icon (or use the file menu).

Figure 2.2 shows the results of loading the file "simple.html" into two different browsers, Netscape on a Mac and Explorer on a PC. Although the content of "simple.html" is not substantial, the thing to note is that the browsers recognize the document as local and use the "file" protocol, as evidenced in the address field of Figure 2.2a.

The first thing to note is that the file URL in Figure 2.2a adheres to the basic "how://where/what" nature of URLs. The "how" is the file protocol and the "where" is "HardDrive", which is simply the hard drive of the Mac on which Figure 2.2a was created. The "what" is the file path, "book/chap2/simple.html", from the hard drive to the file.

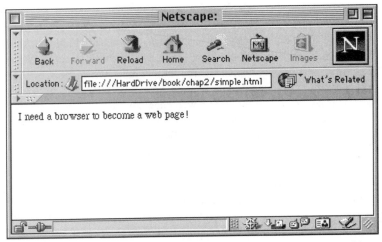

FIGURE 2.2a The local rendering of "simple.html" by Netscape on a Mac.

FIGURE 2.2b The local rendering of "simple.html" by Explorer on a PC.

However, as you can see in Figure 2.2b, the file URL doesn't include the actual file protocol. Rather, the URL only contains the "where," namely the hard drive, "C," of the PC and then the file path from the hard drive to the file "simple.html", Explorer simply chooses to suppress the protocol part of the URL when loading HTML documents locally. However, in the lower right-hand corner of Figure 2.2b, you can see that Explorer does indicate that the file is loaded locally by saying "My Computer." In contrast, when a file is loaded from over the Internet, Explorer shows a similar display indicating "Internet".

We don't provide these contrasting examples to make you understand the details of "file" URLs on different platforms and in different browsers. In fact, it's really not that important. Local files are usually loaded by using the "open file" option of the browser or by dragging or clicking icons, depending upon which platform you are using. It is unlikely that you will ever load a web page locally by typing in a "file" URL as seen in Figures 2.2a and 2.2b. A browser knows the file is local and reacts accordingly by automatically putting its form of "file" URL in the address window. Really, the only significant part of the file URL is the file path, the actual location of the text file on the computer. The lesson to take from this is that we now know that HTML documents can be viewed locally with no Internet connection required.

NOTE
You know enough now to make plain textual web pages locally. All you need to do is to substitute any text you want into the BODY section of "simple.html" and you are good to go. However, putting "simple.html" on a web server for the whole world to see is another matter entirely.

2.4 THE http PROTOCOL

Viewing web pages locally for editing is fine, and even necessary. But, if that's all anyone could do, the Internet wouldn't be much fun. We can't imagine sitting around for a few hours surfing for web pages on our own hard drive. It's pretty clear that web servers are the way to go. But, for now, we will not worry about how to put HTML documents on web servers, but just assume that one is already there.

We have said that the http protocol is designed to transfer web pages over the Internet, but that is an abuse of terminology. Actually, http transports "hypertext" documents. More precisely, it transports HTML documents and, as we discussed above, those are not actually web pages. They generate web pages with the help of browsers. Only after the HTML document traverses the Internet does it become a web page.

We could assume that the file "simple.html" is sitting on a web server somewhere and examine its travels over the Internet but, since that file generates no hyperlinks, we offer a new version that contains a link (hyperlink). Figure 2.3 shows the HTML document named "link.html".

For now, don't focus on the actual HTML code in the document, but be content to realize that it will generate a link when rendered by a browser. Now suppose that "link.html" is stored on the remote web server, "www.uweb.edu", located at the fictitious University of the Web. It doesn't matter where the server is, but you may as well assume that it's thousands of miles away. For simplicity, we assume the file "link.html" is stored in the main root directory of the "www.uweb.edu" domain, as pictured in Figure 1.8, rather than in one of the user accounts.

```
link.html
<HTML>
<HEAD>
</HEAD>
<BODY>
Here is my favorite sports site!<BR>
<A HREF="http://espn.go.com/nfl">Click here to see football news</A>
</BODY>
</HTML>
```

FIGURE 2.3 An HTML file that creates a link.

To pull up this page, we type the URL

http://www.uweb.edu/link.html

into the address field of a web browser. (Recall from Lesson 1 that if it were in one of the user accounts, a URL like "http://www.uweb.edu/~jones/link.html" would be required.) We then hit the return key on the keyboard to initiate the transaction. The browser application then tells our local computer (the one on which it's running) to attempt to find the Internet address as specified in the URL. Of course, by the time the request gets out on the backbone, the named address has been transformed into the associated IP address. When the server is located and has received the request, the two computers have established a line of communication. The "where" part of the URL request has thus been fulfilled.

Since the URL specifies "how" and "what" as well, the server does an "http" transaction by sending our computer the HTML file "link.html". Actually, the file itself has not been sent to us, but a copy of the file. This copy of the file "link.html" is rendered by our browser and we see the web page pictured in Figure 2.4. This copy of "link.html" is now stored in some of our computer memory that has been allocated by our browser. This is called the

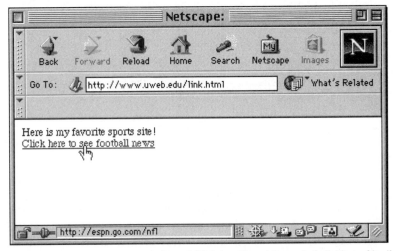

FIGURE 2.4 A browser rendering of "link.html" and the act of clicking of its link.

browser's **cache** (simply pronounced "cash"). This memory is temporary. In other words, the copy of "link.html" that has been sent to us has not been permanently stored on the hard drive of our computer. After some period of time, the copy in the cache memory will be gone.

The main reason for this is so that a recently requested web page can be retrieved quickly. For example, suppose we now click on the link as pictured in Figure 2.4, thereby making a URL request for ESPN's football page. When this new request is granted, copies of all the files associated with the football page are transferred to the cache. We say all of the files associated with the football page because that page is complex, with images and the like. All the objects embedded in a web page also have to come along for the ride or else the page won't be complete. We won't go into that until later in the the text but, for now, we have retrieved the football page and it now appears in our browser.

If we now click the "back" button of the browser to go back to the original page generated by "link.html" you see in Figure 2.4, a new connection to the remote server "www.uweb.edu" does not have to be made. The browser simply pulls the file "link.html" from the cache. This is much faster than making a new request to the server, perhaps thousands of miles away. You can easily notice this feature by loading a slow web page with a lot of graphics, leaving the page, and then going back. It will load much more quickly the second time due to the fact that it is retrieving files from the cache, rather from across the Internet. Figure 2.5 illustrates the situation.

This cache memory is temporary, as we have mentioned. The cache memory allocation is basically of a fixed size. You can only fit so many documents into the cache. Let's suppose for simplicity that our cache can hold five megabytes' worth of files (HTML files, images,

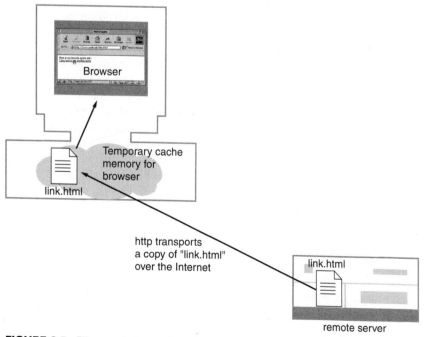

FIGURE 2.5 Files needed to make web pages are temporarily stored in the cache memory so that they can be reloaded quickly.

etc.). After we leave the ESPN football page and surf around enough to copy five megabytes' worth of new files into the cache, the football documents are gone—replaced by the more recently used files. Pulling up the football page again would require a new connection to the server.

> **NOTE**   You can increase the memory allocated to the cache by altering your browser's preferences, but more is not always better. For example, if too many previously cached web pages are present, you could feasibly sit down at your computer to view today's sports news but pull up yesterday's sports page from the cache. However, while such retrieval of outdated pages is possible, certain safeguards are taken by most browsers to avoid this problem.

Perhaps the most important feature of "http" is that it can transport only harmless files, mainly HTML documents and image files. Neither of these kinds of files can sic a virus on your machine from the cache. As we have seen, HTML files are merely text files, the most harmless of files. Image files are just raw organized data and can't foul up your computer. And, although we don't discuss their nature, things like Java applets can't even do damage. Be wary though, "ftp" links in a web page can actually download a potential virus onto your machine. Fortunately, we will discuss that shortly.

> **NOTE**   http transport is harmless and won't unleash viruses on your computer. The files that are transported are merely text and image files, which sit harmlessly in the browser's cache memory.

To make one last observation about "http", recall how we initiated the "http" transaction that acquired "link.html" from the remote server. We typed the appropriate URL into the address location of the browser and hit return on the keyboard. In everyday use, however, it is certainly more common to initiate "http" transactions by simply clicking links. In Figure 2.4, when we clicked a hypertext link, notice that the target of the link appeared at the bottom of the browser in the status bar as the mouse passed onto the link. This target is no more than a URL. In other words, each link has a URL lurking behind it. (You can see this by examining Figure 2.3.) When the link is formally clicked, this URL replaces the old one in the browser's address window as the transaction unfolds. So clicking a link is basically equivalent to typing in the target URL manually and hitting return. One nice consequence of this is that you can check the target of a link before you actually click it. Simply pass the mouse onto the link and observe the target URL in the status bar. In Figure 2.4, you can see the target of the link even though the link has not been clicked. The mouse is simply passed onto the link.

2.5   THE ftp PROTOCOL vs. http

To formally **download** a resource from a remote server, the **file transfer protocol** (ftp) is used. By download, we mean to make a permanent copy of the file from the server to your hard drive. By permanent, we don't mean that you can never erase the file, but rather that it is stored on your hard drive, not in the browser's temporary cache. As we saw above, http transactions make copies of files that merely stick around for a while in the browser's cache. In contrast, a file transported by ftp stays on your hard drive permanently, or at least until you delete it. Figure 2.6 provides an illustration differentiating http from ftp.

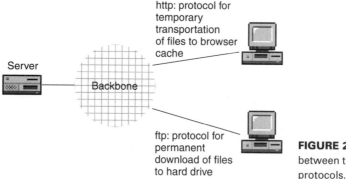

http: protocol for
temporary
transportation
of files to browser
cache

Server

Backbone

ftp: protocol for
permanent
download of files
to hard drive

FIGURE 2.6 The difference
between the ftp and http
protocols.

Much like surfing for web pages by clicking links as depicted in Figure 2.4, ftp transactions can also be accomplished by simply clicking on links rather than having to type long ftp URLs into a browser. In fact, you may have unwittingly initiated an ftp transaction if you have downloaded some freeware or shareware over the Internet. These terms refer to applications that are available for download and are free or ask for a small fee, respectively. The browsers Netscape and Explorer are examples of freeware. You can go to Netscape's or Microsoft's web site and click a link to download the applications onto your computer for free. Since the downloaded application is saved onto your hard drive indefinitely, the transaction is ftp rather than http.

Figure 2.7 demonstrates this by depicting the initiation of a download of Netscape by clicking the appropriate link on Netscape's download page. In this figure, the link has actually been clicked and the browser is attempting to initiate a connection to Netscape's ftp site. This is evidenced in the status bar at the bottom of the browser.

Once the connection is established, a transaction using the ftp protocol begins. Figure 2.8 shows the progress of the file transfer to the local hard drive. A new window has appeared monitoring the progress of the actual download of the file to the local computer.

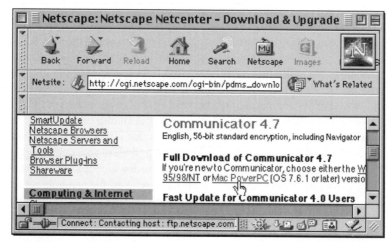

FIGURE 2.7 A link for an ftp transaction as opposed to an http transaction.

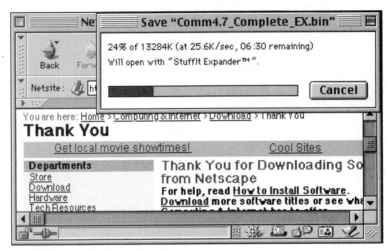

FIGURE 2.8 The result of an ftp transaction.

As the download window in the foreground indicates, the file transfer will be accomplished in roughly six minutes. After the file is saved on the local hard drive, it has nothing to do with the browser; it is just some file on the computer. Even after the browser is exited, the downloaded file is still stored on the hard drive and can be utilized for the purpose for which it was downloaded. Actually, you can see in Figure 2.8 that even during the download, the browser has already loaded the thank-you page that is automatically sent to show appreciation. Even at this point, the browser has done its part of the ftp transaction and is going back to its http work. Note that while Figure 2.8 was generated on a Mac, such ftp transactions on PCs also result in a download-progress window. It just looks somewhat different.

> **NOTE** Completing an ftp transaction by clicking an ftp link is one example of an **anonymous** ftp transaction. Anyone who finds the web page can initiate the transaction and the server sending the file does not care to whom it is sending the file.

Unlike http, there are definite security risks associated with ftp. We have mentioned that http can only transport harmless files, but ftp can definitely transport files that can unleash viruses on your computer. You might be wondering how you can safeguard yourself against such possibilities, especially since links can cause both http and ftp transactions. After all, when you surf the Web you don't always move the pointer onto a link and look at the status bar at the bottom of the browser to deduce the nature of the link before you click it. You could easily click a link that you think is an http link meant to pull up another web page, but inadvertently be clicking an ftp link that puts some file on your computer.

The good news is that simply downloading a file to your computer can't unleash a virus. However, when you double-click the icon of the downloaded file to open it, you can. In other words, a file can't hurt your computer, but opening a file can unleash a virus if it contains one. So if you accidentally acquire some file, don't open it. Just slap it in the trash (recycler on a PC) and delete it. As long as you stick to reputable sites for downloading browsers and other software, you should be fine. Do, however, be wary of downloading strange files.

To digress a bit, the same holds true for e-mail as for http vs. ftp. Simply getting an e-mail ("mailto" protocol) and reading it can do nothing harmful to your computer. However, danger lurks when e-mail messages have attachments. Attachments are separate files that are sent along with e-mail messages. They are usually identified by your e-mail viewer as attachments and often appear as links in your e-mail message. Simply don't click on an attachment from an unknown source. Clicking an attachment causes the attached file to be stored on your computer's hard drive in much the same manner as clicking an ftp link. But, fortunately, the attachment by itself can't harm your computer. You get a final chance to avert malicious viruses by not opening strange attachments, even if you have accidentally caused it to be saved on your hard drive.

2.6 PUBLIC DIRECTORIES ON WEB SERVERS

We have created a simple HTML document and rendered it locally in a browser with the file protocol. Furthermore, we have examined in considerable detail the nature of http transactions once an HTML document is actually served up from a remote server. The missing link is how to put a document like "simple.html" or any other HTML document, onto a remote web server.

The catch here is that you must have an account on a web server. If you are a student, you can typically obtain a web account on your educational institution's web server. If not, your Internet service provider, America OnLine (AOL) or the like, can usually fix you up with one. Having access to the Internet to surf and browse is different from having an account on a web server. When you are surfing, you are just pulling up other people's pages from various web servers. On the other hand, if you want anyone in the world to be able to see your page, you need to physically put your HTML document onto a web server.

Since it is unlikely that you have your own domain name, we will focus on typical user accounts on a web server. Recall Figure 1.8 of Lesson 1. Also recall that user names can have many forms like "dannyjones," "djones," "jonesd," etc., and since they are somewhat arbitrary, we will stick with simply "jones" for simplicity. We will assume that "jones" has a web account on the fictitious web server with address "www.uweb.edu". Also, for simplicity, we assume that "jones" simply wishes to transfer the HTML document "simple.html" to his account. (Although he would probably like to switch the message of the file to something like "This is my first web page!")

But, before we begin the transaction, there is a very important point to be made involving root directories for user accounts on web servers. There is usually another directory inside the root directory into which HTML documents must be put in order to be accessed by http requests. Figure 2.9 depicts the situation. Keep in mind that throughout this book, when we show file directories as in Figure 2.9, you can tell what is in each directory by looking under the name for that directory. So Jones's root directory contains three items, two documents and another directory. In turn, that directory (public) contains the file "simple.html."

What this means is that if Jones were to transfer "simple.html" into his root directory, no one would be able to make an HTTP request for it. However, if he puts it inside the folder named "public," it will be viable for http requests. In other words, if the file is loaded onto the server as depicted in Figure 2.10, the request "http://www.uweb.com/~jones/simple.html" would not pull up his web page.

www.uweb.edu

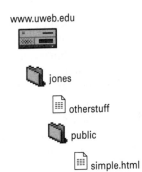

FIGURE 2.9 The document "simple.html" is available to the world for http requests, since it is inside the "public" subdirectory of the root directory. The "otherstuff" and "yetmorestuff" in Jones's account is not accessible to the outside world.

So, effectively, a request for "http://www.uweb.com/~jones/simple.html" bypasses the actual "jones" directory, goes inside the public directory, and looks for the requested file. One advantage to this is that other documents can be stored inside the "jones" folder for safekeeping. For example, you might have a web page not quite finished. Of, course you would be creating and editing the HTML file locally, but you might wish to keep a backup copy on your account on the web server for safekeeping in a location where no one on the Web can find it. Inside the "jones" directory but outside the public directory is one such possible place. This isn't the primary reason for the existence of such public subdirectories, but nonetheless provides a rationale that is easy to remember.

NOTE It is not always the case that an account on a web server requires a special subdirectory. Some server setups don't require this. However, a subdirectory along the lines of the one shown in Figures 2.9 and 2.10 is very common so we choose that setup to cover the majority of cases. Also be apprised that such subdirectories are not always named "public." Other common names for such directories are "www" and "public-HTML." Although such names for the subdirectory comprise the majority of cases, such naming is often at the discretion of the webmaster. We choose "public" because it is indicative of the purpose of the subdirectory. Namely, any HTML files you wish to become public must be put in there.

www.uweb.edu

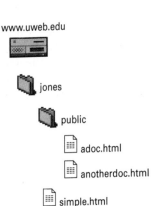

FIGURE 2.10 The request "http://www.uweb.com/~jones/simple.html" comes up empty since "simple.html" is not in the "public" directory. The other two documents are, however, accessible to the world.

2.7 WEB SERVERS AND ftp

Since an HTML document must be permanently saved onto the server, the transaction type must be ftp. However, simply clicking on some ftp link is not going to get your file onto the server. Although some browsers have publishing options that allow you to transfer HTML documents to web servers, that is not the recommended way. You should use a separate ftp application designed to make such transfers. Such ftp applications offer much more versatility for file **upload,** while remaining fairly simple to use. The term upload is often used to describe a transaction involving file transfer from your computer to some remote computer. In contrast, the term **download,** which we have used several times, refers to transfer from a remote computer to your local computer. Such ftp applications often come as standard software on computers. But if one isn't present, there are numerous freeware ftp programs available for download. In fact, links to a few of these can be found in the web site for this book.

NOTE

There are two freeware ftp programs that we recommend, one for Macs and one for PCs. They both function similarly, and are easy to use. In fact, we use these two ftp applications for illustration throughout the rest of this section. Discussion of these two should suffice to explain the nature of ftp applications in general. For Macs, the application is called "Fetch". For PCs, "ws_ftp le" suffices nicely. Note that the "le" stands for limited edition and we believe that "ws" stands for "windows". There is also a deluxe edition of ws_ftp that has more features (and must be purchased), but the limited-edition freeware version suffices nicely for the tasks you need to accomplish throughout this book.

To illustrate such ftp transactions, we will go through the steps required to put "simple.html" into Jones's public directory on "www.uweb.edu". First, we start up the ftp application. We then obtain a connection window that requests the information necessary to connect to the remote server. Figures 2.11a and 2.11b contain Fetch (Mac) and ws_ftp (PC) connection windows, respectively. You may or may not get an ftp window upon starting the application. If you don't and you are using Fetch, one can be obtained by selecting "open connection" from the ftp application's "file" menu. If you are using ws_ftp, the window you see in the background of Figure 2.11b should come up when you start the

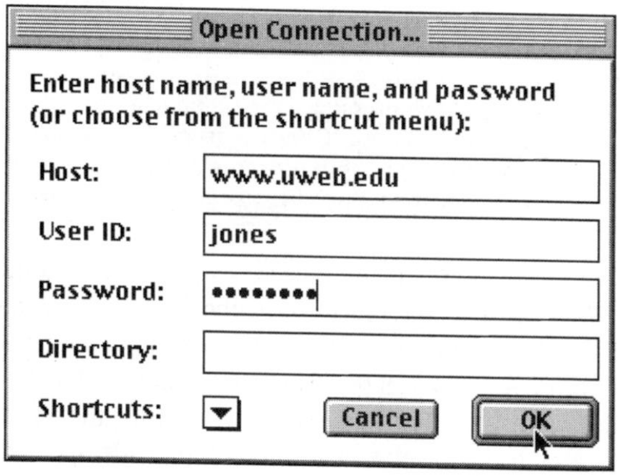

FIGURE 2.11a The connection window given by the Fetch application on a Mac.

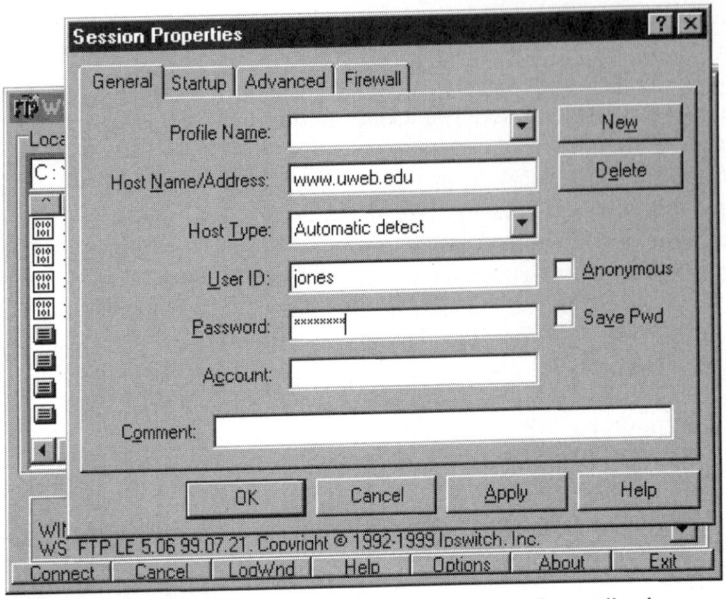

FIGURE 2.11b The connection window given by the ftp application on a PC.

application and it has a "connect" button, as you can see, in its lower left corner. Clicking this button brings up the connection window you see in the foreground.

As you can see in Figures 2.11a and 2.11b, to initiate an ftp connection to the web server, we simply had to specify the named address of the server, the user name for Jones' account and his password. Whoever sets up your web server account should give you detailed information on how to set your password. Setting passwords is quite simple, so we won't go into that right now. We do, however, offer a brief discussion about such matters at the end of this lesson. You may have noticed that other information can be supplied in the connection windows, but you simply need to tell the ftp application where to find the server, tell it which account to go to, and verify that you have the right to access the account by entering your password. Once this information is supplied and you click the "OK" button, the ftp application will make an ftp connection to the remote server (provided that the information is correct, of course).

NOTE Making ftp transactions to a user account on a server is an example of **non-anonymous** ftp. Not just anyone can make such transactions. Only a person armed with the password for the account can make such transactions. In other words, the server has to determine with whom it is dealing before allowing transactions. Such ftp procedures are, thus, not anonymous.

Upon making the connection you will receive a window that facilitates the actual file transfer transactions. We choose to call this window the file transfer window. Figures 2.12a and 2.12b show the file transfer windows of the respective applications. As you can see, the ws_ftp window shows more information than the Fetch window. The Fetch window shows only the file directory of Jones' account on the web server, while the ws_ftp window actually shows both Jones' directory on the web server (on the right side, labeled Remote Site) and

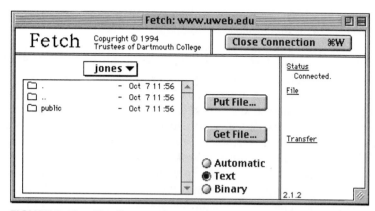

FIGURE 2.12a   The file transfer window in the Fetch application.

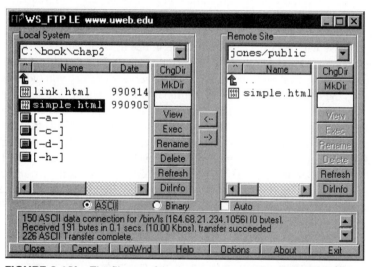

FIGURE 2.12b   The file transfer window in the ws_ftp application.

his directory on his local computer (on the left side, labeled Local System). However, as we shall see, the two applications easily accomplish the same thing.

In the ws_ftp window, you can see that the document "simple.html" has already been transferred into the public directory in Jones' account. This was accomplished by finding the right file on Jones' computer (you can see the file path above the Local portion of the window on the left), highlighting the file by clicking it, and then clicking the arrow button (→) pointing to the Remote Site. This arrow enacts a **put** transaction. In other words, the application puts a copy of the selected file onto the web server. The other arrow button (←) enacts a **get** transaction, getting a copy of a file on a remote computer and storing it onto the local computer. We won't discuss get transactions in detail because their purpose should be clear. We are more interested here in putting HTML files on remote servers than retrieving (getting) files from remote servers. Staying in line with previous terminology, put is for upload and get is for download.

We chose to discuss the ws_ftp transaction first because its window contains more information and will thus aid in describing the Fetch transaction. In Fetch, as in ws_ftp or any other ftp application, you first must select the appropriate directory for the upload. In the Fetch window, you can see that the proper directory has *not* been chosen. If we were to initiate a put transaction by clicking the put button in Figure 2.12a, the file would be transferred into the "jones" directory. However, recalling Figure 2.10 and the surrounding discussion about public directories, we need to transfer the file "simple.html" into his public directory in order for it to be accessible on the Internet. To accomplish this, we simply double-click the public directory folder in the Fetch transfer window to make that the chosen directory. It was in a similar fashion that we selected the public directory in the right-hand side of the ws_ftp window.

Having selected the public directory, the rest is simple. You click the put button and a new window pops up allowing you to choose the file you wish to upload. In this window, you can roam through the directories on your computer until you find the file you wish to upload and, when you choose that file for upload, this temporary window goes away, leaving you with the main Fetch window. Rather than having both windows together as is the case with ws_ftp, they are separate in Fetch. Upon initiating the put transaction, the Fetch application offers a temporary window displaying the local file directories. The file you have uploaded then appears in the web server directory you have chosen. Figure 2.13 shows the result of putting "simple.html" into Jones' public directory with Fetch.

Notice that in both cases depicted in Figures 2.12a and 2.12b, a button has been selected that causes "simple.html" to be transferred as an ASCII file. In the fetch window, the button was simply "Text", and in the ws_ftp window, the button was actually labeled "ASCII". This is crucial if you want your web page to be viable. We have stressed that HTML files are merely text files, and accordingly they must be transferred to the server as such. Binary transfers, another option you see, are used for things like image files. The automatic option will most likely transfer the HTML document as ASCII, but we have chosen the text option for emphasis. We will briefly discuss the automatic option when it becomes pertinent later in this book.

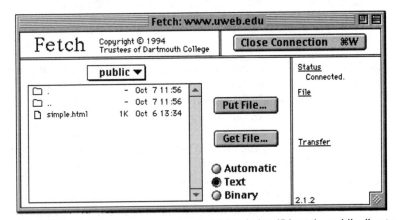

FIGURE 2.13 The completed upload of "simple.html" into the public directory.

Also be wary of your ftp program thinking it is pretty smart. For example, it may notice the fact that a text file is to be transferred and append the file suffix ".txt" onto the file you send. So in the above case, the result would be a file named "simple.html.txt" sitting on the server. This can cause major problems, especially when we start linking to local files with hypertext links. If your ftp program is doing this or something similar, you should be able to correct the annoyance by adjusting its preferences.

NOTE   The moral of the above two paragraphs is that when you transfer a web page to a server, or images as we will learn to do later, you should always check that the transfer was successful. The first way is to check in the ftp window whether the file made it with the right suffix and, perhaps more importantly, whether it made it into the right directory on the server. Even the experienced person accidentally transfers a file into the wrong directory once in a while. Finally, after the transfer crank up your browser, type in the URL of your account, and see if the web page appears as it should.

2.8   HIDING DIRECTORIES ON WEB SERVERS

We have seen several examples of URLs in action up to this point of the text. Moreover, we have discussed in some detail both the "how" part of the URL (protocol) and the "where" part of the URL (server address). The last part of the URL, the "what" part, also warrants more detailed discussion. To reiterate, the "what" portion specifies the exact resource sought by a URL request.

Figures 2.2a and 2.2b, and the surrounding discussion, serve as a good starting point. The "what" part of these file URLs specified the exact local file path to "simple.html" from the computers' (Mac and PC) hard drives. So the "what" in those instances corresponded to the exact locations of "simple.html" on the respective computers. So too, back now in the context of remote web servers, the "what" part of the URL specifies the exact location of the requested HTML document on that server. However, in the remote server case, the location is not specified relative to the server's hard drive, but from the public directory of a particular web domain.

Now that we know how to transfer HTML documents to remote servers, let's assume we have transferred both files "simple.html" and "link.html" to Jones' public root directory in his web account on the server "www.uweb.edu". With the discussion about public root directories behind us, we will henceforth just use the term "public directory" to refer to the actual directory at the domain that makes files public. This will prove less cumbersome linguistically. So anyway, both "simple.html" and "link.html" are in Jones' public directory.

In an attempt to pull up one of his pages, we type the URL "http://www.uweb.edu/~jones" into the address location of our browser and hit return. Figure 2.14 shows the result.

As you can see, we didn't get a web page at all but a listing of the files in his public directory. We simply didn't supply enough of the "what" information in the URL query. As per the discussion about domains and web servers in Lesson 1, it is as if "www.uweb.edu" is the "where" and "~jones" is the "what", the "what" being Jones' web page. As we shall see, that is still true, but in our current situation, it's simply not enough "what".

As was the case in Figures 2.2a and 2.2b, the file URLs terminated with not just the directory that contained "simple.html", but with the file name itself. In like fashion, the

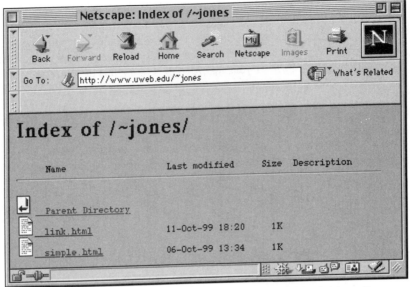

FIGURE 2.14 The result of the URL query "http://www.uweb.edu/~jones".

URL queries

"http://www.uweb.edu/~jones/simple.html"

and

"http://www.uweb.edu/~jones/link.html"

contain the specific "what" information needed to pull up each of Jones' web pages. But, having read Lesson 1, this might put you in a bit of a quandary. We indicated that the URL requests

http://espn.go.com/nfl

and the fictitious

http://www.senatorA.gov

for example, are sufficient to pull up web pages. But neither of these URL queries seem to specify the proper "what" information in the form of the requested HTML file. One might conjecture that "nfl" is the name of their football page and they just forgot to put the ".html" suffix on the file. However, since sites like ESPN are professionally developed and maintained, it is highly unlikely that they would make such a breach of convention and leave off the ".html". Moreover, "www.senatorA.gov" is merely a domain name and apparently has no possibility of referencing a specific HTML file.

In fact, the majority of domain names with which you are familiar don't seem to point to an HTML file. Think of "www.amazon.com" and "www.yahoo.com", for example. Moreover, it is clearly desirable to be able to pull up one of these web sites without having to

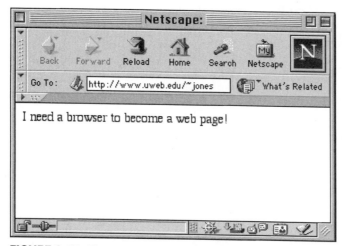

FIGURE 2.15 The request for Jones' public directory has actually pulled up the "index.html" file even though it was not specified in the URL.

remember something like "www.amazon.com/mainpage.html". Well, the solution to Jones' problem as depicted in Figure 2.14, and the thing going on behind the scenes that makes "www.amazon.com" pull up a web page even though none is specified, are one in the same. The best way to demonstrate this is by example.

Suppose Jones renames the file "simple.html" in his public directory with the name "index.html". Now, the exact same URL query that generated Figure 2.14 actually pulls up the HTML document formerly known as "simple.html". You can see in Figure 2.15 that it's the same page, it's just named "index.html".

The reason for this is that any file named "index.html" (or "index.htm") is effectively bound to its directory. That is, a URL request for the directory containing the index file is sufficient to pull up that index file. In Jones' case the request "http://www.uweb.edu/~jones", which merely targets his public directory, is actually targeting the file "index.html" since the index file is stored in his public directory. In like manner, the URLs "http://www.senatorA. gov" and "http://www.amazon.com" both not only target the public directory of each web domain, but the actual index file "bound to" that public directory.

NOTE   Such index files are sometimes called **default** files in the sense that a request for the file's directory automatically defaults to the file itself. In fact, some web servers are actually set up so that these files are called "default.html" (or "default.html") rather than index. But, once again, web server conventions are somewhat arbitrary. We will stick with the "index.htm" convention throughout this book since it is by far the most common.

This indexing behavior is by no means limited to public directories for web domains and accounts. Any other directory contained within the public directory is also given this default behavior. A perfect example is the URL request "http://espn.go.com/nfl", which goes beyond their public directory. As we mentioned above, "nfl" does not refer directly to an HTML document. After the preceding discussion, you may have already deduced that

espn.go.com

public

index.html

mlb

index.html

nba

index.html

nfl

index.html

FIGURE 2.16 URL requests for directories other than the public directory will also automatically pull up an index file, if one is present. Each index file is bound, by the server, to its parent directory. An http URL query for the directory automatically results in the index file being served up.

"nfl" is actually the name of a directory and the NFL football page is actually generated by an index file. Figure 2.16 depicts the situation. Of course, there are many more directories and files inside ESPN's public directory than those depicted, but the figure is sufficient to get our point across. (MLB and NBA stand for Major League Baseball and National Basketball Association, respectively.)

The directory structure depicted in Figure 2.16 is perhaps more complicated than necessary at this point of the text. But just as you organize files in a file cabinet or on your personal computer, it is good to organize files on a web server. Otherwise you have a jumbled mess and it is hard to find things. We discuss organization of web sites in detail in Lesson 5 but, in the meantime, the point to be made is that if a directory on your web server has no index file inside, a URL query for that directory will pull up a listing of that directory's contents much as in Figure 2.15. But, since the directories of Figure 2.16 contain index files, a request to

http://espn.go.com/mlb/index.html

for example, is equivalent to

http://espn.go.com/mlb

It is usually not desirable to have anonymous users perusing your directory listings. Rather, the user should have to follow the links in your web site according to how you have structured the site. But that's a story for another day.

NOTE This notion of having multiple files around, each with the same name, is often a point of confusion. Keep in mind that the files are much different, they just have the same name. For example, you could have two word-processing files named "termpaper.wp" that are totally different. Of course, just as in Figure 2.16, you would need to keep them in different directories to avoid confusion. As your web site expands into multiple directories as this text progresses, you should also have multiple index files. You will have to be extra careful to differentiate among them.

2.9   THE telnet PROTOCOL

Use of the telnet protocol is largely outside the context of the material presented in the first part of this book. However, there is one simple example that pertains to the above discussion and serves to round out our explorations of the various web protocols. When Jones opened an ftp connection to the web server at www.uweb.edu, he had to enter his password. When he first obtained his account on the server he was given a temporary password. In order for him to change this password and set up his permanent password, he had to "telnet" to the web server. Unlike ftp, which handles file transfer to and from a remote computer, telnet allows you to **log on** to or talk to a remote computer.

Most any computer should have some sort of telnet application. Moreover, it should have the word "telnet" in its name. You simply start the application and, if a connection window doesn't appear, you choose something like "open connection" or "open session" from the application's "file" pull-down menu. Since most telnet applications function similarly, we present an example using only telnet on a PC, rather than examples on both platforms. The connection window appears in Figure 2.17a. Upon typing in the address of the server and clicking the connect button, you get the window appearing in Figure 2.17b. We choose to call this the dialog window because you use it to talk to the remote computer.

In this case, Jones simply types in his user name, and is then asked for his temporary password. Upon entering it and hitting return, a new command line appears that asks him to enter a new password. After doing so, he most likely gets another command line that asks him to re-enter his new password. This redundancy in setting passwords is a common way to prevent one from making a typo. Other than remembering his new password, there is nothing more for him to do other than quit the telnet program. He is now ready to start putting web pages on the server with an ftp application.

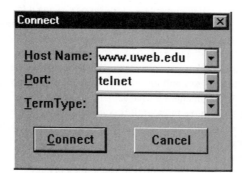

FIGURE 2.17a   The connection window for telnet on a PC.

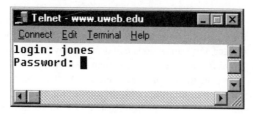

FIGURE 2.17b   The dialog window for telnet on a PC.

Giving computers such command-line instructions was very common just a few years ago. Before computers started using windows, you had to even talk to your local computer in this fashion. Mouses (mice?) were not even required. But with windows-type interfaces being common, the casual computer user may never have to deal with command-line interfaces in any context other than telnet. It is interesting to note that you have no doubt seen telnet in action numerous times at the movies or on television. Most any time you see a computer hacker trying to break into some remote computer, a telnet interface is being used.

2.10 SUMMARY

Key Terms

Platform	platform-independent	file protocol
ASCII file	text file	file suffix
HTML	cache	ftp
anonymous ftp	get	put
upload	download	public directory
index file	telnet	command line
(default file)	logon	

Since HyperText Markup Language (HTML) documents are rudimentary text (ASCII) files, they can be passed around to different computer platforms with little difficulty. Thus, since web browsers make these HTML files into web pages, web page construction is platform-independent. Development and editing of HTML documents is usually done locally, no Internet connection is even required. Local viewing of web pages in browsers is handled with the file protocol. You can usually just drag or click the icon for the HTML document for purposes of viewing it locally in your browser. Even though the "file" protocol is lurking when you view web pages locally, you should rarely have to deal with it directly. You should, however, be aware of the presence of the local file path in the "file" URL.

If a web page has been transferred to a web server, anyone hooked up to the Internet who knows the address of the server should be able to pull up the page using http. Keep in mind that this is an abuse of terminology since HTML documents are what actually sit on a server, and they don't become web pages until someone loads them into a browser. It is convenient, however, to abuse terminology and simply term HTML documents as web pages. You can enact http transactions both by typing http URLs into your browser's address window and by clicking on hypertext links in web pages. The result of an http transaction is that a web page is loaded into your browser. Web pages are not permanently stored on you hard drive, but are temporarily stored in cache memory for quick retrieval by your browser. Moreover, files transported by http sit harmlessly in the cache memory and can't unleash viruses.

In contrast, file transfer protocol (ftp) transactions actually write files onto your hard drive in a permanent fashion and can bring viruses to your computer. However, if you don't open a file transferred by ftp, it can't harm your computer. Ftp transactions can occur anonymously when you click an ftp link. Good examples of anonymous ftp are when you download freeware applications from web pages. When you wish to transfer a web page to your user account on a web server, you need an actual ftp application. Since a password is required, transfers of web pages to servers is non-anonymous. Upon opening an ftp application to put a file on a server, you basically follow these steps:

> **NOTE**
>
> To upload a web page to a remote server:
>
> 1. Put the server address, your user name, and your password in the connection window to access your account.
> 2. Choose the directory on the web server into which you wish to transfer the HTML file. To do this, you can peruse the directories on the remote server in the window provided by the ftp program.
> 3. Locate the HTML file on your computer you wish to transfer using the local directory finder of the ftp application. Then hit the "put" button. In some ftp programs you may not get the local directory finder until after you have hit the put button. In either case, you can peruse the files on your local computer until you find the one you wish to transfer.
> 4. Make sure you transfer HTML files with the text or ASCII option selected.
> 5. Always check to make sure that the file has made it into the right directory on the server and with the appropriate ".html" suffix. Also, pull up the HTML file from the server using the URL for your account to make sure it is actually being served up.

Keep in mind that most web servers require that web pages be placed inside a public directory inside your account in order that they be accessible for http transport. URL requests for your account are automatically shunted into this public directory. However, if you have no file named "index.html" inside your public directory, a request that doesn't contain a reference to a specific file on the end of the URL will actually pull up a listing of the contents of your directory, rather than your web page. Inclusion of an "index.html" file in each of your directories causes a request for the directory to automatically pull up the index file.

Finally, telnet is used to merely communicate or talk to a remote computer, rather than transferring files. To accomplish this, ftp applications provide a command line interface with which you can provide information to the remote computer. One such example is using telnet to talk to a web server to change the password for your account on that server.

2.11 REVIEW QUESTIONS

In most cases, it is not sufficient to answer these from the Lesson Summary.

1. What is a computer platform? Give two examples of platforms. Give an example of a type of computer resource that is platform-dependent. Give an example of a type of computer resource that is platform-independent.

2. Given that web browsers are platform-dependent, why is web surfing with browsers platform-independent?

3. Describe the three specific components of a file protocol URL (don't just say how-where-what). Give an example of when such a URL is used. What form does the file URL take on the computer type you use?

4. An HTML document named "ants.html" is sitting in the main root directory on a remote server with named address "www.aardvark.com". Write the URL necessary to view this document.

5. When you load an HTML document into your browser, what else might get transported into the cache memory along with the HTML document?

6. Why is anonymous ftp called anonymous? Contrast this with non-anonymous ftp.

7. How does an http transaction differ from an anonymous ftp transaction? Discuss the security risks of http vs. ftp.

8. Discuss the nature of a public directory on a web server. What are two other possible names for such a directory?

9. What is a "put" transaction? What is a "get" transaction?

10. Name two ways to check if you have transferred an HTML document to a web server properly.

11. Discuss the purpose of an indexing file. What is another common name for index files (besides "index.html")?

2.12 EXERCISES

1. Find out the name of public directories on your web server. Find the required name of index files on your server. Find out the nature of the URL required to access your web server account.

2. (a) Construct a file whose contents are similar to "simple.html" of Figure 2.1. Use your basic text editor. By "similar" we mean that only the textual content may vary. If you have a web server account, give this file the same name as the indexing file required by your web server. Otherwise, just name it "index.html".

(b) Create a new directory (folder) on your computer to contain this file. If you have a web server account, give this directory the same name as the public directory on your web server. Otherwise, name this directory "public".

(c) Load the file into a browser. Make note of the URL that appears in the browser address field.

3. Find out what ftp application you have access to. If you are working from your own personal computer and don't have one, download a freeware ftp application. (See the Lesson 2 section of the web site.)

4. (a) Transfer the file you made in Exercise 2 into the public directory of your web server account.

(b) In your browser, type in the appropriate URL to pull up this file to make sure the transfer was successful.

5. The point of this problem is to deduce the locations of HTML files at a web site. Go to the homework section for Lesson 2 on the web site for this book and click on the link for Exercise 5. An HTML file named "index.html" will load into your browser. This file is contained in a directory named "mystery". The directory "mystery" contains two other folders named "folder1" and "folder2". The situation is depicted below.

 mystery
    index.html
     folder1
        index.html
    folder2

You can see that folder1 also contains an index file, but folder2 does not. The catch here is that there are also six other HTML files that are not shown above, named "file1.html" through "file6.html". Your task is to figure out which files are in which directories and redraw the above directory diagram with the six other files put in the proper directories. To accomplish this, you can click some links that are provided in the index files. But to find some of the missing files, you will have to proceed by trial and error, adding the missing file names to the end of the URL in the browser's address field.

2.13 PROJECT THREADS

THREAD A

Start thinking about an agenda for your personal home page. It is hard to construct a personal web page without a fixed agenda. Good topics include: hobbies, favorite sports teams, favorite music, etc. Be thinking if your home page will explore several topics with minimal detail or one topic with a lot of detail.

Assignment

(a) Do Exercise 2. In the file, include a paragraph or two about the intended agenda for your home page. Note that the directory you create in Exercise 2b will contain all of your work throughout this book, and will become the public directory for your whole web site.

(b) If you have a web server account, do Exercise 4. It is important to note that you are merely making a copy of your

file on the web server. The local copy still exists on your local computer.

THREAD B

Assignment

(a) Do Exercise 2. In the file, write a paragraph to the effect that this page is where you will be linking to all of your Internet programming assignments. We will refer to this page as your homework page. Note that the directory you create in Exercise 2b will contain all of your work throughout this book, and will become the public directory for your whole web site.

(b) If you have a web server account, do Exercise 4. It is important to note that you are merely making a copy of your file on the web server. Your local copy still exists on your local computer.

LESSON 3

TEXT MARKUP

IN **LESSON 2** we touched on some of the various protocols that allow differing transactions on the WWW. We focused in particular on how HTML documents are passed around the Internet. Since HTML documents generate web pages when loaded into browsers, that is indeed a good foundation upon which to build. However, the Internet is not required to develop most of the material in this book. All you need is a personal computer that has a relatively current web browser. By current we mean Netscape 4 (or later) or Internet Explorer 4 (or later). Although virtually everything presented in this text will work on versions 3 of these browsers, the examples in this book are rendered with versions 4 and 5. Even versions 2 support much of the material covered through Lesson 6, but they don't uniformly support all of the HTML and JavaScript features presented in Lesson 7 and beyond.

The only other thing you need is a basic text editor. Fortunately, one of these is most likely present on whatever type of computer you wish to employ to construct web pages. If you will be using a Macintosh, the appropriate application is called "Simple Text." If you will be using a PC (Windows '95 or later), the appropriate application is called "Notepad." There are special applications, generically called HTML editors, that can be of great help once you learn the fundamentals. However, graduating to such editors before the appropriate understanding is in place will almost certainly result in undue confusion. After mastering the basics of building web pages, we will recommend the use of an HTML editor, but only then. Especially when we progress to creating interactive content with JavaScript will a mastery of the fundamentals of HTML be important.

NOTE As a last note before charging onward, the perfectionist should loosen up a bit at this point. With the realization that HTML causes objects to be configured into web pages by browsers also comes the realization that there are different browsers and, worse yet, different versions of the browsers. Different browsers often interpret HTML's markup instructions differently. These differences are often not drastic, but they are nonetheless a reality. You can spend all day getting your web page looking picture-perfect down to the millimeter in your browser on your personal computer, but if you put the thing on the Internet and someone with a different browser pulls up your page, there are often noticeable differences. Even things like different computer monitors with different resolutions can cause a web page not to look as it was intended. Just concentrate on presenting information in web pages in a relatively pleasing manner and leave absolute perfection to the artist.

3.1 HTML TAGS AND DOCUMENT STRUCTURE

Recall that HTML stands for *HyperText Markup Language.* The term "hypertext" refers to the text's ability to link to other documents. Now for the "markup" part. Many types of objects can appear in a web page. The most fundamental are text, images, and hypertext links. The HTML language does not actually create these objects. For example, an image that appears in a web page is not created by HTML. HTML merely tells a given web browser how and where to display it in a web page. In other terminology, HTML tells the browser how to "mark up" the image. Indeed, these very words you are reading are text and have nothing to do with HTML. However, as we will learn in this lesson, it would require HTML to enable these words to be marked up in a suitable fashion in a web page.

An HTML document is simply a text document. When it is loaded into a browser, the browser must first recognize the text file as an HTML file. Of course, the ".html" (or ".htm") file suffix, as evidenced in Figure 3.1, serves as initial notice to the browser, but the contents of the file itself are at the heart of the situation. This recognition is accomplished using the <HTML> **tag,** which signifies to the browser that it is dealing with an HTML document. The end of the document is signified by the </HTML> tag. The entire document that is to be a web page is contained between the two HTML tags.

The skeleton of any HTML document is shown in Figure 3.1. We have captured how the document appears on the computer screen as a "Simple Text" document to emphasize that it is no more than a text file. The file that we named "skeleton.html" would generate an actual web page. The problem is that the page would be completely blank. The HTML tags that comprise the text file are simply things that the browser recognizes and uses to format the real "stuff" that is to go into a web page. A browser doesn't actually put these tags in the web page it generates.

We mentioned some of the kinds of objects that can go into a web page, but for the time being, we will stick to creating pages that contain ordinary text. A browser only recognizes some text as a tag if the text begins with a "<" symbol and ends with a ">" symbol. So, all

FIGURE 3.1 The document "skeleton.html" generates a blank web page.

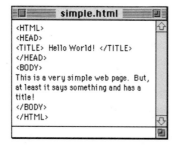

```
<HTML>
<HEAD>
<TITLE> Hello World! </TITLE>
</HEAD>
<BODY>
This is a very simple web page. But,
at least it says something and has a
title!
</BODY>
</HTML>
```

FIGURE 3.2 The document "simple.html" generates a very simple web page.

of the text in Figure 3.1 is formatted as HTML tags. That is why it generates a blank page when loaded into a browser.

The HEAD and BODY tags correspond, as one would expect, to the heading and body sections, respectively, of the HTML document. As we shall see, the HEAD section of an HTML document contains information about the document itself, such as the document's title. The BODY section contains the actual "stuff" that comprises the page—the text, images, links and so forth.

To create a web page that has actual content, we add something to each of the HEAD sections and BODY sections. To the HEAD section, we add the title of the web page. The title will be displayed as the page's title at the top of the browser. The title must be placed between TITLE tags.

<TITLE> The page's title goes here. </TITLE>

To the BODY section we add some ordinary text. Any text in the BODY of the document that is not contained within HTML tags "<>" is just that, text. Consider the HTML document named "simple.html" displayed in Figure 3.2. The result of loading "simple.html" file into a browser is displayed in Figure 3.3. The file was loaded into the browser locally. Hence the "file" protocol that you see in Figure 3.3 in the address field of the browser. Since we

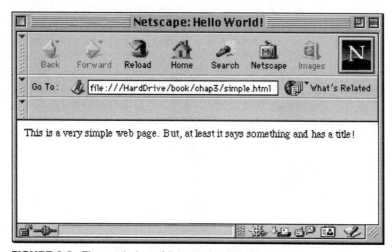

FIGURE 3.3 The rendering of "simple.html" in Netscape 4 on a Mac.

didn't go get "simple.html" from a remote web server, the address field shows a "file" URL with the local file path to "simple.html".

The browser did, in fact, treat the sentence in the BODY section as ordinary text since it wasn't marked as a tag with <>. Since the sentence wasn't a tag, it became part of the actual web page. The title, "Hello World", of the web page is seen in Figure 3.3 at the top of the browser window. Note that the title of the actual web page as defined by the TITLE tags in the HTML document is distinct from the name of the HTML document itself, "simple.html". The actual HTML file that was loaded into the browser is, of course, indicated at the end of the URL in the address window of Figure 3.3.

N O T E Since all HTML documents you will create have the same skeletal structure, it is recommended that you keep a copy of "simple.html" handy. It's like a template from which you can begin each time you wish to make a new web page. Just open the template, do a "save as" from the file menu, and choose a name for your new document. So, in theory, you only need to type the basic tags once. There is certainly no need to retype them each time you wish to make a new page.

Before continuing, there is a point that needs to be made. In an HTML document, space is not really space. That sounds dubious, but it's true. Consider   the large amount of space we left after the word "consider" in this sentence (no, that's not a typo).   That is real space; when this book was printed from a computer file, that space went along for the ride. Obviously, right, we can see it. Even the space after this very sentence and before the next paragraph is real space.

Notice all the space in the document in Figure 3.2; that is not real space. But we can see it, can't we? The document, "simple2.html", displayed in Figure 3.4 produces *exactly* the same results as in Figure 3.3, the rendering of "simple.html". The space in Figure 3.2 simply did not go along for the ride when the browser formatted the web page. Formatting is the job of the tags. Browsers do, however, recognize single spaces. Otherwise words in a sentence would run together.

The browser reads an HTML document from the top down and from left to right, much as you read a page in a book. If all the spaces were removed from this book the content would still be the same, it would just be very difficult for a human to read it. (It might freak out the spell checker as well!) The extra spaces we leave in an HTML document are only for the human reader. As HTML documents get longer and longer, it becomes harder to read them and detect possible errors. Although "simple.html" and "simple2.html" are simple (imagine that!), even the contrast between Figures 3.2 and 3.4 should convince one of the

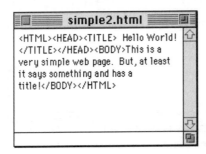

FIGURE 3.4 The space in simple.html is not real. The document simple2.html will produce the same results when rendered by a browser.

practicality of adding the extra space to make the document more readable by humans. Many of the rest of the HTML documents in this book were created not only with extra space but with indentations to emphasize certain things. The browser, however, couldn't care less.

A last point regarding HTML documents in general is that the HTML tags are case **in**-sensitive. That is, the following two tags are both perfectly fine:

<title>

</TiTle>

It is, however, a widely adopted convention to put tags in all capital letters. This again contributes to readability. For instance, even in the jumbled mess of Figure 3.4, the HTML tags stand out nicely from the other text.

3.2 CONTAINER ELEMENTS

Now that we have created a very simple web page, it's time to discuss in detail the nature of the HTML tags. The four sets of tags we have used, HTML, TITLE, HEAD, and BODY, each begin with a **start tag,** which is of the form <...>, and terminate with an **end tag,** which is of the form </...>. A unit such as

<BODY>...</BODY>

is called an HTML **element.** Elements of this type, that is elements with both start and end tags, are called **container elements.** In fact, each of the four elements we have used thus far are container elements. We have not yet seen any elements that are not container elements.

A container element tells the browser what to do with whatever the element contains between its start tag and end tag. Anything contained between the start and end tags of the HEAD element should be information about the document. Such information is always contained in another HTML element such as TITLE. There are only a handful of elements allowable inside the HEAD element. They all carry "meta-information" about the document, not the actual content that you see as part of the page. For the time being, TITLE is the only element we will use in the HEAD section.

Any text (images, links, etc.) that is to be part of the actual page is contained between the start and end tags of the BODY element. Any text, as we saw in Figure 3.3, in the BODY element is simply rendered as text in the generated web page. However, to tell the browser to do something with the text other than just display it as is requires yet more elements. After all, that's what HTML is for—to tell the browser what to do with "stuff." There are close to 100 types of elements that can be included within the BODY element. Some are for formatting text, some are for creating links, and others are for, well, other things. The collection of all these elements tells a browser what to do with the actual objects that are to comprise the web page.

There is an important point regarding container elements. They should be **nested;** that is, they should appear one inside another and not overlap. See Figure 3.5. Failing to nest container elements properly can cause a web page not to be rendered properly by a browser, or not to be rendered at all. This is not as important an issue as it used to be, however. Most

FIGURE 3.5 HTML container elements should be nested. They shouldn't overlap one another.

current browser versions are smart enough to correct for minor overlap infractions. But, nonetheless, nesting is still a practice to which you should strictly adhere.

3.3 FORMATTING TEXT

Standard text editors, such as "Simple Text" or "Notepad", format text for you. You can increase the size of text or make it boldface simply by pressing the right buttons on the keyboard or using the pull-down menus. For example, consider the HTML file in Figure 3.6. When the document "bold.html" is rendered as a web page in Figure 3.7, the browser has no clue that the text in the body section is intended to be large and bold.

Indeed, a browser must be told how to "mark up" virtually anything. Of course, to tell the browser to format text as boldface (or whatever else is desired), HTML elements are required. Rather than entering into an elaborate discussion about these new elements, it is best simply to proceed by example. The HTML document in Figure 3.8 displays a few of the most common HTML elements used for instructing browsers how to markup text. The resulting web page is displayed in Figure 3.9.

The purposes of the two container elements that surround the first two sentences should be apparent. There is one element that might seem strange, however. The

element, which you see at three different spots in the document, is not a container element. It is simply an element. It is not designed to enclose some text for the browser to format, but simply to cause something to happen. Namely, it causes a line break to occur in the web page—just like hitting return when typing. Its use in "textformat.html" was simply to put each formatting example on a new line in the web page. There are a couple of other such

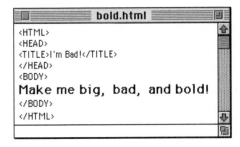

FIGURE 3.6 An HTML document with enlarged boldface text.

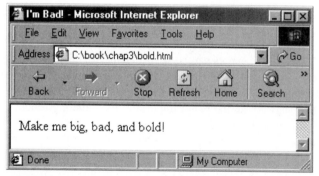

FIGURE 3.7 The rendering of the document of Figure 3.6 in Explorer 5 on a PC. The boldface text in the body of "bold.html" is ignored.

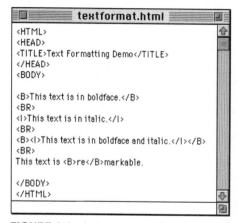

FIGURE 3.8 A document with various text-formatting elements.

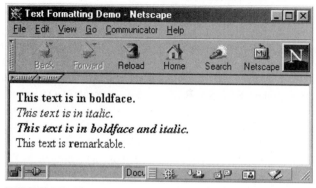

FIGURE 3.9 The rendering of the document in Figure 3.8 in Netscape 4 on a PC.

noncontainer elements that we will see shortly. However, nearly all HTML elements are of the container variety.

There are a couple of points to be made about the document "textformat.html". First, these text-formatting elements can be used together to create a multiple effect, as in the third sentence of the document. But, of course, the elements are properly nested, as you can see. The italic tags are on the inside and the boldface tags are on the outside. The order in which these tags are nested is not important; the italic tags could easily be put on the outside and the same effect would be generated.

The second point is slightly more subtle. In the fourth sentence, we placed only the "re" prefix between the boldface tags. The rest of the sentence, not being affected by any HTML tags, is just marked up as plain text. Even with all of these tags and elements floating around, if the browser finds text not within a container element, it marks it up as plain text. Moreover, the tags are completely gone by the time the web page appears in the browser in Figure 3.9. Even though the end tag of the boldface element seems to chop the word "remarkable" into two pieces, the word appears whole when rendered in the browser. The bold tags, having told the browser what to do with the "re" prefix, simply don't make it into the browser window. Remember, tags simply tell the browser how to format things, they don't show up in the generated web page.

> **N O T E**   There are a few other HTML elements used for basic text formatting. Some of these are rarely used, not supported by most browsers, or have been **depreciated,** which means that future browser versions may not recognize the tags. Two examples are the "<CENTER>... </CENTER>" and "<U>...</U>" elements, which center and underline the enclosed text, respectively. Even though they are used in many existing web pages, it is recommended that they be avoided in current page construction. However, since centering text is worthwhile, we will learn the recommended way to center text in Lesson 4, but will forgo underlined text completely. The author is not fond of underlined text since links are underlined and underlining plain text can cause undue confusion.

3.4 HORIZONTAL AND VERTICAL SPACE

Without the
 (line break) tags in "textformat.html", the document in Figure 3.8, the four sentences would be rendered much as the sentences of this paragraph, with no line breaks forced at the end of each sentence. Of course there are line breaks in this paragraph, but they are forced because of the right margin, not because the typist (unfortunately the author) hit return on the keyboard. In similar fashion, you don't always have to force line breaks in a web page with the <BR> tag. Browsers have automatic wraparound just like the word processor that created this paragraph. Figure 3.10 shows "textformat.html" displayed in a browser where the window has been made smaller. In other words, Figure 3.10 was obtained from Figure 3.9 simply by dragging the window smaller on the author's computer screen.

Notice that the line breaks forced at the end of each sentence by the <BR> tags are still enforced. The other line breaks are forced by the browser so that the text doesn't flow out of the browser window. You will also notice that the text is left-justified but not right-justified. In other words, the text's left margin is even whereas the right margin is not. In contrast, the text of this paragraph is fully justified (hence right-justified). Most browsers simply

This text is in
boldface.
This text is in italic.
***This text is in
boldface and
italic.***
This text is
remarkable.

FIGURE 3.10 Browsers force text wraparound based upon the size of the display window. However, regardless of window sizing, the line breaks forced by the <BR> tags are still observed.

don't support full justification. Even when we learn to right-justify text in Lesson 4, the left margin will be unjustified. In almost any browser, you simply get one or the other, but not both. This is the first blow to the perfectionist. You are most likely not going to get your text fully justified. Even if you find a browser version that does support full justification and design a web page accordingly, most other people will not be able to appreciate the fruits of your labor.

Two other noncontainer type elements that are useful in controlling line breaking (and vertical spacing in general) are the paragraph element, <P>, and the horizontal rule, <HR>. Once again, demonstration of these by example seems to fill the bill: see Figures 3.11

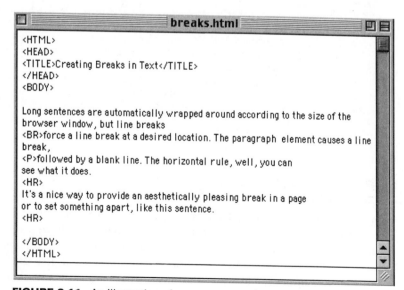

FIGURE 3.11 An illustration of some non-container elements.

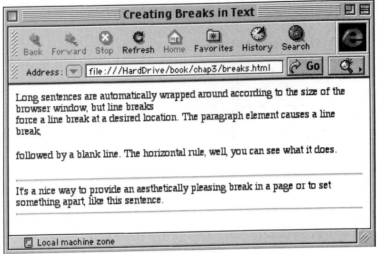

FIGURE 3.12 The rendering of the document in Figure 3.11 in Explorer 4 on a Mac.

and 3.12 for the document and its rendering, respectively. Rather than entering into a discussion about the specifics of these two elements, we have provided some commentary in the document itself.

> **NOTE**
>
> Having seen a variety of HTML elements and tags, you can see that creating HTML documents can be somewhat tedious. You have to type in all the "<" and ">" symbols as well as the strange names of the elements themselves. To do this you are going to have to spend a good bit of time at your computer. But that is just the nature of things. In the process, you are going to make some errors, primarily typos. What happens if you type in ">HR>" or "<RH>" by accident?
>
> The good news is that it won't cause your computer to explode. That would be a bummer! The way browsers deal with this is that if a browser sees an HTML tag that it doesn't recognize, it simply ignores it as if it weren't even there. So for example, if it encounters "<RH>" it is not going to say, "OK, the dude meant '<HR>' so I'll put one in." It's simply going to pass right over it and not mark up anything. This is one of the first levels of error detection. If you load a page and something doesn't appear that's supposed to, just check the associated tags for errors. Note that if you butcher a tag really badly, like just putting "HR" so that the browser doesn't even realize that it is supposed to be a tag, it will mark it up as ordinary text. That is also easy to detect.

3.5 HEADER ELEMENTS

We have not yet caused the browser to display text of varying sizes or colors. We delay discussion on fully controlling text size until Lesson 4 where the necessary HTML features are explored. There are, however, some very handy elements used for creating headers that do affect text size. By headers, we mean text that stands out, like the lesson titles at the beginning of each lesson in this book or the smaller subtitles that break up each lesson into sections. Headers come in varying sizes and are typically used to break up long documents

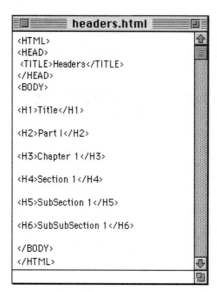

FIGURE 3.13 An illustration of the HTML heading elements.

into distinct units like chapters, sections, subsections, and the like. There are six HTML elements that make headers of varying sizes. Figures 3.13 and 3.14 serve to illustrate them.

In Figure 3.14, it is apparent that the header elements all render the enclosed text in boldface and that the font sizes range from quite large in the H1 element to quite small

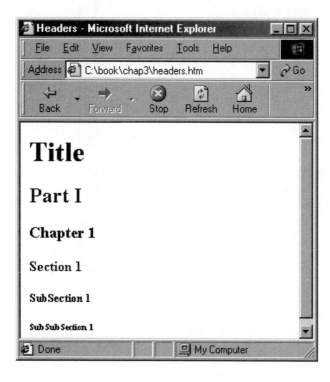

FIGURE 3.14 The rendering of the document in Figure 3.13 in Explorer 5 on a PC.

in the H6 element. But once again, this is at the discretion of the particular browser you are using. Also note that the header elements automatically provide a line break in the web page together with some vertical space to offset it from any text that is to follow.

3.6 PREFORMATTED TEXT AND QUOTED MATERIAL

We have seen several ways to create vertical space within a web page, but have used no HTML elements that can create horizontal space. One HTML element that can accomplish this is the

<PRE>...</PRE>

container element which preserves any preformatting that its contents may have. In other words, extra spaces within text contained in the <PRE>...</PRE> are rendered, rather than ignored. Another HTML element that affects horizontal spacing is the

<BLOCKQUOTE>...</BLOCKQUOTE>

container element, which causes its contents to be rendered as if it were quoted material in a book. The quoted material is rendered with exaggerated margins.

```
cdonline.html

<HTML>
<HEAD>
 <TITLE>CDs Online</TITLE>
</HEAD>
<BODY>
<H1>Welcome to CDs Online</H1>
<HR>
<B>Our Mission:</B>

<BLOCKQUOTE>
We strive to give you a no-hassle shopping experience, with
the best selection and the lowest prices in the world.
</BLOCKQUOTE>

<HR>
<B>Today's specials on overstock:</B>

<PRE>
  Santana:  Supernatural
          $8.99

  Metallica: Master of Puppets
          $7.99
</PRE>
</BODY>
</HTML>
```

FIGURE 3.15 An HTML document using preformatted text and quoted material.

FIGURE 3.16 The rendering of the document of Figure 3.15 in Netscape 4 on a PC.

Rather than entering into an elaborate explanation of these two elements, we present an example that uses both of them. The functionality of these two elements can be observed by examining the HTML document of Figure 3.15 and its rendering in Figure 3.16. You can see in Figure 3.16 that the sentence contained within the <BLOCKQUOTE>... </BLOCKQUOTE> element is simply indented at both the left and right margins. The text contained within the <PRE>...</PRE> element is rendered with all of the extra blank spaces preserved. But note that the spacing is not exactly preserved. In the HTML document the prices are somewhat offset from the names of the CDs, whereas in the rendered version the prices line up flush with the CD names. In practice, it sometimes takes a bit of trial and error to get things rendered as desired.

NOTE When creating horizontal space within the <PRE>...</PRE> element, avoid using tab spacing. Tabs are somewhat arbitrary and various browsers interpret them differently. Instead, just use a bunch of blank spaces created by the space bar. Moreover, since original paragraph formatting is preserved, you can't use <P> and <BR> tags inside the <PRE>...</PRE> element to force paragraph formatting with HTML. You can, however, use other HTML elements that force text formatting rather than paragraph formatting.

NOTE	There are two other elements related to BLOCKQUOTE that you may run across, but they are only supported by Internet Explorer 4 (and presumably subsequent versions). They are <Q>...</Q> for quoted material and <CITE>...</CITE> for citations. Since Netscape and older Explorer versions don't support them, we recommend using other means.

3.7 SUMMARY

Key Terms

Tag	start tag	end tag
element	container element	nested
depreciated		

All you need to create web pages is a computer with a browser, preferably version 4 or later, and a basic text editor, "Simple Text" on a Mac or "Notepad" on a PC. Every HTML (HyperText Markup Language) document has the same basic skeletal structure, but there are a variety of HTML elements that can be used in the <BODY>...</BODY> section to format text. A list of those elements that are widely supported by browsers and are not depreciated follows.

Container Tags	Function
<B>...</B>	boldface text
<I>...</I>	italic text
<H1>...</H1>	largest section header
⋮	⋮
<H6>...</H6>	smallest section header
<PRE>...</PRE>	preserve paragraph formatting of text
<BLOCKQUOTE>...</BLOCKQUOTE>	offset quoted material

NonContainer Tags	
 	line break (carriage return)
<HR>	horizontal rule (line across page)
<P>	paragraph (line break then blank line)

The container elements "act on" any text that they enclose, whereas the noncontainer elements simply cause something to happen. Container tags should be nested, meaning that they shouldn't overlap. Capitalization of the tags and extra spaces in the HTML document are for the benefit of humans. Browsers recognize single spaces only in order to keep words separate.

Information in the <HEAD>...</HEAD> section of an HTML document is not what appears in the web page, but information about the document. The only HTML element allowed in the HEAD section we have seen thus far is the <TITLE>...</TITLE> element. The title, which is contained between these tags, appears in the bar at the very top of the browser once the page is loaded. This is different from the actual name of the HTML document, which appears as the file name at the end of the URL in the address window.

> **NOTE**
> You may have noticed that the examples in this lesson are rendered using a variety of browsers. In fact, the versions of Netscape and Explorer that were the most current at the time this was written were used. Moreover, both Netscape and Explorer were used on each of the Mac and PC platforms—that's four different browsers. The only version-5 browser that was available was Explorer for PC. We anticipate that, at the time you read this, versions 5 (or even higher) of all of these browsers will be available.
>
> Rather than playing the browser shuffle throughout the remainder of this book, we render the rest of the examples in Netscape 4 on a Mac. This is for no specific reason other than they're simply the browser and platform to which the author is most accustomed. Just keep in mind that the same web pages may look slightly different in your browser on your computer. In fact, the reader is encouraged to upgrade (it's free!) to the most current browser versions for their platform and view the examples from this section and the rest of the book to note any slight differences. Both the examples and links to the upgrade sites can be found on the web site for this book.

3.8 REVIEW QUESTIONS

In most cases, it is not sufficient to answer these from the Lesson Summary.

1. Are HTML tags case-sensitive?

2. Explain the function of the HEAD section of an HTML document. Contrast this with the function of the BODY section.

3. Give an example of HTML tags that are not properly nested.

4. When you make boldface text in the actual HTML document using your text editor, how does that affect what gets marked up in the web page? Discuss the effect of inserting extra blank spaces in the HTML document. When you hit return to cause a new line in the HTML document, how does that affect the web page when it is marked up?

5. When a browser sees an HTML tag that it doesn't recognize, what does it do?

6. What is a depreciated HTML element? Name two.

3.9 EXERCISES

1. Deduce, by experimentation, the purposes of the following elements, which were not discussed in this lesson: BIG, SMALL, SUB, SUP, STRONG (they are all container elements).

2. Make a web page that uses the PRE element to create a table with three columns. List five of your favorite CDs in the following format. (If you don't know the year, guess.)

Artist	*CD*	*Release Date*
Corrosion of Conformity	Blind	1995
Black Sabbath	Paranoid	1970
:		

You should also use several of the other HTML elements from this lesson in the page.

3. Go to the homework section for Lesson 3 on the web site for this book. Under Exercise 3, you will find the picture of a web page. Make a web page with approximately the same appearance.

4. Go to the homework section for Lesson 3 on the web site for this book. Under Exercise 4, you will find the picture of a web page. Make a web page with approximately the same appearance.

5. Go to the homework section for Lesson 3 on the web site for this book. Under exercise 5, you will find the picture of a web page. Make a web page with approximately the same appearance.

3.10 PROJECT THREADS

THREAD A

If you have not yet done so, do the assignment for Thread A in Section 2.13.

Assignment

(a) Embellish your home page with many of the features presented in this lesson. Of course, if you have any refinements or additions to the agenda for your home page, you should include them.

(b) If you are to do any of the Exercises above, put that file(s) in your public directory with your home page. You will later link to this file(s).

(c) If you have a web server account, transfer all updates and new pages to the web server. It is important to note that you are merely making a copy of your files on the web server. The local copies still exist on your local computer.

THREAD B

If you have not yet done so, do at least one of the research questions from Section 1.15. Also, do the assignment for Thread B in Section 2.13.

Assignment

(a) Give your homework page a title. Also, give the page itself a large bold heading.

(b) Make each of your research assignments from Lesson 1 into a web page, and put the pages in your public directory. Embellish the pages with many of the HTML elements from this lesson. Supply links to each of the informational web sites that support your research. (See Figures 2.3 and 2.4 from Lesson 2 for making simple links.)

(c) If you are to do any of the Exercises from this lesson, put those file(s) in your public directory. You will later link to the file(s).

(d) If you have a web server account, transfer all updates and new pages to the web server. It is important to note that you are merely making a copy of your files on the web server. The local copies still exist on your local computer.

CONTROLLING TEXT MARKUP

WE HAVE seen several examples of HTML elements. In the case of the container elements like the one for boldface, <B> . . . </B>, the browser is told to mark up in boldface whatever text is contained within the element's tags. In the case of a noncontainer element, like the horizontal rule <HR>, the browser is told to insert a horizontal line into the web page. The key here is that these elements told the browser what to do, but not how to do it.

4.1 DEFAULT SETTINGS

When a browser is not expressly told how to do something, but just what to do, it reverts to what is called a **default setting.** For example, when a browser renders a web page it defaults to some standard background color for the page. This is determined by the particular browser that is rendering the page, but a typical default is a light gray background, since that provides good contrast for the black text. You can see from the various examples in Lesson 3 that the author's browser has been set to default to a plain white background.

NOTE The background color default setting is not necessarily dependent on the browser type or version, but can be chosen on a given browser application by altering the preferences for that browser. In fact, almost any application has preference settings that can be altered to provide desired default behavior. As a common example, even word processors such as Word Perfect and MS Word have preference settings that can be changed to provide a different default color for text or background. Most people, whether or not they are aware of preference settings, just leave black as the default text color on their word processor. Similarly, for the casual user, it is advisable to leave most preferences for a browser unchanged. Besides, as we shall see, many web pages override the defaults anyway.

It is an abuse of terminology to say that browsers have a default background color for web pages. In actuality, the default is for the <BODY> . . . </BODY> element. However, this amounts to roughly the same thing since the body element generates the entire content of the web page. So when the browser is told what to do, namely mark up the contents of the <BODY> . . . </BODY> element as the web page, it simply reverts to the default. Similarly, virtually all HTML elements have default standards. For a familiar example, the <HR> element just told the browser to put in a horizontal line, it didn't say how wide or thick of a line to put in. As it turns out, the default for the width of the line the <HR> element inserts in a web page is just "make it span the page." We saw this in several examples in Lesson 3. So once again, when the browser is only told what to do and not how to do it, it reverts to the default.

4.2 THE HR ELEMENT AND HTML ATTRIBUTES

There is an important feature of HTML that allows you to provide instructions for the browser to override an element's default behavior. This feature provides for the use of HTML **attributes** that supplement the information an element gives to a browser. As we have emphasized, an element by itself tells the browser what to do. The use of attributes in conjunction with elements provides a means of telling the browser not only what to do, but how to do it. So, basically, the element is the "what to do" and the attribute is the "how to do it".

To illustrate what HTML attributes are and how to implement them, we begin with the <HR> element. This element has several attributes that are easily understood, and thus serves as a fine starting example. In terms of the utility of <HR> in building web pages, the length of the discussion below could be considered overkill. However, the fact that <HR> has several attributes whose value types will be used throughout this book makes it the perfect target for a lengthy discussion about attributes.

Once again, an attribute is the "how to" component of an element. As the terminology of the last sentence attests, the attribute is a component (part) of the element. Well, the HR element consists of only the solitary tag <HR>, so the only place for an attribute is, thus, inside the tag itself. For example, the following endows HR with a WIDTH attribute:

```
<HR WIDTH="50%">
```

This attribute is kind of a unit, a property of the HR element together with a value. The value determines the property of the element. For example,

```
<HR WIDTH="75%">
```

sets the value of the WIDTH attribute to 75%, creating a line 75% the width of the browser window. Of course, then, the first example above would set the WIDTH attribute of the line to 50%, creating a line 50% the width of the browser window. In this way, the value of the attribute can be changed from case to case to yield a line of a desired width.

HTML elements typically have more than one attribute. The HR element has three common attributes, WIDTH, SIZE, and ALIGN. The SIZE attribute is used to determine the thickness of the line and the ALIGN attribute to determine the alignment (left, right, center) of the line in the browser window. When an element has multiple attributes, they may be used together in combinations within the element to fine-tune the rendering of the element. Thus, if desired, all three of the attributes above can be used simultaneously in the HR element.

Their use is best demonstrated by example. Figure 4.1 displays an HTML document containing several HR elements, each of which contains varying combinations and values of these attributes. The web page generated by Figure 4.1 is displayed in Figure 4.2. The appearance of the first three instances of the <HR> element in Figure 4.1 should come as no surprise. The way they are rendered is apparent from their definitions. The fourth instance, whose SIZE attribute has the value of 1, appears as just a black line. Most browsers mark

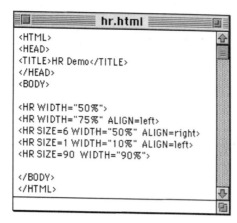

```
                    hr.html
<HTML>
<HEAD>
<TITLE>HR Demo</TITLE>
</HEAD>
<BODY>

<HR WIDTH="50%">
<HR WIDTH="75%" ALIGN=left>
<HR SIZE=6 WIDTH="50%" ALIGN=right>
<HR SIZE=1 WIDTH="10%" ALIGN=left>
<HR SIZE=90  WIDTH="90%">

</BODY>
</HTML>
```

FIGURE 4.1 The <HR> element with several combinations of its attributes.

up the HR element with a shaded effect, kind of a perceived depth. With a specification of SIZE=1, there is no room for this effect.

The fifth instance, whose SIZE attribute has the value of 90, appears as a box rather than a horizontal line. That is to be expected since it is so thick. It is apparent that the last HR element takes up about 90% of the width of the browser window as expected, since its WIDTH attribute is set at 90%. However, its SIZE attribute is also set at 90 but it clearly doesn't take up 90% of the height of the browser window.

The values of the SIZE attributes of the last three of the HR elements in Figure 4.2 are not given as percentages but just as numbers. These non-percentage values determine the thickness of the respective HR element as a number of **pixels.** The term pixel stands for

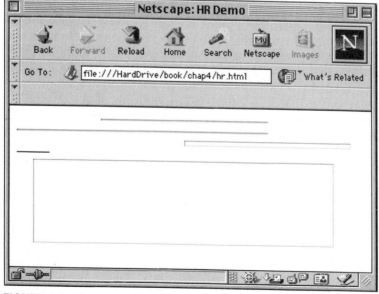

FIGURE 4.2 The rendering of the document of Figure 4.1.

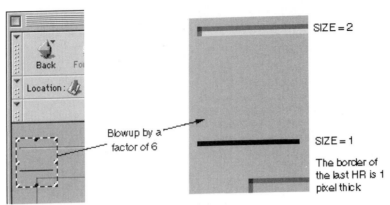

FIGURE 4.3 A blowup containing portions of the second, fourth, and fifth HR elements of Figure 4.2.

*pic*ture *el*ement and refers to the myriad small "dots" that a computer monitor (or TV for that matter) uses for display. Typical computer monitors use a half million or more pixels to make images on the screen.

For example, Figure 4.3 contains a blowup of part of the upper left portion of the web page shown in Figure 4.2. We have, however, added a gray background for contrast.

The effect that makes the line look almost three-dimensional in a web page is created by bordering the HR with pixels of contrasting shades of grey, as shown in Figure 4.3. The HR element in Figure 4.3 whose SIZE is two pixels was defined in Figure 4.1 by

<HR WIDTH="75%" ALIGN=left>

There is no mention of the SIZE attribute in this definition, yet its thickness is two pixels. This is the default size for the <HR> element. So, in the context of HTML elements, the default setting is the value that is automatically given to the attribute if the attribute is not present in the element. For example, the basic HR definition

<HR>

has no mention of any attributes. Thus, when it is marked up, the default settings for each of the missing attributes are used by the browser. The default settings for the three attributes of the HR element are WIDTH="100%", SIZE=2, and ALIGN = center. If any or all of these attributes are not present in the definition of a HR element, the browser simply resorts to the default settings. Refer back to Figure 3.11 to see the markup of an HR element using only the default settings.

NOTE The size of pixels varies from computer to computer. It depends both on the intrinsic resolution of the computer's monitor and on the resolution set by the computer's operating system. For a typical computer there are about 72 pixels per inch (about 30 per centimeter). So, for example, if you want an <HR> about two inches wide, you should specify WIDTH = 144. But, once again, there is no guarantee that it will be two inches wide on every computer.

One other feature of HTML attributes is that they may be able to take multiple types as their values. For instance, not only can the WIDTH attribute take percentages as values,

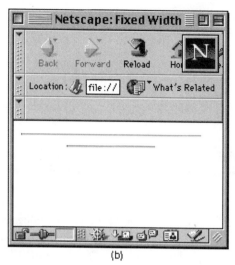

(a)   (b)

FIGURE 4.4 (a) The default 100% is roughly the same width as 87 pixels;
(b) the second HR is still 87 pixels, but the default 100% is adjusted to the new
window size.

but it can also take values in pixels. The following two HR definitions

<HR>

<HR WIDTH=96>

each produce roughly the same width line when viewed as in Figure 4.4a. However, in
Figure 4.4b, when the window is made somewhat larger, the first HR with the default
setting of 100% adjusts to the window size whereas the second HR with the setting of
WIDTH = 96 pixels remains the same size, 96 pixels.

Finally, some kinds of attributes take no value at all. The HR element has an attribute
called NOSHADE that causes the browser to override the default shading effect. Figure 4.5

FIGURE 4.5 The rendering of two HR
elements using the NOSHADE attribute.

shows the markup of the following two HR elements:

<HR SIZE=4 NOSHADE>

<HR SIZE=10 WIDTH=20 NOSHADE>

The rendering of the two HR elements in Figure 4.5 is done with all black pixels. The default shading effect was overridden by the NOSHADE attribute.

4.3 HTML ATTRIBUTES IN GENERAL

The goal of the previous discussion of the HR element is to make ourselves familiar with the notion and use of HTML attributes. Certainly HR provides a handy tool when constructing web pages, but its utility alone does not warrant a discussion as lengthy as the above. However, what did warrant such a protracted discussion is the fact that both the types of attributes that HR takes and the particular values these attributes accept are widely used in this lesson and in subsequent lessons of this book.

In general, an HTML element may or may not make use of attributes. Many elements, such as the HR element, may be used without any attributes whatsoever. In this case, the attributes are called optional. When an optional attribute is not present in an HTML element, the browser simply resorts to the default setting for that attribute. The use of default settings is particularly necessary when the attributes correspond to physical characteristics of the object the element is to mark up. Since each markup of such an object must be endowed with physical characteristics, there must be default settings or else the browser would be confounded.

Attributes may or may not have values. If the attribute has a value it can *always* be included in quotes after the attribute:

ATTRIBUTE="value"

In general, one can't go wrong by always including the value of an attribute in quotes. In cases where the value is strictly numerical (SIZE = 5), the quotes may be omitted. Also, if the values come from a fixed set of options (ALIGN = center), the quotes can often be omitted. However, in many cases the quotes are required. For instance, when the values contain special characters, such as a percent sign (WIDTH="75%"), quotes are often required. The newer browser versions are somewhat more tolerant of attributes that are not in quotes, but there are attributes whose values absolutely must be contained within quotes. At the appropriate junctures, we will remind you of this.

Often, the values accepted by HTML attributes correspond to quantities with which are familiar. Quantities such as 75% are intuitively clear, as are quantities such as left, right, and center. In fact, we process information using quantities such as these on a daily basis in everyday life. For example, we center pictures on a wall or note that the gas tank is 50% full (or 50% empty!). However, HTML attributes also use values that one doesn't use on a daily basis. Examples are pixels and hexadecimal color representations. When the time comes to deal with colors, we will include an appropriate mention of hexadecimal color representations.

In contrast, some attributes don't have values at all. For example, the NOSHADE attribute of the HR element has no value. If it is present, it overrides the default setting.

Such attributes could actually be given values, as in the following hypothetical case. Suppose NOSHADE had two possible values, true and false. The default would then be NOSHADE = false, and overriding the default would be NOSHADE = true. In such a way, such attributes could have values. The advantage of not including values in attributes like NOSHADE is clear: less typing. The previous hypothetical example of NOSHADE with values illustrates how it works; it's a true/false or on/off kind of attribute. Other HTML elements have such on/off type attributes that typically require no value.

HTML attributes must be defined within the actual tags that comprise the element. For noncontainer tags this is straightforward, since there is only one tag that defines the element:

<TAG ATTRIBUTE="value">

When an attribute is to be included in a container tag, it must be defined in the start tag of the element:

<TAG ATTRIBUTE="value">.........</TAG>

Many HTML elements have attributes that are not optional. In general, when an attribute has no natural default for the browser to fall back upon, the attribute is inherently non-optional. For example, the anchor element, which we discuss in detail in Lesson 5, is used to create hypertext links to other HTML documents. You saw this element in Figure 2.3 in Section 2.4. Acting as a link, it must provide reference to some other HTML document by specifying a URL. Such reference is given by an attribute of the anchor element. If the attribute were optional, there would need to be a default setting—some default HTML document to automatically link to. Clearly, there is no call for one universal HTML document to which all links throughout the world default. So elements such as the anchor element have mandatory attributes.

As a final note, we mention that when an element has several attributes, it doesn't matter in what order they appear in the element. For example, the following two element definitions are equivalent:

<TAG ATT1="value"   ATT2="value"> . . . </TAG>

<TAG ATT2="value"   ATT1="value"> . . . </TAG>

In other words, if you are going to put several attributes in an HTML element, just put them in there and don't worry about the order in which they appear.

NOTE

A very common mistake that causes an element not to be marked up properly is the inclusion of extra blank space. Throughout Lesson 3, we emphasized that space in an HTML document doesn't matter. There are some subtle spacing issues that do matter, however. First, the fact that attributes can be placed in tags makes it necessary for browsers to be tolerant of

<TAG   >...</TAG>   **OK**

where there is some extra space added after the start tag where attributes would be placed. Since attributes can be placed only *after* the start tag, browsers are not tolerant of

<   TAG>...</TAG>   **OOPS!**

where space has been added before the tag name. In fact, most browsers would not even recognize the preceding as an HTML tag at all and would render the actual character string "<   TAG>...</TAG>" as text in the web page. Finally, most browsers are not tolerant of space before or after the equals sign of an attribute. For example,

<TAG ATTRIBUTE=   "value">...</TAG>   **OOPS!**

would most likely cause problems since there is blank space after the equals sign.

4.4 PARAGRAPH ALIGNMENT

We have seen the paragraph element as a noncontainer tag, <P>. It functions little differently from the BR element. They both cause the subsequent text to begin on a new line. However, on most browsers, the P element also inserts an extra blank line whereas the BR element does not. The P element causes, in effect, a carriage return followed by a blank line. The P element can also be used as a container element to align paragraphs. Appropriately, it takes the ALIGN attribute. The ALIGN attribute of the P element works basically in the same way as the ALIGN attribute of the HR element. It takes only left, right, and center as values, and the values cause the paragraph to be aligned appropriately. Of course, when used as a container element, the attribute must be defined in the start tag of the element:

<P ALIGN=left> The paragraph to be aligned. </P>

The above paragraph element, even though it contains the ALIGN attribute, still displays the paragraph using the default setting for paragraph alignment. That is because the default for paragraph alignment is ALIGN=left. Clearly it is natural for the default for paragraphs that they be aligned to the left margin of a page, whether we're dealing with paragraphs in a book or in a web page. With a natural default, the ALIGN attribute of the P tag is optional.

In practice, its use is straightforward and is best demonstrated by example. Figure 4.6 displays a document with variously aligned paragraphs. The rendering of the document is given in Figure 4.7.

```
Palign.html
<HTML>
<HEAD><TITLE>Paragraph Demo</TITLE></HEAD>
<BODY>
I am a normal paragraph. I am thus aligned to the left margin of
the browser window by default. My left alignment does not necessarily
reflect my political views.
<BR>
<HR WIDTH="50%">

<P ALIGN=center>
I am a paragraph that, for emphasis, has been placed in the
middle of the browser window.
</P>

<HR WIDTH="50%">

<P ALIGN=right>
I am a paragraph that is right-aligned. Once again,
please don't take this as a political statement.
</P>
</BODY>
</HTML>
```

FIGURE 4.6 A document using attributes with both container elements and noncontainer elements.

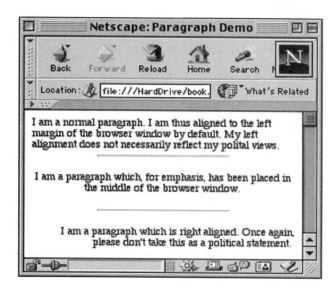

FIGURE 4.7 The rendering of the document of Figure 4.6.

One of the main things to note in Figure 4.7 is that the alignment of the paragraphs is sloppy. For example, the right-aligned paragraph, although each line is flush with the right margin, has an unjustified left margin. Moreover, the left-aligned paragraph has a jagged right side. The only aesthetically pleasing paragraph is the centered one. Once again, there is really no way around this short of using the <PRE> . . . </PRE> tags for preformatted text. But note that most web pages that contain a decent amount of text just use the P element for alignment of paragraphs and simply have one or more unjustified margins.

NOTE Actually, ALIGN does take a "justify" value that fully justifies text. However, this attribute is only supported by some browsers. The newest browser versions seem to fully align text pretty well.

In Figure 4.6, one should contrast the use of attributes in the noncontainer element HR with the use of attributes within the container version of the P element. The attributes of the self-contained HR element have an internal effect on the object it marks up. The attributes don't affect anything external to the HR tag itself. In contrast, the attribute of the container element P affects its entire contents. In other words, the attribute acts on the contents of the element rather than the element itself.

4.5 ATTRIBUTES OF THE BODY ELEMENT

Since the <BODY> . . . </BODY> element of an HTML document contains virtually everything that is to be marked up in the web page, it is natural to expect that any attributes of the BODY element will affect properties of the entire web page. Indeed, that is true. Perhaps the most desired effect is to provide a nice colorful background for the entire web page. The BGCOLOR attribute of the BODY element provides an easy way to set the ambient color of a web page. For example,

<BODY BGCOLOR="blue">

gives a web page a blue background. It's that simple. Note that, as with any attribute, the BGCOLOR attribute is placed inside the start tag of the body element. Since the BODY tags are always present in an HTML document, one simply places the BGCOLOR attribute in the pre-existing <BODY> start tag.

The drawback to this is that there are only a limited number of **named colors,** such as "blue", that browsers recognize. By named color, we mean that the color has a name like "blue". There are actually about 17 million colors that most modern computers can display. To represent that many colors, **hexadecimal** color representations are required. The term hexadecimal refers to a base-16 number system, unlike the base-10 numbers we use in day-to-day life. We won't go into detail about hexadecimal colors here, but complete coverage can be found in Appendix C. A hexadecimal color is a six-digit "number" in which each digit can be one of the integers 0–9 or one of the letters A–F. For example,

<BODY BGCOLOR="#66BBFF">

gives a mild light blue background to the web page. In practice it is advantageous to understand hexadecimal colors, but not necessary.

The bad news is that there are only 256 colors that many browsers will actually display in a web page. However, in reality, due to different browser types and versions, only 216 colors are termed **browser-safe** or **web-safe.** This means that if you stick to these web-safe colors, any browser on any platform will render that color exactly as intended. If a browser can't render a particular color, it approximates the color using one of its available colors. Straying from the web-safe colors can lead to substantial differences in your color scheme on different browsers.

Well, it there are only 216 web-safe colors, why even deal with hexadecimal colors at all? For starters, naming colors is somewhat arbitrary. If you've looked inside a box of crayons lately, you have no doubt seen some pretty strange names for colors. With all of the bizarre color names, it is not surprising that different browsers and different browser versions don't support the same set of named colors. There are perhaps only 150 or so named colors that any browser should recognize. But, even some of the ones that are apparently supported on most browsers are strange. For example, "blanchedalmond", "lightgoldenrodyellow", and "papayawhip" are supposed to be supported by both Netscape and Explorer. However, on the author's computer, even some of these were not recognized.

> **NOTE** The moral of all this discussion about colors is that you're better off using a color-picking application to generate hexadecimal colors for you. There are several freeware applications that you can download to generate hexadecimal colors for you. Some of these are referenced in the web site for this book. In these applications, you can visually pick a color you like and the corresponding hexadecimal color representation will be generated for you. Moreover, some of these applications have a web-safe option that allows you to stick to the safe colors. There is also a web-safe color palette referenced in the web site for this book. Either a color-picking application or the color palette will give you far more versatility than trying to remember various named colors that may or may not work. But remember that **any hexadecimal color must be preceded by the pound sign, #.**

It is OK to use named colors, like "blue" for instance. In fact, if you stick to common color names you will probably not run into too many problems. But another drawback stems from the fact that many named colors are quite bold. For instance, "blue" produces such a rich background that the default black text hardly stands out from the blue page. Once again, rather than using named colors, it's best to pick a nice soft hexadecimal color for your background.

There are some other attributes of the BODY element that also take colors for values. First there is a TEXT attribute that takes either named or hexadecimal colors as values. For example,

<BODY BGCOLOR="#000000" TEXT="#FFFFFF">

produces a black web page with white text. Just be careful that there is adequate contrast between the background color and text color you choose. Again, one of the color-picking applications or the color palette should be helpful.

Finally, there are attributes that control link colors in a web page. Although we do not discuss links until the next lesson, we present here the three attributes that can be used to set link colors. The LINK attribute sets the color of any link in a web page that has not been visited. The ALINK (active link) attribute sets the color of an active link. Click your mouse on the link and hold the mouse button down and you should see the color set by ALINK. Finally, VLINK sets the color of any link that has already been visited. In practice, LINK and VLINK are considerably more useful than ALINK. For example,

<BODY BGCOLOR="#FFFFFF" LINK="#009900" VLINK="#990000">

renders a page with white background, the default black text (since the TEXT attribute is not present), green links, and visited links that are red.

NOTE Browsers have preferences with which you can specify a default setting for all of the above attributes of the BODY tag. Thus, if a web page has none of these attributes present, the colors set in the browser's preferences will appear in the web page. However, it is not advisable to alter these preferences in your browser. For example, if someone's web page has been set with a green background color but has not specified link colors with the LINK attribute, and your browser's preferences have been set to render links in green, your browser will render links in the same color as the background of the page. Hence, you would not be able to see the links.

4.6 THE FONT ELEMENT (DEPRECIATED)

In order to have more control over the size, color, and type of text in a web page, the <FONT> ... </FONT> element is commonly used. However, as the section title above indicates, it has been depreciated. So, at some point in the future, it will likely not be a standard HTML element, although, at the time of writing, it is still in widespread use. The eventual replacement for the FONT element is the use of Cascading Style Sheets (CSS). Section 4.8 presents the basics of CSS. But, even in version-4 browsers, CSS is somewhat inconsistent. For our later discourse on CSS, we have therefore chosen a streamlined subset of style-sheet elements that should work on almost any version-4 browser or later, and on any platform.

In the meantime, we do present the FONT element since it is still in widespread use and you will no doubt run across it. The same is true of the <CENTER> . . . </CENTER> element, which we mentioned was depreciated in Lesson 3. Even though we have presented means of centering text, namely

<P ALIGN=center> . . . </P>

it is advantageous to be aware of it since you will no doubt run across it before it gets retired.

The main properties of text that it is desirable to control are size, color, and font face. Indeed, when you use a word processor, you make decisions regarding these text properties all the time. For example, when writing this book, we had to choose a text size and font. It was pretty clear that we just wanted black text, rather than some bright color as might be desirable in a web page. In our case, we chose 10-point text in the Times Roman font. Points (pt) refer to the size of the given text. Common sizes for text are 10 pt and 12 pt. Titles are often rendered in larger sizes, like the 12 pt section headings in this book. Font refers to font types like Helvetica, Courier, and Geneva, just to name some common ones. Setting such text properties in a word processor is easy and should be familiar to you. However, controlling them in a web page requires HTML elements and attributes.

The <FONT> . . . </FONT> element takes as attributes the three text properties we mentioned in the preceding paragraph, namely, SIZE, COLOR, and FACE. The values of the SIZE attribute are not specified in points as in a word processor, but in absolute and relative sizes. The SIZE attribute takes the values 1, 2, 3, 4, 5, 6, and 7 for absolute font sizes. The typical default SIZE on most browsers is SIZE = 3, which is roughly equivalent to 10-pt or 12-pt font in word processing. So, for example,

<FONT SIZE=5>some text</FONT>

renders the enclosed text two sizes larger than the default SIZE of 3. The SIZE attribute can also take on the relative sizes of ±1, ±2, . . . , and so forth. For example,

<FONT SIZE="+2">some text</FONT>

renders the enclosed text two sizes larger than whatever the browser's default SIZE is set at. If the browser has the typical default of SIZE=3, then SIZE="+2" is equivalent to text of size 5.

These relative sizes add some extra insurance given different default sizes for browsers. For example if you wish a certain block of your text to be small and you specify SIZE=2, your text could actually be the same size as the rest of the text if the browser defaults to a size of 2. However, SIZE="−1" should always make the desired block of text one step smaller than the rest.

The COLOR attribute takes on either a named color or a hexadecimal color. For example,

<FONT COLOR=red>This sentence is red.</FONT>

renders the whole sentence in red. The FACE attribute simply takes on one or more font faces. For example,

<FONT FACE="arial">This sentence will be rendered in Arial font.</FONT>

sets the font face of the sentence as Arial, a common font. The bad news here is the fact that different browsers and different computers often support different font faces. In practice, this is not a major problem since a browser simply will revert to a default font if it can't find the one you are telling it to use. Some common faces that most any computer or browser should support are listed below in their respective styles.

Arial

Chicago

`Courier`

Geneva

Helvetica

Monaco

New York

Palatino

Times

If you feel adventurous, you can check to see what fonts your browser recognizes by looking in its preferences to see what options are presented for font face. Or you might crank up a word processor and see what font options it can find on your computer. There is a decent chance that if you word processor can find the font, so can your browser. There are some pretty cool ones you can find. For example,

𝔅𝔩𝔞𝔠𝔨 𝔉𝔬𝔯𝔢𝔰𝔱

is in "BlackForest" font, which is kind of a gothic-looking font. But once again, if you try to use this font in a web page and the browser can't find it, the browser will simply resort to the default. If you are a perfectionist and you don't wish to resort to having to use a browser's default font, you can specify a list of fonts:

    <FONT FACE="EngraversGothic BT Regular, BlackForest, Arial">This text will be rendered in whichever font the browser can find, starting from left to right.</FONT>

and the browser will start checking for them from the left to right. If it can't find one it just checks for the next one. In the above case, if it can't find the first two, it will most likely find Arial.

NOTE	Font names are *not* case-sensitive. So "blackforest" works just as well as "BlackForest". However, font names *are* space sensitive. So, if you specify "Black Forest", the browser won't be able to find the font, even if it is present on the computer.

4.7 PUTTING IT ALL TOGETHER: A PRACTICAL EXAMPLE

Now that we have seen attributes used for various purposes, it is appropriate to present an example that uses many of the features we have explored. For illustration purposes, we design an abbreviated lunch menu for a hypothetical sandwich shop. As when building

```
                                karen.html

<HTML>
<HEAD>
<TITLE>Karen's Lunch Menu</TITLE>
</HEAD>

<BODY BGCOLOR="#CC99CC">
<P ALIGN=center>
<FONT SIZE="+2" FACE="BlackForest" COLOR="#003399">Karen's Sandwich Shoppe</FONT>
</P>
<HR>
<FONT SIZE="+1" COLOR="#003399">Daily Special:</FONT> Liverwurst with salami and
mushrooms on rye.</FONT>
<BR>
<P ALIGN=right>
<FONT COLOR="#003399">Regular:</FONT> $3.99
<BR>
<FONT COLOR="#003399">Triple Decker:</FONT> $5.99
</P>
<HR>
<FONT SIZE="+1" COLOR="#003399">The SCOOBY:</FONT> Ham and sardines on wheat with extra
pickles and artichokes.
<BR>
<P ALIGN=right>
<FONT COLOR="#003399">Regular:</FONT> $4.99<BR>
<FONT COLOR="#003399">Triple Decker:</FONT> $6.99
</P>
<FONT SIZE="+1" COLOR="#003399">The SHAGGY:</FONT> Pastrami on white topped with hot
fudge and spinach.
<BR>
<P ALIGN=right> <FONT COLOR="#003399">Regular:</FONT> $4.99<BR>
<FONT COLOR="#003399">Triple Decker:</FONT> $6.99
</P>
</BODY>
</HTML>
```

FIGURE 4.8 A document utilizing various font-controlling HTML elements.

nearly any web page, there are numerous ways it can be done. In the example below for Karen's Sandwich Shop, we have chosen a format that illustrates the use of text formatting elements and attributes, as well as some use of different colors.

Figure 4.8 displays the HTML document that generates the lunch menu for the sandwich shop. Figure 4.9 displays the web page it generates. It is best for you to spend a few minutes examining the document and the web page it generates. The best way to do this is to start from the top down in the HTML document and see how the various elements and their attributes affect the text that gets marked up in the resulting web page. However, to see the different colors, you need to visit the Lesson 4 section of the web site.

The first feature you should note is the subtle violet background color set by BG-COLOR in the BODY tag. We simply used the web-safe hexadecimal color chart to pick the color. Next, we chose a cool font for the text "Karen's Sandwich Shoppe", beefed up the font size by two sizes, and chose a nice blue for the text. Notice that this text is centered using the ALIGN attribute of the P element.

Each different sandwich (I'm getting hungry just talking about them!) basically adheres to the same format. The sandwich name is stepped up one font size and is rendered in

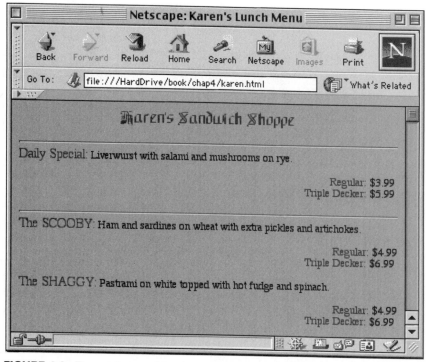

FIGURE 4.9   The rendering of the document of Figure 4.8.

the same color as the page's centered header using the FONT element. Since the sandwich descriptions are not contained within these FONT elements, they are simply rendered as the default black text. We just left the sandwich name and description aligned to the default left, so no extra alignment was required. However, the sandwich prices are aligned right, again using the ALIGN attribute of the P element. There are yet more FONT tags surrounding "Regular" and "Triple Decker" to give these choices a blue text color. However, the actual prices are not contained within these FONT tags, and are thus rendered in black. You will note that a line break, BR, was required between two sandwich types so that they would both be flush right. That is, a line break is forced after each "Regular" option so that each "Triple Decker" option is on its own line and can be right aligned.

NOTE

To someone not used to writing computer code, Figure 4.8 could appear quite daunting given the amount of symbols. But if you take the right approach and put in your time, you will get the hang of it. There is no way to learn to build web pages without spending many hours becoming buddies with your computer.

There are some things you can do to make the process a little easier, however. First of all, make a sketch of the page you intend to design before you start typing in the HTML code. Then remember that the browser renders the HTML document from the top down. So simply start at the top of your sketch and type in the required HTML elements as needed.

Second, keep in mind that there is a lot of redundant code in Figure 4.8. We didn't have to type in all that code. For example, each sandwich unit (the name, description, and pricing) requires the exact same HTML code. Once we got the first sandwich unit coded, we simply copied and pasted all of this code to create the other sandwich units. Of course we had to change the names and descriptions, but that is trivial compared to rewriting all of the HTML code. In like manner, you could expand Karen's sandwich menu to contain 50 sandwiches, for example, without writing new HTML code.

Finally, be prepared to load the HTML document into the browser as you go along. For example, once we got Karen's Sandwich Shoppe at the top coded for the blue color and fancy font, we loaded the incomplete page into the browser to see if what we had so far was working as intended. Once we had this part, we set up the first sandwich and then checked the browser again. Of course, there were some minor problems (typos for instance), but we were easily able to correct those. Building your pages piece by piece and checking often to see if things work will save you some headaches.

4.8 STYLE SHEETS (OPTIONAL)

As we mentioned above, the actual term is Cascading Style Sheets (CSS), but the "cascading" part is somewhat beyond the scope of this book, so we won't go into that. What CSS is about is setting styles for fonts and other things in the HEAD section of the HTML document. You then call upon these styles whenever you need them in the BODY of the document you are creating. Although, in practice, CSS may be more difficult than simply slapping attributes into FONT tags, CSS is the future of page design with HTML. We only go into some basics here and don't even attempt to give a deep coverage of the subject, but this exposure will be valuable to you as CSS proliferates and the depreciated FONT element is eventually put to rest.

To include a style sheet into your document you use the STYLE element in the HEAD section of the document as follows:

<STYLE><!- -

Your style definitions go here.

- -></STYLE>

The <STYLE>...</STYLE> container element is not hard to comprehend. It is simply an HTML element designed to tell the browser that its contents are style rules. However, the "<!--" and "-->" require some explanation. These symbols are a means to mark text in an HTML document that the browser should simply ignore. In common programming jargon, markers like these are called **comment symbols.** For example, you might include a comment in the document "karen.html" of Figure 4.8 that says

<!- - remember to add the Monster sandwich next week - ->

so that when you are editing the document to change the daily special, you will see a reminder. This is perhaps a lame example since you would probably just leave a sticky note on your computer with the reminder. But the point to be made is that the browser would completely ignore the text within the comment symbols and it would not get marked up in the web page.

The purpose of the comment symbols in the STYLE element is that CSS is a fairly new HTML tool. In fact, version-3 browsers, many of which are still being used, don't understand very much of CSS. Recalling the note from Lesson 3 that a browser will ignore any tags it doesn't recognize, a version-3 (or earlier) browser would most likely ignore the STYLE tags and get completely baffled by the style rules contained inside. With the comment symbols surrounding the style rules, even if a browser fails to recognize the STYLE tags, it will then proceed to ignore the style rules since they are hidden from it by comment symbols. In this way, an old browser will still be able to view your page without freaking out, just without your style rules. However, new browsers will see the STYLE tags and realize why you included the comment symbols, so all will be well. For the most part, we don't have sympathy for people using archaic browsers, but version-3 browsers aren't that outdated. Since nearly everything else presented in this book works on version-3 browsers (and newer), the above conversation seems warranted.

OK, so we put style rules inside the <STYLE><!--....--></STYLE> element. But what is a style rule? The first style rules we will explore suffice to replace the FONT element. A new element has been created to create style on the text level. It is the

<SPAN> . . . </SPAN>

element. This is basically a generic element that does nothing but mark a span of text for the application of style rules. For example,

<SPAN>some text</SPAN>

would do nothing to the enclosed text. But if we define a special **class** of the span element in a style sheet

```
<STYLE><!--
SPAN.bigblue {color:blue ; font-size:20pt}
--></STYLE>
```

we can use the CLASS attribute of SPAN to utilize the predefined style. For example,

```
<SPAN CLASS="bigblue">mark me up big and blue, please</SPAN>
```

would invoke the "bigblue" style class and mark up the enclosed text as blue and 20-pt size. Another example should help to clarify the point. Consider the style sheet in the HTML document of Figure 4.10, which defines three types of font for use in the web page. Figure 4.11 shows the rendering of the document in Figure 4.10.

Once the different style classes for SPAN have been defined, you simply use the SPAN element and call on the desired style class with the CLASS attribute. In practice it is quite simple to use styles once you have defined them, but the act of defining them requires some further discussion. In general, the definition for a style class has the form

TAG.class {property1:value1 ; property2:value2 ; . . . }

where each property:value pair is separated from other pairs with a semicolon. The properties and their values are separated by colons. Some common style properties and some value

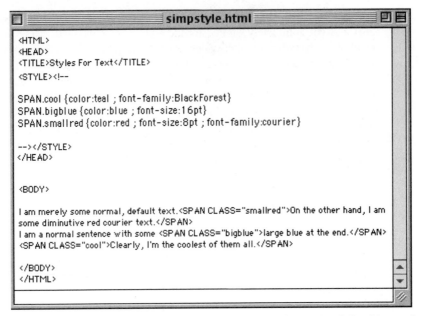

```
                        simpstyle.html

<HTML>
<HEAD>
<TITLE>Styles For Text</TITLE>
<STYLE><!--

SPAN.cool {color:teal ; font-family:BlackForest}
SPAN.bigblue {color:blue ; font-size:16pt}
SPAN.smallred {color:red ; font-size:8pt ; font-family:courier}

--></STYLE>
</HEAD>


<BODY>

I am merely some normal, default text.<SPAN CLASS="smallred">On the other hand, I am
some diminutive red courier text.</SPAN>
I am a normal sentence with some <SPAN CLASS="bigblue">large blue at the end.</SPAN>
<SPAN CLASS="cool">Clearly, I'm the coolest of them all.</SPAN>

</BODY>
</HTML>
```

FIGURE 4.10 An HTML document with three different font styles defined in a style sheet.

types they take are given in the table below.

Property	Values	Example
color	named color, hexadecimal color	red, #FF0000
font-size	pt	14 pt
font-family	named font	Times
text-align	left, right, center, justify	
text-indent	inches, centimeters	.5 in, 3 cm
line-height	integer	1, 2, 3, 4, . . .
margin-left	inches, centimeters, pixels	2 in, 1 cm, 72
-right	" "	" "
-top	" "	" "
-bottom	" "	" "

This is by no means a comprehensive list of style properties, but certainly provides an adequate list for purposes of explanation in this section. Note that the color property is the only one that doesn't require a hyphen (-). The first few should be self-explanatory. The "text-indent" property provides a means of indenting things, like the first sentence of this paragraph. The "line-height" property provides a means of double spacing lines of text, for example. The four "margin" properties provide a means of creating your own space around blocks of text. The utility of these might not be readily apparent, but we will provide examples shortly.

These style properties can not only be used to set styles for the generic SPAN element, but can override default behavior of other HTML elements as well. For starters, every HTML element has been endowed with the CLASS attribute, so that style classes can be specified

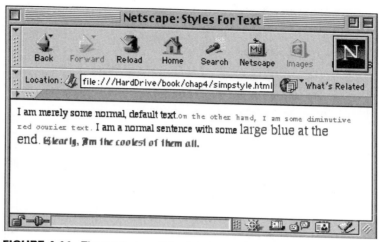

FIGURE 4.11   The rendering of the document of Figure 4.10.

within the element. For example,

> H1.centered {text-align:center}

> H1.fancy {color:#3366FF ; font-family:BlackForest ; text-align:center}

create two different styles that can be used with the H1 (header1) element. Thus, the following

> <H1 CLASS="centered"> I am a centered header</H1>

> <H1 CLASS="fancy"> I am a somewhat fancy header</H1>

would produce some nonstandard headers when used in the body section of the HTML document. Note that the default font size for the H1 element would still be carried through when the headers are marked up, since no specification was given for font size in the definitions of the styles.

To illustrate the use of the space-creating margin properties and the "line-height" property, we offer another example. In Figure 4.12 these properties are used to create a paragraph that has a margin around it of the sizes specified in the "P.double" style class and in which the lines are double spaced. The rendering of the document appears in Figure 4.13.

One point worthy of note is that, even though we used a style sheet to do most of the dirty work, we still used HTML attributes to position the <HR> underneath the text in the upper right. In other words, the use of style sheets does not limit your ability to use other HTML features, you just get some added flexibility. In particular, the text is perfectly justified, a feature that is highly unreliable if you use the ALIGN=justify attribute with the <P> or <FONT> elements. But note that full justification, even when done with style sheets, is not completely reliable in all browsers.

We conclude this introduction to style sheets by making a version of Karen's Lunch Menu, the web page for which is pictured in Figure 4.9, that utilizes style sheets. By doing this, we emphasize two points clarifying the utility of style sheets. First of all, when you

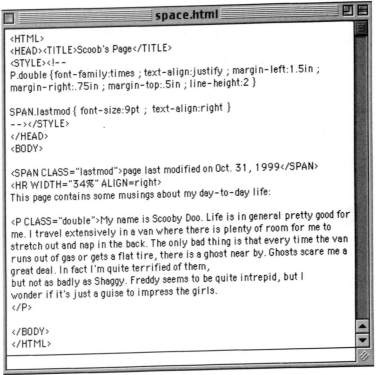

```
space.html
<HTML>
<HEAD><TITLE>Scoob's Page</TITLE>
<STYLE><!--
P.double {font-family:times ; text-align:justify ; margin-left:1.5in ;
margin-right:.75in ; margin-top:.5in ; line-height:2 }

SPAN.lastmod { font-size:9pt ; text-align:right }
--></STYLE>
</HEAD>
<BODY>

<SPAN CLASS="lastmod">page last modified on Oct. 31, 1999</SPAN>
<HR WIDTH="34%" ALIGN=right>
This page contains some musings about my day-to-day life:

<P CLASS="double">My name is Scooby Doo. Life is in general pretty good for
me. I travel extensively in a van where there is plenty of room for me to
stretch out and nap in the back. The only bad thing is that every time the van
runs out of gas or gets a flat tire, there is a ghost near by. Ghosts scare me a
great deal. In fact I'm quite terrified of them,
but not as badly as Shaggy. Freddy seems to be quite intrepid, but I
wonder if it's just a guise to impress the girls.
</P>

</BODY>
</HTML>
```

FIGURE 4.12 An HTML document with two style classes defined, one using "margin" properties and the "line-height" property.

peruse the document "karen.html" pictured in Figure 4.8, you see quite a mess of tags and attributes. In fact, in general if you wish to use special formatting for a given part of a web page over and over again, you must write quite a bit of redundant code. For example, when we marked up the sandwich names, we repeated a good bit of code:

<FONT SIZE="+1" COLOR="#003399">Daily Special:</FONT>

<FONT SIZE="+1" COLOR="#003399">The SCOOBY:</FONT>

<FONT SIZE="+1" COLOR="#003399">The SHAGGY:</FONT>

A preferable approach is to make a style for the sandwich names:

SPAN.san {color:#003399 ; font-size:16pt }

and then just call the style class to mark up the sandwich names:

<SPAN CLASS="san">Daily Special:</SPAN>

<SPAN CLASS="san">The SCOOBY:</SPAN>

<SPAN CLASS="san">The SHAGGY:</SPAN>

Thus, you only have to write the desired styles once in the style definition, rather than

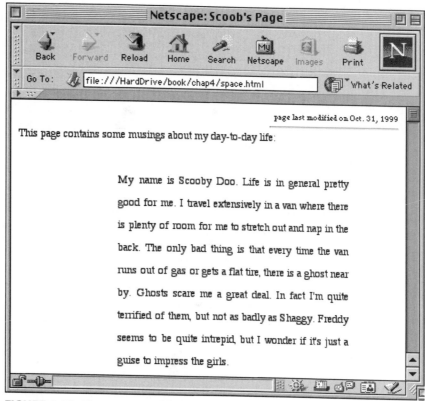

FIGURE 4.13 The rendering of the document of Figure 4.12.

carrying the desired attributes with every sandwich definition in the web page. It is simply a cleaner approach. Especially if we were to add a couple of other attributes in the FONT element to format the sandwich names, the amount of redundant code carried throughout the document would be significant.

The second point involves the use of a style sheet with multiple documents. For example, Karen might wish to have separate breakfast, lunch, and dinner menus. Rather than making a new style sheet for each web page, she can create one style sheet and use it for all three web pages. Not only does this eliminate more redundancy, but it helps to create a uniform style among her different menus. To accomplish this, she first needs to create a text document that contains *only* the style definitions and not the STYLE tags, as in Figure 4.14. Notice the suffix ".css" given to the file name. This is not imperative, but it certainly helps in the file-management process.

To import this style sheet into her menu documents, the LINK element is used:

<LINK HREF="menustyles.css" REL="STYLESHEET" TYPE="text/css">

The first attribute, HREF, of the LINK element specifies the name of the CSS file that is to be referenced. The other two attributes, REL and TYPE, are simply necessary and must be present. So in practice, if you wish to import a style sheet, just make a copy of the

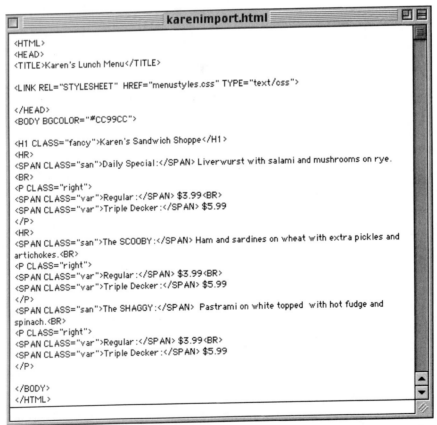

```
menustyles.css

H1.fancy {color:#003399 ; text-align:center ; font-family:BlackForest }
P.right {text-align:right ; margin-top:0 ; margin-bottom:0 }
SPAN.san {color:#003399 ; font-size:16pt }
SPAN.var {color:#003399 ; font-size:14pt }
```

FIGURE 4.14 A text document that contains the style definitions for each of Karen's breakfast, lunch, and dinner menu web pages.

above LINK element in the HEAD section of the HTML file that is to make use of the style sheet. The only thing you will need to change is the name of the actual style file you are using. Figure 4.15 shows the style-sheet version of Karen's lunch menu using the external style sheet shown in Figure 4.14, and Figure 4.16 shows the rendering of the document in Figure 4.15.

```
karenimport.html

<HTML>
<HEAD>
<TITLE>Karen's Lunch Menu</TITLE>

<LINK REL="STYLESHEET" HREF="menustyles.css" TYPE="text/css">

</HEAD>
<BODY BGCOLOR="#CC99CC">

<H1 CLASS="fancy">Karen's Sandwich Shoppe</H1>
<HR>
<SPAN CLASS="san">Daily Special:</SPAN> Liverwurst with salami and mushrooms on rye.
<BR>
<P CLASS="right">
<SPAN CLASS="var">Regular:</SPAN> $3.99<BR>
<SPAN CLASS="var">Triple Decker:</SPAN> $5.99
</P>
<HR>
<SPAN CLASS="san">The SCOOBY:</SPAN> Ham and sardines on wheat with extra pickles and
artichokes.<BR>
<P CLASS="right">
<SPAN CLASS="var">Regular:</SPAN> $3.99<BR>
<SPAN CLASS="var">Triple Decker:</SPAN> $5.99
</P>
<SPAN CLASS="san">The SHAGGY:</SPAN> Pastrami on white topped with hot fudge and
spinach.<BR>
<P CLASS="right">
<SPAN CLASS="var">Regular:</SPAN> $3.99<BR>
<SPAN CLASS="var">Triple Decker:</SPAN> $5.99
</P>

</BODY>
</HTML>
```

FIGURE 4.15 An HTML document that uses the LINK element to import an external style sheet.

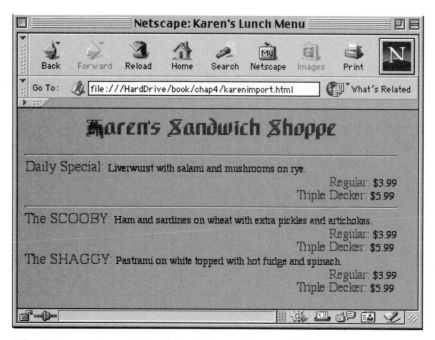

FIGURE 4.16 The rendering of the document in Figure 4.15.

As you can see, the style-sheet version of her lunch menu looks very similar to the one pictured in Figure 4.9. In fact, we constructed the style sheet with that purpose in mind. The definitions of the "san" (sandwich) and "var" (variety) styles is straightforward. We simply chose a color and sizes for the text. For the title at the top, we created a "fancy" version of the H1 element. To get the varieties and the prices to the right margin, we defined a "right" class of the P element. Recall that we also used the P element (<P ALIGN=right> . . . </P>) in the previous version of the lunch menu to accomplish this. There is a difference worth noting, however.

In Figure 4.9 there is substantially more vertical space above and below the prices than in Figure 4.16. This is because the paragraph, P, element automatically puts some space above and below each paragraph it creates. So in Figure 4.9 the space is put automatically by the P element. In the style definition for the "right"-aligned paragraph class in Figure 4.14, you will notice that we chose to override this spacing behavior of the P element by setting the top and bottom margins of the "P.right" style to zero. Now, in terms of appearance, you might actually prefer the menu in Figure 4.9 over the one in Figure 4.16. The purpose here is to give one last illustration of the added flexibility of style sheets.

NOTE Only version-4 (and later) browsers will recognize the attempt to import an external style sheet as depicted in Figure 4.15. So, if you choose to use this technique, be apprised that your styles will not show up in older browsers. This is not really a big deal, however. For example, if the styles in Karen's lunch menu failed to be applied, the same information would still be on the web page. You just wouldn't see the fancy fonts and the prices would be on the left margin as opposed to the right.

Also note that, for the purposes of this lesson, an external style sheet should be kept in the same folder (directory) as the HTML documents that are to use the style sheet. Only after you learn about relative URLs in Lesson 5 will you be able to store your external style sheets in other folders. After learning about relative URLs you will understand the significance of this paragraph.

4.9 SUMMARY

Key Terms

Default setting	attribute	pixel
named color	hexadecimal color	web-safe color
CSS		

HTML elements have default settings. That is, if no attributes are supplied in the element, the browser resorts to a predetermined standard to mark up the element. For example, <HR> defaults to a SIZE (height) of two pixels and a WIDTH of 100% of the browser window. The use of attributes in the <HR> element, and other HTML elements, serves to override the default settings. With this in mind, HTML elements can be characterized by supplying information like the following for HR:

<HR>

Attributes	Possible Values	Default
WIDTH	%, pixels	WIDTH="100%"
SIZE	pixels	SIZE=2
ALIGN	left, right, center	ALIGN=center
NOSHADE		Shaded markup

This serves to illustrate that elements can have several attributes and that each attribute can have several possible value types that can be assigned to it. It is also possible to have attributes, like NOSHADE, that don't take values and function like an on/off switch. When used with container elements, attributes must be placed in the start tag after the tag's name. When using more than one attribute in a given element, the order in which you supply the attributes does not matter. The quotes surrounding the value of an attribute are not always required, but it can't hurt to include them when in doubt to avoid errors.

The paragraph element can be used as a container element <P> ... </P> to aid in formatting text in a web page.

<P> ... </P>

Attributes	Possible Values	Default
ALIGN	left, right, center	ALIGN=left

The <BODY> ... </BODY> element has several attributes that are extremely useful when formatting a web page. It is best to use hexadecimal color representations rather than the named colors since color names are somewhat arbitrary. Moreover, it is best to stick to the 216 web-safe colors given in the Lesson 4 section of the web site.

<BODY > ... </BODY >

Attributes	Possible Values	Default
BGCOLOR	named color, hex color	BGCOLOR=white, BGCOLOR="#FFFFFF"
TEXT	named color, hex color	TEXT=black, TEXT="#000000"
LINK	named color, hex color	these default to different
ALINK	named color, hex color	colors depending on the
VLINK	named color, hex color	browser and platform

The LINK, ALINK, and VLINK attributes specify the color of unvisited, active, and visited links, respectively. The TEXT attribute can be used to set the text color for the entire web page. While this is useful, the <FONT> ... </FONT> element provides more versatility since it can be used to change the color of groups of text or even single words, rather than merely setting a text color for the entire document.

<FONT > ... </FONT > (depreciated)

Attributes	Possible Values	Default
COLOR	named color, hex color	COLOR=black COLOR="#000000"
SIZE	absolute size (1,...,7), relative size (± 1, ± 2,...	SIZE=3
FACE	named font family	browser-dependent

Even though the <FONT> ... </FONT> element has been depreciated, it is still in widespread use. In fact, the eventual disappearance of this element will make it somewhat more difficult for the beginner to learn how to format text in web pages since the alternative is to use style sheets (CSS).

(Optional)

The use of style sheets is somewhat more difficult than using attributes of the <P> ... </P> and <FONT> ... </FONT> elements, but they provide much more flexibility. In particular, one style sheet can be imported for styling into several HTML documents. When using an internal style sheet, it is defined in the head section of the HTML document inside the <STYLE> ... </STYLE> element:

<STYLE><!--

Your style definitions go here.

--></STYLE>

To define a style class, you can use the generic <SPAN> ... </SPAN> element to define an entirely new style class:

SPAN.bigred {color:red ; font-size:20pt}

or you can define a new twist on some existing element:

B.centered {text-align:center}

In this case, the <B> (boldface) element will retain any of its default settings that are not redefined in the style definition. To invoke a style rule in the BODY section of an HTML document, you use the CLASS attribute. For example,

<SPAN CLASS="bigred">some text</SPAN>

and

<B CLASS="centered">some text</B>

would cause the above predefined style classes to be invoked upon the enclosed text. The following table contains a good set of useful style settings and their values for the beginner.

Property	Values	Example
color	named color, hexadecimal color	red, #FF0000
font-size	pt	14 pt
font-family	named font	Times
text-align	left, right, center, justify	
text-indent	inches, centimeters	.5 in, 3 cm
line-height	integer	1, 2, 3, 4, . . .
margin-left	inches, centimeters, pixels	2 in, 1 cm, 72
-right	" "	" "
-top	" "	" "
-bottom	" "	" "

If you are going to use an external style sheet to format an HTML document, the external style sheet should be an ordinary text file just like an HTML file, but should be suffixed with ".css". To import the external style sheet you supply the name of the style sheet in the following link element:

<LINK HREF="sheetname.css" REL="STYLESHEET" TYPE="text/css">

This link element goes in the HEAD section of the document that will be using the style sheet. You should substitute the name of your style sheet into the HREF attribute, but should leave the other parts of the LINK element alone. Also note that the external style sheet should be kept in the same directory (folder) as the HTML file that will be linking to the style sheet. The external style sheet contains only the style rules, not the STYLE element tags. In fact, when you use external style sheets, you don't need to use the STYLE element at all.

4.10 REVIEW QUESTIONS

In most cases, it is not sufficient to answer these from the Lesson Summary.

1. Explain the role of the actual HTML element as opposed to attributes of the element.

2. About how many pixels per inch are displayed in a typical computer monitor? How many per centimeter? If you wish a HR to be 2.5 inches long (about 6.25 centimeters), how many pixels should you specify its SIZE to be?

3. It is always OK to use quotes to enclose the value of an attribute. Under what circumstances is the use of quotes imperative?

4. What does the term pixel stand for?

5. Explain the functionality of attributes that take no values. If you were to design such an attribute to take two values rather than none, what are the natural choices?

6. List an HTML element with a mandatory attribute. Explain why it is mandatory.

7. Give two examples when blank space (other than between two words) actually matters in an HTML document.

8. Explain how the P element, when used as a noncontainer element, differs from the BR element.

9. Discuss the limitations of using named colors.

10. How can you give a browser several font face options to fall back upon in case it can't find a particular font?

11. Are names of font faces case-sensitive?

4.11 EXERCISES

GENERAL

1. Find out if you have access to an RGB color picker. If you are using your own computer and don't have one, download a freeware color picker and/or bookmark one of the color palettes. (See the Lesson 4 section of the web site.)

2. Go to the homework section for Lesson 4 on the web site for this book. Under exercise 2 you will find the picture of a web page. Make a web page with approximately the same appearance. *Optional:* use an internal or external style sheet.

3. Go to the homework section for Lesson 4 on the web site for this book. Under exercise 3, you will find the picture of a web page. Make a web page with approximately the same appearance. *Optional:* use an internal or external style sheet.

4. Go to the homework section for Lesson 4 on the web site for this book. Under exercise 4, you will find the picture of a web page. Make a web page with approximately the same appearance. *Optional:* use an internal or external style sheet.

4.12 PROJECT THREADS

THREAD A

Assignment

(a) Rename your home page "version1.html". Create a new file named "index.html" (or whatever the indexing file name is on your web server) and copy the contents of your version-1 home page into this file. This is your version-2 home page. Add any new or refined ideas you have for your home page. Also, embellish the page using many features from this lesson, including a color scheme. *Optional:* Use an internal or external style sheet.

Important: Keep your version-1 home page. You will use it again in Lesson 5.

(b) If you are to do any of the Exercises above, put the file(s) in your public directory with your home page.

(c) If applicable, transfer all files to the web server when completed. Check to make sure the transfer was successful.

THREAD B

Assignment

(a) Add a color scheme to your homework page that features a background color and text color(s).

(b) Embellish the research pages you made in Lesson 3 using many features from this lesson. In particular, use a color scheme that features a background color, text color(s), and colors for the visited and unvisited links. If you have more than one research page, use a common color scheme.

Optional: Use an internal or external style sheet. If you have more than one research page, use an external style sheet to provide uniformity among the pages.

(c) If you are to do any of the Exercises above, put the file(s) in your public directory with your homework page.

(d) If applicable, transfer all files to the web server when completed. Check to make sure the transfer was successful.

HYPERTEXT MARKUP
AND WEB SITES

WHILE IT is nice to be able to create textual HTML documents that can be viewed around the world, the concept of text markup certainly doesn't utilize the full power of the WWW. Sure, with a given URL, anyone in the world with a browser hooked up to the Internet can type that URL into the browser and see what the web page at that location has to say. But that is not really in the spirit of surfing the Web.

As we all know, one can sit at a browser for hours on end and cruise to various web sites around the world without knowing a single URL, or even what a URL is, for that matter. Most browsers can pull up a search engine at the click of a button. Once at the search engine, with the typing of a word or two, a surfer can be given tens of thousands of hypertext links to pursue. Any one of the web pages that one of these links pulls up probably has more hypertext links from which to choose. A surfer can end up virtually anywhere, following link after link.

What does it take to create such links? Well, all it takes is an HTML element, an attribute of that element, and a URL. As luck would have it, we are at this point fairly well versed in all three.

5.1 HREF ANCHORS (LINKS)

Now that we are familiar with attributes of HTML elements, it's time to move on to the real power of HTML. This power, with which we are all familiar, is the ability to link to other documents. Linking is accomplished with the **anchor** element. The anchor element is a container element and is comprised of start and end anchor tags:

<A>. . .</A>

The anchor element has one attribute that is mandatory. Actually, one of the two attributes, HREF or NAME, is mandatory. One or the other must be present to allow the anchor element actually to do something. We will only discuss the HREF attribute in this section. The HREF attribute (**H**ypertext **REF**erence) specifies the URL to which the anchor element is to link. The URL is given as the value of the HREF attribute. The anchor element,

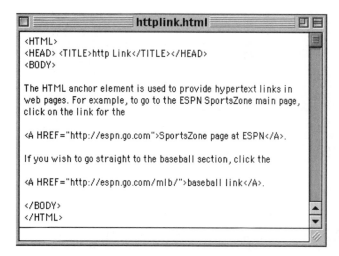

FIGURE 5.1 A document with two hypertext links.

being a container element, contains the actual text that is to represent the link in the web page. The basic form is

<A HREF="SomeURL">click here</A>

In this case, the text which the anchor element contains, namely "click here", would appear as an underlined link in the web page:

<u>click here</u>

We choose to call such anchors **HREF anchors.** The URL specified by the HREF attribute lurks behind the scenes; it does not appear in the web page itself. When the underlined link in the page is clicked, the page at the location given by the URL is loaded into the browser. For a simple example, consider the document displayed in Figure 5.1. It contains two hypertext links to ESPN's SportsZone web site. The text contained within the anchor elements is marked up as underlined links. This can be seen in Figure 5.2.

Clicking on either of the links causes the HTML document to which that link points to be loaded into the browser. Most browsers underline active links, as in Figure 5.2, to make them stand out from the text. Also, unless you have specified colors with the LINK and VLINK attributes of the BODY element (see Section 4.5), a browser will simply use its default color settings for links. Typically unfollowed links (LINK) are rendered in one color and previously activated links (VLINK) in another. That way, one can see at a glance what links have already been explored and which ones have not.

Even though the URL to which an anchor points is lurking behind the scenes and is not apparent from looking at the page, most browsers display the URL of a given link when the mouse pointer passes on top of the link. To reiterate what we mentioned in Lesson 2, this display is typically at the bottom of the browser and is called the status bar. You can see this in Figure 5.2 where the mouse has been moved onto the baseball link and the URL to which that link points appears in the status bar.

Some links are not very descriptive. For example, what the two links in Figure 5.2 are for is apparent from the surrounding text. But if the surrounding text were not there,

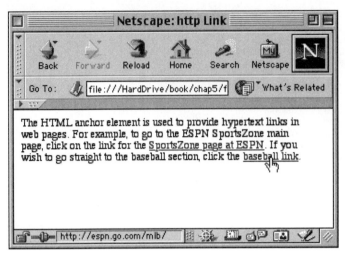

FIGURE 5.2 The rendering of the document of Figure 5.1.

the purpose of each link might not be clear. Especially the <u>baseball</u> link: baseball what? Sometimes the status bar can at least give a hint of the destination of a link if the link is not descriptive. In practice, links should be as descriptive as possible, whether by the supporting context or the underlined text of the link itself.

5.2 ABSOLUTE AND RELATIVE URLs

We have seen how to link to a remote web page by putting the URL of that page as the value of the HREF attribute in an anchor. In fact, you might be surprised how easy linking to other web pages actually is. All you need to know is the URL for that web page. Armed with the URL, using the anchor element is quite simple. To introduce some terminology, a complete http URL such as "http://espn.go.com/mlb" is called an **absolute URL.** It specifies the absolute location of a web server and a resource on that server. We choose to call a link that uses an absolute URL an **absolute link.**

In contrast, not all links are absolute. For example, if two web pages are in the same account on a web server, absolute links are not required to link the two pages together. There is a more local style of link to accomplish such local linking. The true flavor of local linking comes into play when designing a web site with several subdirectories and numerous web pages. For purposes of illustrating local linking, we turn again to our old friend Jones and his account on the hypothetical web server "www.uweb.edu".

NOTE If you skipped Lesson 2 so that you could charge straight into web page construction, now would be a good time to a read through that lesson. In particular, we explored the nature of Jones' web account on www.uweb.edu, and web accounts in general, in Sections 2.6–2.8. Or perhaps, if you have already read Lesson 2, be prepared to refer back to it as necessary if you need to clarify a point made in this lesson.

Well, now that Jones has read Lessons 3 and 4, he is armed with the ability to create textual presentation-type web pages, replete with color and some other fancy things. With

www.uweb.edu

public
  hobbies.html
  index.html
  professional.html

FIGURE 5.3 There are three HTML documents in Jones' public directory on the web server.

this knowledge, he has made several web pages and transferred them to his account on the web server. All these pages collectively comprise his **web site.**

Typically, a web site has a main page that has hypertext links to other subsidiary pages at the site. This is indeed the case with Jones' web site. His web site has a main page and, for simplicity, only two subsidiary pages: one for his professional interests and one for his hobbies. The organization of his files on the web server is depicted in Figure 5.3. All three of the files are in his public directory on the web server.

A browser request made to the URL

http://www.uweb.edu/~jones

results in the "index.html" document in his public directory being pulled up. Remember from Section 2.8 that a request for a directory that doesn't specify a particular file automatically pulls up the index file (or default file) if present. It is clear then that the document "index.html" is the one that generates his home page. To directly access one of his other two pages from your browser, the "hobbies.html" page for example, you would type in the URL

http://www.uweb.edu/~jones/hobbies.html

which specifies the exact file requested. You should be starting to get the point here. Chances are, you know that "http://www.uweb.edu/~jones" is the address for Jones' web site (after all, he is your buddy). But it is unlikely that you know the names of all the HTML documents in his site. Nor should you have to. You would clearly expect only to be able to find his home page and then click hypertext links to access his other pages.

Of course, to provide a hypertext link to "hobbies.html", for example, from his home page, he can include the following link in his "index.html" file:

<A HREF="http://www.uweb.edu/~jones/hobbies.html"> hobbies </A>

This link uses an absolute URL. But this is not the desired way to accomplish his local linking. The absolute URL, in this case, provides more information than is necessary. For starters, if you are viewing his home page, you have already established a link with his web server. If Jones uses an absolute URL to link to his hobbies page from his home page, the full URL would cause your browser to initiate a new connection to the server.

The preferable way is to use a **relative URL.** By relative URL we mean a partial URL that points to the desired document without using the protocol and server address. All Jones has to do is provide a file path relative to the document "index.html" in which the link appears. In this case, since the index and hobby files are in the same directory, the relative URL pointing to "hobbies.html" from "index.html" merely consists of the document's name, "hobbies.html". So the anchor

<A HREF="hobbies.html">Click here to see my hobbies page.</A>

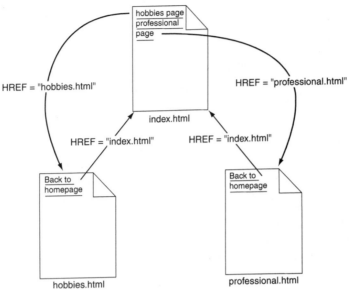

FIGURE 5.4 Since all of the HTML documents are in the same directory, the URLs required to link them together are just the file names.

is sufficient to establish a **local link** from "index.html" to "hobbies.html". Similarly, using relative URLs, Jones can link his entire web site together as depicted in Figure 5.4. A substantial advantage to this relative linking is that, when you click one of his links, your browser can use the existing server connection to initiate the transfer, rather than initiating a new connection as would be the case with an absolute link.

NOTE

This is your first lesson in web site design. All of your web pages should be linked together in a predictable way so that navigation around your site is easy and quick. For example, the navigational links should be handily located on your pages. Until we learn more advanced page-layout techniques, your navigational links should be at or near the top of the web page. However, if a web page is no larger vertically than the browser window (i.e., no use of the scroll bar is required to see all of the page), the bottom is also a viable location. You often see navigation links in a nice concise format like

[link1][link2][link3][link4]

for example.

Of course, it is often desirable to have links in the body or your page that are fully supported with text, even if some of these links duplicate your navigational links. The navigational links simply provide quick access to other pages of the site. In this way, a frequent visitor can navigate the site without always having to scroll through the page to find links.

Further to illustrate the use of relative URLs, we provide a slightly more complicated version of Jones' web site as shown in Figure 5.5. We will assume that Jones has been industrious and has beefed up his web site. Since his hobbies pages began to proliferate, he chose to create a new directory in which to keep all of them. Appropriately, the directory is simply called "hobbies".

www.uweb.edu

```
[===]

   public
      hobbies
          billiards.html
          index.html
          volleyball.html
      index.html
      professional.html
```

FIGURE 5.5 A more complicated version of Jones' site with a subdirectory named "hobbies".

Note that Jones has chosen to rename his hobbies page "index.html". (Again, if you don't know why this is, you should refer back to Section 2.8.) Just keep in mind that the two index files have different content, even though they have the same name. The index file in the hobbies folder generates his hobbies page, whereas the index file in his public folder generates his main home page.

When subdirectories are involved, the relative URL works in essentially the same way except that the full file path must be specified rather than just the file name. For example, the following anchor provides a link from the page "professional.html" to the document "billiards.html":

<A HREF="hobbies/billiards.html"> Click here for my billiards page. </A>

Since the document to which the link points is one directory "below" the "professional.html" document, the complete file path relative to the index document must be provided. In other words, "hobbies/billiards.html" basically says that the link should 'look inside the hobbies folder and find the "billiards.html" file.'

However, the two documents, "billiards.html" and "volleyball.html", are in the same directory, so the document name is sufficient. In other words, the relative file path is just the file name since the documents are in the same folder. The following anchor provides a link from "billiards.html" to "volleyball.html":

<A HREF="volleyball.html"> Click here for my volleyball page. </A>

Providing a link using a relative URL from "volleyball.html" to "professional.html", for example, presents more of a problem since the "professional.html" document is one directory "above" the "volleyball.html" document. The notation "../" means go back up one directory. (It's just two periods followed by a forward slash.) So the file path

../index.html

means go up one directory and find the document "professional.html". In other words, "../index.html" says look directly "outside" of the current folder and find the file "professional.html". The following anchor provides a link from "volleyball.html" to "professional.html":

<A HREF= "../professional.html">Click here to go to my professional page. </A>

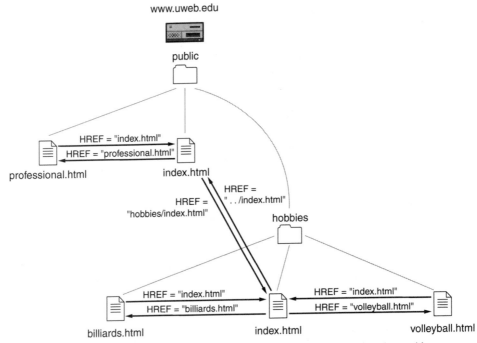

FIGURE 5.6 The relative URLs to provide internal linking for the web site pictured in Figure 5.5.

Figure 5.6 illustrates some of the partial URLs that would provide a good system of internal links for Jones' site as shown in Figure 5.5. In this way, relative file paths provide an effective linking system for the documents at a particular web site.

> **NOTE**
>
> You can note that every file is not linked to every other file at the web site. For example, in the examples preceding Figure 5.6, we wrote down a link from "volleyball.html" to "professional.html". However, in Figure 5.6 we don't provide such a link. Rather, each index file contains links to all of the files contained in its directory. Moreover, the index files are linked together. This provides an adequate linking structure for the web site. It is not necessary to link every page together. Including a link from every page to every other page in Figure 5.6 would actually require 20 different links, while the above linking scheme only requires eight links to make the site navigable. This is an example of hierarchical site design, a topic to which we give more consideration in a later section of this lesson.

As a last note about relative URLs, consider Figure 5.7, which depicts a "two-deep" directory structure. Inside "public" is the file "file.html" and the folder "folder1". Inside "folder1" is the file "file1.html" and the folder "folder2". The directory "folder2" contains only the file "file2.html". We won't provide a complete linking structure for this example, but just link a couple of the documents together for illustrative purposes. To put a link in "file.html" that points to "file2.html", the required URL must provide the complete file path

HREF="folder1/folder2/file2.html"

www.uweb.edu

public
file.html
folder1
file1.html
folder2
file2.html

FIGURE 5.7 A depiction of a web site that goes two directories deep.

which basically says 'look inside folder1, then look inside folder2, then find the file "file2.html"'.

To provide a link in "file2.html" that points back to "file.html", we must provide the reverse file path:

HREF="../../file.html"

which basically says 'back up one directory, then back up another, then look for the file "file.html".' Using similar reasoning you should be able to extend the above example to handle even larger file directories. Some "deeper" directory sites are presented in the homework problems at the end of this lesson.

NOTE

Be careful when you are defining your hypertext links. For example, the hypertext reference

HREF="hobbies/biliards.html"

would cause the link *not* to work since billiards is misspelled (one l). URLs must match the file path *exactly,* letter-for-letter. But it even gets worse. URLs, both absolute and relative, are **case-sensitive.** That is, in a hypertext reference like

HREF="hobbies/Billiards.html"

the link will not work since the capital B in billiards does not match the file name, "billiards.html", which begins with a small letter. Similarly,

HREF="Hobbies/billiards.html"

would not work since the capital H in hobbies does not match the actual folder name, "hobbies".

It is very important for you to have a consistent way to name your files and directories. It is best to adopt the policy of naming all of your folders and files with strictly lower-case letters. This will take some of the tedium out of writing hypertext links. Moreover, you should not put any spaces in the names you choose. For example, "my hobbies" is a poor choice for the name of a directory. Any spaces would also have to be matched in a URL. Taking these precautions will save you some time in error detection and prevention over the long haul, but you are still going to have to be careful with your spelling.

Finally, don't fall into the "local trap". Just because it works on your computer doesn't mean it will work on a web server. Some computers, especially Macs, will let you get away with case or space errors. However, web servers are almost always inexorable. In fact, many won't even allow blank spaces in file or directory names.

> **NOTE** If you are used to working on a PC, where directories are preceded with the back slash "\" rather than the forward slash "/" used in URLs, you needn't be concerned. Go ahead and use the forward slash "/" for your relative URLs, even if you are developing your web site on a PC. Browsers on PCs will handle either type of slash. If you have no idea about what we are talking about here, just forget that this note exists!

5.3 SITE PORTABILITY

One advantage to using relative URLs rather than absolute URLs to hook up a web site internally revolves around the issue of **portability** of a web site. For example, if Jones were to transfer to another university or just desire to host his web site at a different address, the fact that he used relative URLs would be a huge plus. But before discussing such a drastic change, let's discuss the process of developing his site in the first place.

It is almost always more convenient to design web pages locally and then upload them to the server. Although this was discussed to a small extent in Lesson 2, some further explanation is in order. Let's suppose that Jones has been reading this book diligently and knows how to make textual web pages with some smooth formatting. Now that he has learned how links work, he envisions his web site as pictured in Figure 5.3. Let's also make the assumption that he plans to develop his site at home on his personal computer. Being the smooth operator he is, he decides that he doesn't even want to mess with an ftp program or the web server until he has his entire site working at home. So what he does is create an exact replica of the site pictured in Figure 5.3 on his computer at home. In other words, he creates a folder named "public" somewhere on his hard drive and, each time he creates a new page for his site, he puts in his local public folder.

Now, it's pretty clear that he doesn't want to use absolute URLs when he makes links on his personal computer. Recall that absolute URLs (absolute to a personal computer rather than a web domain) use the file protocol. So, in the local setting, a link using an absolute URL to point to his hobbies page, for example, would have the form

<A HREF="file:///HardDrive/public/hobbies.html"> Click here for my hobbies page.</A>

if he is using a Mac or

<A HREF="C:\public\ hobbies.html"> Click here for my hobbies page.</A>

if he is using a PC. In either case, this link certainly would not work upon transferring his site to the web server, even though it would in the local setting.

So he uses all relative URLs to link his site together. He gets his web pages built, verifies that all of his links work, and gets everything just right. Only then does he transfer his site to the web server www.uweb.edu. So he cranks up his ftp application and sets about transferring the files into his public directory on the server. After he accomplishes the ftp transactions, he still has the local copy of the web site on his computer. Moreover, being wise, he checks to see if everything got transferred properly by pulling up the new web site from the server with his browser. The key is that the links work even though he has transferred to site to the web server. The use of relative URLs has made his web site completely portable.

Suppose that Jones now has all of his web site as pictured in Figure 5.3 on the web server and working properly. He then has some free time and wishes to augment his site with some more pages. His goal is to upgrade the site to the state pictured in Figure 5.5. The process is simple: he goes to the local copy of his web site on his computer, makes the desired changes and upgrades, tests all of the links to make sure they work, and then, once satisfied, transfers the new site to the web server. But, again, since Jones is pretty smooth he is going to pull up his pages from off the server with his browser and make sure everything got transferred properly.

Finally, relatively linked sites can even be moved from server to server without fear of faulty URLs. One never knows when www.uweb.edu will go antiweb! But anyway, if you are keeping a local copy of your web site, you could put it on any server, anywhere, provided you have an account.

> **NOTE**
>
> If you make some changes to only one or two files in your local copy of the web site, it makes sense to transfer just those two files to the server after you are satisfied with the changes. However, you have to be *very* careful, especially with multiple index files in your web site. For example, assume that Jones' site is now as pictured in Figure 5.5. If he makes some local changes to the index file for his hobbies page but accidentally transfers that index file into his public folder, rather than into the hobbies folder, he would completely overwrite the index file that generates his home page since it has the same name. That would completely mess up his web site.
>
> The moral here? Well, be careful when you are transferring stuff to the server. Even the veteran ftp'er makes mistakes sometimes. Conceptually, it's easy, but you have to pay close attention. If you do make a mistake, it's not the end of the world. You still have the local copy of your web site and can try again.
>
> One way to avoid such mistakes is basically to copy all the contents of your local public folder to the web server. Almost any ftp application has a feature with which you can pick whole groups of files and folders to transfer as a group. If you look around in the pull-down menus of the ftp application, you should find such an option. Then you simply select the entire contents of your local public folder to be transferred as a group. That way, it's harder to make a mistake (although still possible). The drawback to this is the fact that if you web site gets large, such group transfers can take a good bit of time.

5.4 WEB SITE DESIGN STRATEGIES

In Figure 5.6 and the surrounding discussion, it was indicated that certain strategies can be used to effectively link a web site together. Without the use of a linking strategy, a web site can be very unpredictable and hard to navigate through. For example, Figure 5.8 shows a web site with 10 pages. The arrows in the diagram represent links from one page to another.

Assuming that you start your navigation through the site at the home page (home), you can pull up various other pages, but there are problems. For example, you can't even get to page C by following links. The page is isolated on the site. The only way to pull it up would be to know the actual name of the file and append it to the end of the URL, assuming, of course, that you know the directory path to the file as well. Clearly, that is a ridiculous expectation. The two pages A and B form what can be termed a closed circuit. Sure, you can get to either of the pages from the home page by following links, but once there all you can do is to toggle back and forth between page A and page B. Of course, you could use

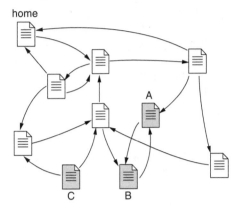

FIGURE 5.8 A web site with 10 web pages and no planned site structure.

the "back" button or "recent history" option on your browser to escape from the circuit, but a nicely designed web site shouldn't require such "escape" procedures.

Well, why not just link each of the of the pages to each other page? For starters, that would require a *lot* of links. Each page would have to have nine links, one for each of the other pages. Given that there are 10 pages, that's 90 links! While this approach is feasible, it is not desirable. There are two structured approaches that can be employed to link all of the pages together in an effective way. We have already seen an example of a **hierarchical** structure in Figure 5.6. Indeed, we will discuss that in more detail shortly. Another approach is called a **linear** structure. Figure 5.9 depicts a linear site structure for a site with 10 pages.

The home page has links to each of the nine other pages so you can go directly to each of them. Each of the nine other pages, in turn, has a link back to the home page. So, for example, if you are viewing page 3 and wish to go to page 10, you can hit home and then select page 10 from the home page. Another way to navigate through the site is to simply use the next and previous links. This provides a kind of sequential path through the documents. There are still quite a few links required, but 36 (three links in each of the pages 2 through 9, two links in page 10, and 10 links in the home page) is certainly better than 90.

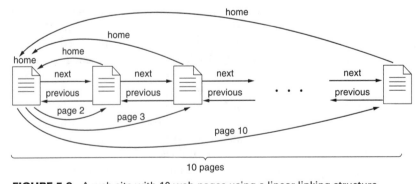

FIGURE 5.9 A web site with 10 web pages using a linear linking structure.

Linear site design is ideal for things such as online books and online tutorials. In sites of these types, you might wish to go straight through the pages in order the first time you visit the site, but might wish to refer straight to page 8, for reference, the next time you visit the site. Keep in mind that the links should be placed conveniently on the pages. For example, you might wish to put the direct page links at the top of the home page:

[page2][page3][page4][page5][page6][page7][page8][page9][page10]

while putting the sequential links and home links at the bottom of the other pages:

[prev][next][home]

so that the reader can decide where to go after reading the page. Of course, the home page would only have a [next] at its bottom and the last page would only have [prev][home] at its bottom. But, once again, this is just one viable suggestion. When we learn more advanced page-layout techniques, other desirable placements for the links will be pointed out.

Perhaps the most useful site structure is the hierarchical design. It is particularly useful for web sites that tend to have different categorical groups of pages. For example, in Figure 5.10, the home page could index a gardening help site. Page A could be the non-organic gardening page and index three non-organic subtopic pages like fertilizers, herbicides, and pesticides. Page B could be the organic gardening page and index three organic subtopic pages like manures, composting, and natural pesticides. As you can see in the figure, Page C, the composting page, indexes yet two more subtopics like proper mixtures and using worms. In a categorical site such as this it should be apparent why the hierarchical structure is preferable.

Having discussed a gardening site to emphasize the categorical rationale, will explain Figure 5.10 without using the gardening terms. (Somehow worms and hierarchy don't work well in the same sentence!) All that is required of the home page is to link to pages A and B,

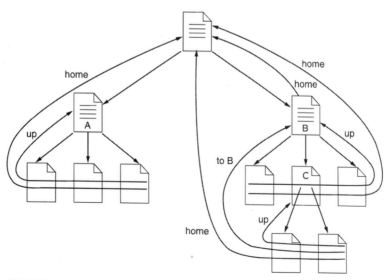

FIGURE 5.10 A web site with 11 web pages using a hierarchical linking structure.

the next level of indexing pages. In turn, this next level simply has to link to the third level. Finally, page C has to link to the fourth level of the hierarchy. Each page in a given level of the hierarchy contains links back to the indexing files in each previous level of its branch of the hierarchy. For example, each page in the fourth level would contain

[up][to B][home]

But each page in the third level only has to contain

[up][home]

The two indexing files in the second level merely have to point back home. Even though there are 11 files in hierarchical web site, as opposed to only 10 files in the linear site in Figure 5.9, only 30 links are required to make the site effectively navigable. Recall that the linear site with only 10 files utilized 36 links. However, both site strategies are very effective, depending upon the desired functionality of the site.

> **NOTE**
>
> What we haven't mentioned is where you store all the files for the web site. For example, should you just keep all of them in the public directory or should you create new subdirectories to organize your files? Organizing your files in a web site is much like organizing paper documents in a filing cabinet. You don't have to have a good scheme, but it sure makes life easier in the long run. The organization scheme is largely a matter of personal preference. For example, if two different secretaries are each asked to create a new filing scheme for an office, they would likely construct substantially different schemes.
>
> You will simply have to use your common sense. For example, in the hierarchical site, it makes sense to have a folder for each category or level of the hierarchy. This is indeed how Jones chose to organize his hierarchical site in Figure 5.6. If he were to add more professional-related files, he would probably create a new "professional" folder to contain them. If a linear collection is part of your site, you may wish to keep all of that collection in its own directory. However, if there are a large number of image files (Lesson 6) associated with each page of the collection, it may be desirable to keep all of the files associated with each document of the collection in a separate directory.
>
> Once again, just use your common sense. On Jones' limited web site, it's not really a big deal, but as we learn to associate image files and other things with a given web page, you will have to organize a decent-size collection of files. If you go overboard on subdirectories, local linking becomes a headache. On the other hand, if you don't use enough subdirectories to give some semblance of order to your files, that can be a headache as well.

5.5 NAMED ANCHORS

If an anchor element does not contain an HREF attribute, it must contain a NAME attribute. Remember, there is no built-in default to handle the absence of both the NAME and HREF attributes. Well, there kind of is: the default is that the anchor accomplishes absolutely nothing if neither of these two attributes are present.

The inclusion of the NAME attribute in an anchor causes the anchor element to function as a bookmark in the web page. We choose to term anchor elements that use the NAME attribute rather than the HREF attribute as **named anchors.** An ordinary bookmark for a bound paper book is used so that a particular spot in the book can be readily accessed. In a long web page, it is also desirable to have bookmarks of some sort. For example, suppose a web page contains text markup of a book on how to make web pages. Navigating through the chapters of such an online book involves using the scroll bar on the right of the browser window to make the chapters roll by. To go directly to Chapter 3, for instance, might take a good bit of scrolling. As we all know, scrolling through even 25 or 50 pages takes some time. Of course, you would probably wish to break the book up into a linear collection of documents, one for each chapter. But even then, each chapter would contain several pages' worth of text. You might wish to bookmark each section of a given chapter for easy reference. Of course, there are ways to drag the scroll bar to a particular spot, like halfway down, but even that involves trial and error.

As we have mentioned, the anchor element together with the NAME attribute provides such a bookmark. Since a web page is more like one long continuous page than like a book with distinct pages, we choose the term **pagemark.** A named anchor thus provides a fixed pagemark in the web page:

<A NAME="chap2">...</A>

Such an anchor element provides a fixed location in the document that can be instantaneously accessed. The means of access is provided in the same way that access to web pages is provided, by a hypertext link. Of course, hypertext links are also defined with the anchor tag, but with the HREF attribute rather than the NAME attribute:

<A HREF="#chap2">Click here to go straight to chapter 2.</A>

Clicking on this HREF link causes the web page to go instantly to the anchor named "chap2". The actual position of the named anchor (or pagemark) becomes the top of the display shown in the browser window. The actual terminology for the name of a named anchor is **fragment identifier.** While the general URL identifies a protocol and a possibly remote location, the fragment identifier merely names a page location within a web page. The value of the above HREF attribute of the hypertext link, "#chap2", consists of a "#" character followed by the fragment identifier. The "#" character tells the HREF attribute that a fragment identifier rather than a URL is to follow.

Well, this might seem a bit strange at first, but as usual an example will help clarify things. We return to the above discussion about an online book to illustrate the pagemarking ability of the named anchor. For simplicity the book has only three chapters and mimics a book with purpose similar to this one. The HTML document representing the online book is displayed in Figure 5.11.

In Figure 5.12, where the document is rendered, you can only see the title and part of the first chapter. However, you can deduce from the document in Figure 5.11 that the other two chapters are there. You would simply need to use the scroll bar to scroll down and see them. There is, in effect, a hypertext table of contents directly below the book's title. It provides an HREF link to each of the book's three chapters. The HREF attribute of each anchor comprising the table of contents specifies a fragment identifier, which points to one of the named anchors. The named anchors are placed at the beginning of each chapter. That way, when the hypertext link for Chapter 3, for example, is clicked, the named anchor that marks the beginning of Chapter 3 is instantaneously positioned at the top of the browser window. Such an action is depicted in Figure 5.13.

Notice in Figure 5.11 that there is no actual content of the named anchors. In an HREF anchor the content of the anchor gets marked up as the underlined text of the link.

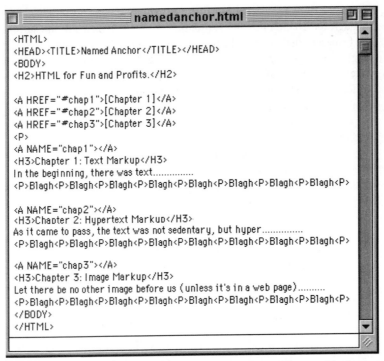

FIGURE 5.11 A document containing named anchors referenced by hypertext links.

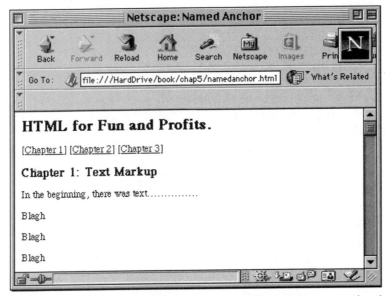

FIGURE 5.12 The rendering of the document of Figure 5.11 representing the top of an online book.

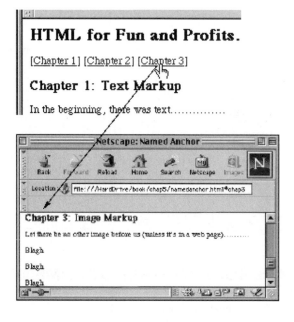

FIGURE 5.13 When a hypertext link that points to a fragment identifier is activated, the browser instantaneously goes to the appropriate named anchor and puts it at the top of the browser window.

For named anchors, this is not desirable. The named anchor is to simply provide a reference point in the web page. It doesn't even need to be marked up visually in the web page. You may be speculating that we left the contents of the named anchors empty precisely for that purpose. Since the named anchors are simply for reference, we didn't supply any text for them. As it turns out, that was not our reasoning. We left them empty just out of convenience.

Since named anchors are strictly for reference points in a page, even if we were to supply some text as content of a named anchor, it would *not* be rendered as underlined text as it would be with a HREF anchor. For example,

> Since this is a named anchor it only provides a reference point in the page.
> <A NAME="spot"> Thus, these contents will *not* be marked up as an underlined link.</A> However, all of this text would be, in effect, bound to this anchor.

would contain no underlined text when marked up. In fact, if you were to view the above in a web page, you would not even perceive that there is a named anchor in the second sentence. As indicated by the text of the example, there is another point to be made here, however. If an HREF link were clicked that points to the anchor named "spot", you would likely see the results pictured in Figure 5.14.

NOTE

Browsers tend to group stuff together in blocks. In fact, as we just pointed out, a whole block of stuff could basically be bound to a named anchor, even text which precedes it. If you want your named anchor to go at the absolute top of the browser window when targeted, it is recommended that you put a <P> or <BR> tag immediately before it. Since both of these elements cause a formal line break, no previous text will be bound to the named anchor.

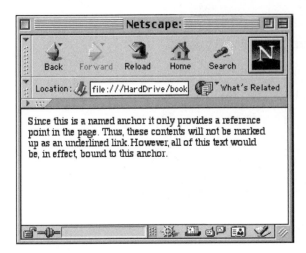

FIGURE 5.14 When the named anchor, "spot", is targeted, the previous text is transported to the top of the browser, rather than just the contents of the anchor being targeted there.

5.6 LINKS TO NAMED ANCHORS IN OTHER DOCUMENTS

Normally, when an anchor points to another HTML document, whether using an absolute URL for a remote document or a relative URL for a local document, that document is loaded and is displayed from its top. However, if an HTML document has a named anchor, a link in a different web page can point straight to that anchor. The way this is accomplished is by appending the fragment identifier of the named anchor onto the URL of the page that contains the named anchor. Notice in Figure 5.13 that the fragment identifier was actually appended to the URL in the location field of the browser after the link was targeted. So, effectively, not only can a URL give the exact file path to a document, it can point to a named anchor within that document. You simply have to append the fragment identifier for the named anchor onto the URL following the "#" sign.

For example, if Jones had the named anchor

<A NAME="8ball">Here are</A>the rules for 8-ball .....

in his "billiards.html" page as pictured in Figure 5.5, there would be many ways of pointing straight to that named anchor. The use of the absolute URL

<A HREF="http://www.uweb.edu/~jones/hobbies/billiards.html#8ball">
Click here to go straight to Jones' 8-ball rules.</A>

could point straight to his 8-ball rules from any web page. You can also append fragment identifiers onto relative URLs. So, for example, the link

<A HREF="hobbies/billiards.html#8ball"> Click here to go straight to my
8-ball rules.</A>

would directly target his 8-ball rules from his home page.

For a concrete example, refer back to the HTML document displayed in Figure 5.11 and rendered in Figure 5.12. Suppose somebody has taken a liking to Chapter 2 of that book

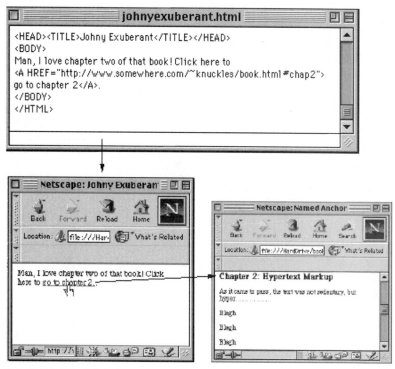

FIGURE 5.15 A link that points to an anchor in another document.

and wishes to make a link straight to that chapter. Assume the location of the document of Figure 5.11 is given by "www.somewhere.com/~knuckles/book.html". The following anchor creates a link which points straight to Chapter 2 of the book:

> <A HREF="http://www.somewhere.com/~knuckles/book.html#chap2">Go straight to chapter 2 of Knuckles' book.</A>

Figure 5.15 gives a file containing the above link and depicts what happens when the link is clicked.

5.7 THE MAILTO LINK

The last topic of this lesson involves not any new HTML tags or attributes, but a protocol we haven't discussed yet. The purpose of the **mailto** protocol should be obvious from its name. It can be used in a web page to activate an e-mail transaction. This is a simple matter, so we don't enter into a lengthy discussion. A simple example should get the idea across. Suppose Jones has an e-mail account with address "jones@uweb.edu". If he wishes to put a link in one of his web pages that can initiate an e-mail transaction, he simply includes

> <A HREF="mailto:jones@uweb.edu">Click here to send me some e-mail.</A>

which we call a **mailto link.** Note that the mailto link is still an HREF anchor, just using the mailto protocol.

When such a link is clicked, an e-mail window should appear on top of the browser window. The user simply types in a message and hits send. The e-mail window goes away and the user can keep perusing Jones' site, or can surf elsewhere.

> **NOTE** An important observation is that the mailto URL is the only absolute-type URL that uses only a colon (:) rather than the usual :// after the protocol. Also, mailto links can be somewhat unreliable. In order for the link to work, the user's browser has to be able to find an e-mail program to accomplish the transaction. In older browsers, you often had to tell it where to find an e-mail program by setting one of its preferences. However, since most current browsers have some sort of e-mail application built in, mailto links are pretty reliable today.

5.8 SUMMARY

Key Terms

HREF anchor	mailto link	portability	local link
web site	absolute URL	named anchor	hierarchical site
relative file path	relative URL	absolute link	fragment identifier
linear site			

Links are created in web pages with the anchor (<A>. . . </A>) container element. The contents of the element are marked up as the actual underlined text of the link. The web page to which the link points is specified as the value of the HREF attribute. We term these as HREF anchors. The value of the HREF attribute can be an absolute or relative URL. Absolute URLs are basically complete URLs that include the http protocol, the server address, and perhaps a specific resource at that address. Absolute URLs are used to link to remote web sites. Internal linking, linking to pages within one's web site, is accomplished using relative URLs. We often call linking within one's web site local linking. A relative URL is the file path to the desired document, relative to the document in which the link appears. If the target file is in the same directory as the document that contains the link, the necessary relative URL is just the name of the target file. For a relative URL to look inside a directory, the name of the directory is required. However, to back up a directory (look outside the current directory), the "../" structure is required.

> **NOTE** If a local link is not working, the problem is most likely one of the following:
> 1. The relative URL does not specify the correct file path to the target file.
> 2. The directory names or file names used in the relative URL do not exactly match the actual directory or file names. By *exactly,* we mean capital letters, blank spaces and all. (It is best to use all small letters and no spaces in your directory and file names to help alleviate such problems.)

A major plus that comes from using relative links to link all of your web pages together locally is that your web site is then portable. This means your web site works on your personal computer and also works on a web server. In fact, if you are building or maintaining a web site on a web server, you should keep an exact replica on your personal computer, right down to the public directory. When you make changes to your local copy and are satisfied with the results, ftp the whole site or just the changes to the server. Once transferred, the links should be checked.

NOTE

If your web site works locally but a link fails on the server, the problem is most likely one of the following:

1. You have been lax about problem 1 above and your personal computer is tolerant. For example, file names might not be case-sensitive on the personal computer. The web server, however, is not being so kind.

2. You transferred one or more pages into the wrong directory on the server. This causes the relative file paths specified in your links no longer to be correct.

3. You accidentally transferred one or more of your HTML documents to the server as something other than "text" or ASCII" (see Section 2.7).

Most web sites are structured in a hierarchical fashion. That is, each level has a main page that links to the other subsidiary pages on that level. Main pages for the different levels are linked together in such a way as to make the web site easily navigable. For certain types of web sites, such as an online tutorial, linear sites are ideal. This is where you have a main page and can tour through the other pages in a sequential fashion with [next][back] type links. Links can also be provided so that you can bypass the sequential order and choose any of the pages. But, regardless of the type of site design, the navigational links should be placed conveniently on each page. Also, the number of different directories you create to organize all of the different files in a given type of web site is a matter of personal preference and common sense.

One of the two attributes HREF or NAME is mandatory in an anchor element. When used with the NAME attribute, an anchor element's functionality is perhaps more indicative of its name. A named anchor serves as an anchor within a given web page. When a named anchor is targeted by an HREF link, not only does the page containing the named anchor load into the browser, but the position of the named anchor is brought to the top of the browser window. To target a named anchor with an HREF link, you have to append the name of the anchor onto the URL after a # symbol. Such an appendage is called a fragment identifier and can be applied to the end of a relative or absolute URL. However, if the named anchor is in the same page as the HREF anchor that points to the named anchor, only the fragment identifier is required.

Finally, a mailto link uses an HREF anchor to enact an e-mail transaction. The required value of the HREF attribute is a mailto URL. A mailto URL consists of the mailto protocol, followed by a colon, and then an e-mail address. If the user's browser can find an email program, when the link is clicked an e-mail window will appear that is addressed to the e-mail address specified in the link.

The following table summarizes the anchor element up to this point of the text.

<A> ··· </A> (One of the Two Attributes Must be Present.)

Attributes	Possible Values	Default
HREF	absolute URL, relative URL, fragment identifier	none
NAME	textual name	none

5.9   REVIEW QUESTIONS

In most cases, it is not sufficient to answer these from the Lesson Summary.

1. Give two disadvantages of using absolute URLs to link the pages of a web site together.

2. Differentiate between the notions of the actual text of a link and supporting text for a link. If a link, is not well supported, how can you use your browser to deduce its nature before you click it?

3. Describe the advantages of navigational links in a page, even if they are redundant with better supported links in the page.

4. Give a strategy for naming files and directories that will help avoid links which won't work. What's wrong with the reasoning: "it works on my computer, why won't it work on the web server?"

5. Explain the difference between http-absolute URLs and file-absolute URLs.

6. Discuss the "design-test-transfer-test" process of web development. Discuss two different strategies for the transfer part.

7. Discuss potential ftp transfer errors and their ramifications.

8. Explain when the functionality of a linear site design might be appropriate, and when hierarchical design might be appropriate.

9. How is the content of a named anchor marked up in a web page?

10. How are URLs using the mailto protocol structurally different from absolute URLs using other protocols?

5.10   EXERCISES

GENERAL

1. Write three absolute URLs, where each points to one of the files of Figure 5.7.

2. Consider the directories shown below. Write down the HTML code for a link in the first file that points to the second file. Use relative URLs.

(a) Link from "file.html" to "file3.html"

(b) Link from "file3.html" to "file.html"

(c) Link from "file4.html" to "file1.html"

(d) Link from "file1.html" to "file3.html"

(e) Link from "file3.html" to "file2.html"

```
public
    file.html
    folder1
        file1.html
        folder2
            file2.html
    folder3
        file4.html
        folder4
            file3.html
```

3. Answer parts (a), (b), and (c) for Exercise 2 above. However, assume that there is a named anchor with NAME="findme" in the "to" file to which you are linking. Write down the HTML code for a link that points straight to this named anchor.

4. Design the web site of Figure 5.10. Each web page should contain a short (one sentence or less) description of what that page is. In other words, each page is almost blank. The emphasis here is on the navigational links and the linking structure. However, to emphasize the hierarchy, give all of the indexing pages the same background color. Moreover, distinguish among the levels of the hierarchy by making all the pages on a given level, aside from the index file, have a common background color.

5. (This file is used for Exercise 8.9.4 as well.) Go to the homework section for Lesson 5 on the web site for this book. Under Exercise 5, you will find a link to a web page named "dsl.html" that discusses DSL Internet connections. This page has a title and four sections, numbered 1 through 4. Download the source HTML file for this page and add the following features. (Do a "save as" and select source while viewing the page.)

(a) Put a named anchor at the beginning of each of the four sections. Put navigational links at the top of the page that target each of the four named anchors.

(b) Put links near the title of each of the four sections that point back to the top of the page. These links need only be of the form <u>back to top</u>. In this way, the viewer can go straight to one of the sections and then right back to the top without having to use the scroll bar.

(c) Section 4 has several subtopics. Put named anchors at each of the subtopics of Section 4. Put links at the beginning of section 4 that target these subtopics.

(d) Make a separate web page that serves to index all the named anchors you have added to the file. Include a link that points to the page itself, links that point straight to each of the four named anchors for the main sections, and links as a sublist to the link for section 4 that point to the named anchors that mark the subtopics of section 4. This page serves as an external table of contents.

6. (The files you create here are used for Exercise 8.9.5 as well.) Go to the homework section for Lesson 5 on the web site for this book. Under Exercise 6, you will find a link to a web page named "dsl.html" that discusses DSL Internet connections. This page has a title and four sections, named 1 through 4. Download the source HTML file for this page and make this page into a linear collection of pages as follows:

(a) Make a brief title page using the title of the document.

(b) Make each of the four sections into its own web page.

(c) Add links to each of the pages making this collection of five pages into a linear collection. The title page is the main indexing page for the collection.

(d) Section 4 has several subsections. Put a named anchor at each of these subsections. In addition to the link on the title page that points to the page for section 4, add links that point straight to the named anchors marking the subsections.

5.11 PROJECT THREADS

THREAD A

It is now time to make the separate web pages you have into a fully linked web site. Reread Section 2.8.

Assignment

(a) Rename your home page "version2.html". Create a new file named "index.html" (or whatever the indexing file name is on your web server) and copy the contents of your version-2 home page into this file. This is your version-3 home page. Add any new or refined ideas you have for your home page. Also, include at least two links to external sites that relate to or support the theme(s) of your home page.

(b) Create another directory (folder) inside your public folder named "homework". Move your old home page versions into this folder. Also, move any other homework assignments you have created into this folder. Create an index file to run this new directory. The situation is depicted below.

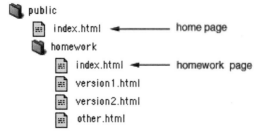

This new index file is your homework page and will be used to organize links to all of your homework assignments. Your homework page can be simple, perhaps with a heading as to the purpose of the page, and some color(s).

Link your web site together with *relative* links according to the following guidelines:

(i) Your home page will have a navigational link near its top that points to your homework page. Your homework page will have a navigational link near its top that points back to your home page.

(ii) Your homework page will contain links to each of the homework assignments. At this point, that means the two previous versions of your home page and any other assignments you have done. The links should be well supported so that it is apparent to what they point.

(iii) Each assignment referenced on your homework page will have navigational links at its top that point back to your homework page.

(c) If you are to do any of the Exercises above, put those files in your homework directory and add the required links.

(d) If applicable, transfer all files to the web server when completed. Check to make sure the transfer was successful. Especially, check to make sure all of the links work.

THREAD B

It is now time to make the separate web pages you have into a fully linked web site. Reread Section 2.8.

Assignment

(a) Create a new directory (folder) named "research" inside your public directory. Move your research page(s) into the new directory. If you have only one research page, rename it "index.html" (or whatever the indexing file name is on your web server). Otherwise, if you have more than one research page, make a new page named "index.html" inside your research folder that has links to each of your research pages.

(b) Do Exercise 5 above. Create a new directory (folder) named "ex5_5" inside your public directory to contain the files from that exercise. Name the table of contents page from 5d "index.html".

(c) You should have a web site as pictured. Supply links so that the site is a fully linked hierarchical web site. Of course, use relative links. The links in the homework page that point to the assignments should be well supported in terms of to what the links point. Strictly navigational links like back to homework page should be placed at the very tops of pages.

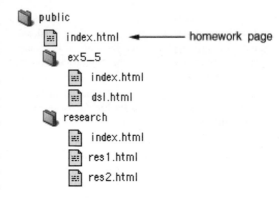

(d) If you are to do any other Exercises above, put those files in your root directory with your homework page and supply necessary links.

(e) If applicable, transfer all files to the web server when completed. Check to make sure the transfer was successful. Especially, check to make sure all of the links work.

LESSON *6*

IMAGE MARKUP

IN THE early days of the WWW, the content of web pages was mostly textual. In fact, many early browsers didn't even support graphical images. Even without images, there was a lot of information available on the Web. But, as the old saying goes, "a picture is worth a thousand words." As browsers that could render graphical images, like Netscape and Internet Explorer, became widely available, the popularity of images on the WWW burgeoned. But even then, their use was cumbersome. Images are typically very large files and take up lots of computer memory.

But now with blazingly fast computers (and the actual Internet connections getting faster) images are not overly cumbersome objects to include in web pages. In fact, almost any web page you pull up on the Internet nowadays is replete with images, going from small icon-like images to large photograph-like images. Of course, these images are not simply likenesses put onto paper as with the traditional photograph, but digitized, computer-readable images. Digital processing of images has reached such an advanced level that many new cameras and video recorders even store images in digital format. In fact, there is really no difference between how an image from a digital photograph is stored and how the digital images you see in web pages are stored.

6.1 IMAGE FILES

Images that are used in web pages are of two varieties, ".gif" and .jpeg". That might sound a bit strange, but these two image varieties are no more than two file types. The ".gif" and .jpeg" designations are the file suffixes used to identify the two image types. As we mentioned above, digital image files tend to be quite large. To help ease the burden of transporting large image files on the Internet, file-compression techniques are used. In other words, files are digitally compressed so that they take up less computer memory. The key is that the image files must be compressed in such a way as not to affect the clarity or sharpness of the image. Since file compression is beyond the scope of this book, we will have to be content with saying that ".gif" and ".jpeg" represent two different types of image-file compression, two different ways digital images are "compacted" so they take up less computer memory. Rather than referring to the two image types by the file suffixes, we will use **GIF** and **JPEG**.

FIGURE 6.1   A GIF image file and the actual image it contains.

N O T E   As a general rule, icon-type images are usually created as GIF images and photograph-type images are usually created as JPEG-type images. The GIF compression type provides for greater flexibility, as we shall see, whereas the JPEG compression type provides for greater sharpness and clarity with more colors, as is desirable with photographs.

Because the images we will use for demonstration in this lesson are small icon-type images, we will use GIF images for the examples. However, as you do more and more web development, you will no doubt encounter JPEG images. In terms of the HTML required to mark up the two image types in web pages, there is no appreciable difference, so GIF images suffice nicely for demonstration. As a last note on JPEG, is also very common to see ".jpeg" images appended with only the suffix ".jpg". So for a given JPEG image file, say "mypicture.jpeg", the file name "mypicture.jpg" could also be used.

Figure 6.1 depicts a basic GIF image file named "funnyman.gif". As you see it on the left, it doesn't look like an image at all, just a computer file. That's because that's what it is, just a compressed bunch of digital information. In order to see the contents of an image file, you have to load the file into an application that can decompress and display the file's contents. In the context of web development, the application of choice is usually a graphic editor or a web browser. Upon opening the image file, you can then see the graphic it generates. In this case, it is the icon of a cartoon-like guy you see on the right side of Figure 6.1. In case you were wondering about the strange name of the image file, it is advisable to give image files descriptive names so that you can easily keep track of them in your website file directories.

As for graphic editors, you can find reference to some freeware and/or shareware editors on the web site for this book. However, the good ones like Adobe Photoshop cost a good bit of money (like several hundred dollars). We will not go into the details of using graphic editors, but they are a means by which you can create, view, and alter images. Next time you see an image containing Bill Clinton's head on a bodybuilder-type body, you will be seeing evidence of graphic manipulation with a graphic editor.

Since we are focusing on web page development, the chosen image-viewing application for this lesson is the web browser. As it turns out, an image doesn't have to be embedded in a web page to be displayed by a browser. Figure 6.2 shows the result of loading "funnyman.gif" into a browser from a local computer. You can see in the address window that we are indeed viewing a GIF image rather than an HTML file, which would end with the suffix ".html" rather than ".gif".

If you look at the top of the browser window in Figure 6.2, you can see that Netscape has given the dimensions of the actual image in pixels. Note that Explorer also gives you the dimensions of an image when you load it by itself, not embedded in a web page. In this case the image is 33 × 33 pixels, 33 pixels wide and 33 pixels high. In fact, every image has inherent dimensions and the standard order for these dimensions is

WIDTH × HEIGHT

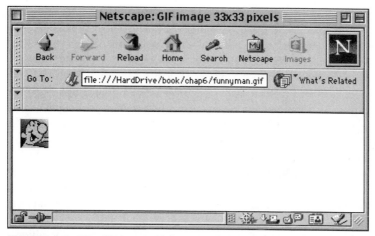

FIGURE 6.2 The GIF image "funnyman.gif" loaded into a web browser from the local hard drive. It's not in a web page.

So, for example, you could have two image files sitting on your computer:

one being substantially larger that the other. Let's say that "image1.gif" is 40×30 pixels and "image2.gif" is 600×700 pixels. Then image1 is small, roughly the size of "funnyman.gif", but is rectangular (somewhat wider than high). In contrast, image2 is very large, but also rectangular (somewhat higher than wide). In fact, image2 is so large that it would barely fit inside the browser window, if at all. In other words, you would only see part of the image in the browser and would have to use the scroll bars to see the other parts.

So, even though the icons for the images look the same, the actual images are drastically different. But the fact that the icons are similar doesn't mean the actual images files are similar. Remember that, in general, larger images take up more computer memory than smaller images. In reality, "image1.gif" might take up 4K or so of computer memory, whereas "image2.gif" might take up 50K, or more, of computer memory.

NOTE

To summarize, the **image size** (or **image dimensions**) refers to the actual size, WIDTH × HEIGHT in pixels, of the image once it is displayed by an application that can display images. In contrast, the **file size** of an image refers to the amount of computer memory, in K (kilobytes), that it takes to store the image. In general, there is a direct correlation between the image dimensions and its file size. In other words, larger images typically come from larger image files. We say "in general" and "typically" in the previous two sentences because there are exceptions. Things like the type of compression being used and the actual resolution of the image also affect the file size.

Perhaps the most urgent question you might be pondering is, "How in the heck do I get my hands on some images to put in my web page?" The hard way is to make them yourself. Many of the images used in this book, like the image1 and image2 icons above, were created by taking a screen shot of the author's computer screen. Taking a screen shot basically amounts to capturing a digital image of the computer screen, exactly as you see it. Then a graphical editor can be used to cut out the desired parts. However, the details of such a process are beyond the scope of this book.

Another way to create an image is to use a **scanner.** A scanner is a piece of equipment that can be used to scan a physical image, like a photograph or piece of paper, to create a digital file for the image. Scanners can be purchased for anywhere from around $100 to several hundreds of dollars, depending on the desired versatility and quality. You simply put your physical image into the scanner, much like putting it into a copy machine, and scan the thing. In fact, it is much like using a copy machine, except that the result is a digital computer file rather than another physical likeness of the image. But, once again, a more detailed discussion of this is beyond the objectives of this book. Besides, if it is just a photograph that you are interested in getting on a web page, and you happen to own a digital camera, you should be good to go.

The good news is that you can download tons (millions or billions) of images for free over the Internet. In fact, many web sites offer libraries of image files explicitly so that you can download some of them for your use. The web site for this book offers links to some of these resources. You might be surprised to learn that, aside from image libraries designed expressly for image download, virtually any image you find in a web page while surfing is downloadable. The procedure is outlined in the following note.

NOTE

If you find an image in a web page, image library or otherwise, you can click your mouse on the image and hold the mouse button down. (On PCs it's the right mouse button.) When you "click and hold" on the image, a menu should pop up providing you with several options. One of these will be "save image as" or simply "save as". Choose this option to download a copy of the image onto your hard drive. This is basically a quick anonymous ftp transaction accomplished by your browser. The best way to learn is just to play with a few images in web pages until you get the hang of it.

It is **very important** to note that you should avoid an image that could be copyrighted. In other words, don't pirate the official logo from some company and put it on your web page. Perhaps the infinitive "to pirate" (as in "to steal and pillage") is too harsh here (but it's a cool verb). Anyone who puts an image on the Web should be aware that it is fair game for download. There are, in fact, ways to safeguard images against download. However, the vast majority of images on the Web are not safeguarded. In general, pirating images is kind of a fuzzy issue, and there is a gray area between right and wrong. If you stick to image libraries, you should not have to worry too much about this issue. The best advice at the present time is to use your best judgment. In practice, it is a simple matter to avoid pirating an image if you think copyright could be an issue.

Throughout the remainder of this lesson, we will use the verb "pirate" to mean the anonymous downloading of an image from the Web. We think it's a cool verb and don't mean that images should be stolen. In fact, as we mentioned above, you should stringently avoid any possibility downloading copyrighted material.

6.2 IMAGE MARKUP

Now that we know how to pirate images, it's time to learn how to put images into a web page. The HTML element used to embed an image into a web page is the IMG (image)

FIGURE 6.3 An HTML document "imagedemo.html" into which the image "funnnyman.gif" is to be embedded. They are both sitting in some public directory that could be on a web server or simply on your computer.

element. Its basic form is

<IMG SRC="URL">

The IMG element is not a container element (it doesn't contain anything) and has one mandatory attribute, the SRC attribute. SRC stands for "source" and gives the location (or source) of the image. The tag tells the browser to mark up an image and the SRC attribute points the browser to the right image file. That's why SRC is mandatory in the IMG tag. Without this, the browser does not know where to find the image. The SRC attribute can either take an absolute URL or relative URL.

If the IMG element uses an absolute URL, it would look something like

<IMG SRC="http://www.somewhere.com/an_image.gif">

where the absolute URL points to some remote server and specifies the desired image file. However, it is unlikely that you would want to embed an image in your web page from some remote server. The best bet is to store all of the image files that will be used in your web site right with the HTML documents that generate the web pages. In this way, you just have to specify a relative URL, which, of course, is just a file local path.

For a concrete example, we need an image. A convenient choice is "funnyman.gif" of Figure 6.1 which, for your reference, was pirated from a free online icon library. Figure 6.3 shows a public web directory that contains a very simple HTML document named "imagedemo.html" and the image "funnyman.gif".

Figure 6.4 shows the file "imagedemo.html", which uses the IMG element to embed the GIF image. You will note that the relative URL used by the SRC attribute is just the name of the image file since the image file is in the same directory as the HTML file. The rendering of this HTML file is shown in Figure 6.5.

The main thing to note here is that the image is thrown right in with the text in the web page. In many respects, the default behavior of image markup is that images behave

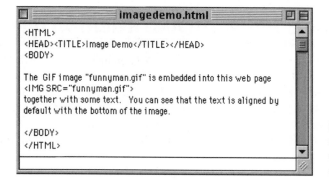

FIGURE 6.4 The HTML document "imagedemo.html", which uses the IMG element to embed a GIF image.

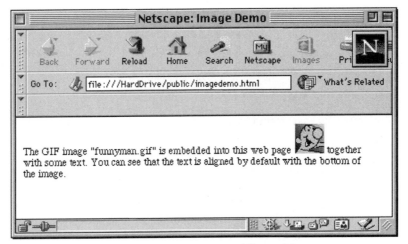

FIGURE 6.5   The rendering of the document of Figure 6.4.

like ordinary text. For example, when we put in some larger text in this sentence, the bottom of the larger text lines up with the bottom of the adjacent text. So, too, the image appears right in with the text and its bottom is aligned with the adjacent text.

> **NOTE**
>
> In general, the larger the image file, the longer it takes the web page that contains the image to load into the browser. An image file the size of "funnyman.gif", maybe 4K or so, will load almost as quickly as the text. However, if you put a bunch (maybe 25 or 30) of images of that size into the same web page, the page would load noticeably more slowly. If you include a large image, say with file size of 100K or more, that will also slow down the browser. Several large image files can bring the browser to a standstill for several seconds or even minutes.
>
> The point to be made here is that, while images are good in web pages, don't go hog-wild and load your pages to the hilt with images. You need to create some balance between image content and the speed that the page will load into a browser. This was a particularly big deal just two or three years ago. But computers now are getting blazingly fast and can process images very quickly. But even with smokin' fast computers, there are still issues of transporting huge images or large numbers of smaller images over the Internet. Even if a web page loads smokin' fast on your computer, that doesn't mean that everyone else will be able to download that page quickly over the Internet.

6.3   CREATING SPACE: THE WIDTH AND HEIGHT ATTRIBUTES

The two most fundamental attributes of the IMG element are the WIDTH and HEIGHT attributes. You will notice in Figures 6.4 and 6.5 that there is no mention of these attributes. In that case, the image was marked up with the default dimensions of the image. If you recall, that's 33×33 pixels. The WIDTH and HEIGHT attributes of the IMG tag can be used to override the default dimensions. Figure 6.6 shows three different renderings of "funnyman.gif" using these attributes. Rather than providing the HTML file that generates the figure, we offer some discussion.

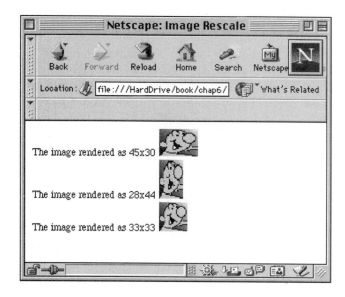

FIGURE 6.6 The rendering of the funnyman image with various dimensions specified by the WIDTH and HEIGHT attributes of the IMG element.

The HTML required to format the three versions of image amounts to no more than

<IMG SRC="funnyman.gif" WIDTH=45 HEIGHT=30>

<IMG SRC="funnyman.gif" WIDTH=28 HEIGHT=44>

<IMG SRC="funnyman.gif" WIDTH=33 HEIGHT=33>

in the same order, of course, that the images appear in the example web page. It's pretty clear that, in the first two instances, the image has been distorted from its original form by the WIDTH and HEIGHT attributes. In the third instance, the attributes did no more than specify the actual dimensions of the image. In other words, the image would have been marked up to be that size even if the attributes had not been present.

So why then did we include the attributes in the third instance, if they were not needed? The reason is that you should *always* use these two attributes with the IMG element, even if you don't intend to resize the image. The reason for this is as follows. Of course, there is a bit more to it than we indicate, but this basic reasoning is easy to comprehend.

Before a browser can start marking up a web page, it has to determine how much space to allocate for any images that are to be embedded in the page. If the WIDTH and HEIGHT attributes are not used, the browser has to completely load all of the image files from the remote server in order to see their dimensions. Once the browser knows all of the dimensions, it can then start to render the web page. The problem with this is that image files tend to load slowly. So, basically, you would be sitting and looking at a blank browser screen waiting for the browser to load all the image files into its memory cache. Then, once it has determined the image dimensions, it begins to render the web page, which again takes some time.

Now, picture the scenario where WIDTH and HEIGHT attributes have been included in *all* of the IMG elements, even if they are not needed to resize the image. Before the browser has loaded all of the images, it has read the HTML code and knows how much space to allocate for the images because of the WIDTH and HEIGHT attributes. So it starts rendering the web page. Since all of the images are not yet acquired from the remote server, it simply creates space in the web page into which it will eventually load each image. So, what this means is that the browser can lay out the whole web page, leaving empty boxes for the images, at the same time it is attempting to acquire all the images from the remote server. As the various images arrive, they are simply inserted into the vacant spaces that have been appropriated ahead of time because of the WIDTH and HEIGHT attributes.

So, the use of WIDTH and HEIGHT attributes can produce a substantial savings in loading time for a given web page. In fact, almost any web page you will find when surfing will have these attributes in all its IMG tags. You can actually see some empty boxes being "drawn" in the page while it is loading. Then, eventually, the images will arrive, and you will see them appear in the spaces that were allocated ahead of time.

NOTE

If you wish to reduce the size of an image, say for space considerations, and you wish not to distort the image as in the first two cases in Figure 6.6, there may actually be a little algebra involved. Suppose you need an image near the top of your web page that is exactly 30 pixels high. (You will see reasons why you would want something such as this as we progress in later lessons to more advanced ways to create page layout.) If the image is a square image like "funnyman.gif", it is easy. You just set the attributes to mark up the image as 30 × 30.

The problem comes in when an image is not square. For example, suppose you go and pirate a suitable image, but the image is 26 × 37. Now, you know that you want to set HEIGHT=30. But how do you know what to set the WIDTH to so that the image doesn't get distorted? You could guess, maybe 19 × 30, but guessing can leave you with a slightly distorted image. The proper way is to preserve the width/height ratio. You don't know the new width, so just let the desired width be *w*. Then the equation

$$\frac{26}{37} = \frac{w}{30}$$

old ratio = new ratio

provides the desired requirement for the variable *w*. Solving the equation by cross multiplying, you get that $w = 21.08$. Of course we can't request fractions of pixels, so we round to the nearest whole number 21. The desired dimensions are thus 21 × 30.

6.4 POSITIONING IMAGES WITH TEXT

Just as there are ways to create custom text alignments using attributes of text markup elements, there are attributes of the IMG element that provide some latitude in the way images are aligned within the text. Moreover, there are ways to make the text actually flow around an image, much as in a magazine or newspaper. All that is required to better align images on the page is a few attributes of the IMG element. But, of course, that should come as no surprise.

First, there is the ALIGN attribute. The values

ALIGN=bottom

ALIGN=middle

ALIGN=top

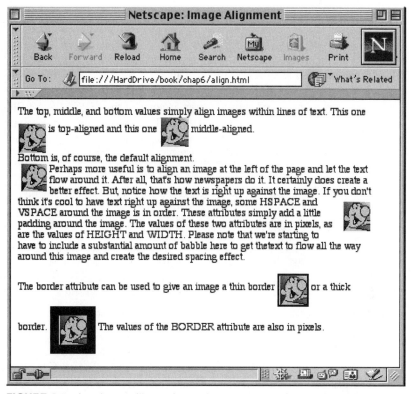

FIGURE 6.7 A web page illustrating various attributes of the IMG element.

are used to set how adjacent text is aligned with the image. We saw in Figure 6.5 and again in Figure 6.6 that text is aligned with the bottom of the image by default. The above values provide some added flexibility, as you can see in the first two images in Figure 6.7. However, it is often not desirable to place images right in with text. As you can see, the placement of images within text causes the lines of text to be separated by differing amounts of space. The second and third lines of text are separated by around twice as much space as the first and second lines. That's kind of an ugly effect.

However, the values

ALIGN=left

ALIGN=right

actually cause the text to flow around the images, as evidenced by the third and fourth images in Figure 6.7. Notice how the text that flows around the third image is right up against the image. The HSPACE and VSPACE attributes provide for some extra horizontal and vertical padding, respectively, around the image. These attributes take pixels for values. For example, the attributes

HSPACE=10

VSPACE=5

```
align.html

<HTML>
<HEAD><TITLE>Image Alignment</TITLE></HEAD>
<BODY>
The top, middle, and bottom values simply align images within
lines of text. This one
<IMG SRC="funnyman.gif" WIDTH=32 HEIGHT=32 ALIGN=top>
is top-aligned and this one
<IMG SRC="funnyman.gif" WIDTH=32 HEIGHT=32 ALIGN=middle>
middle-aligned.<BR>
Bottom is, of course, the default alignment.<BR>
<IMG SRC="funnyman.gif" WIDTH=30 HEIGHT=30 ALIGN=left>
Perhaps more useful is to align an image at the left of the page and let the text
flow around it. After all, that's how newspapers do it. It certainly
does create a better effect. But, notice how the text is right up
against the image.
<IMG SRC="funnyman.gif" WIDTH=32 HEIGHT=32 ALIGN=right HSPACE=10 VSPACE=5>
If you don't think it's cool to have text right up against the image,
some HSPACE and VSPACE around the image is in order. These attributes
simply add a little padding around the image. The values of these two
attributes are in pixels, as are the values of HEIGHT and WIDTH.
Please note that we're starting to have to include a substantial amount of babble here to get
thetext to flow all the way around this image and create the desired spacing effect.
<P>
The border attribute can be used to give an image a thin border
<IMG SRC="funnyman.gif" WIDTH=32 HEIGHT=32 BORDER=2 ALIGN=middle>
or a thick border.
<IMG SRC="funnyman.gif" WIDTH=32 HEIGHT=32 BORDER=10 ALIGN=middle>
The values of the BORDER attribute are also in pixels.
</BODY>
</HTML>
```

FIGURE 6.8   The HTML document that generates Figure 6.7.

create a 10-pixel padding beside the image and a 5-pixel padding above and below the image. This is evidenced in the fourth image of Figure 6.7, but since the text is not right-justified, it's a bit hard to perceive the exact HSPACE.

The purpose of the BORDER attribute should be clear from the last two images of the example. It can be used to create a black border around an image. It also takes pixels. For your edification, the HTML document that generates Figure 6.7 is shown in Figure 6.8.

The last attribute of the image element we mention in this section is the ALT attribute. It provides for a text ALTernative for images. By text alternative, we mean some string of text that will be displayed in place of the image if a browser can't display images or has image display turned off. ALT was a bigger deal back when image display was not standard fare on all browsers. But, still today, some people like to go to the browser's preferences and turn off the image display feature. Then they get text-only web pages, which load much more quickly. This is, in fact, a good option for people using very slow computers or very slow phone modems for their Internet connection.

So, whatever the case, the inclusion of something like

ALT="picture of cartoon man"

in an IMG tag provides a text alternative to the image. If for whatever reason the image does not appear in the web page, the browser will display the string of text instead.

6.5   IMAGES AS LINKS

It is also possible to have images act as hypertext links. We choose to term images that are active as links as **image links.** So rather than clicking on a normal underlined hypertext link to go somewhere, the surfer can actually click on an image and be transported. To accomplish this, the IMG tag pointing to the image is simply placed inside an anchor element whose HREF attribute points to the desired URL:

<A HREF="URL"> <IMG SRC="imgname.gif"> </A>

Note that the IMG tag comprises the content of the anchor element. It is *not* placed in the start tag with the HREF attribute. Figure 6.9 shows the result of placing image tags inside anchor elements.

It is apparent that the images are actually links. Indeed, the mouse cursor pointing to the bomb has caused the URL for Terrorists Anonymous to be displayed in the status bar of the browser. Rather than displaying the whole document, "outlaws.html", that created the page in Figure 6.9, we give the definitions of the two anchor elements that create the image links. The rest is of the document is quite simple.

<A HREF="http://www.piratehelp.com">
<IMG SRC="jollyroger.gif" WIDTH=45 HEIGHT=45 ALIGN=middle BORDER=0>
</A>

<A HREF="http://www.terroristhelp.com">
<IMG SRC="bomb.gif" WIDTH=45 HEIGHT=45 ALIGN=middle BORDER=0>
</A>

Again we emphasize that the image tags are contents of the anchor elements, not part of the start tags. One interesting thing to note about this example is that normally when you put an

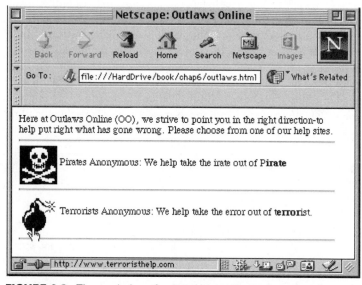

FIGURE 6.9   The rendering of a document with two images acting as hypertext links.

image inside an anchor element to make it a link, the browser will render a border around the image. For a textual link, the browser underlines the text to emphasize that it is in fact a link. In similar fashion, it will wrap that underline all the way around an image link to emphasize that it is a link. This looks just like an image border, except that it's blue or whatever color the browser defaults to for links. In this case, we didn't want a colored border around the images, so we forced the browser to suppress it with BORDER=0 in the IMG element.

We also mention that it is advisable to support image links with text of some sort. If an image link is just sitting off to the side somewhere, it might not be apparent that it is a hypertext link, especially if you suppress the blue (or whatever color) border that the anchor element tries to give the image.

A common practice that involves images as links is called thumbnailing. (The spell checker is bound to catch that one!) Given a moderate or large image, whether big in file size or image dimensions, it is often desirable to create a **thumbnail** of the image. A thumbnail is a small version of the image, perhaps icon-sized, that is used to represent the image. For an example, consider an online realtor selling houses. It might be desirable for a certain web page on their site to contain a brief description of several houses, together with a small thumbnail picture for each house. Since the actual house pictures are quite large, it is not practical to display them all in the page for space considerations. Moreover, it is not advisable for them all to be in the same page because of potential loading delays.

With small thumbnails, the viewer can quickly load the thumbnail page, get a quick look at all of the houses and descriptions and, if interested in one, click on a thumbnail to see the full version of the house. Of course, in this case the thumbnails are image links and the HREF attributes point to the larger image that each thumbnail represents. Moreover, the actual house picture to which each thumbnail link points does not even have to be embedded in a web page. Recall that back in Figure 6.2 we loaded an image into a browser that was not part of a web page. In that case, the relative URL simply points to the image file, rather than an HTML document.

There is one crucial point here, however. Suppose a given house image is 600×400 pixels. That's a 3/2 width over height ratio. So why not just proportionally squash the image with the WIDTH and HEIGHT attributes to 60×40? The problem is that the image size has been reduced, but the actual image file size remains the same. So, if the realtor were to use this method to create the thumbnails, the actual thumbnail page would have a bunch of tiny images, each of which is generated by a huge image file. That defeats the purpose of thumbnailing in the first place. Unfortunately, there is no solution short of learning to use a graphic editor application skillfully. Since the details of graphic editors are beyond the scope of this book, there is not much more to say about thumbnailing. Thumbnailing is, nonetheless a technique with which you should be familiar.

NOTE One use of image links that has become very common is to use button icons as image links. The following two buttons are typical. They are just small image files.

Home and Next

When using such buttons, there is usually no need for supporting text since the supporting text is built right into the image. Such button images can be found in abundance in various image and icon libraries around the Internet. Just be sure to suppress the border the anchor element will try to draw around the button. Otherwise, it looks a bit funny.

6.6 ORGANIZING IMAGE FILES

Perhaps the easiest way to organize the image files on your web site is just to put each image file in the same folder as the web page that is to use the image. That way, the required relative URL is just the name of the image file. Indeed, all the examples presented thus far in this lesson use this sort of URL. You may have noticed that every single IMG element example just pointed to the file using SRC="someimage.gif". But this need not be the case.

For a concrete example, let's go back to Jones' web site, as pictured in Figure 5.5 of Section 5.2, where he has a home page, a professional page, and some hobbies pages. Being the Web-savvy dude that he is, Jones has decided to put buttons, similar to the ones pictured just above, in his pages to function as links. Since he has a hierarchical site design, he knows that he wants a "Home" button in each of the subsidiary pages. Moreover, he wants a "Mail" button for the "mailto" link (see Section 5.7) in his homepage. He decides for simplicity that he should just keep all of his images in a common "image" directory. This is not necessary per se, but he figures since the four subsidiary web pages will all use the same "Home" button, he might as well just keep one home button around and use it in each of the four pages. Figure 6.10 depicts his web site updated with the new directory in which he has put the files for the two buttons.

Three of the required relative URL's have been pictured. The bottommost two simply have to point inside the image folder and specify the desired image file. The file path from the index file in the hobbies folder that points to the "home.gif" button is more complicated, however. Note the two dots at the beginning of this URL. It has to point back out of the hobbies folder into the public folder, then into the images folder, then specify the desired image file.

> **NOTE**
>
> We are not necessarily saying that you should organize your images as pictured in Figure 6.10. In fact, it is largely a matter of personal preference. If you just have a few images, it makes sense just to put them with the HTML documents that will use them. However, if you have a lot of images or some images that you will use in more than one web page, it makes sense to organize the images a little better, perhaps in an image folder. Just be careful. Just as with relative URLs in links, you have to get the file path right. Also, the file and directory names are case-sensitive. So if you don't match exactly, your image won't show up.

If a browser can't find an image, it's really no big deal. The page containing the image will still be displayed, but the image will simply not be present. Most browsers

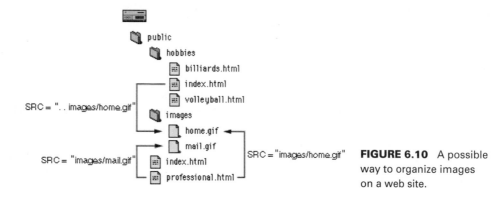

FIGURE 6.10 A possible way to organize images on a web site.

will insert a generic icon-looking image where the missing image should be displayed. It's quite obvious (and annoying) when an image doesn't show when it's supposed to. One should *always* check to see if everything works on the local copy of your web site before transferring it to the web server.

6.7 PUTTING IMAGES ON A WEB SERVER

Speaking of web servers, how do you get your images on the server? The answer is simple: you just transfer them over like you would any other file. But there is one difference. While HTML documents must be transferred to the web server as text or ASCII, images must be transferred as **raw data.** You should easily spot this option on your ftp program.

Remember, transfer web pages to the server as text or ASCII but transfer images as raw data. Otherwise you site will not work on the server, even if it has been working locally. On most any ftp application, there should be a third option, namely **automatic.** Keeping this option selected should keep your transfers in order. But this varies slightly among ftp applications. This option is something you might wish to experiment with to see if is reliable on your ftp application.

As a last note, just as when you are transferring web pages to the server, you have to be very careful which directory you upload them into. If you put an image in the wrong directory, it won't show up in the page because the URL won't match any more. This is perhaps another good reason to keep your images well organized on your web site.

6.8 TRANSPARENT GIFs AND ANIMATED GIFs

We mentioned towards the beginning of this lesson that GIF images are considerably more flexible than JPEG images. While JPEG is, in general, better for high resolution real-life types of images, GIF images provide two features that make them "cool" for use in web page construction. The first cool type of GIF image is the **transparent GIF.** This doesn't mean that you can see right through the image, but that the image's background will adapt to whatever background color is in the web page. In this sense, the image is in the foreground and the image's background is like a chameleon. The image's background automatically blends in with the web page's background.

The following GIF image "arrow.gif" is an example of a transparent GIF. In order to demonstrate its dimensions, we display it below with a border drawn around the image. This was simply done by setting BORDER=1 in the IMG element.

The image is 40 × 30 pixels and appears to consist of a blue arrow on a white background. However, Figure 6.11 shows the same image (without the border) on both a white background and light blue background web page. So, even though the image is a 40 × 30 rectangle, it appears to be just an arrow shaped image floating on the page. The good news is that you don't have to use any special HTML tags to make a GIF transparent. Some are just made that way. Moreover, they abound in free icon libraries, out there ready for pirating.

FIGURE 6.11 The background of the transparent GIF adapts to the background of the web page in which it is embedded.

The second cool type of GIF image is the **animated GIF.** These GIFs are like short cartoons: they run through a sequence of similar images to create a motion effect. Once again, you don't have to do anything special to put one in your web page. Just go find one in a free image library and put it in your web page with the IMG element. There is really no more explanation required. Furthermore, it is hard to illustrate an animation in a static book. So, our advice is just to go find one and check it out.

N O T E

We have pretty much skirted around the topic of how to use a graphic editor, and will do so once again. If you load an animated GIF into almost any graphic editor, you can actually change the speed setting for the image. That is, you can set the rate at which the different frames of the animation are displayed. You can make the animation go really fast or really slooooooow. While setting animation speed is pretty easy, it takes quite a while to learn how to do various things with such editors. That might make a good project once you are done with this book!

6.9 BACKGROUND IMAGES

One of the things you may have noticed while surfing is that many web pages have textured backgrounds, rather than just colored backgrounds. Some of these textured backgrounds are very subtle and some are quite elaborate, like clouds, for example. Such effects are quite easy to produce; all that is required is an image file that is suitable for a background and an attribute of the BODY element.

Consider the image in Figure 6.12. You can see that it presents just a mildly textured surface, maybe like a rough cloth or a marbled tile. Such images are ideal for backgrounds since they do not overpower the page and provide a good background for text. Once again, such images can be found in numerous icon and image libraries. In fact, many of these contain only background-type images, or have a special section for background images.

To set an image file as the background for a web page you use the BACKGROUND attribute of the BODY element.

<BODY BACKGROUND="URL of image">

bg.gif

FIGURE 6.12 An image suitable for a web page background.

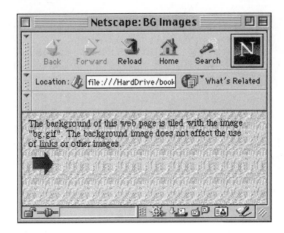

FIGURE 6.13 A web page with background created by the image of Figure 6.12.

Assuming for simplicity that "bg.gif" is in the same directory as the web page which is to use it,

<BODY BACKGROUND="bg.gif">

causes the image "bg.gif" to appear as the background of the page.

Figure 6.13 shows a web page that uses "bg.gif" for its background. For illustrative purposes, this web page contains some other things. In particular, it contains another image that appears on top of the background image. In other words, the background won't affect other objects in the web page. They are superimposed on top of the background image. You can even note that the arrow image is the same transparent GIF that was used as an example in the previous section. The transparent background of the arrow even absorbs the background image.

You are probably wondering how the small image in Figure 6.12 (it's 65×65) can create a background that fills the whole browser window. The background effect is a **tiling** of the small background image. The background image is put in the web page much as floor tiles are placed in a kitchen or bathroom floor. So the page in Figure 6.13 actually contains many copies of the small image. No matter how big the browser window is made, enough copies of the background image will be included to cover the whole page.

NOTE The inclusion of a background image is the only image markup you will do that involves an attribute of the BODY element rather than the IMG element. All other image markup in this lesson is accomplished with the IMG element. But, given that the BODY element also has a BGCOLOR attribute that sets a background color, there could be a conflict of interest here. In other words, if you put a background image and a background color in the same web page, which one wins? The answer is simple. The background image wins and the BGCOLOR is simply not displayed.

6.10 IMAGE MAPS (OPTIONAL)

Perhaps you have seen an image in a web page in which you can click different parts and be transported to different web pages depending upon which region of the image you have

FIGURE 6.14 An image suitable for making an image map.

clicked. In other words, the image as a whole acts as multiple links, but separate regions link to different pages. Such setups are called **image maps.** As usual, the best way to proceed is to provide a concrete example. Figure 6.14 shows part of a map of the western United States. For this example, we will simulate a tourist information page where someone can click on a state and be transported to an information web page for that state. For simplicity, we will focus on only the states of Oregon, California, and Nevada.

The first thing to note is the (x,y) coordinate display in the upper right corner of Figure 6.14. The reason this appears is that the image is loaded into a graphical editor program. There is really no way around using such a program if you wish to learn the nuts and bolts of making image maps. Once again, reference to several graphical editors is given in the web site for this book. The good news is that you don't have to know much about the editor. All you need to do is determine some (x,y) coordinate pairs using it.

With respect to images, the (x,y) coordinate system works as follows. The upper left pixel of the image is (0,0). Then coordinates for the other pixels are assigned according to the following scheme:

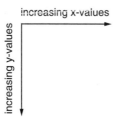

So, if the image in Figure 6.14 is 175 × 225 in dimensions, then the coordinates of the lower left corner are (0,225), the coordinates of the lower right corner are (175,225), and the coordinates of the upper right corner are (175,0). That serves to illustrate how pixel coordinates are assigned in images, but really all you need to know how to do is point your cursor at the image and read the coordinate display.

For example, in Figure 6.14 you can see the mouse pointer at the corner between California, Oregon, and Nevada. In the upper right of the image you can see that the coordinates of that point are (95,94). That's really all there is to it. Sure, different graphical editors will have different displays, but it should be no problem to put the mouse pointer on the image to deduce coordinates.

The reason for needing to deduce coordinates is that you can outline different regions of the image for use in an image map by specifying certain coordinates. The first way to designate a region is to specify the center of a circle and a desired radius:

SHAPE="circle"

COORDS="x,y,r"

This sets a circular region with center at (x,y) and with radius r. Here the radius is given in pixels. The second way is to specify the upper left and lower right coordinates of a rectangle:

SHAPE="rect"

COORDS="X_1,Y_1, X_2,Y_2"

The third way is to specify the vertices of a polygon. Given the irregular shapes of the states in Figure 6.14, we will use polygons to lay out the image map we are creating. So, to illustrate the use of polygons, we proceed with our concrete example, rather than in generality.

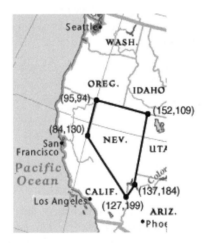

The polygon is defined by specifying its vertices (corners). The key is that the vertices are listed in order starting from (152,109). That makes sense, though. Since each vertex will be connected to the next one specified, you have to go in order or else the lines would cross each other.

N O T E

Since defining a polygon region is not as straightforward as the circle and the rectangle, we offer these hints.

1. Find the desired points using a graphic editor. List them in order. You can go clockwise or counterclockwise. If you don't go in order, the lines will cross and your image map won't work.

2. Don't list the first coordinate twice. In other words, whichever coordinate you list first, don't list it last as well.

In similar fashion, we have outlined California and Oregon as polygons. To set this up as an image map, you just include the image in the web page as a link.

```
<A HREF=" "> <IMG SRC="westusa.gif" ISMAP USEMAP="#themap"
BORDER=0> </A>
```

There is no need to specify a URL in the HREF attribute of the anchor element since the linking will be handled by the image map (once we define it). In the IMG element, we have pointed to the source of the image, namely "westusa.gif". The following two attributes are necessary. First, ISMAP takes no value and simply indicates that the embedded image is to function as an image map. Second, the USEMAP attribute specifies which map to use to set the regions in the image. Finally, the BORDER attribute is not necessary but, since the anchor element will draw a colored border around the image, it's a good idea to suppress it.

The above HTML suffices to embed the image in the web page and set it up as an image map. The MAP element is a separate chunk of HTML code that actually sets the regions in the image and the URL to which each region points.

```
<MAP NAME="themap">
  <AREA HREF="neva.html" SHAPE="poly"
    COORDS="152,109,137,184,127,199,84,130,95,94">
  <AREA HREF="oreg.html" SHAPE="poly"
    COORDS="78,29,138,48,123,100,56,78">
  <AREA HREF="cali.html" SHAPE="poly"
    COORDS="95,94,84,130,130,208,121,226,95,221,65,189,48,99,56,78">
</MAP>
```

The MAP element has a NAME. Remember, we had to call the map by name when we set the image up as an image map in the IMG element. You then include an AREA tag for each area you wish to define. The HREF attribute of the area tag specifies a URL (relative or absolute). This URL points to the web page to which that area is to link. After that, the attributes that define the actual area and its coordinates are included.

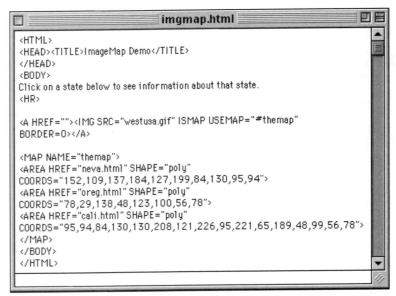

```
<HTML>
<HEAD><TITLE>ImageMap Demo</TITLE>
</HEAD>
<BODY>
Click on a state below to see information about that state.
<HR>

<A HREF=""><IMG SRC="westusa.gif" ISMAP USEMAP="#themap"
BORDER=0></A>

<MAP NAME="themap">
<AREA HREF="neva.html" SHAPE="poly"
COORDS="152,109,137,184,127,199,84,130,95,94">
<AREA HREF="oreg.html" SHAPE="poly"
COORDS="78,29,138,48,123,100,56,78">
<AREA HREF="cali.html" SHAPE="poly"
COORDS="95,94,84,130,130,208,121,226,95,221,65,189,48,99,56,78">
</MAP>
</BODY>
</HTML>
```

FIGURE 6.15 An HTML document that generates an image map for California, Oregon, and Nevada. Clicking on any of these states loads a different web page.

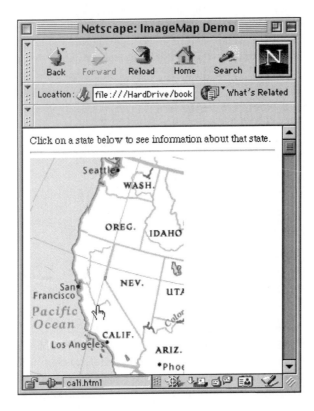

FIGURE 6.16 The rendering of the document of Figure 6.15.

For reference, we offer the complete document for our western USA example and its rendering in Figures 6.15 and 6.16 respectively. The HTML document that generates the image map is called "imgmap.html". Since the HREF attributes of the AREA tags only point to a file name, it is apparent that the web pages to which the image map points are in the same directory as "imgmap.html". You can also note in Figure 6.16 that the mouse pointer is on California and the desired web page, the target of that region, is shown in the status bar at the bottom of the browser.

NOTE In practice you don't have to be extremely accurate when you set up your regions. If there is some "dead space" where no region covers, nothing happens when you click on that space. If two regions overlap, the link URL for whichever of the overlapping regions appears first in the MAP definition is used.

6.11 SUMMARY

Key Terms

GIF	animated GIF	raw data	thumbnail
image size	JPEG	background image	transparent GIF
button	image link	file size	tiling

By far the most common types of images used in web pages are GIF and JPEG. The suffixes ".gif" and ".jpeg" (or ".jpg") are appended to the respective file names to help distinguish between the image types. You typically can't visually distinguish between the two image types since they differ in the types of compression used to store the digital information. However, GIFs are more versatile for icon-type images since they can be transparent or animated, and JPEG images tend to provide better clarity for photograph-type images. Whatever the type of image, a browser can display it even if it's not in a web page.

The size of an image file is the amount of computer memory required to store the file, whereas the image size refers to the dimensions of the image. The size of an image is given in pixels and is of the form WIDTH × HEIGHT. In general, an image with large dimensions requires a large file size, but resolution is also a factor that figures into the file size of an image. You can create your own images with a digital camera, scanner, or by capturing a likeness of your computer screen and trimming out the part you want. However, the easiest way is to simply copy them from other web pages. In fact, many web sites have icon libraries made expressly for this purpose. To copy an image you simply click and hold on the image with the mouse button (right button, if applicable) and select "save as". Be sure to avoid copying an image that might be copyrighted.

To put an image in a web page you use the IMG element (noncontainer) and specify the URL of the image as the value of the SRC (source) attribute. The URL of the image can be an absolute or relative URL, but you should locally store the images you use in your web pages and use relative URLs. Using the HEIGHT and WIDTH attributes of the IMG element, you can control the dimensions of the image as it appears in the web page. But even if the image does not need to be resized, you should still include the HEIGHT and WIDTH attributes. That way, the browser knows in advance how much space to allocate for the image in the web page and can thus start laying out the page before all of the images arrive.

If you wish to control the way images are aligned with text, the ALIGN, HSPACE, and VSPACE attributes can be used in the IMG element. The ALIGN attribute helps position the image on the page and can cause text to flow around an image. The HSPACE and VSPACE attributes create padding around an image to help offset text that might be flowing around the image.

To use an image as a hypertext link, you simply put it inside an anchor element whose HREF attribute points to the desired web page. Just as textual links are automatically underlined by the anchor element, an image used as a link will be given a colored border by the anchor. Since this is often not desirable, the BORDER attribute of the IMG element can be set to 0 pixels to suppress the border given by the anchor. A common use of image anchors is to create small thumbnails of an image that are active as links and that, when clicked, cause the larger original image to be displayed. Another common use is to find button icons that indicate the nature of the link and use them for image links. That way you don't need much, if any, text to support the intent of the image link.

Below is a summary of the features of the IMG element we have discussed. Note that the last two attributes listed are covered in the optional section on image maps.

<IMG>

Attribute	Possible Values	Default
SRC	absolute URL, relative URL	–
ALIGN	left, right, center, top, middle, bottom	left, bottom
HSPACE	pixels	browser-dependent
VSPACE	pixels	browser-dependent
BORDER	pixels	0
ALT	"text string"	No alternate text
ISMAP	–	–
USEMAP	"#text string"	–

The easiest way to organize image files on a web site is to just put each image in the directory as the HTML document that is to use the image. That way, only the name of image file is required by the SRC attribute. However, if you plan to use the same image file in more than one web page (maybe if you are using link buttons to provide consistency throughout the site), it makes more sense to keep all of the images in an "images" directory. But such an arrangement complicates the relative URLs required to access the images. Since the relative URLs used to access image files are governed by the same rules as the relative URLs used to link to other web pages, the tips below are very similar to those of Lesson 5. But given their importance, we repeat them in their entirety.

NOTE   If an image is not showing up in your web page when it's supposed to, it's most likely one of the following problems:

1. The relative URL does not specify the correct file path to the image file.

2. The directory names or file names used in the relative URL do not *exactly* match the actual directory or file names. By exactly, we mean capital letters, blank spaces and all. (It is best to use all small letters and no spaces in your directory and file names to help alleviate such problems.)

When you transfer images to a web server, they have to go as "raw data". Otherwise, browsers can't display them. You simply have to make sure the raw data option is selected when you transfer image files (as opposed to "text" or "ASCII" for HTML files). However, almost any ftp application has an "automatic" option that will take care of this for you, but you should nonetheless make sure that this option is reliable by testing it.

> **NOTE**
>
> If an image appears in your web page locally but fails to appear in your web page on the server, the problem is most likely one of the following:
>
> 1. You have been lax about problem 1 above and your personal computer is tolerant. For example, file names might not be case-sensitive on the personal computer. The web server, however, is not being so kind.
>
> 2. You transferred one or more images into the wrong directory on the server. This causes the relative file paths specified as the values of the SRC attributes no longer to be correct.
>
> 3. You accidentally transferred one or more of your image files as "text" or ACSII" rather than "raw data."

Two of the features that make GIF images more useful in web pages are transparent and animated GIFs. The background of a transparent GIF adapts to the background color of the ambient web page. Thus, even though the image is square or rectangular (as are all images used in web pages), the main features of the image appear to float on the web page. An animated GIF image is a series of images that act like a cartoon. The different frames of the image appear sequentially, creating the effect of motion. Even though there are several different images comprising an animated GIF, it is still one image file that is no harder to embed in a web page than a normal image.

The only type of image that is not included in a web page using the IMG element is a background image. This is not a new type of image, but usually a GIF image that presents a background pattern for a web page. Such images are (usually) not overpowering so that when they are tiled to provide a complete background for the web page, other objects (text, links, etc) in the web page stand out nicely. A background image is included by providing a relative URL pointing to the image as the value of the BACKGROUND attribute of the BODY element. The BACKGROUND attribute takes precedence over the BGCOLOR attribute and transparent GIF images will adapt to a background image.

Optional

Image maps can be used when you would like different regions of an image to function as links and point to different web pages. To embed an image for use in a web page, you use the IMG element as usual, but include the ISMAP attribute, which takes no value, and the USEMAP attribute, which takes the name of the map to be used as its value. You must use a # symbol before the map name. These two attributes are summarized above with the other attributes of the IMG element.

The map itself is used to define different regions of the image. It is defined by the MAP element, which uses a NAME attribute so that the USEMAP attribute of the IMG element can call on the map by name. Each different area of the image map must be defined by an AREA element. Each area element must take a SHAPE attribute that can specify one of three basic shapes, circle, rectangle (rect), and polygon (poly). Next, the COORDS attribute gives the actual specifications of a given region. A circular region requires the (x,y) coordinates of the center of the circle and a radius in pixels. A rectangular region requires the (x,y) coordinates of both the upper left and lower right corners of the rectangle. A polygon requires the (x,y) coordinates of each vertex of the polygon, which must be listed in order (clockwise or counterclockwise) so that the edges of the polygon don't overlap. Finally, each AREA tag must contain an HREF attribute whose value points to the web page that area is to access.

In order to find the (x,y) coordinates, you will need to use a graphic editor. In practice, this is easy since all you need to do is point the mouse to a spot in the image and the graphic editor should display the coordinates. It's no big deal if the regions you define overlap a bit. In the event that a user clicks a spot in an image map where two or more images overlap, whichever region is defined first within the MAP element is used. Such overlapping is usually preferable to having "dead space" in an image map.

6.12 REVIEW QUESTIONS

In most cases, it is not sufficient to answer these from the Lesson Summary.

1. Summarize the difference between image files and images.

2. Name two applications that can load an image for viewing, even if the image is not in a web page.

3. What is the disadvantage of using a large number of images in a web page? How can a web page be made to support a large number of images in such a way as to circumvent this problem?

4. An image is 127 × 111. Resize the image so that it is 100 pixels high but is not distorted.

5. Describe the use of the ALT attribute.

6. Discuss two strategies for organizing image files in file directories.

7. Describe transparent and animated GIFs. What special HTML tags are needed to mark them up?

8. What does automatic mean when referring to an ftp application?

9. What happens if a web page is given both a background color and background image?

10. Why not just use the HEIGHT and WIDTH attributes to create thumbnails?

6.13 EXERCISES

GENERAL

1. Go to the homework section for Lesson 6 on the web site for this book. Under Exercise 1, you will find the picture of a web page. Make a web page with approximately the same appearance. The images required for the page are available for download as well.

2. Go to the homework section for Lesson 6 on the web site for this book. Under Exercise 2, you will find the picture of a web page. Make a web page with approximately the same appearance. The images required for the page are available for download as well.

3. Go to the homework section for Lesson 6 on the web site for this book. Under Exercise 3, you will find the picture of a web page. Make a web page with approximately the same appearance. You will need to find suitable images on the Internet.

4. Go to the homework section for Lesson 6 on the web site for this book. Under Exercise 4, you will find the picture of a web page. Make a web page with approximately the same appearance. You will need to find suitable images on the Internet.

5. (optional) Go to the homework section for Lesson 6 on the web site for this book. Under Exercise 5, you will find an image to be made into an image map. Each region of the image is a different color and contains the name of a major commercial web site. Make a web page in which this image functions as an image map. Each region is to link to the corresponding web site.

6. (optional) Go to the homework section for Lesson 6 on the web site for this book. Under Exercise 6, you will find an image to be made into an image map. Each region of the image is a different color and contains the name of a major university in the USA. Make a web page in which this image functions as an image map. Each region is to link to the web site for that university.

6.14   PROJECT THREADS

THREAD A

On the web site under Lesson 6, you can find links to several online icon libraries. These will be useful in parts (b) and (c) below.

Assignment

(a)   Find two or more images to support the agenda of your home page. You may have to do some searching for these. If you have access to a scanner, you may make your own images.

(b)   Find a small icon of a computer and put it near the top of your home page. Make it active as the link to your homework page. Find a small icon of a mailbox and put it at the bottom of your home page. Make it active as a mailto link. Find a suitable "home" icon (or something similar) and put it at the top of your homework page. Make it active as the link back to your home page.

(c)   Do Exercise 6 from Lesson 5. Create a new folder named "ex5_6" inside your homework directory to hold all of the new files. Name the main page for the linear collection "index.html" (or whatever the indexing file name is on your web server). Find icons for the navigational links in the linear collection. Use arrows for the "next" and "previous" links. Of course, you should put a link to this new index file in your homework page, and supply a link in the new index file back to your homework page. (You need not put such links in the other pages of the linear collection.)

(d)   If applicable, transfer all files to the web server when completed. Check to make sure the transfer was successful. Especially, check to make sure all the links work.

THREAD B

Assignment

(a)   Do one or more of the exercises from this lesson. Create a new folder in your public directory to contain the files (images and otherwise) for each exercise. Name any new directories accordingly, "ex6_3" for example. Of course, you should provide a link from your homework page to any new page, and vice versa.

(b)   If applicable, transfer all files to the web server when completed. Check to make sure the transfer was successful. Especially, check to make sure all the links work.

LESSON 7

HTML LISTS AND TABLES

SOME HTML elements require more structure than just a couple of tags and some attributes. We have deferred discussion of these elements until this lesson. But since you have been working with various HTML elements for some time, these structures shouldn't pose many conceptual difficulties. However, these structures up the ante on both typing demands and the number of attributes and value types that must be dealt with. Having progressed through Lesson 6, you are familiar with the core basics of HTML and web site structure. Indeed, most of what you have learned is worthy of committing to memory.

With the introduction of these new HTML structures, we don't necessarily recommend that you memorize each and every one of the attributes. While it is important to know the basic tags and to have a working knowledge of the various attributes, committing all of these to memory involves what we term extraneous thought. At some point, memorization of details can tend to obscure the underlying concepts. But armed with a working knowledge of the concepts and a reference list, one can accomplish greater feats than armed with mere facts.

7.1 HTML EDITORS

With this in mind, we recommend that you employ an HTML editor at this point. An HTML editor takes a good bit of the typing out of the picture. Moreover, a good HTML editor can even help you to avoid many of the pitfalls (like typos) associated with writing HTML code. Numerous freeware and shareware editors are referenced in the Lesson 7 section of the web page for this book. While these are very useful, the really powerful editors cost an appreciable amount of money. Perhaps among the most popular commercial HTML editors (at the time of printing) are Adobe Pagemill, Macromedia DreamWeaver, and Claris Homepage. These editors can be purchased in the range of $50–$125.

NOTE The best way to choose an HTML editor is as follows.

1. If your educational institution supports a good commercial editor, use theirs.
2. If that is not the case and you don't plan to buy commercial-grade editor, use the references in the web site for this book to download a freeware or shareware editor.

> **3.** Fork over the money and buy a good commercial editor. In this case, it is certainly a good idea to ask around and see which editor people like best on the computer platform you use.

It is not imperative that you adopt an editor at this point. Aside from the construction of elaborate HTML tables, you can accomplish all of the exercises in the rest of this book with a standard text editor. However, to become a skilled web-page author, it is almost unthinkable not to learn to use an HTML editor. The bad news is that there will be some startup time involved. But, armed with an understanding of the fundamental HTML concepts, the startup time should not be that substantial. It's kind of like learning to use a new word processor. You know the word-processing fundamentals, you just have to learn where the right buttons are. The good news is that, in the long run, an HTML editor will save you an untold amount of typing, and will allow you to exploit advanced HTML features that would otherwise involve remembering myriad tags and attributes.

With the above discussion in mind, we move on to the HTML topics for this lesson. Given all of the different editors available, it would be futile to attempt to explain how to use one here. It shouldn't take more that a couple of hours of experimentation to learn how to exploit the basic features of an HTML editor. Mastery of the more advanced features will come gradually over time as you progress further through this book.

7.2 UNORDERED LISTS

There are a couple of structured HTML elements that can help to organize information in a web page. They create ordered lists and unordered lists of information. We first discuss unordered lists.

The basic definition of an **unordered list** is

```
<UL>
   <LI>list item</LI>
   <LI>list item</LI>
   ⋮
   <LI>list item</LI>
</UL>
```

The UL (*U*nordered *L*ist) start and end tags define the list itself and the LI (*L*ist *I*tem) start and end tags define the individual items comprising the list. List items can consist of text, links, images, and almost anything else that HTML can mark up. List items can even contain other lists.

The browser shot in Figure 7.1 shows a basic unordered list followed by a more complicated list. The list items of the second list are themselves unordered lists. We refer to lists whose items are themselves lists as nested lists. Figure 7.2 shows the HTML code necessary to produce the lists of Figure 7.1.

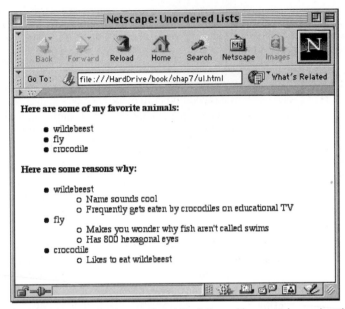

FIGURE 7.1 A simple unordered list followed by nested unordered lists.

```
<B>Here are some of my favorite animals:</B>
<UL>
    <LI>wildebeest</LI>
    <LI>fly</LI>
    <LI>crocodile</LI>
</UL>
<B>Here are some reasons why:</B>
<UL>

    <LI>wildebeest
    <UL>
        <LI>Name sounds cool</LI>
        <LI>Frequently gets eaten by crocodiles on educational TV</LI>
    </UL>
    </LI>

    <LI>fly
    <UL>
        <LI>Makes you wonder why fish aren't called swims</LI>
        <LI>Has 800 hexagonal eyes</LI>
    </UL>
    </LI>

    <LI>crocodile
    <UL>
        <LI>Likes to eat wildebeest</LI>
    </UL>
    </LI>

</UL>
```

FIGURE 7.2 HTML code that produces the two unordered lists of Figure 7.1. The second list demonstrates nested lists.

NOTE You can see that Figure 7.2 contains a substantial amount of structured HTML code. The code was generated with an HTML editor. That's why the HTML tags are rendered in bold and the list item tags are indented. So not only did we not have to type in all of the tags, the editor formatted the code so that it is easy (perhaps easier) to comprehend. You can imagine just from the relatively short lists pictured in Figure 7.1, and the substantial amount of code required to generate the lists, that a web page with several lists could easily require an HTML document with several pages of HTML code. Of course, not every editor will format the HTML code exactly as in Figure 7.2, but it should offer substantial improvement over a plain text editor.

The browser automatically includes the symbol that sets each list item apart. The typical default is the solid disk as you see in the outer lists in Figure 7.1. But, as can be seen in the nested lists (or inner lists), there are other symbols available. The browser has defaulted the items in the second layer of the unordered list to a circle. It is typical for browsers to default to different symbols for each new layer of a nested unordered list. Of course, these defaults will vary among browsers. But the number of these symbols is limited. In fact, there are only three types: disk, circle, and square. The first two you see in Figure 7.1 and the square is simply a small hollow square.

If you wish, you can override the defaults in unordered lists by using the TYPE attribute. The TYPE attribute can take as its value any of the three available symbols. For example,

```
<UL TYPE="square">
    <LI>...</LI>
        :
    <LI>...</LI>
</UL>
```

creates an unordered list whose items are set apart by small squares.

NOTE One common use of unordered lists is to organize a list of hypertext links. Simply put the required anchor elements within the list item tags, and you have a nice structured list of links.

7.3 ORDERED LISTS

Ordered lists are very similar to unordered lists except that the list items are ordered with numbers, letters, or Roman numerals, rather than symbols. The ordered list has the same structure except that it is defined with the OL (*Ordered List*) element. Like the unordered list, the ordered list also uses LI tags to define its items:

```
<OL>
    <LI>list item</LI>
    <LI>list item</LI>
        :
    <LI>list item</LI>
</OL>
```

```
<H2>Internet programming for fun and profit.</H2>
<OL>

   <LI>Introduction.
   <OL TYPE="i">
      <LI>The Internet.</LI>

      <LI>The World Wide Web.</LI>
   </OL>
   </LI>

   <LI>Basic HTML.
   <OL TYPE="I">
      <LI>The HTML document.</LI>

      <LI>HTML tags.</LI>
   </OL>
   </LI>

</OL>
```

FIGURE 7.3 Some HTML code with nested ordered lists. The ordering scheme has been set by the TYPE attribute in the inner lists.

The OL element also uses the TYPE attribute. With the OL element, TYPE takes the values "1", "A", "a", "I", and "i". Figure 7.3 contains some HTML code that makes use of three of the six possible TYPE values. The resulting lists are rendered in Figure 7.4.

The outer list has no TYPE attribute so the browser has used the default setting. The default corresponds to TYPE="1" and results in ordering the list items with regular numbers (integers). The first inner list sets TYPE="i" and orders its items with lower-case Roman numerals. Similarly, TYPE="I" in the second inner list has caused upper-case Roman numerals to be used. The values we have not used, "A" and "a", result in orderings using upper- and lower-case letters, respectively.

If for some reason, the items of a list need to start at something other than 1, there is a START attribute that takes integers as values and specifies where the items of a given OL start. For example,

<OL START=7> . . . </OL>

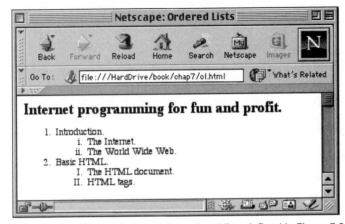

FIGURE 7.4 The rendering of the ordered lists defined in Figure 7.3.

orders the list with the sequence (7, 8, 9, . . .) and

<OL TYPE="a" START=7> . . . </OL>

orders the list with the sequence (g, h, i, . . .).

7.4 HTML TABLES

Another useful markup tool is the HTML table. As one might expect, an HTML table is defined with the TABLE element. Tables are built row by row. Within the TABLE element, TR (*T*able *R*ow) tags define each row.

The basic structure is

```
<TABLE>
  <TR>...</TR>
  <TR>...</TR>
    ⋮
  <TR>...</TR>
</TABLE>
```

The contents of each TR element define each individual row of the table. However, contents of table rows must be distinguished with TD (*T*able *D*ata) tags. For a very simple example, Figure 7.5 shows the code for an HTML table with four rows. The contents of each row is simply the text string "item". The resulting rendering of the table is also shown.

We have included the BORDER attribute in the TABLE start tag so that the table has a distinguishable border, as can be seen in Figure 7.5. Setting BORDER=2 gives the entire table a border two pixels thick. Just like the HR element, the pixels of the border are shaded to produce a three-dimensional effect. The default setting in most browsers is BORDER=0 which, of course, leaves no distinguishable border around the table and between the table data items. When using a table to present typical tabular text data, it is usually desirable to

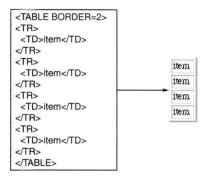

FIGURE 7.5 The definition of a table with four rows and its markup.

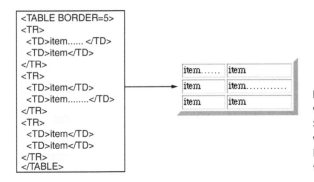

FIGURE 7.6 The code for a table with three rows and two columns. Since there are two TD elements within each TR element, the browser has created two columns for the table.

include the BORDER attribute; otherwise, the rendering of the table in Figure 7.5 would simply look like

item

item

item

item

There are uses for borderless tables, but we will discuss that later.

Of course, tables usually have both rows and columns. Surprisingly, there is no column tag to create columns to complement the rows in a table. The creation of columns is accomplished with the TD (*Table Data*) tag. Inserting more than one TD element within a table row creates an extra column for the extra TD element. Figure 7.6 shows the definition of a table with both columns and rows. This table exhibits a five-pixel border that gives the table a slightly more three-dimensional effect.

> **N O T E** Note that the columns of the table in Figure 7.6 have been automatically formatted by the browser to accommodate the largest item present in each column. Given a table definition, most browsers format the table as optimally as possible. That is, the table is made just large enough to accommodate all of its contents.

7.5 CONTROLLING TABLE PROPERTIES

Such use of TR and TD tags can be used to create tables with any number of rows and columns. There are, however, some attributes that can be used to fine-tune table building. First, there are two attributes that help to control space in a table. The CELLPADDING attribute creates space around the contents of the table's cells. The CELLSPACING attribute creates space between the actual cells of the table. Figure 7.7 illustrates their use.

The BGCOLOR attribute may also be used in table definition to help the table stand out from the rest of the page. The BGCOLOR attribute causes only the cell interiors to be colored. In the cases of the CELLPADDING and CELLSPACING attributes of Figure 7.7, the BGCOLOR attribute serves to emphasize what the spacing attributes actually

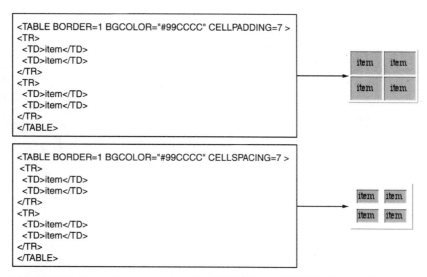

```
<TABLE BORDER=1 BGCOLOR="#99CCCC" CELLPADDING=7 >
<TR>
 <TD>item</TD>
 <TD>item</TD>
</TR>
<TR>
 <TD>item</TD>
 <TD>item</TD>
</TR>
</TABLE>
```

```
<TABLE BORDER=1 BGCOLOR="#99CCCC" CELLSPACING=7 >
<TR>
 <TD>item</TD>
 <TD>item</TD>
</TR>
<TR>
 <TD>item</TD>
 <TD>item</TD>
</TR>
</TABLE>
```

FIGURE 7.7 Two tables using the CELLPADDING and CELLSPACING attributes, respectively. The BGCOLOR attribute has also been included to emphasize the spacing. In the first table, the CELLPADDING is applied around the text of the cells. In the second table, the CELLSPACING is applied between the actual table cells.

accomplish. Typical default settings that are used in the absence of the spacing attributes are CELLPADDING=1 and CELLSPACING=2.

As we have mentioned, browsers typically create tables of the minimum size to accommodate contents of the table cells. Indeed, the tables created in Figures 7.5, 7.6, and 7.7 are as small as possible to contain the contents of the cells. There are, however, WIDTH and HEIGHT attributes that can be used to specify the exact dimensions of a table. The WIDTH and HEIGHT attributes can take both percentages and pixels as values. For an example of their use, see Figure 7.8.

The assignment WIDTH="100%" causes the table to be made to cover 100% of the width of the browser window. The pixel assignment HEIGHT=75 causes the table to be made exactly 75 pixels high. If the browser window in Figure 7.8 were resized to fill up the whole computer monitor, the table would still cover the width of the browser window, but would still be drawn exactly 75 pixels high. With the dimensions of the table specified, the cells are constructed to all be of the same size and to fill the table. Although in Figure 7.8 the WIDTH is given as a percentage and the HEIGHT in pixels, percentages and pixel values can be used interchangeably as values of either of the two attributes, depending upon the need.

A final attribute of the TABLE element we mention here is the ALIGN attribute. This attribute takes the values left, right, and center. This attribute works exactly like the ALIGN attribute of the IMG element. For example, setting ALIGN=right will cause the whole table to be right-aligned on the page with text flowing around the table. So, if you have a small table, the ALIGN attribute can certainly make your presentation smoother by allowing text to flow around the table. However, if your table is large, you would probably not use this attribute. The default is left-aligned with text above and below the table, not flowing around the table.

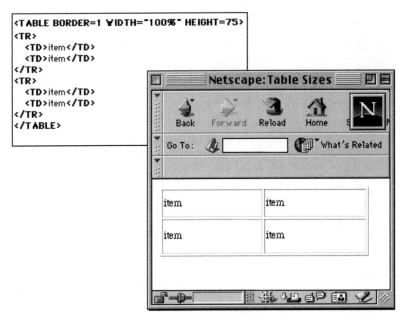

```
<TABLE BORDER=1 WIDTH="100%" HEIGHT=75>
<TR>
  <TD>item</TD>
  <TD>item</TD>
</TR>
<TR>
  <TD>item</TD>
  <TD>item</TD>
</TR>
</TABLE>
```

FIGURE 7.8 A table that uses the WIDTH and HEIGHT attributes to create a table of a certain size.

7.6 CONTROLLING ROW PROPERTIES

There are three attributes of the TR element that are useful when it is desired to control markup within a whole table row. Rather than supplying an example, we defer that to the next section where we examine how to control properties of individual cells. Properties of individual calls are controlled with attributes of the TD element. Controlling the properties of individual cells at the TD level provides more flexibility than controlling row properties at the TR level. In fact, even more attributes are available for the TD element than for the TR element. Many HTML editors don't even like to control cell properties at the TR level. In other words, if you put some attributes into a TR element, your HTML editor might just up and move them into the TD tags to spite you.

7.7 CONTROLLING PROPERTIES OF INDIVIDUAL CELLS

For starters, there is an alternative HTML element that can be used to create heading-type table cells. This is the TH (*T*able *H*eading) element. When used in place of the TD element, TH creates table cells in which the text is rendered in boldface. For example, TH is desirable for defining the cells in the top row of a table that is to have column headings. Figure 7.9 serves to demonstrate the point without undue discussion.

However, the fact that we slipped some ALIGN attributes into the TD tags is worthy of discussion. It's clear from Figure 7.9 that the ALIGN attribute serves to center the contents of the cell horizontally. As evidenced in Figure 7.8, the default is ALIGN=left. In general, ALIGN sets the horizontal alignment within a table cell and takes the values left, right, and center. The TD element also takes VALIGN and BGCOLOR attributes. VALIGN sets

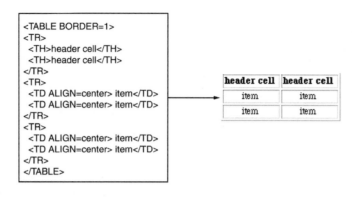

```
<TABLE BORDER=1>
<TR>
 <TH>header cell</TH>
 <TH>header cell</TH>
</TR>
<TR>
 <TD ALIGN=center> item</TD>
 <TD ALIGN=center> item</TD>
</TR>
<TR>
 <TD ALIGN=center> item</TD>
 <TD ALIGN=center> item</TD>
</TR>
</TABLE>
```

FIGURE 7.9 A table in which the cells of the top row are defined with TH rather than TD tags so that the top cell of each column acts as a heading for that column.

the vertical alignment within each cell and takes the values bottom, middle, and top. The BGCOLOR attribute takes a hexadecimal or named color and sets a background color for a table cell.

The TD element takes the BACKGROUND attribute. Its value is a URL pointing to a background image. That background image is tiled as the background of the table cell in which the BACKGROUND attribute appears. The TD element also takes HEIGHT and WIDTH attributes so that you can control the sizes of individual table cells. As usual, the HEIGHT and WIDTH attributes take percentages and pixels as values. Figure 7.10 demonstrates the use of several of the attributes discussed above.

There are yet two more attributes of the TD element, namely ROWSPAN and COLSPAN. Since the role of these two attributes is quite significant, we provide a detailed

```
<TABLE BORDER=1 WIDTH="100%" >
<TR>
    <TH VALIGN=bottom BGCOLOR="#99CCCC" HEIGHT=30>
    header
    </TH>
    <TH VALIGN=bottom BGCOLOR="#99CCCC" HEIGHT=30>
    header
    </TH>
</TR>
<TR>
    <TD ALIGN=center BACKGROUND="bg.gif" HEIGHT=100>
    item
    </TD>
    <TD ALIGN=center BACKGROUND="bg.gif" HEIGHT=100>
    item
    </TD>
</TR>
</TABLE>
```

header	header
item	item

FIGURE 7.10 A table in which the cells use various attributes of the TD element. In particular, the heights of the cells are controlled precisely. Also, the cells in the second row use a background image rather than a BGCOLOR.

explanation later in this lesson. We mention them here to emphasize the fact that memorization of all of these attributes could prove to be futile. Rather, they are all succinctly organized for reference in the summary for this lesson, and again in Appendix A. Your best bet is to let your editor do much of the work for you and use all of these attributes in a reference capacity.

NOTE There are two points worthy of note regarding attributes of the TD element.

1. All of the attributes of TD can also be used with TH. In fact, in general, TH and TD are very similar. TH just renders cell text in bold. In Figure 7.10, we have used attributes in the TH tags as well.

2. The ALIGN, VALIGN, and BGCOLOR attributes can also be used in the TR element. That is, you can control these three properties for a whole table row in one fell swoop. However, this approach offers no real advantages over control at the individual cell level. In fact, many HTML editors automatically format at the cell level rather than the row level, even if the properties apply to the whole row. In Figure 7.10, for example, the VALIGN and ALIGN attributes could have been put in the respective TR tags since the alignment settings apply to the whole row. However, for simplicity in the remainder of this lesson, we format exclusively at the cell level rather than the row level. Besides, there is added flexibility at the cell level since TD supports more attributes than TR.

7.8 HTML TABLES AS PAGE ORGANIZERS

The examples of tables we have seen are useful when information needs to be presented in a structured tabular form, like a multiplication table for example. But, perhaps the most useful utility of HTML tables is their use to format entire web pages. The first key is that table cells can contain not only text, but most other HTML elements themselves. Figure 7.11 shows a table whose cells contain many of the major HTML features we have discussed in this book.

The upper left cell contains two ordinary hypertext links, the upper right cell contains an image, the lower left cell contains an unordered list, and the lower right cell contains its own background image. In each case, the HTML elements needed to define the different cell contents are simply placed between the proper table data (TD) tags. Well, the exception is the background image, which is inserted with the BACKGROUND attribute of the TD element in the start tag. Such versatility of tables goes a long way toward organizing a web page but it still doesn't look very neat. Imagine if newspapers had lines drawn between the different sections as in Figure 7.11; it's not aesthetically pleasing.

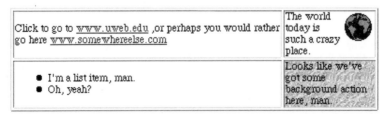

FIGURE 7.11 A table whose cells contain various HTML elements.

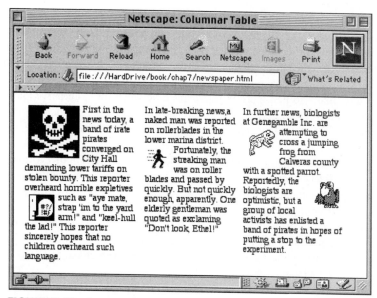

FIGURE 7.12 A page using a borderless table with one row and three columns to create a newspaper-like presentation.

```
<HTML>
<HEAD>
   <TITLE>Columnar Table</TITLE></HEAD>
<BODY>
<P><TABLE BORDER=0 CELLSPACING=5 WIDTH="100%" HEIGHT="100%">
   <TR>
      <TD VALIGN=top>
         <IMG SRC="jollyroger.gif" WIDTH=66 HEIGHT=66 ALIGN=left>
         First in the news today.........expletives
         <IMG SRC="curse.gif" WIDTH=36 HEIGHT=35 ALIGN=left>
         such as "aye mate,....... overheard such language.
      </TD>
      <TD VALIGN=top>
         In late breaking news,...... in the lower marina district.
         <IMG SRC="streak.gif" WIDTH=30 HEIGHT=30 ALIGN=left>
         Fortunately, ...... "Don't look, Ethel!"
      </TD>
      <TD VALIGN=top>
         In further news, biologists at Genegamble Inc.
         <IMG SRC="frog.gif" WIDTH=40 HEIGHT=38 ALIGN=left>
         <IMG SRC="parrot.gif" WIDTH=36 HEIGHT=40 ALIGN=right>
         are attempting to cross ...... a stop to the experiment.
      </TD>
   </TR>
</TABLE>
</BODY>
</HTML>
```

FIGURE 7.13 The document that creates the page in Figure 7.12. Much of the text has been deleted, but all the HTML is present. Note that all of the content of the web page is defined within the table calls.

So the second key is to simply use borderless tables to organize a page. In this way, the page can be split up into sections with no apparent borders. For one practical example, in Figure 7.12 we use such a technique to create a newspaper-like web page with three columns of text. In Figure 7.13 we display a version of the document that created

Figure 7.12, but with much of the text deleted. Using a table to format a web page completely makes the document somewhat complicated. In order to format the page in this manner, all the contents of the page are contained within the TD tags. In the case of Figure 7.13, the entire contents of each column are placed within the TD tag that defines that column. Moreover, the CELLSPACING attribute in the TABLE start tag has been set to five pixels so that there is some space between the columns. Otherwise, the columns would be right up against each other. Since there is only one row in the table, there is only one set of TR tags, and this one TR element contains all of the TD tags defining the columns.

Such columnar page presentations certainly do add another formatting option to page design. A very common practice along these lines is to have a colored column on the left of the page that contains many of the page's hypertext links for quick reference. The WWW is replete with pages using this type of presentation. In fact, it has become one of the more standard formatting techniques. Figure 7.14 shows a fictitious web page using such a presentation. It consists of two columns, a colored one on the left for some links and a larger column on the right containing the bulk of the web page. The HTML document that generates the page is shown in Figure 7.15.

In the main table, the one that creates the page layout, the left column (first TD element) has been set to 100 pixels. That way the left column will always be rendered as a narrow strip, but wide enough to accommodate the links. Since the HEIGHT and WIDTH have been set to 100% in the TABLE tag, the page layout will cover the whole page. In particular, since WIDTH=100%, the right column is expanded to fill the remaining space, the space that the 100-pixel column leaves unfilled. You can see from Figure 7.15 that the HTML code is pretty complicated-looking, especially with all of the attributes

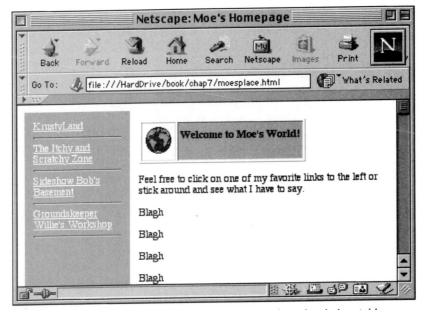

FIGURE 7.14 A very common type of page layout using a borderless table.

```
<HTML>
<HEAD><TITLE>Moe's Homepage</TITLE></HEAD>
<BODY LINK="#FFFFFF" VLINK="#FFFF99">
<TABLE BORDER=0 CELLSPACING=0 CELLPADDING=10 WIDTH="100%" HEIGHT="100%">
    <TR>
        <TD VALIGN=top WIDTH=100 BGCOLOR="#99CCCC">
            <A HREF="http://krusty.com">KrustyLand</A>
            <HR>
            <A HREF="http://itchscratch.com">The Itchy and Scratchy Zone</A>
            <HR>
            <A HREF="http://bob.com">Sideshow Bob's Basement</A>
            <HR>
            <A HREF="http://willie.com">Groundskeeper Willie's Workshop</A>
            <HR>
        </TD>
        <TD VALIGN=top BGCOLOR="#FFFFFF">
            <TABLE BORDER=1 BGCOLOR="#99CCCC" CELLPADDING=2 HEIGHT=33>
                <TR>
                    <TD WIDTH=33 BGCOLOR="#FFFFFF">
                        <IMG SRC="world.gif" WIDTH=33 HEIGHT=33>
                    </TD>
                    <TD>
                        <H4>Welcome to Moe's World!</H4>
                    </TD>
                </TR>
            </TABLE>

            <P>Feel free to click on one of my favorite links to the
            left or stick around and see what I have to say.
            <P>Blagh<P>Blagh<P>Blagh<P>Blagh<P>Blagh<P>Blagh
        </TD>
    </TR>
</TABLE>
</BODY>
</HTML>
```

FIGURE 7.15 The document that produces the page in Figure 7.14.

for both TABLE properties and cell (TD) properties floating around. Adding further to the mess is the fact that yet another table is defined within the main part of the page. We certainly would not have wanted to create that document without an HTML editor.

NOTE Page layouts in which various regions are colored to offset them from the rest have become extremely popular on the Web. In particular, having a colored strip on the left, or perhaps across the top in which some links are organized has come to be standard. Such colored regions are often termed **navigation bars**. If you start surfing some commercial web sites, it shouldn't take long at all to find various navigation bars. You will quickly encounter web pages where there are all sorts of different regions, colored or otherwise, set up with borderless tables. In fact, you would be surprised to see how elaborate many of the borderless table structures that create page layout actually are.

7.9 SPANNING ROWS AND COLUMNS

The COLSPAN and ROWSPAN attributes of the TD element enable very elaborate borderless-table web page layout designs. We provide such an example in the next section. In the meantime, we return to standard tables to illustrate the COLSPAN and ROWSPAN

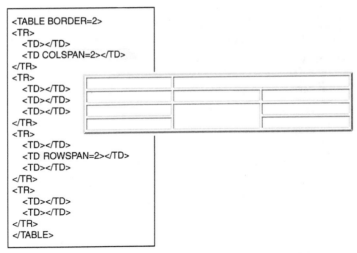

```
<TABLE BORDER=2>
<TR>
  <TD></TD>
  <TD COLSPAN=2></TD>
</TR>
<TR>
  <TD></TD>
  <TD></TD>
  <TD></TD>
</TR>
<TR>
  <TD></TD>
  <TD ROWSPAN=2></TD>
  <TD></TD>
</TR>
<TR>
  <TD></TD>
  <TD></TD>
</TR>
</TABLE>
```

FIGURE 7.16 A table that makes use of the COLSPAN and ROWSPAN attributes.

attributes. Figure 7.16 shows a table with four rows and three columns in which these two attributes have been employed. In the first row, the second column (second TD element in that row) has been endowed with COLSPAN=2. You can see that this has caused that table cell to span two columns. In the third row, the second column (second TD element in that row) has been endowed with ROWSPAN=2. You can see that this has caused a similar effect, except in terms of rows.

In conceptual terms, this should be self-explanatory. The COLSPAN and ROWSPAN attributes take positive integers $(1, 2, 3, \ldots)$ as values and cause a given table cell to span that many columns or rows. Of course, the defaults are COLSPAN=0 and ROWSPAN=0. But there is one subtlety worthy of elaboration. The spanning effect is applied to the right and down. In other words, COLSPAN causes a table cell to span columns to its right and ROWSPAN causes a table cell to span rows below that cell. Figure 7.17 shows how the spanning effect was applied in the table of Figure 7.16.

As a consequence of the spanning action, there are fewer cells left in the table. In Figure 7.16, the first row is left with only two cells (two TD elements) and the fourth row is left with only two cells (two TD elements). In practice, an HTML editor will help you to keep track of such things.

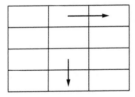

FIGURE 7.17 How the browser created the table in Figure 7.16. The spanning action of a table cell is always applied to the right and down.

7.10 ADVANCED PAGE LAYOUT

The COLSPAN and ROWSPAN attributes can be used to create all kinds of web page layouts. Figure 7.18 shows a web page that makes good use of these attributes. Among the main features of the page are the two navigational bars, one on each side. The first contains links to other sports pages on the site, and the other contains links to information about each of this week's games. In between the two navigational bars are two more table cells. The

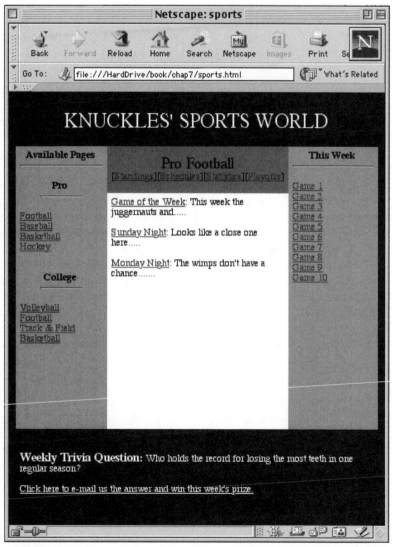

FIGURE 7.18 A web page with left and right navigational bars and with other information organized by table cells.

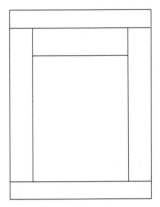

FIGURE 7.19 The tabular layout of the web page shown in Figure 7.18.

top contains this particular page's topic and some informational links. Just below that is a table cell containing the main topics of discussion. Finally, both above and below all this structure there are two additional table cells with white text on a dark background, one for the page's title and the other for the weekly trivia question. Figure 7.19 depicts the page layout.

Rather than displaying the HTML code for the sports page, we examine the steps necessary to create such a page. Besides, the HTML document that creates the page contains about two and a half pages of code. The first observation is that the table outline in Figure 7.19 contains four distinct rows and three distinct columns. So it is necessary to start with a complete table with four rows and three columns. The basic procedure necessary to create the desired tabular structure is outlined in Figure 7.20.

Once the tabular structure is in place, all that is left to do is set the background colors and place the other stuff in the table cells. By saying "all that is left to do," we don't mean that it's trivial. But with the help of an HTML editor, the whole process is not too bad.

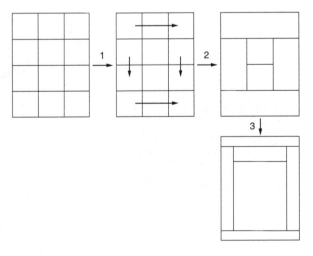

FIGURE 7.20 Creating the tabular layout for the sports page of Figure 7.18. (1) Figure out the necessary spanning action. (2) Set the spans and see if the desired effect is obtained. (3) Use the HEIGHT and WIDTH attributes of the TD elements to obtain the desired cell sizes. (This usually involves some trial and error.)

NOTE	The first task in making an elaborate tabular layout is designing the layout. It is one thing to understand the HTML basics and put an HTML editor to work for you. But conceiving of web page designs takes imagination. Perhaps the best method is to surf around and notice the layout structure of some commercial pages. That way you can get some ideas about what you like. Once you have an idea for the structure of a page, it helps to make some sketches similar to Figure 7.19 to refine your ideas. After that, just figure the necessary spanning actions and set about coding the web page.

7.10 SUMMARY

Key Terms

HTML editor	header cell	navigation bar	table cell
nested lists	unordered list	list item	span
table row	table data	table	

Armed with the larger HTML structures presented in this lesson, it will behoove you to learn to use an HTML editor. There will be some startup time, but in the long run it will save you lots of time and effort. Most any HTML editor will generate HTML tags for you at the click of a button.

HTML lists come in two types, ordered and unordered. The ordered lists are defined with the OL element and unordered lists are defined with the UL element. Items within each type of list are defined with the list item element LI. Furthermore, both lists take the TYPE attribute, which changes symbols used for the list items. The two list types are summarized below.

<UL>... </UL>

Attribute	Possible Values	Default
TYPE	circle, disc, square	disc

<OL>... </OL>

Attribute	Possible Values	Default
TYPE	1 (integers), i, I (lower- and upper-case Roman numerals), a, A (lower- and upper-case letters)	(integers)
START	integer	1

<LI>... </LI>

Used to create list items with the <UL>...</UL> and <OL>...</0L> elements.

HTML tables can be used to organize information within a web page. An HTML table is defined with the TABLE element. Rows in table are created with the TR (table row) element. The TH (table header) element can be used in place of the TD element and also creates a table row, but one in which any text is rendered in boldface. Actual cells in a table are created with the TD (table data) element. Each TD element defines a table cell within a row, and hence a column of the table. The attributes that can be used in the TABLE element to control properties of the entire table are summarized below.

<TABLE>... </TABLE>

Attribute	Possible Values	Default
ALIGN	left, center, right	left (text not flowing around table)
BGCOLOR	hexadecimal color, named color	inherits background (color or image) from web page
BORDER	pixels	0
CELLPADDING	pixels	1
CELLSPACING	pixels	2
HEIGHT	pixels, percent	minimum to accommodate content
WIDTH	pixels, percent	minimum to accommodate content

There are three attributes that can be used to control table properties on the TR level. However, controlling table properties on the TD level provides more flexibility, and is recommended.

<TR>... </TR>

Attribute	Possible Values	Default
ALIGN	left, center, right	left
VALIGN	top, middle, bottom	middle
BGCOLOR	hexadecimal color, named color	inherits background (color or image) from web page

<TD>... </TD>and <TH>... </TH>

Attribute	Possible Values	Default
ALIGN	left, center, right	left
VALIGN	top, middle, bottom	middle
BACKGROUND	URL of image	—
BGCOLOR	hexadecimal color, named color	inherits background (color or image) from web page
HEIGHT	pixels, percent	conforms to cell contents
WIDTH	pixels, percent	conforms to cell contents
COLSPAN	integer	0
ROWSPAN	integer	0

While HTML tables are useful for organizing information within a web page, they can produce remarkable results when used without a border to lay out a whole web page. Any HTML element we have discussed can be contained within a table cell. Thus, you can use a table set to WIDTH=100% and HEIGHT=100% to create a layout for the web page. In this case, the entire contents of the page are contained within the table cells.

One common page layout involves a colored column on the left side or a colored row across the top that contains links for the page. Such a colored strip, replete with links, is often called a navigational bar. With the use of the COLSPAN and ROWSPAN attributes, quite elaborate page layouts can be created. However, in practice this can be a bit tricky. We recommend the following procedure.

NOTE

To create a tabular page layout:

1. Conceive of a page design and draw a sketch of the tabular structure.
2. Count the total number of distinct columns and distinct rows.
3. Start with a standard table with that many rows and columns. Figure out the spanning action needed to create the desired layout. Remember, COLSPAN spans to the right and ROWSPAN spans downward.
4. Create the table and make sure that the spanning actions have done what they are supposed to do.
5. Resize the table cells to fine-tune the layout. This usually involves trial and error.
6. Start putting stuff into the table cells.
7. Repeat 1–6 as necessary for fun on a rainy day.

Important note: It is sometimes desirable to use an empty colored table cell to provide a colored stripe across the page, for example. But you have to be careful. Some browsers will not render empty table cells. If you wish to use an empty cell, an easy way to make sure that it gets rendered is to put a character (an "x", for example) in the cell that is the same color as the background for the cell. That way, the colored cell still appears empty, but the cell is sure to be rendered by any browser.

7.11 REVIEW QUESTIONS

In most cases, it is not sufficient to answer these from the Lesson Summary.

1. Discuss the difference between a UL and OL. How can you make a OL start numbering from something other than 1?

2. What is the difference between CELLPADDING and CELLSPACING?

3. What are the default alignments (horizontal and vertical) for the contents of a table cell?

4. When using a table for an entire page layout, why don't you want to use pixel values for the HEIGHT and WIDTH attributes of the TABLE element?

5. Suppose you are specifying the HEIGHT and WIDTH attributes at the cell level. What happens if you make one cell of a row higher than the rest of the cells of that row?

6. When you specify a COLSPAN or ROWSPAN, how is it determined which rows or columns get spanned?

7. How is the ALIGN attribute different when used in the TABLE element from when it is used in the TD element?

7.12 EXERCISES

1. Get access to an HTML editor.
2. (These images can be used in Exercise 8.9.2. as well.) Acquire eight images suitable for background images in a web page. Make two 3 × 3 tables that display these images. The middle cell of the each table should contain a link(s) to the site(s) where you found the images. In the first table,

put the images in the table cells as regular images:

<TD><IMG SRC="img1.gif"></TD>.

In the second table, put the images as background images of the table cells:

<TD BACKGROUND="img1.gif"></TD>.

See the diagram below.

img	img	img
img	—	img
img	img	img

3. Make a web page approximately like the one pictured in Figure 7.18. For a better picture of the page, see Exercise 3 in the Lesson 7 section of the web site.

4. Go to the homework section for Lesson 7 on the web site for this book. Under Exercise 4, you will find the picture of a web page. Make a web page with approximately the same appearance. The required images are available for download as well. The borderless table structure is given below.

5. Go to the homework section for Lesson 7 on the web site for this book. Under Exercise 5, you will find the picture of a web page. Make a web page with approximately the same appearance. The required images are available for download as well. The borderless table structure is given below.

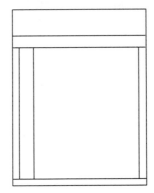

6. Go to the homework section for Lesson 7 on the web site for this book. Under Exercise 6, you will find the picture of a web page. Make a web page with approximately the same appearance. The required images are available for download as well. The borderless table structure is given below.

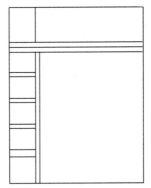

7.13 PROJECT THREADS

THREAD A

(a) This assignment creates the final version of your home page.

Assignment

(a) Rename your home page "version3.html" and keep it handy. You don't have to put a link to it in your homework page, but you should save it for a while.

(b) Create a new file named "index.html" (or whatever the indexing file name is on your web server) to be your final home page version. Spend some time and construct a borderless table layout that will nicely organize the content of your home page. A big timesaver is to copy parts of your version-3 page and paste them into your table cells. Since you may wish to use some empty colored table cells to help with the organization of the page, see again the important note at the end of Section 7.10. You may also need to employ this trick if you wish to preview your tabular structure before you have added the final content to cells.

(c) Use a list to organize the links in your homework page. When appropriate, use nested lists, for example if you have more than one link for a given lesson.

(d) If applicable, transfer all files to the web server when completed. Check to make sure the transfer was successful. Especially, check to make sure all of the links work.

THREAD B

Assignment

(a) Do one or more of the exercises from this lesson. Create a new folder in your public directory to contain the files (images and otherwise) for each exercise. Name any new directories accordingly, "ex7_3" for example. Of course, you should provide a link from your homework page to any new page, and vice versa.

(b) Use a list to organize the links in your homework page. When appropriate, use nested lists, for example if you have more than one link for a given lesson.

(c) If applicable, transfer all files to the web server when completed. Check to make sure the transfer was successful. Especially, check to make sure all of the links work.

HTML FRAMES

HTML TABLES provide a great deal of flexibility when designing the layout for a web page. However, there is a certain degree of functionality that is sometimes desired and that tables don't provide. It is often desirable to have a navigation bar that "stays put." For example, consider Figure 5.11, which shows a simulated online book. There are links at the top that reference each chapter of the book. The linking in that document is done with named anchors so that, when the link for Chapter 3 is clicked, Chapter 3 is brought to the top of the browser window. The disadvantage to this is that once Chapter 3 is moved to the top of the browser window, the navigational links are no longer visible since they are at the very top of the web page. One solution is to repeat the list of navigational links at the beginning of each chapter, but a drawback to this is having to use repetitive code. Another drawback is that if you read enough of Chapter 3 that you make use of the scroll bar, the navigational links are once again not on the screen anymore.

HTML frames provide the potential to leave the list of navigational links at the top of the screen, even though various other parts of the book are visible. In fact, as we shall see, the navigational links will be present regardless of what part of the book is visible, so there will be a "fixed" navigational bar at the top of the browser window. Such is the flexibility of frames. Frames were first supported by Netscape Navigator version 2, and are fully supported by both Navigator and Explorer versions 3 and later.

8.1 FRAMED WEB PAGES

Before showing the actual HTML code necessary to create framed web pages, we discuss the nature of such documents. Framed web pages actually display more than one web page at a time. It's rather like one of those picture frames with several openings. You can display several pictures in the same frame. Figure 8.1 demonstrates this concept in the context of framed web pages. For simplicity, the framed document has only two frames.

Going back to the picture-frame analogy, one HTML document is required to generate the picture frame. Then, to fill each of the "holes" in the picture frame, additional HTML documents are required, one for each "hole." As Figure 8.1 depicts, three distinct HTML documents are required to create a FRAMESET page with two frames. The result would be an

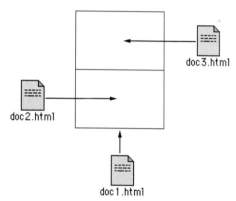

FIGURE 8.1 One document creates the FRAMESET (or picture frame, if you will). For each frame in the FRAMESET, another HTML document is required to provide content.

HTML document showing two different web pages. The contents of "doc3.html" will be displayed in the top frame and the contents of "doc2.html" will be displayed in the bottom frame.

The documents "doc2.html" and "doc3.html" that are marked up into the two frames are just ordinary HTML documents like the ones you have been learning to create. However, as you can imagine, the document that creates the actual FRAMESET is of a different nature.

One important thing to note from Figure 8.1 is that the actual content of the framed document comes from the two web pages that are "loaded into" the two frames. That being the case, the document that creates the FRAMESET has no BODY section. The BODY section is replaced by the FRAMESET element. Within the FRAMESET element are FRAME elements that point to the web pages that are to provide content for the frames. Figure 8.2 shows a document "doc1.html" that is sufficient to generate the FRAMESET as pictured in Figure 8.1. We say that "doc1.html" is sufficient to generate the FRAMESET of Figure 8.1 because there are several possible attributes that can be used to change the appearance of a framed document. However, since Figure 8.1 gives the structure of the FRAMESET rather than its actual appearance in a browser, we just give the minimal HTML code necessary to illustrate the nature of framed documents.

The FRAMESET element is a container element that *entirely* replaces the BODY element. The contents of the FRAMESET element are the FRAME elements themselves. FRAME elements are noncontainer elements that point to the actual documents load into the frames via SRC (source) attribute. The SRC attribute is mandatory in the FRAME tags to the extent that, without them, there would be no content for the frame. While a framed page can be rendered without SRC attributes, the result would be a blank web page with a

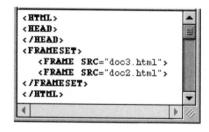

```
<HTML>
<HEAD>
</HEAD>
<FRAMESET>
   <FRAME SRC="doc3.html">
   <FRAME SRC="doc2.html">
</FRAMESET>
</HTML>
```

FIGURE 8.2 There is no body section, since the body of the framed page comes from the other HTML documents that are loaded into the frames.

horizontal divider across the middle as shown in Figure 8.1. Just as with the SRC attribute when used with the IMG element, the SRC attribute of the FRAME element takes a URL, relative or absolute, as its value. It might seem funny to have two distinct web pages, each displayed in half of the browser window, but there are several applications, as we shall see.

NOTE Above, we supplied only the names of the source files as values of the SRC attribute. Of course, since the value of SRC is a relative URL, the exact file path to the source document is required. So, above, it is implicit that all of the source files are in the same directory as the document containing the FRAMESET. Moreover, since there will be a lot of different files floating around in the remainder of this lesson, we will stick to this convention for simplicity.

You can use an absolute URL to point to the source file but you would rarely wish to do this. If the source file is on your web site, it is more efficient to use a relative URL. If the source file is not on your site, you probably shouldn't be loading it into one of your frames anyway. It's kind of uncool to load other people's web pages into your frames.

8.2 ATTRIBUTES OF THE FRAMESET ELEMENT

The attributes of the FRAMESET element simply control the layout of the framed page. Once again, the contents of the frames themselves can be *any* web pages. We will see concrete examples shortly. First are the COLS and ROWS attributes. For example,

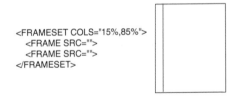

```
<FRAMESET COLS="15%,85%">
  <FRAME SRC="">
  <FRAME SRC="">
</FRAMESET>
```

creates a frameset as pictured with two columns, where the first column covers 15% of the width of the browser window and the second covers 85%. The default is for rows of equal size.

As another example,

```
<FRAMESET>
  <FRAME SRC="">
  <FRAME SRC="">
  <FRAME SRC="">
</FRAMESET>
```

creates the pictured frameset, although it is recommended that you always use COLS or ROWS to specify a frameset. The previous is roughly equivalent to

<FRAMESET ROWS="33%, 33%, 34%" >

We say "roughly equivalent" because the percentage values must be given in whole numbers, and three times 33% is only 99%. We thus added an extra percentage onto the third column so that the total is 100%. It is not imperative that the total of your rows or columns add up to 100% since the browser will figure an approximation, but it is recommended.

An alternative is to specify rows and columns in terms of pixels. For example, rather than specifying 15% for the first column in the "15%, 85%" column set above, it might be desirable to specify that the first column be, say 100 pixels wide. The dilemma this creates is that you don't know how many pixels wide the second column should be. Indeed, this depends on the size of the browser window (and even the resolution of the particular computer monitor). The solution is the symbol "*" which, in this context, means "the rest". So

<FRAMESET COLS="100,*">

specifies that the first column should be 100 pixels wide and the second should take up the rest of the width of the browser window. This method is even fairly flexible. The frameset

<FRAMESET ROWS="150,*, 100">

specifies the size in pixels of the first and third rows, and leaves the middle row to take up the remaining space.

Two additional attributes of the FRAMESET element are BORDER and BORDER-COLOR. BORDER specifies in pixels the size of the border that separates the frames, and BORDERCOLOR specifies the color of the border. The default is BORDER=5. Like any color-specifying attribute, BORDERCOLOR takes named or hexadecimal colors. The default is usually gray. The use of these two attributes will be clear in the following examples. But keep in mind the actual content, and hence colors, of the frames' interiors come from the actual documents that are loaded into the frames.

N O T E

It is possible that your HTML editor will automatically put numbers in front of any "*" symbol you use. These numbers represent a "weighting" of the unspecified frames. For example

<FRAMESET COLS="150,1*,3*,100">

will cause the two middle rows to be weighted as 1/4 and 3/4, respectively, of the remaining space in the middle. (The total for the unspecified space is $1 + 3 = 4$.) It is unlikely that you would need to make a framed page with four columns, but even in a smaller frameset, your editor might automatically specify ROWS="150,1*". That is no big deal since "1*" is equivalent to "*". This is, nonetheless, something about which you should be aware.

It is also possible that your HTML editor will automatically insert a FRAMEBORDER attribute in the FRAMESET element. FRAMEBORDER, which provides an alternative between a three-dimensional and standard border, is somewhat browser-dependent and unreliable.

8.3 ATTRIBUTES OF THE FRAME ELEMENT

Explaining the attributes of the FRAME element requires a concrete example. So we turn to the "fixed navigation bar" as mentioned in the introduction for this lesson. Figure 8.3 shows a frames version of the online book used for an example on named anchors in Figure 5.11. There are several things to be learned from Figure 8.3. The first has already been alluded to several times. There are two separate HTML documents on display. The one in the top frame is named "links.html" and the one in the bottom frame is named "chap1.html". Rather

FIGURE 8.3 A frames web page with a fixed navigational bar at the top. When a navigational link is clicked, the lower frame receives the new web page and the top frame stays put.

than showing the whole frameset document, which you can see from the address field of Figure 8.3 is named "book.html", we just give the FRAMESET element that creates the page. Just remember that this FRAMESET replaces the BODY element in "book.html".

```
<FRAMESET ROWS="65,*" BORDER=1>
<FRAME SRC="links.html" NAME="top" MARGINWIDTH=5 MARGINHEIGHT=5 >
<FRAME SRC="body.html" NAME="bottom" MARGINWIDTH=5 MARGINHEIGHT=5>
</FRAMESET>
```

Next, the MARGINWIDTH and MARGINHEIGHT attributes of the FRAME elements create some padding between the borders of the frame cells and their contents. They basically function like the CELLPADDING attribute used with tables. For example, without the specification MARGINHEIGHT=5 in each FRAME tag, the phrases "HTML for Fun and Profits" and "Chapter 1: Text Markup" would be flush up against the tops of the two frame cells, rather than having the five-pixel cushion you can see in Figure 8.3. These two attributes provide added functionality over CELLPADDING in tables in the sense that you can control vertical padding and horizontal padding separately within frame cells.

One subtlety is the scroll bar you see at the right of the bottom frame. If the web page that provides a frame's content is longer than the frame, the browser will automatically provide a scroll bar so that you have access to all of the frame's content. We choose not to provide it in this example, but the SCROLLING attribute can be used in a FRAME element to force or deny the presence of a scroll bar. SCROLLING takes the values "yes", "no", and "auto." The "yes" value forces the presence of a scroll bar, even if one is not necessary. The "no" value causes a scroll bar not to be present, even if it is needed. Finally, the "auto" value is the default and lets the browser decide if one is necessary.

You may be wondering why we have skirted discussion of the NAME attributes present in the FRAME elements of Figure 8.3. Well, the NAME attributes don't really have any purpose unless there are links in the documents comprising the frames. Since there

```
<HTML>
<HEAD>
</HEAD>
<BODY BGCOLOR="#FFFFFF">
<H2>HTML for Fun and Profits.</H2>

<A HREF="chap1.html" TARGET="bottom">[Chapter 1]</A>
<A HREF="chap2.html" TARGET="bottom">[Chapter 2]</A>
<A HREF="chap3.html" TARGET="bottom">[Chapter 3]</A>
</BODY>
</HTML>
```

FIGURE 8.4 The HTML document that provides the content for the top frame in Figure 8.3.

are links in "links.html", the document contained in the top frame, the NAME attributes certainly have a purpose in this example. Their use, however, is a topic worthy of its own discussion.

8.4 TARGETING LINKS TO FRAMES

We begin by showing in Figure 8.4 the document "links.html", which appears in the top frame of Figure 8.3. The first thing you will probably notice is that the anchor elements contain a TARGET attribute. This attribute was not mentioned in the lesson on hypertext links because it has no use outside of a frames setting. Notice that each of the links points to a different HTML file, one for each chapter of the online book. The TARGET attribute of each link simply mandates that, when the link is clicked, the HTML file to which the link points is loaded into the bottom frame. Figure 8.5 depicts the situation.

In this way, the document in the top frame, the one with the navigational links, stays put while the various chapters of the book can be loaded into the bottom frame. The fact that we used the TARGET attribute in the links to target the different chapters to the bottom frame is crucial. For example, if we fail to target "chapter3.html" to the bottom frame

<A HREF="chap3.html">[Chapter3]</A>

the result is that the document "chap3.html" would be loaded into the same frame that contained the link.

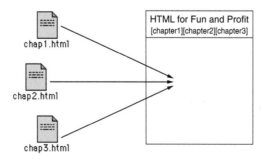

FIGURE 8.5 An example of a fixed navigational bar. The links in the top frame target the HTML files for the chapters into the bottom frame. Meanwhile, the content of the top frame remains fixed.

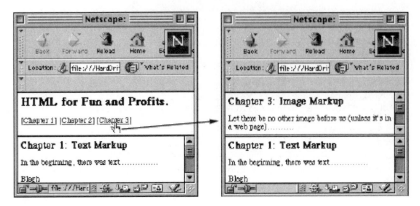

FIGURE 8.6 Failure to target a link to the desired frame causes the document to be loaded into the frame in which the link appears.

> **NOTE**
>
> An interesting thing happens in most browsers if you specify that a link should target a particular frame, but a frame of that name does not exist. The page which the link pulls up will actually be loaded into a completely new window. For example, if you target a link to a frame, but misspell the name of the frame, the browser will be completely confused about which frame to insert the document into. Rather than using the default behavior of inserting the new page into the same frame in which the link was clicked, the browser will create a new window, on top of the original window, and display the new page there.

Figure 8.6 exhibits the default behavior for links contained in frames. If no target frame is specified, the new file is simply inserted into the frame in which the link was clicked. As usual, there is a value of the TARGET attribute that also produces the default behavior. In the context of Figure 8.6, the following two links are equivalent:

<A HREF="chap3.html">[Chapter3]</A>
<A HREF="chap3.html" TARGET="_self">[Chapter3]</A>

In other words, TARGET="_self" is the default behavior. This just means to load the new web page into the same frame. Here the value "_self" is preceded by an underscore so that the browser recognizes the value as a special targeting value. You should never put an underscore before a normal frame name.

As a last note on targeting, it is possible to escape from the frame environment entirely. Suppose a FRAMESET has two rows similar to the online book example we have been using and that the following link appears in the top frame:

<A HREF="newpage html" TARGET="_parent"> Get me out of here!
I've been framed.</A>

The special value "_parent" of the TARGET attribute allows the new web page to appear in the "parent window" of the FRAMESET. That is to say, TARGET="_parent" allows you to escape from the frame environment. Without this, you could only load web pages into frames within the FRAMESET. Figure 8.7 illustrates this.

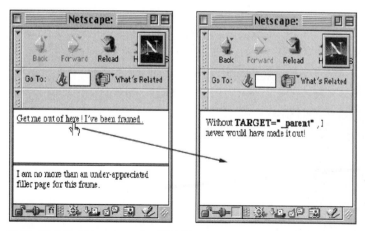

FIGURE 8.7   Using the value TARGET="_parent" causes the web page to which the link points to escape from the FRAMESET and appear in the "parent window."

N O T E

A good example of linking to named anchors in other documents can be derived from the online book example above. Figure 8.5 depicts three different HTML files, one for each of the three chapters of the book. That need not be the case. For example, one could combine all three chapters into one HTML file and simply include a named anchor at the beginning of each chapter. If the file containing the combined chapters were called "allchapters.html", the link in the top frame pointing to chapter 3, for example, would take the form

```
<A HREF="allchapters.html#chap3" TARGET="bottom">[Chapter3]</A>
```

Exercises 8.9.4 and 8.9.5 below emphasize the distinction between chopping a document into pieces for display and using the whole document for display with named anchors for each section.

8.5   NESTED FRAMES

It is possible to "nest" frames. Indeed, if you wish to make a frames page that has both rows and columns it is necessary to do so. In terms of page layout, frames are less flexible than tables. But, as we have seen, frames add a degree of flexibility that tables don't provide. To illustrate this further, we offer a contrived version of an online music history page. A screenshot of the initial loading of the page is shown in Figure 8.8. The primary functionality of this page is realized by a list of music categories in the upper left frame. When one of the categories is clicked, a list of subcategories for that music genre is then displayed in the lower left frame. The user can then choose from one of these subcategories and see a history page displayed in the main frame on the right.

Certainly, the first topic worthy of discussion is the actual FRAMESET required to generate the document in Figure 8.8. Figure 8.9 shows the FRAMESET element used to create the layout in Figure 8.8. In order to create the layout, we first create a FRAMESET with two columns and no border. Then, instead of using the FRAME element to create the first column of the FRAMESET, we used another FRAMESET element to create the two rows of the first column. Finally, the second column is given content using the FRAME element. The content of the upper left frame is given by the HTML document "categories.html", the

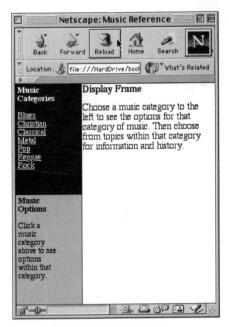

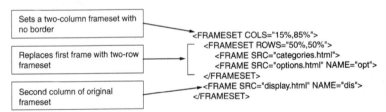

FIGURE 8.8 An online music history page making use of nested frames.

FIGURE 8.9 In order to nest frames, you must use a new FRAMESET in place of one of the FRAME elements.

content of the lower left frame is given by the HTML document "options.html", and the initial content of the main frame on the right is given by the HTML document "display.html". The actual contents of those documents are apparent in the respective frames of Figure 8.8.

With that in place, each link in the upper left frame must be made to target the lower left frame so that the options for a category appear there when its link is clicked. Figure 8.10 shows the result of clicking the Metal link.

Since the name of the options frame is given as "opt" in Figure 8.9, each link in the web page of the upper-left frame must specify TARGET="opt". So the link for the Metal category has the form

<A HREF="metal.html" TARGET="opt">Metal</A>

So, upon clicking the Metal link as depicted in Figure 8.10, the page "metal.html" then provides content for the lower left frame.

Finally, all of the links for the different options must target the main frame on the right. Figure 8.11 depicts the result of clicking on the Grunge link in the lower left frame.

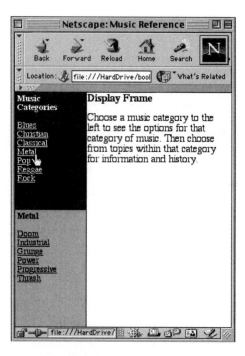

FIGURE 8.10 When a category link is clicked, the page of subcategory links for that category is targeted to the lower left frame.

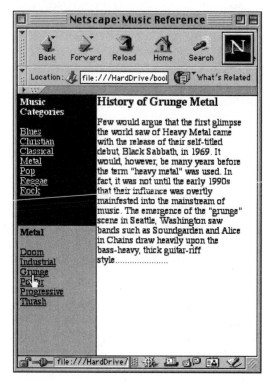

FIGURE 8.11 When an option link is clicked, the page for that option must be targeted to the right frame.

Since the name of the display frame is given as "dis" in Figure 8.9, each link in the web page of the lower-left frame must specify TARGET="dis". So the link for the Grunge option has the form

<A HREF="grunge.html" TARGET="dis">Grunge</A>

N O T E
The above music example used a new FRAMESET to create two rows in the first column of the original FRAMESET. You can do it the other way around as well. In other words, you could start with a ROWS page and use a new FRAMESET to create COLS in one of the rows. The thing to note is that, regardless of how many FRAMESET elements you use to set up the frames page, there is always one FRAME element for each frame. This in is evidence in Figure 8.9.

8.6 THE PROS AND CONS OF FRAMES

The obvious disadvantage of frames is that the page layout options are somewhat more limited than with tables. The obvious advantage, as we have emphasized, is that a fixed navigation bar can be provided. However, many commercial sites with elaborate tabular layouts also make use of what we term a "pseudo-fixed" navigation bar. Such pseudo-fixed navigation bars basically serve the same purpose.

For an example, consider the Knuckles' Sports World page of Figure 7.18. In that discussion we were concerned with the layout of that page itself, and not with what the whole web site might entail. For starters, if the user clicked on the College Volleyball section, the only parts of the page that should change are those table cells to the right of the left navigation bar, and perhaps the weekly trivia question. In other words, even if the user were looking at the volleyball page, it would still be desirable that the exact same navigation bar be present at the left. To accomplish this, one would simply have a template (or master page) common to each of the sports pages. That is, each sports page would be constructed from the same master file, and only the contents of the appropriate table cells would be altered. Then, each time a different sports page is requested, the same navigation bar appears. In this way, it would be pseudo-fixed: it would be in the same spot on each page. This requires some redundant code, but has its advantages.

One glaring advantage of the pseudo-fixed navigation bar type of site is that each page is available for bookmarking by a user's browser. If a user wants to check the basketball page every couple of days, he/she simply chooses "add bookmark" or "add favorite" in the browser's pull-down menu and can go straight to the basketball page at will. Suppose, on the other hand, that a web site is designed with a fixed navigation bar using frames as with the music reference site in the above example. If the user wishes to bookmark the History of Grunge page, for example, there are problems.

When a frames page is loaded into a browser, only the document with the FRAMESET is listed in the address field of the browser. In the above case, the FRAMESET document is called "music.html". No matter how many links the user clicks to load various subsidiary pages into different frames, the FRAMESET document is still the document that appears in the address field of the browser. So, even though the History of Grunge page is present in the main frame, a bookmark (or favorite) will only select the FRAMESET document, "music.html". When the bookmark is activated, the FRAMESET document and the original source files for the frames will be loaded. You would then have to click a couple of links to retrieve the Grunge page.

The majority of major commercial sites are set up with tabular structures. If the site is deep, users can still bookmark any part of the site. However, there are some commercial sites that use frames. In practice, for a personal web site it probably doesn't make much difference. If you desire an elaborate page layout, use tables. If you like a slide-show style of presentation with a fixed navigational bar, frames may be the right choice. Based upon your need, it basically boils down to the desired functionality and to common sense.

As a last note, both tables and frames are widely supported by modern browsers. However, frames offer one feature for dealing with clients with old browsers that tables don't. The following NOTE suffices to explain.

NOTE

If you are using an HTML editor to create your frames pages, there is a good chance that it will automatically insert the NOFRAMES element into your documents. It may appear before, after, or even inside the FRAMESET element. It has the following form:

```
<NOFRAMES>
<BODY>
    ⋮
</BODY>
</NOFRAMES>
```

This element is optional and provides a body for the web page in case the viewing browser doesn't support frames. In that case, whatever is in the BODY section of the NOFRAMES element is rendered as the web page, and the FRAMESET tags are ignored. If it is not imperative that viewers with old browsers see the page, you can simply write "Sorry, you need a browser that supports frames to see this page." If it is crucial to reach all surfers, it is common to provide a link to an alternate no-frames page: Click here for a no-frames version of this page.

8.7 SUMMARY

Key Terms

frameset	frame	parent
target	nested frames	fixed navigation bar

Framed web pages are actually several web pages in one. The FRAMESET document creates the structure for the page, but other HTML documents provide the content for each frame. The FRAMESET element replaces the BODY of the FRAMESET document and has attributes as defined in the following table.

<FRAMESET >···</FRAMESET >

Attribute	Possible Values	Default
COLS	pixels, percent, *	*
ROWS	pixels, percent, *	*
BORDER	pixels	browser-dependent (about 5 pixels)
BORDERCOLOR	hexadecimal color, named color	browser-dependent (often gray)

The FRAMESET element just creates the layout. The FRAME element actually specifies the content for each frame. In order to provide content for a frame, there should be exactly one FRAME element present for that frame. Remember, a frame is allocated by the COLS and ROWS attributes of the FRAMESET element. The FRAME element actually fills the allocated frames.

<FRAME >

Attribute	Possible Values	Default
SRC	URL	–
NAME	character string	–
MARGINHEIGHT	pixels	browser-dependent (about 10)
MARGINWIDTH	pixels	browser-dependent (about 10)
SCROLLING	yes, no, auto	auto

When nesting frames, a FRAMESET element takes the place of a FRAME element, so that the content provider for a frame is another FRAMESET. In this way, you can subdivide a frame into more frames. The FRAME element still provides content for the nested frames.

The NAME attribute of the FRAME element really has no use other than in targeting a link to a frame. The TARGET attribute of the anchor (<A>...</A>) element actually does the targeting.

<A >···</A >

Attribute	Possible Values	Default
TARGET	name of a FRAME, _self, _parent	_self

The HTML document indicated by the HREF attribute of an anchor is loaded into the frame specified by the TARGET attribute of the anchor element. If no target is specified, the document is loaded into same frame in which the link appears. This is the default behavior and is the same as TARGET="_self". If frames are not nested, TARGET="_parent" is sufficient to cause the document to be loaded into the parent window. This is kind of like escaping from the FRAMESET into the whole window.

Significantly more commercial web sites are designed with tables than with frames. One of the main disadvantages of frames is that a web page displayed in a frame can't be directly bookmarked. On the other hand, frames are ideal when a fixed navigation bar is desired for a slide-show style presentation. Deciding which method of page layout to use is largely a matter of personal preference and the desired functionality of the site.

If your frames page is not working as planned, the following will help you trouble-shoot.

| **NOTE** | If your frames page is not being rendered at all, the problem is likely one of the following: |

If your frames page is not being rendered at all, the problem is likely one of the following:

1. You have not supplied the same number of FRAME elements as you have allocated frames with the FRAMESET element.

2. You have improperly nested FRAMESET elements.

If one of your frames is coming up initially empty, the problem is likely one of the following:

1. You have forgotten to specify the source file for a frame with the SRC attribute.

2. The name of the document specified by the SRC attribute does not *exactly* match the name of the actual document.

3. The relative URL specified by the SRC attribute doesn't provide the correct file path to the document.

If one of your links is malfunctioning, check the following symptoms:

1. The link causes the document to be loaded in the same frame as the link: You have forgotten to TARGET the name of a frame with the link.

2. Clicking the link causes the new page to come up in a *completely* new window, on top of the window containing the frames page: The name specified by the TARGET attribute of the link does not *exactly* match the name of the intended frame. Check the spelling and cases (upper-case vs. lower-) of both the frame names and the value of TARGET. If a frame of the name as specified by TARGET is not found, a new window is created.

8.8 REVIEW QUESTIONS

In most cases, it is not sufficient to answer these from the Lesson Summary.

1. Describe the picture frame analogy as it pertains to framed web pages.

2. What is the default if several FRAME elements are included in a FRAMESET, but neither of the attributes COLS nor ROWS is used in the FRAMESET element?

3. Explain the effect of ROWS="3*,2*,10%". Explain the effect of COLS="100,2*,*". It will help to draw sketches of the layouts.

4. What degree of flexibility do MARGINHEIGHT and MARGINWIDTH for frames offer over CELLPADDING for tables?

5. How is scrolling within frames controlled? What is the default?

6. What is the NOFRAMES element for? Explain the purpose of the BODY element within NOFRAMES.

7. Explain the rolls of "_parent" and "_self" when targeting web pages to frames.

8. Explain in words (without writing down HTML code) how you nest frames.

9. Contrast the advantages of frames and tables. What do we mean by a pseudo-fixed navigation bar as opposed to a fixed navigation bar?

8.9 EXERCISES

1. Go to the homework section for Lesson 8 on the web site for this book. Under Exercise 1, you will find the picture of a framed web page. The links in the various frames of the web page specify which frames or windows they target.

Make a dummy page for the links to pull up. The dummy page should be of a different color from the source pages of the frames. Make a framed web page with approximately the same appearance and make each of the links target the dummy page to the appropriate frame or window.

2. (See Exercise 7.13.2. You may use the same images.) Acquire eight images suitable for background images in a web page. The objective of this exercise is to make a slide-show type presentation for the images using frames.

(a) Use one frame for a "fixed" navigational bar that contains links to each of the eight images. Use another frame to display the images. For each image there should be a link pointing to the image file (HREF="img1.gif"), and another link pointing to an empty web page that uses the image as a background image (HREF="img1.html"). That way, the viewer can choose to see the actual image or the image tiled as a background image of a page.

(b) Do part (a) using nested frames. One frame should contain two links, one for viewing the actual images, and one for viewing the images tiled as backgrounds of web pages. If the link for the actual images is clicked, a second frame displays a list of links pointing to the eight image files. If the link for the images tiled as backgrounds is clicked, the second frame displays a list of links pointing to the eight web pages which use the images as backgrounds. A third frame is used for the display.

3. Make a web page approximately like the one discussed in Figures 8.8–8.11. You can trim the page down to three music categories. You can make up your own categories if you like. Each category need only have two subcategories or options within that category. The actual description pages can be minimal "dummy" pages or, if you have music opinions, feel free to amuse me.

4. (See Exercise 5.10.5. The file you created for that exercise can be adapted for use here.) Go to the homework section for Lesson 8 on the web site for this book. Under Exercise 4, you will find a link to a web page named "dsl.html" that discusses DSL Internet connections. This page has a title and four sections, named 1 through 4. Download the source HTML file for this page and make a frames page with two frames for this document as follows:

(a) When the frames page loads, the navigational frame contains links to each of the four sections of the document, as well as a link for the top of the document. The initial source for the display frame should be the document.

(b) Put a named anchor at each of the four sections of the document. The four links in the navigational frame should bring each of the four sections respectively of the document to the top of the display frame. The link in the navigational frame that points to the top of the document simply causes the top of the document to appear at the top of the display frame.

(c) Section 4 has several subsections. Put a named anchor at each of these subsections. In the navigational frame, put links that cause each of these named anchors to appear at the top of the display frame. These links should be organized as a sublist to the link for section 4.

5. (See Exercise 5.10.6. The files you created for that exercise can be adapted for use here.) Go to the homework section for Lesson 8 on the web site for this book. Under Exercise 5, you will find a link to a web page named "dsl.html" that discusses DSL Internet connections. This page has a title and four sections, named 1 through 4. Download the source HTML file for this page and make a frames page with two frames for this document as follows:

(a) When the frames page loads, the navigational frame contains a link to a title page for the document, and links to each of the four sections of the document. The initial source for the display frame should be the title page.

(b) Make a brief title page for the document, and make a separate page for each of the four sections of the document. These are the pages that the links in the navigational frame pull up.

(c) Section 4 has several subsections. Put a named anchor at each of these sub-sections. In the navigational frame, put links that point straight to each of these named anchors. These links should be organized as a sublist to the link for section 4.

8.10 PROJECT THREADS

THREAD A

Assignment

(a) Do one or more of the exercises from this lesson. Since several files are needed for each exercise, create a new folder in your homework directory to contain the files for each exercise. Name any new directories accordingly, "ex8_3" for example. Of course, you should provide a link from your homework page to any new page, and vice versa.

(b) If applicable, transfer all files to the web server when completed. Check to make sure the transfer was successful. Especially, check to make sure all of the links work.

THREAD B

Assignment

(a) Do one or more of the exercises from this lesson. Create a new folder in your public directory to contain the files (images and otherwise) for each exercise. Name any new directories accordingly, "ex8_3" for example. Of course, you should provide a link from your homework page to any new page, and vice versa.

(b) If applicable, transfer all files to the web server when completed. Check to make sure the transfer was successful. Especially, check to make sure all of the links work.

WHAT IS JAVASCRIPT?

WELL, IT'S time to move on to JavaScript. Cool. JavaScript must be how I put audio files and video files and other fun things into my web page. The answer is an emphatic no. Most anything that shows up in a web page is rendered because of HTML instructions. Well, if we are moving on to JavaScript, why didn't we learn how to do audio and video in the HTML lessons? The answer is simple. You have learned the fundamental, core issues surrounding the construction web pages and web sites. The building blocks that make up your foundation of HTML knowledge are the following:

- Using HTML tags and attributes.
- Linking to other documents, and linking structures for web sites.
- Using images for various purposes.
- Page layout techniques: tables vs. frames.

Certainly, audio and video are not at the core conceptual level as are the above. In fact, if you wish to put an audio clip on a web page, since you are now armed with the above fundamentals, you can easily find a short tutorial online telling you how. Actually, depending upon what type of audio you want to put in your web page, it probably only requires a single HTML element to include it. The hard part is actually creating the audio file. There are numerous formats of audio, and it usually requires special software to create them. Much as it is not practical to include tutorials on various graphical editors in a book such as this, it is not practical to give tutorials on creating audio files. Besides, it is certainly not in line with the goal of this book—to provide a solid conceptual basis for interactive programming on the Internet.

If you sit down and watch TV for a while and visit the first 10 or 15 commercial web sites you see advertised (that might not take long these days), you will likely not run into any significant use of embellishments such as audio or video on the front ends of these sites. What you will encounter is the skillful use of nearly every HTML fundamental you have learned thus far, together with the fruits of labor of their skilled graphic artists. A mastery of the fabrication of graphics is really the only thing (besides more practice) keeping you from being able to create such professional-looking web pages. For example, see the images that accompany Exercise 7.13.5 on the web site for this book, especially the file tabs menu bar.

However, these commercial web sites do contain important HTML structures that we have not yet covered. These structures are for obtaining input, or data, from the user. You have no doubt seen web pages with text fields into which you enter your name and address. Perhaps you have seen checkboxes providing you with different options from which to choose. Pull-down menus are often present in web pages that allow you to choose from a variety of options. Moreover, almost any web page with such structures has buttons for you to click to submit the information for processing. Such structures are parts of HTML forms.

HTML forms are easy to create, especially if you are becoming adept with an HTML editor. The first part of this lesson gives an overview of the various features that HTML forms provide, together with the HTML elements necessary to create them. But HTML forms alone do not provide the capability of processing data and interacting with the user. That is where JavaScript enters the picture. The second part of this lesson gives some insight into the role of JavaScript as it is used to handle data entered into HTML forms, and into the role of JavaScript with respect to interactive programming on the Internet in general.

9.1   OVERVIEW OF HTML FORMS

Figure 9.1 shows an HTML document containing an **HTML form.** The form contains most of the various **form elements** we will be exploring. The form is not meant to be a

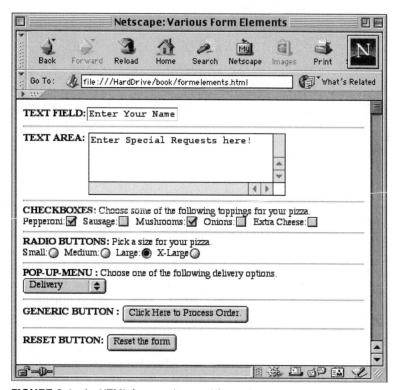

FIGURE 9.1 An HTML form and several form elements.

viable pizza order form, but to demonstrate the general nature of each of the various form elements. Preceding each form element in boldface is the name by which we will refer to each type of form element. The various form elements have numerous attributes, many of which are needed only so that JavaScript can process the form. To concisely illustrate the HTML required to generate such a form, below Figure 9.1 we provide a brief discussion about the form and each form element. Discussion about other attributes and features of HTML forms is deferred until the necessary JavaScript background is in place. Moreover, a full reference for HTML forms can be found in Appendix A.

All of the form elements must be defined as contents of the HTML FORM element

<FORM> . . . various form elements are defined here . . . . </FORM>

In fact, every bit of markup you see in Figure 9.1 is contained in a FORM element. The text descriptions actually need not be but, rather than using a different set of FORM tags to surround each form element, we simply included all of the form's elements and textual support inside one set of FORM tags.

We next explain each form element, but not necessarily in the same order that they appear in the form above. One HTML element, the INPUT element, can generate most of the form elements. The INPUT element is a noncontainer element and takes the TYPE attribute. By specifying a different type, you can create five of the seven types of form elements you see in Figure 9.1. Those types should be apparent from the INPUT elements below.

<INPUT TYPE=text VALUE="Enter Your Name" SIZE=15>
<INPUT TYPE=button VALUE="Click Here to Process Order.">
<INPUT TYPE=reset VALUE="Reset the form">
<INPUT TYPE=checkbox>
<INPUT TYPE=radio>

As you can see, the VALUE attributes contain a text string that appears inside the actual form element. In the case of the text field (TYPE=text), the VALUE attribute determines the initial contents of the text field. The text field is typically used to obtain a short piece of information from the user. Often, one sets VALUE="" so that the text field is initially empty. Either way, the user types information into the field. The length, in characters, of the text field is set by the SIZE attribute. So, the above text field can display 15 characters.

The generic button (TYPE=button) is used to cause some action (i.e., call some JavaScript into action). When the user clicks the mouse on the button, something happens. In the above example, the pizza order might be totalled for your final approval. Its VALUE determines the text that appears on the button. Usually the text is some sort of indication of what is to happen when the button is clicked. The reset button (TYPE=reset) works exactly like the generic button, except that its action is predetermined. It simply resets the form to its original state. For example, if you start adding information into the various form elements and then change your mind, you can simply click the reset button to return the form to the state in which it was originally loaded into the browser.

The checkbox (TYPE=checkbox) allows one or more options to be chosen. We have not included the VALUE attribute in the checkbox definition, since its value is not relevant in the context of HTML. Each checkbox is just a small square on the web page and thus doesn't need a value for its display (like the text appearing on a button, for example). Since there are five checkboxes in Figure 9.1, five INPUT elements of TYPE=checkbox were required. The supporting text for the checkboxes is just text. It doesn't originate from an HTML attribute.

Radio buttons (TYPE=radio) function almost exactly like checkboxes. In fact, their name is poorly chosen since they are really not buttons in the sense of generic and reset buttons. They are simply round checkboxes. When you click one of them, it is filled in with a black circle, rather than a check. Radio buttons do, however, offer one important advantage over checkboxes. You can select any number of checkboxes, but radio buttons can be set up so that only one of them can be selected. For example, in Figure 9.1, if you were to click the "small" option, the black circle would disappear from the "large" option, leaving only the "small" option chosen. In contrast, you can choose any number of the checkbox toppings, and the rest still stay checked. As with checkboxes, it requires one input element to create each distinct radio button. However, we will not learn how to set them up so that only one can be selected until Lesson 14.

The other two types of form elements appearing in Figure 9.1 are not created with the INPUT element. The text area is created with the TEXTAREA container element:

> <TEXTAREA ROWS=4 COLS=30>Enter Special Requests here!</TEXTAREA>

The initial text comes from the content of the TEXTAREA element, rather than from a VALUE attribute as with the text field. The text area is often used to obtain lengthy comments from the user. The ROWS and COLS attributes determine the size of the text area. So, the above text area can display four rows, each 30 characters in length.

The pulldown menu, sometimes called a popup menu, is used to provide a list of options for the user. When the user clicks and holds on the compacted menu, the full menu appears containing several options. In fact, these menus are very similar to the popup menus you use regularly at the top of your computer screen. In practice, a popup menu works just like a bunch of radio buttons, except that it is more compact. Until you click on the menu to open it, most of the options are hidden from view. This is ideal for a large list of options, such as the 50 states, which would clutter the form if created with radio buttons. It should come as no surprise that these menus are created with HTML tags. The menu appearing in Figure 9.1 is created with the SELECT element,

> <SELECT>
> <OPTION>Pickup
> <OPTION>Delivery
> <OPTION>Eat In
> </SELECT>

and the OPTION tags designate each option that appears in the menu. Of course, there are other attributes, but they only have relevance when armed with a programming language such as JavaScript.

Well, that's it for the overview of HTML forms. There's nothing fancy here, just some HTML elements. You can sit down right now and make all the forms you like. In fact, with a good HTML editor, you can whip up a form in no time flat. However, don't expect to be able to do anything with the form yet. You can at least get familiar with the HTML form elements so that they won't seem mysterious when it comes time to supply programming to make them functional.

N O T E Just keep in mind two things:

1. Even though the form elements appear to be stand-alone HTML elements, they must be defined within the HTML FORM tags.
2. If your HTML editor throws some strange attributes at you, they are most likely useful only in conjuction with a programming language like JavaScript. The attributes presented above are sufficient to create the physical form elements.

9.2   THE CLIENT-SERVER MODEL

OK, so what happens when the user clicks a "submit form" or "process form" button? There are basically two answers. The information entered into the form is processed on the client's computer or it is sent back to the web server for processing. JavaScript is used for **client-side processing.** In Section 2.4 we discussed http transactions. When a user requests a web page, a copy of the HTML file is sent from the web server to the computer of the person who has made the request. This person (actually his or her computer) is called the **client.** In this respect, HTML is called **portable code:** the HTML code required to generate the web page is actually transported to the client. JavaScript is another example of portable code. In fact, JavaScript code is contained within an HTML document. Thus, the JavaScript code is physically transported to the client and executed by the client's browser to process the data from the HTML form. Hence the term client-side processing.

Another possibility is to send the data from the form back to the web server. Accordingly, this is called **server-side processing.** While JavaScript has some utility in server-side processing, other languages are better suited for that purpose. Indeed, programming languages like C++, Perl, Java, and Visual Basic are often employed for server-side processing. Sending HTML form data to a web server for processing requires a standardization for how browsers can send form data to the web server. This standardization is called the **Common Gateway Interface (CGI).** Thus, server-side programs are often called CGI programs. Figure 9.2 illustrates the above discussion and the associated terms.

A main advantage of portable code (like JavaScript) is its direct accessibility to the web page. As we shall see in subsequent lessons, JavaScript can interact directly (and immediately) with HTML forms, and even other components of a web page. On the other hand, CGI programs on the web server require extra transactions between the client and web server, causing a time delay (sometimes significant). But there are serious advantages to CGI programming. The most glaring advantage is the capability of CGI programs to interact directly with a database. At the present time, large databases are certainly not portable. In other words, it is not practical to send large databases to the client along with an HTML document. Those databases intended for interaction with web pages are typically kept on the web server (or another easily accessible computer in the local network of the server). Not only does proximity enable CGI-type programs to be more efficient data-access and data-retrieval vehicles than client-side programs, but the programming languages used for CGI are themselves more database-friendly. But this comes at a price—these languages are also tend to be much more complicated than client-side languages like JavaScript.

In reality, server-side and client-side processing don't present a "one or the other" prospect. Advanced form processing often entails a mixture of the two techniques. Figure 9.3

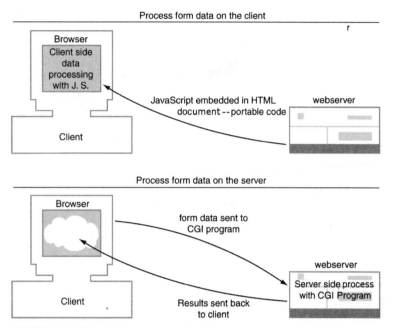

FIGURE 9.2 There are two fundamental ways to process data from an HTML form.

depicts how the input from an HTML form might be handled in a real instance, such as submitting an HTML form to a search engine.

1. An HTML document, replete with JavaScript, is sent to the browser of a client.
2. When the user submits the form, the form data is checked and cleaned up with client-side processing using JavaScript.
3. The data is sent to a CGI program on the server.
4. The CGI program interacts with a database.
5. The results are sent back to the browser on the client in the form of a new web page.

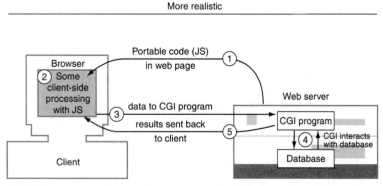

FIGURE 9.3 A sequence of events in which HTML form data is processed on both the client and on the server.

To make this a little more concrete, it serves to employ the search engine example since we all should be somewhat familiar with such transactions. When you pull up a search engine, you get a web page containing an HTML form. Often this form just contains a text field for your query and a button to submit the form. Sometimes there are checkboxes, radio buttons, or pulldown menus providing options with which you can refine the search. When you click the submit button, the form is processed on the client side with JavaScript. This processing might entail simply checking to see if you left the text field blank, or perhaps organizing the form data before delivering it to the server-side CGI program that is to receive the query. The data is then sent to the CGI program. The CGI program searches the database for links that contain key words from your query. Finally, any matches are sent back to the client in the form of a new web page.

Sounds simple? Well, it's not! It takes professional programmers to develop search-engine-quality interfaces between web pages and databases. In fact, such advanced constructs are well beyond the scope of this book. But in theory, the concept as depicted in Figure 9.3 is fairly straightforward. In our exploration of JavaScript, we will look at some issues of form verification on the client side with JavaScript, as well as numerous other uses.

NOTE

You have no doubt seen evidence of form data being submitted to the web server for processing. For example, the following was copied out of the address window of a browser after typing "heavy metal" into the query field of the Dogpile search engine and hitting the submit button (actually, the button is labeled "Fetch").

http://www.dogpile.com/texis/search?q=heavy+metal&geo=no&fs=web

The first part of the URL is basically the location of the server-side processing program on the server for www.dogpile.com, and the stuff after the question mark is called a **query string**. It contains the text that was typed into the search field, as well as some other unintelligible information useful only to the CGI program.

9.3 INTERPRETED PROGRAMMING LANGUAGES

In Section 2.1, we discussed the general issue of platform independence. In particular, HTML documents are merely text (ASCII) files that are **interpreted** by browsers. This means that the browser reads the HTML file and interprets the markup instructions to the best of its ability. If the same HTML file is loaded into the browser again, the browser has to reinterpret the markup instructions. In like manner, JavaScript, which is contained in HTML files, is also interpreted by browsers. The advantage to this is that the same JavaScripts can be passed around the Internet, from client to client, getting interpreted by various browsers on virtually every type of computer. This transcends the platform issue.

In contrast, most of the programming languages in wide use today are **compiled** rather than interpreted. A good example of a compiled language is C++. Many (if not most) of the applications you use on a regular basis (word processors, HTML editors, etc.) are written in C++. Just like HTML, C++ code is typed into a text file by the programmer. However, what happens next is quite different. The text file containing the C++ code is compiled into an executable program or application. The result is nothing like a text file. An executable file, like MS Word, is actually a computer program that comes to life when you activate it, usually by double-clicking on its icon.

You have no doubt been using such a word processor for years without realizing that the application is the result of compiling a (very large) text file. A compiler is basically an interpreter that creates an application by interpreting the programming code. In contrast, a browser interprets programming code and makes a temporary web page, rather than a permanent application. The key here is that a compiled application has to "talk" directly to the computer (Mac, PC, or otherwise) on which it is to be used. This is why the same word processor has to have two different compiled versions, one for Mac and one for PC, for example. Such applications created by compiled languages are thus platform-dependent.

Now back to the Internet. Clearly, if computer code is to be passed around the Internet to process HTML form data and the like, it can't be compiled into a platform-specific program. Rather, it is interpreted time and time again as the client's needs necessitate. This is starting to change the fundamental way the client-server model operates. The idea of a "fat client" is that, any time a certain type of processing needs to be done, a platform-specific compiled application has to be constructed for that purpose and installed on the client. The idea of a "thin client" is that one compiled application, like a web browser, is installed on the client, and the processing needs of that client are handled by portable programming code that is temporarily sent to the client's browser and interpreted there. The current model is still pretty client-fat. However, as the speed of the Internet and client computers increases, the model is likely to become more client-thin. There is no telling how "thin" the client will become, but languages like Java and JavaScript are certainly starting to make an impact.

9.4 JAVASCRIPT IS NOT JAVA

With all the current Internet craze, you have no doubt heard about Java. In fact, you may be wondering how Java is different from JavaScript. At its first conception by Sun Microsystems, Java (then under a different name) was to be a language for programming consumer electronic devices like microwave ovens, electronic clocks, dishwashers, and virtually any other electronic device that you can think of. Given the myriad different manufacturers of electronics, it was important for Java to be *ubiquitous*. The adjective is defined in Webster's unabridged dictionary as "seeming to be present everywhere at the same time; existing everywhere; omnipresent." The term is evolving in colloquial computer jargon to embody much the same concept as platform independence. Thus, Java needed to be ubiquitous, at least relative to various consumer electronic devices.

Java was basically designed to be able to be interpreted by various types of operating systems. That way, one Java program would be able to "talk to" different devices. However, Java never gained popularity in the consumer electronics industry. With the growing popularity of the Internet, however, Sun soon realized that such a language could be very valuable. To make a long story short, Sun started giving Java away for Internet usage. Java is a very powerful object-oriented programming language. In fact, Java is powerful enough to create behemoth applications like word processors and web browsers. But that involves compiling Java code into executable applications. In this respect, it is not a purely interpreted language, but close enough for the context of this discussion. Java's main claim to fame is its use as a language interpreted by browsers and servers.

Java programs created for use in web pages are called **applets** (kind of the little brother of application). Numerous applets can be found for free download on the Internet, and all you need to embed them in a web page is the <APPLET> . . . </APPLET> HTML container element. With just a little searching, you can find all sorts of applets and instructions on how to use them. Even things like video games can be embedded in a web page in the form of a Java applet. So they are quite powerful. To provide you with some perspective, some Java applets can be found in the Lesson 9 section of the web site.

Perhaps the key here is the word "embedded." Java applets are embedded in a web page in much the same way as images. HTML APPLET tags allocate space for the applet, and then the code for the applet is transferred to the browser, interpreted, and executed only within that allocated space. Like an image, an applet is not part of the HTML document, but is sent by the server as needed and "lives" only within its allocated space in the web page. In general, it is not safe to pass around powerful programming code. But the fact that Java is limited to manipulating objects within "its space" keeps malicious programmers from writing portable Java code that could harm other files on your computer.

JavaScript was developed independently of Java (again under a different name at first) to provide a simple programming language for use in the Netscape browser to enhance the interactivity of web pages. As such, it needed actually to be part of the web page, rather than some external object embedded in the page. When the use of Java applets in web pages came on to the scene, JavaScript was augmented so that it could interact with Java applets. For example, upon a certain user event, JavaScript can activate a Java applet. So, by its very nature, JavaScript had to be able to access nearly all components of a web page. Thus, while not as powerful as Java, JavaScript has much more control over the web page itself. As browser capabilities have evolved, so has JavaScript. In fact, JavaScript can now be used directly to access and control many components of a web page, including HTML forms.

To sum this up, Java is very powerful but has control only over what it is doing in its allocated space in a web page. In contrast, JavaScript is not as powerful a programming language, but has access to the entire web page. One fact not to overlook in all this talk of how the "Java" languages evolved is the fact that they have only existed in their current form since around 1995. But such is the Internet.

9.5 WHY LEARN JAVASCRIPT?

Java is more powerful and CGI programs provide good database interaction capabilities, so why start with JavaScript? For starters, to learn any programming language, one must learn the basics of programming. As it turns out, the same set of basics is common to virtually any programming language. That is, the same logical structures that make programming powerful basically drive all programming languages. Thorough its evolution JavaScript has been endowed with all of the necessary features. With the more powerful capabilities of languages such as Java also comes a great deal more complexity. Learning JavaScript will arm you with the programming fundamentals necessary to explore languages such as Java and those used for CGI, with much less headache.

Another factor that makes JavaScript an excellent beginning language is its object capabilities. The most powerful languages (Java, C++) are called object-oriented languages. Much of their power arises from capabilities related to objects. In practice, object capabilities are very difficult to learn if you are not already equipped with the programming fundamentals. The joy of JavaScript is that many objects, like HTML forms, can be created with HTML. JavaScript is then used to control the objects. This provides a gentle introduction to programming with objects, which in general can be a daunting undertaking.

Finally, you can write simple interactive programming behind HTML forms without overly rigorous study of programming theory. Moreover, future versions of HTML and future browsers are slated to allow even more control over objects in web pages through client-side programming. In fact, languages like JavaScript will be given so much control over HTML markup that the acronym DHTML (Dynamic HTML) is being used to term this "marriage" of HTML and client-side programming. At the time of this writing, Netscape and Explorer have different implementations of DHTML that are not compatible. However, the future should see more commonality in this respect. DHTML technology provides the capability to impact the fundamental ways we interface with electronic information. In the not-so-distant future, such technology will no doubt pervade even what we see on a TV screen.

9.6 RELATED TECHNOLOGIES

One possible cause for concern in the above sections is the lack of the mention of the name Microsoft. Indeed, the Windows operating system fairly dominates the desktop computer market. However, Microsoft recognized the importance of portable code to support web pages and introduced Jscript in Internet Explorer version 3. Jscript is very similar to JavaScript. In fact, there is a world consortium that has undertaken the standardization of client-side programming. Both Jscript and JavaScript have adapted to this standardization. Versions 4 (and above) of both browsers support roughly the same Jscript/JavaScript capabilities. With this in mind, the remainder of this book sticks to this commonly supported scripting standard. We simply refer to it as JavaScript.

Microsoft has also introduced ActiveX, a "language" that can embed objects into web pages in much the same way as Java. However, many argue that ActiveX lacks the security features of Java Applets. Moreover, ActiveX is currently supported only by Explorer. The current language of choice among most web developers is Java. Microsoft has even introduced its own environment for Java development, namely J++.

Other Microsoft technologies have failed to dominate the web. Active Server Pages (ASP) is a Microsoft technology that allows nice server-client interaction using Visual Basic on the server side. But this currently works only on Microsoft web servers. ASP is, however, supported by the Netscape browser. Next time you are surfing and you see a web page whose HTML file ends with ".asp", you are looking at an active server page, most likely being served off of a Microsoft-powered web server. But unlike the desktop computer market, the majority of web servers are not Microsoft-based, so ASP is still the exception, rather than the norm.

9.7 SUMMARY

Key Terms

form	PERL	JavaScript	CGI
client-side processing	form element	ASP	compiled
server-side processing	portable code	client	Jscript
interpreted	Java applet		

User input can be obtained from a web page using HTML forms. There are several types of form elements that can collect information in different ways. They are summed up below.

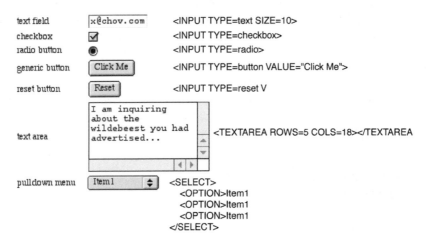

text field	`<INPUT TYPE=text SIZE=10>`
checkbox	`<INPUT TYPE=checkbox>`
radio button	`<INPUT TYPE=radio>`
generic button	`<INPUT TYPE=button VALUE="Click Me">`
reset button	`<INPUT TYPE=reset V`
text area	`<TEXTAREA ROWS=5 COLS=18></TEXTAREA`

pulldown menu	`<SELECT>`
	`<OPTION>Item1`
	`<OPTION>Item1`
	`<OPTION>Item1`
	`</SELECT>`

The *value* attributes of the generic and reset buttons specify the text that appears on the button. The *value* attribute can be used with the text field to cause text to be displayed in the field when the page is loaded. Instead, we supplied some text manually, after the page was loaded in a browser. Initial text can be displayed in a text area by including the text between the TEXTAREA start and end tags. Again, we have manually added text after the page is loaded. It is important to note that *all* form elements must be defined within the HTML

<FORM> . . . </FORM>

element.

Processing form data requires a programming language such as JavaScript. JavaScript is used to process form data on the client (the computer that has loaded the web page). We call this client-side processing. Since JavaScript code is transported to the client with the web page, it is called portable code.

More serious processing is done on the server, where databases to support the form are kept. We call this server-side processing. Currently, the most common programming language used for this is PERL. The standardization that handles submission of form data to web servers is called Common Gateway Interface (CGI). Thus, PERL programs written to handle form data are called CGI programs. In many situations where form data is to be collected, the processing involves the use of JavaScript on the client and a language like Perl on the server side.

JavaScript is different from Java. Java applets are programs that are embedded into web pages and have control only over the space into which they are embedded. JavaScript is not as powerful, but has much more access to components of the web page. The fact that JavaScript is interpreted, rather than compiled, makes it portable to any computer on the Internet that has a relatively current browser. This is one of the factors that has helped make the web interactive while remaining platform-independent.

Microsoft's answer to JavaScript is Jscript. The two are very similar. In fact, this book uses a common subset of JavaScript/Jscript. Microsoft's answer to CGI programming comes in the form of Active Server Pages (ASP), using Visual Basic on the server-side. Since UNIX/LINUX servers dominate the Web rather than Microsoft servers, ASP is not as prevalent as JavaScript and Perl for CGI.

9.8 REVIEW QUESTIONS

In most cases, it is not sufficient to answer these from the Lesson Summary.

1. Explain a difference between checkboxes and radio buttons.

2. Explain the steps that might occur when a "submit" button is clicked on a search engine page.

3. Explain the difference between an interpreted and a compiled programming language.

4. What do we mean by the terms "fat client" and "thin client"?

5. For about how long have the "Java" languages been around?

6. What does Microsoft call its Java environment? What does it call its version of JavaScript?

9.9 EXERCISES

1. Make an HTML form for an online retailer (e-tailer). It should have four text fields for users to enter their name, address, zip code, and e-mail address. A pulldown menu should be provided for users to chose their state of residence (just pick 10 states). The form should have radio buttons for users to choose from among several types of credit cards with which to pay. It should have a generic submit button and a reset button. A text area should be supplied for any additional comments and should initially contain the message "Additional comments."
Optional: Organize the form elements with a borderless HTML table.

9.10 PROJECT THREADS

Throughout the remainder of this book, you will be doing individual JavaScript homework exercises from each lesson. Each exercise will involve creating a new web page supported with JavaScript. Regardless of whether you have been working Thread A or B, you have a homework page. Your homework page is to contain a link to each new assignment. The following guidelines apply to any JavaScript

JavaScript assignments throughout the rest of this book are to go in that folder.

(b) The links to your JavaScript assignments in your homework page are to be organized in an HTML table. This table should be placed at the top of your homework page, before the links to your HTML assignments.

| Put a description here that indicates what the page behind the link does. | JS Assignment #1 |
| Put a description here that indicates what the page behind the link does. | JS Assignment #2 |

assignments that you do throughout the rest of this book.
(a) Create a new folder and name it "javascript". Put it in the same directory as your homework page. All of your

(c) Each JavaScript assignment should have a link back to your homework page. The links should appear at the very top of the assignment page.

PROCESSING USER INPUT

WITH ALL of the discussion about HTML forms in Lesson 9, you are probably ready to create some fancy interactive web pages. However, JavaScript programming (or any programming) is significantly more difficult than HTML markup. In fact, most programmers don't consider writing HTML code to be programming at all. Even processing a pizza order form similar to the one of Figure 9.1 requires significant programming skill. Several programming lessons are necessary to provide that foundation. So, in the meantime, we must depart from discussing HTML forms and focus on some JavaScript basics. By Lesson 13, the proper fundamentals will be in place, and we will apply what we learn in Lessons 10–12 to processing input from HTML forms.

10.1 USING JAVASCRIPT TO GENERATE HTML

JavaScript code is included in an HTML document using the HTML SCRIPT element.

<SCRIPT>

JavaScript statements...

</SCRIPT>

The SCRIPT tags enclose JavaScript code that, for the most part, will take the form of distinct statements. In almost any programming language, a statement is an instruction for the computer to execute. Much as a recipe is a set of instructions for a cook, a program is basically a series of instructions (statements) for the computer to follow. For example, the following is a very basic statement in JavaScript:

```
document.write("Hello!");
```

This statement is recognized by the JavaScript interpreter as meaning: Take the text string included between the quotes and write it to the HTML document. The semicolon at the end signifies the end of the statement. To see how the previous JavaScript statement can be executed within an HTML document, consider the HTML file in Figure 10.1 and its rendering in Figure 10.2.

There is no difference between the two words "Hello!" and "Goodbye!" in terms of their presentation in the browser window, although "Hello!" was produced using a JavaScript statement and "Goodbye!" was produced as ordinary text in the body of the

```
<HTML>
<HEAD></HEAD>
<BODY>

<SCRIPT LANGUAGE=JavaScript>
document.write("HELLO!");
</SCRIPT>

<BR>
GOODBYE!

</BODY>
</HTML>
```

FIGURE 10.1 An HTML file that executes a JavaScript statement.

```
Netscape:

 Back    Forward   Reload    Home        N

HELLO!
GOODBYE!
```

FIGURE 10.2 The rendering of the document of Figure 10.1.

HTML document. For practical purposes, one can produce the "Hello!" just as easily as the "Goodbye!" without any knowledge of JavaScript. However, as we shall see, the *document.write()* statement provides a means to echo input back to the user.

The *document.write()* statement can also be used to write HTML tags to the document. Figure 10.3 shows an HTML document that, except for the HTML, HEAD, and BODY tags, uses JavaScript to create the entire content of the web page. The document is rendered in Figure 10.4. In this case, the text string inside the *document.write()* statement contains HTML tags as well as ordinary text. As can be seen in Figure 10.4, the markup effect of the HTML tags is no different than if they were included in the document with no use of JavaScript at all. The HTML tags simply instruct the browser to render "Scooby Doo" in bold, followed by a line break, followed by "Where are you?" in plain text. Moreover, all of the text is to be centered.

One limitation of the *document.write()* statement has to do with line breaks. For example, the following makes use of two JavaScript statements:

```
<SCRIPT LANGUAGE=JavaScript>
document.write("Dear Scooby, ");
document.write("Were you able to elude the werewolf...");
</SCRIPT>
```

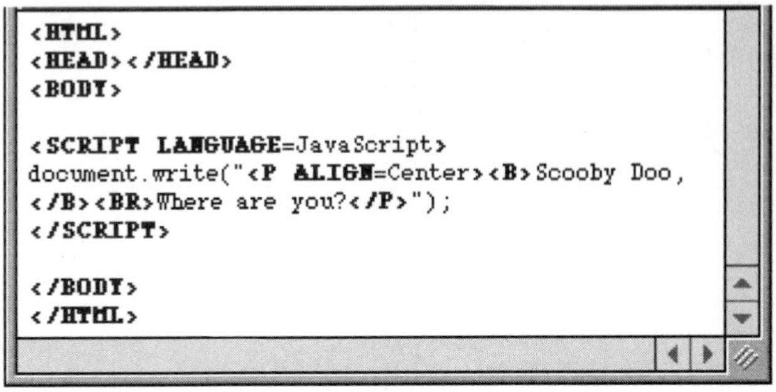

```
<HTML>
<HEAD></HEAD>
<BODY>

<SCRIPT LANGUAGE=JavaScript>
document.write("<P ALIGN=Center><B>Scooby Doo,
</B><BR>Where are you?</P>");
</SCRIPT>

</BODY>
</HTML>
```

FIGURE 10.3 An HTML document that generates a web page whose entire contents are created with a document.write() statement.

FIGURE 10.4 The rendering of the document of Figure 10.3.

Rather than showing the whole document, we included only the SCRIPT tags. Like HTML, JavaScript is read from the top down. The first statement executes, followed by the second. The result is

> Dear Scooby, Were you able to elude the werewolf . . .

being written to the HTML document and, subsequently, to the web page. Notice that the *document.write()* statement does not cause a line break. To write the same text to the document in the form

> Dear Scooby,
> Were you able to elude the werewolf . . .

requires

```
<SCRIPT LANGUAGE=JavaScript>
document.write("Dear Scooby, <BR>");
document.write("Were you able to elude the werewolf ...");
</SCRIPT>
```

where a line break is forced using the standard HTML BR element.

10.2 INTERPRETING JAVASCRIPT AND HTML

We have now seen examples of using JavaScript to include both text and HTML markup instructions into an HTML document. Indeed, the above examples use both HTML markup instructions included as normal in the document and those included by Javascript. Since JavaScript can produce HTML instructions, it is necessary that the JavaScript be interpreted first by the browser. Then, any resulting HTML is interpreted by the browser.

Think of the browser as having two different brains, one for HTML and one for JavaScript. When a web page is first loaded, the JavaScript brain (interpreter) takes over and reads all the JavaScript contained in the document. Then the HTML brain (interpreter) takes over and handles the necessary markup. Since there are various browser types and versions, there are slight variations and subtleties to this order of interpretation but, in principle, that's how it works.

Further to illustrate this point, consider Figure 10.3 again. As its name indicates, the *document.write( )* statement writes its contents to the actual HTML document, not the resulting web page. But this should be clear since the content of the statement contains HTML code that should not appear in the actual web page. When the page loads, the browser's JavaScript brain first executes the JavaScript. The result is that the contents of the *document.write( )* statement are written to the document. When the JavaScript brain is done and the HTML brain takes over, it sees only the results of the JavaScript, not the JavaScript statements themselves. So, in effect, after the JavaScript executes, the HTML brain sees

```
<HTML>
<HEAD></HEAD>
<BODY>
<P ALIGN=Center><B>Scooby Doo,</B><BR>Where are you?</P>
</BODY>
</HTML>
```

since the *document.write( )* statement has already done its job.

10.3 WHERE CAN JAVASCRIPT BE LOCATED?

The SCRIPT tags can be used in either the HEAD or the BODY sections of an HTML document. For example, Figure 10.5 shows an HTML document with some JavaScript in its head section as well as in the body section.

After the JavaScript interpreter is done, the HTML interpreter sees

```
<HTML>
<HEAD></HEAD>
<BODY>

<B>I'm first, man!</B>
OK, buddy. That's fine.<BR>
Last but not least.
</BODY>
</HTML>
```

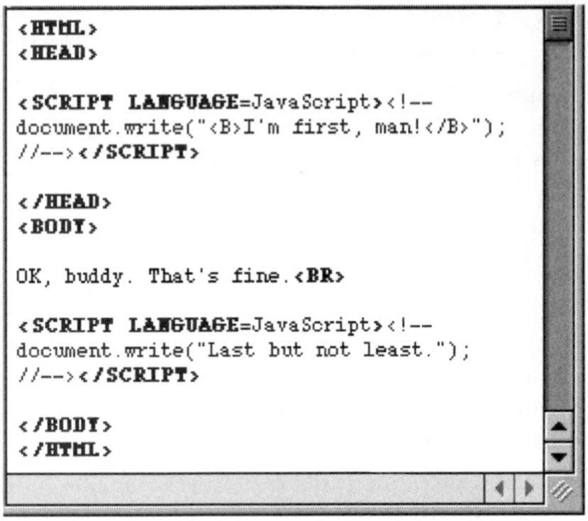

```
<HTML>
<HEAD>

<SCRIPT LANGUAGE=JavaScript><!--
document.write("<B>I'm first, man!</B>");
//--></SCRIPT>

</HEAD>
<BODY>

OK, buddy. That's fine.<BR>

<SCRIPT LANGUAGE=JavaScript><!--
document.write("Last but not least.");
//--></SCRIPT>

</BODY>
</HTML>
```

FIGURE 10.5 JavaScript statements can be defined in the HEAD section or the BODY section.

and the resulting markup in the web page generated by the document of Figure 10.5 is

I'm first, man!

OK, buddy. That's fine.

Last but not least.

The first thing to note is that the JavaScript statement in the HEAD section actually writes its contents into the BODY section of the document. Also, the JavaScript in the head section is written at the very top of the BODY section. This is not surprising since JavaScript is read from the top down and the *document.write()* statement in the HEAD section is interpreted first. However, the JavaScript in the BODY section takes its place according to where it is defined. Even though the JavaScript interpreter goes first, it knows not to violate the order of the code in the body section. So, "Last but not least" is written after "OK, buddy. That's fine.", since that's the original order of things.

One other note hardly worthy of comment is the fact that the JavaScript from the HEAD section is written followed by a line break and a blank line, even though no breaks were specified. This is one of those browser nuances, and really doesn't warrant further comment or thought on your part.

The strange symbols

<!--   //-->

that surround the JavaScript inside the SCRIPT tags in Figure 10.5 probably seem mysterious. Indeed, their purpose is not apparent from the context. This purpose is twofold. First, these symbols hide JavaScript statements from any browser that doesn't understand scripts. If an old browser can't understand the SCRIPT tags, it just ignores them, just as it does any other tags it doesn't recognize. However, JavaScript statements are not HTML tags and would not be ignored. The result would be that the actual JavaScript statements would be marked up as text in the web page. Clearly, that is not desirable. On the other hand, if you have no sympathy for people using old or text-only browsers, this is not a very compelling reason to use these symbols.

A more compelling reason involves the nature of the HEAD section itself. Remember, very few HTML elements can be defined inside the HEAD section. In particular, the <B> . . . </B> tags are not allowed in the HEAD section. Even though these boldface tags are used in a JavaScript statement, the HTML interpreter of some browsers will still "see" these tags in the HEAD section and revolt by failing to render the page properly, if at all. This is even true of some browsers that understand scripts. So, it is best to just get in the habit of using these symbols to hide JavaScript from the HTML brain of browsers.

> **N O T E**
> It is best at this point to make a JavaScript template and keep it handy. That way, each time you create a new web page replete with JavaScript, you can just open up the template, do a "save as", and type away. In fact, most of the JavaScript programs you will write will appear in the HEAD section of the HTML document. So a template with SCRIPT tags (and the symbols to hide the JavaScript from the HTML brain) in the head section should be sufficient. This is preferable to typing in the SCRIPT tags and symbols time after time. Even though most HTML editors will generate SCRIPT tags for you, a given editor may not put them in the head section, and also may not include the hiding symbols. A standard template which you can reuse is the way to go.

10.4 PROMPTING FOR AND STORING USER INPUT

It's finally time to get down to business and acquire some input from the user. Until we have the sophistication necessary to deal with HTML forms for user input, we will use the *prompt()* function. Figure 10.6 shows a prompt window. Of course, the appearance of this window will vary depending upon what type of computer you use, but the general effect is the same. The user, Bubba in this case, is to enter some information and then hit the OK button. The key question here is, what happens to the information that the user enters?

For that purpose we need to make use of a JavaScript **variable.** The best way to think of a variable is that it is a named memory location inside a computer. The statement necessary to create a variable is

```
var name;
```

which tells the computer "set up a memory location (variable) inside the computer and call it *name*." Think of the variable as a box inside the computer in which you can store

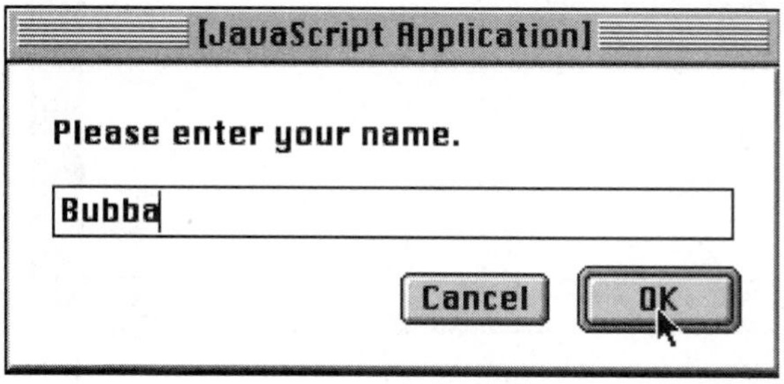

FIGURE 10.6 A prompt window that requests user input.

information and the name of the variable as a label put on the box. A perfect analogy is a box you place in a closet that you will use to store an item and retrieve it later. It is natural to write a name on the box for identification purposes. The name of a variable serves in much the same way: it is used to allocate the memory location so that its contents can be retrieved.

Once the variable has been declared, the statement necessary to prompt the user for information takes the form

```
name=prompt("Please enter your name.","");
```

which tells the computer to "prompt the user to enter a name, and then put the results into the variable *name*". Figure 10.7 depicts this process. We have already termed the act of creating a variable as **declaring the variable.** The act of putting data into the variable is called **initializing the variable.**

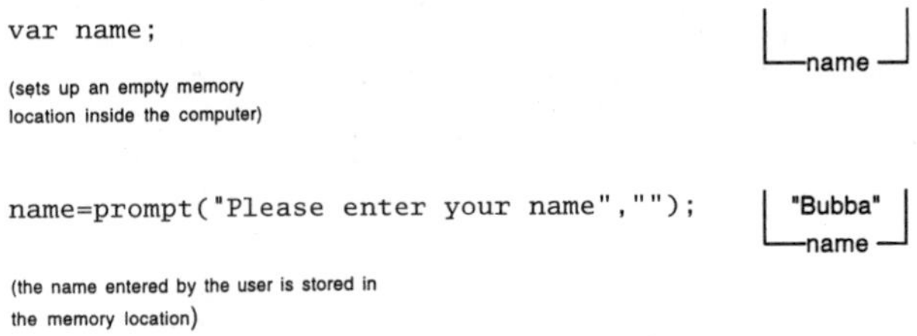

```
var name;
```
(sets up an empty memory
location inside the computer)

└─name─┘

```
name=prompt("Please enter your name","");
```
(the name entered by the user is stored in
the memory location)

"Bubba"
└─name─┘

FIGURE 10.7 Creating a variable and storing user input in the variable.

Now that we have stored the information entered by the user in the variable, all that is required to retrieve the information is to call the variable by name. The statement

document.write(name);

says to the computer, "get the contents of the variable *name* and write these contents to the HTML document." Note that the name of the variable is not surrounded by quotes. You *never* refer to a variable by using quotes. But more on that later. To put all this together, Figure 10.8 shows the file containing our first interactive web page—albeit minimal. This document puts the ideas of the above discussion together into an actual program.

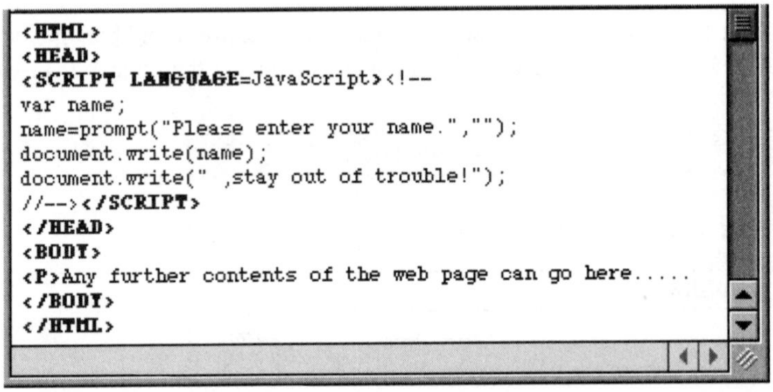

```
<HTML>
<HEAD>
<SCRIPT LANGUAGE=JavaScript><!--
var name;
name=prompt("Please enter your name.","");
document.write(name);
document.write(" ,stay out of trouble!");
//--></SCRIPT>
</HEAD>
<BODY>
<P>Any further contents of the web page can go here.....
</BODY>
</HTML>
```

FIGURE 10.8 An interactive web page that prompts the user for a name and then gives the user a personalized message.

Let's briefly summarize the sequence of events that occurs when Bubba loads this file into his browser. The JavaScript executes, setting up the *name* variable, although Bubba has no perception of this. The first thing Bubba sees when he loads the page is the prompt window. When he enters Bubba and hits OK, as in Figure 10.6, the final two JavaScript statements execute. Almost immediately, Bubba sees the resulting web page, which contains the following:

> Bubba, stay out of trouble!
> Any further contents of the web page can go here.....

Before we conclude this section with a brief discussion about the *prompt( )* function itself, we wish to emphasize the **top-down logic** of the program:

-Define a variable to store the input

-Prompt for the input

-Output a message using the stored input

Always remember, JavaScript is read from the top down, and thus you must write the program following top-down logic. In this case, the logic is simple, but that is not always the case. The order of the JavaScript statements is very important. For example, you can't give the personalized message until you have obtained the user's input.

The *prompt( )* function itself might seem a little strange. Two sets of quotes are used and, in the above example, we have left the second pair empty. Here's how the statement works.

```
prompt("this text appears as instructions on the prompt
    window", "any text here would actually be placed as
    the initial contents of the data entry field");
```

In Figure 10.8, we chose to leave the contents of the second pair of quotes empty so that the data entry field would initially be empty. That is, when Bubba first loaded the web page and saw the prompt window, the field into which he entered his name was empty. He then entered his name.

10.5   USING VARIABLES TO PROCESS INFORMATION

Not every variable is declared in order to store user input. You can also create variables to help you process the information that the user has entered. For example, we wish to write a program that requests the user's age and then converts that age into the equivalent in dog years. The convention is that every human year is equivalent to seven dog years. Of course, we will have to store the age that the user enters into a variable. But then we have to calculate the equivalent age in dog years. To store this new information, we define another variable. The top-down logic is as follows:

-declare a variable to store the age

-prompt for the user's age

-declare a variable to store the dog age

-calculate the dog age and store it in this second variable

-write the results using the information stored in the two variables

```
<HTML>
<HEAD>
<SCRIPT LANGUAGE=JavaScript><!--
var age;
age=prompt("Please enter your age.","");
var dogage;
dogage=age*7;
document.write("You may be ");
document.write(age);
document.write(" years old but, if you were a dog, you would be ");
document.write(dogage);
document.write(" years old!");
//--></SCRIPT>
</HEAD>
<BODY>
</BODY>
</HTML>
```

FIGURE 10.9 An interactive web page that prompts the user for an age and then uses a second variable to convert that age into dog years.

The program that implements this logic is displayed in Figure 10.9. Once again, the entire program is contained in the HEAD section. It could be in the BODY, but for reasons you will understand later, we choose to put it in the HEAD of the document.

The act of prompting for the age and storing it into the *age* variable is familiar, so we won't discuss that further. The next two statements, however, warrant discussion. Let's suppose that the user has entered 45 into the prompt box. What happens next is depicted in Figure 10.10.

After this, some output is generated using several *document.write()* statements. Since both the person's age and his or her age in dog years are stored in variables, the output

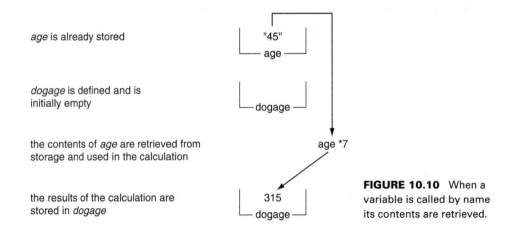

age is already stored

"45"
── age ──

dogage is defined and is initially empty

└ dogage ┘

the contents of *age* are retrieved from storage and used in the calculation

age *7

the results of the calculation are stored in *dogage*

315
└ dogage ┘

FIGURE 10.10 When a variable is called by name its contents are retrieved.

statements can retrieve both pieces of information. Note that the contents of *age* were retrieved twice, once for the calculation and once for the output. Such is the nature of variables. Once you have information stored, you can retrieve it as often as you like. If the user enters 45, the resulting web page would contain.

You may be 45 years old but, if you were a dog, you would be 315 years old!

The user never perceives the variables working behind the scenes. Rather, the user sees the retrieved contents of the variables accessed by calling them by name in the *document.write()* statements.

> **NOTE** Calculations using variables can make use of the standard arithmetic operations: addition, subtraction, multiplication, and division. The symbols for these operations should come as no surprise:
>
>   + addition
>
>   − subtraction
>
>   * multiplication
>
>   / division

When more advanced types of operations are required to process information, these arithmetic operations can also be employed. For example, if you wish to raise a number to the third power, use multiplication as follows:

```
var num;
num=prompt("Enter a number to be cubed.","");
var numcubed;
numcubed=num*num*num;
```

So, if the user enters "2", the variable *numcubed* would be assigned the value of 8. Many beginning programmers find this restrictive. Why such a crude method to cube a number when my calculator has built-in ways to accomplish the same task? Well, programming is all about telling the computer *exactly* what to do. You might be surprised to know that your calculator computes powers of numbers in a manner similar to the above.

10.6 VARIABLE NAMES

Since variables are named memory locations in which to store and retrieve information, some consideration needs to be made of the names that are given to variables. In the above examples, the variables that were created had names indicative of the purposes (*name, age, dogage*) for which they would be used. In general, you should adopt this practice. In simple programs like those above, if the variables were simply named *x* or *y*, little confusion would arise. However, in longer programs where numerous variables are employed for various purposes, descriptive variable names make programs much easier to understand, and thus errors and other problems can be detected more easily. This will become apparent as we progress through subsequent lessons.

There are specific rules in JavaScript governing the names of variables. Variable names can be composed of letters, the digits 0...9, and the underscore "_". They can't, however, begin with a number. For example, the following are valid variable declarations:

```
var total1;
var total2;
var grand_total;
var dog_age;
```

The first three would be fine descriptive names for variables in a program that calculates some preliminary totals and then a final total for a customer's bill, for example. The underscore is ideal for providing spaces in multiword names; *grand_total* and *dog_age* would be preferable to some programmers to *grandtotal* or *dogage*. We concede that *dogage* sounds a bit strange (e.g., a man is walking his dog when a passerby comments "That's some fine dogage you have there!").

The following are not valid variable declarations and would result in errors when loading the program that contains them into a browser:

```
var grand total;              (OOPS!)
var 1total                    (OOPS!)
var sum&total;                (OOPS!)
```

Spaces, beginning numeric digits, and non-letter characters are not allowed. In addition, unlike HTML tags, variable names are case-sensitive. That is,

```
var Total;
var total;
```

would declare two distinct variables. One last pitfall involves the use of certain words that are reserved for other uses by JavaScript. For example,

```
var var;
```

yields an error since "var" is a word already utilized in JavaScript. A list of common reserved words is provided in Appendix B.

10.7 VARIABLE TYPES

OK, so variables are named storage locations, and there are rules that govern how we can name the variables. But what types of information can we store in variables? The answer might seem simple: the information that the user enters, or perhaps the result of a calculation. That is true, but that matter is not that simple. The values that variables contain are often called **literals.** Using this terminology, variables are flexible memory locations that can store different types of literal values. The two literal value types we discuss in this section are **numeric literals** and **string literals.** The term "literal" will gain further relevance in future lessons. In the meantime, we will frequently refer to the two literal types as simply **numbers** and **strings.**

We first discuss strings. Think of the term "string" as meaning character string. A string is basically just a group of characters you can produce with your keyboard. A string might be meaningful or just gibberish. These four strings illustrate this:

"hello there"

"*jhft%$cd0qˆub   nf'q92834r*&6"

" years old!"

"45"

Strings must be defined with quotes "", so that the exact set of characters comprising the string is well defined. For example, consider the string " years old!" that was used in Figure 10.9. This string begins with a blank space (made with the space bar on the keyboard). So the actual string contains 11 characters, including the initial space and the space between the words. Without the defining quotation marks, there would be no way to define the initial space at its beginning. For another example, how many characters are in the following string?

xyz pdq

It's not apparent. Maybe the string is "xyz pdq", or perhaps "   xyz pdq   ", which is a much longer string given all of the extra spaces. You can see further evidence of including extra spaces in strings in Figure 10.9. Without the extra spaces, the retrieved contents of the variables would butt right up against the other words of the sentence when marked up in the web page:

You may be45years old but, if you were a dog, you would be315years old!

It's not that such spacing issues are a big deal, but they certainly help motivate the necessity for defining character strings with quotation marks.

Variables can also contain numbers. Looking back to the list of four strings just above, you might be tempted to say that the string "45" is a number. This is quite a subtle distinction, but in terms of the way computers store information, it is no more than a string with two characters. To illustrate this, we define two variables below and store different types of literals in them. The variable x is declared and initialized to contain the *number* 45, and the variable y is declared and initialized to contain the *string* "45".

```
var x;           |    45    |
x=45;            |___ x ____|


var y;           |   "45"   |
y="45"           |___ y ____|
```

This is not going to make that much sense at the moment, but you will soon see the reason for it. For now, just realize that character strings are stored in variables using quotes, while numbers are stored just by themselves. The most simplistic reason for this distinction is that computers pass information around as strings of characters, but need a different numeric format in order to carry out calculations. We'll get back to this notion shortly.

To introduce yet more terminology, numeric literals come in two varieties, **integers** and **floating-point** numbers. Integers consist of the positive and negative "whole numbers":

$$\ldots, -5, -4, -3, -2, -1, 0, 1, 2, 3, 4, 5, \ldots$$

and floating-point is a fancy term for numbers with decimal places. Think of the "point" as meaning decimal point. For example, 3.14 is a floating-point number. Other than introducing the terminology, we again defer further discussion on this matter.

To motivate yet one more term, we return to strings. Recall the discussion of the client-server model in Section 9.2. In particular, we discussed the notion of sending information from a client to a web server for processing. When information is passed between computers in this fashion, it is passed as a character string. Refer back to the note at the end of Section 9.2 where we mentioned how a search-engine query (on the Dogpile search engine) for "heavy metal" gets sent back to the server. In particular, we mentioned that the query *string* on the end of the URL is delivered to the server. The web server receives the long string

"q=heavy+metal&geo=no&fs=web"

and parses the string into the specific pieces of information that it contains. To **parse** a string means to chop it up and convert it into smaller or more useful pieces of information. To summarize this, the information from the HTML form is gathered into a long character string, passed to the server, and then parsed to extract the smaller chunks of information that it contains. It contains the query for "heavy metal," the instruction not to limit the search geographically, and the instruction to look for web pages (rather than newsgroups, for example). The & symbols in the query string are markers separating the three different chunks of information. This facilitates the parsing process.

10.8   CONCATENATION OF STRINGS

Before returning to discussing the difference between numeric literals and string literals, we explain the concatenation operation on strings. To **concatenate** means to join together. Although the plus sign + is obviously used to add numbers, it carries a different significance when used with strings. Consider the following variable declaration and initialization:

```
var dog;
```

— dog —

```
dog="Scooby "+"Doo";
```

"Scooby Doo"
— dog —

The *dog* variable is assigned the string "Scooby Doo" which is the concatenation of the two smaller strings "Scooby " and "Doo". The concatenation operator + has basically fused the two smaller strings together into one string. Notice the extra space defined at the end of the "Scooby " string. Without this space, the result of the concatenation would be "ScoobyDoo".

The assignment

dog="Scooby"+" "+"Doo";

would also cause *dog* to contain "Scooby Doo". Here we have concatenated three strings, the middle one being a string consisting of only one white space.

Since calling upon a variable by name results in the contents of the variable being retrieved, the following variable assignments cause *dog* to contain the string "ScoobyDoo":

```
var first;
first="Scooby";
var last;
last="Doo";
dog=first+last;
```

If we had wished to put the extra space back in the middle to obtain "Scooby Doo", we could have assigned

```
dog=first+" "+last
```

10.9 VARIABLE ASSIGNMENT

One term we used repetitively in the previous section is "assign." In particular, we assigned some strings to variables. Variable assignment is accomplished with the = sign. Indeed, we have been using the = sign to store values into variables for several sections. In JavaScript, = does *not* mean equals. In the simplest case, such as

```
var x;
x=10;
```

the first statement obviously creates a variable named *x*. However, the second statement does *not* assert equality between *x* and the number 10. Remember, *x* is the name of a storage location. The statement says, "take the number 10 and store it in the variable location named *x*." But that is a simple instance. In general, the assignment operator = does the following:

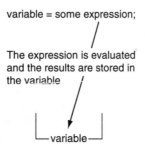

The type of expression can have numerous forms. Reconsider the assignment statements of Figure 10.9:

```
age=prompt("Please enter your age.","");
dogage=age*7;
```

The second assignment is depicted in Figure 10.10. It does not assert that "*dogage* equals age*7", but rather that the expression *age**7 should be evaluated and stored in the variable named *dogage*. Note that the contents of *age* are not changed. The number stored in *age* is merely retrieved so that the expression can be evaluated. In the first assignment in Figure 10.9, the expression on the right of the assignment operator does not involve a calculation. Rather, when the computer evaluates the prompt function, it stores the user's input into the variable *age*.

The type of expression on the right of an assignment operator can be quite complicated, such as

```
var x;
x=((23*11)+19)/10;
```

which causes the variable *x* to contain the floating-point number 27.2, or can be trivial, such as

```
var y;
y=27.2;
```

which simply puts the number 27.2 into the variable *y*. Moreover, we have seen that the expression can contain other variables whose contents are retrieved and used in the calculation. To emphasize that variables used in the expression side of variable assignment are not changed, consider the following code:

```
var x;
var y;
y=10;
x=11;
y=x;
```

The result of these five lines of code is that both the variables *x* and *y* contain the number 11. The assignment y=x takes the value from *x* and stores it in *y*. The value of *x* is not changed, but merely retrieved for the assignment.

To emphasize in a compelling manner that the assignment operator is not an assertion of equality, consider the statements

```
var z;
z=2;
z=z+1;
```

Without knowing that the last statement enacts variable assignment, an algebra teacher would cringe. Indeed, to solve the equation z=z+1 using algebra, you would subtract variable *z* from each side of the equation, leaving the simplified version 0=1, which is absurd. (If 0 equals 1, the very fabric of the universe unravels!)

Now, let's interpret the three statements as the JavaScript interpreter would. In fact, let's speak as the interpreter. We set up an empty variable location named *z* and then put the number 2 into *z*. We then encounter the third statement and evaluate the expression on the right. Since *z* contains 2, the calculation results in the number 3. We then assign this result to *z*. The end result is that *z* contains the number 3, and the number 2 is gone.

10.10 PARSING USER INPUT

In Section 10.7, we hinted at the fact that computers pass around information in the form of strings. In fact, we motivated the term "parse" by using the example of passing a string of information to a web server for processing. Even in the local setting information is passed as strings. For example, the *prompt( )* function *always* assigns the user's input to a variable in the form of a string.

In the program of Figure 10.8, the variable *name* was assigned the string "Bubba". Although it didn't carry any significance at the time, Figure 10.7 depicts the input as a string when it is stored in the variable. But if user input is always stored as strings, how about the number 45 that the user entered in the program of Figure 10.9? You can see from the depiction in Figure 10.10 that we did indicate that the user's input was stored as the string "45" rather than the number 45. Thus, the calculation actually consisted of multiplying the string "45" by the number 7. Now, computers use numbers rather than strings in calculations, so the JavaScript interpreter quickly parsed the string "45" into the number 45 before doing the calculation:

$$\text{"45" * 7} = ? \text{ (makes no sense)} \quad \text{—parse} \rightarrow \quad 45 * 7 = 315$$

In this context, the term "parse" means that it converted the string into a number. So, given both contexts in which we have used the term parse, it can mean to chop up a string into smaller, more useful, pieces or simply to convert the string to a number. Either way, parsing is a means to extract usable information from a character string.

You are probably thinking, "Isn't this getting a little nitpicky?" Well, no! Welcome to programming a computer. To see why this actually is a big issue, consider an interactive program that is to acquire two numbers from the user and find their average. The top-down logic of the program is as follows:

-declare a variable for the first number (num1)

-prompt for the first number

-declare a variable for the second number (num2)

-prompt for the second number

-declare a variable to store the average (avg)

-calculate the average: avg = (num1+num2)/2

-output the results to the user

Let's depict the sequence of events by supposing that the user enters the two numbers 50 and 100 into the two prompt boxes:

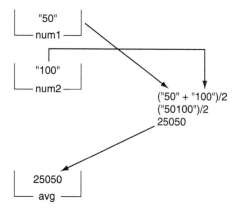

All prompt information is stored as strings. When the string values that the user enters are retrieved for the calculation, the computer is confronted with ("50"+"100") as part of the calculation. Thus, it concatenates the two strings into the string "50100". When confronted with "50100"/2, the computer quickly parses the string into a number and finishes the calculation 50100/2, which yields 25050.

So you see, this program does not work as planned. The average of the two numbers clearly should be 75. This really serves to drive home an understanding that strings and numbers are different beasts. The primary way that JavaScript passes around user input is in string format. When left with no alternative like "50100"/2, the Javascript brain is smart enough to parse the string "50100" into a number. When confronted with "50"+"100", however, it does the natural thing and concatenates the two strings.

When numeric input is acquired from the user, we recommend that you *always* parse it into a number. As we have seen, JavaScript may or may not be smart enough to do so for you. To accomplish this, use the *parseFloat()* function. This function parses a string into a floating-point number. Consider the following three statements:

```
var num1;
num1=prompt("Please enter the first number you wish to
      average.","");
num1=parseFloat(num1);
```

We are familiar with the first two. For example, if the user types 50 into the prompt box, the string "50" is stored in *num1*. Of course, since the third statement is variable assignment,

```
<HTML>
<HEAD>
<SCRIPT LANGUAGE=JavaScript><!--

var num1;
num1=prompt("Please enter the first number.","");
num1=parseFloat(num1);

var num2;
num2=prompt("Please enter the second number.","");
num2=parseFloat(num2);

var avg;
avg=(num1+num2)/2;
document.write("The average of ");
document.write(num1);
document.write(" and ");
document.write(num2);
document.write(" is ");
document.write(avg);
document.write(".");

//--></SCRIPT>
</HEAD>
<BODY>
</BODY>
</HTML>
```

FIGURE 10.11 An interactive program that averages two numbers entered by the user.

the expression on the right is evaluated. What happens is that the current content of *num1*, namely "50", is parsed into the number 50. Completing the variable assignment statement, this value is then placed into the variable *num1*. So the third statement just serves to replace the content of *num1* with its numeric equivalent. (The name indicates that the string should be parsed into a floating-point number but, in this case, since 50 does not require a decimal point, it is not given one. In other words, JavaScript would rather use 50 than 50.0.)

We now provide a version of the average program that actually works. Rather than reiterating the top-down logic for the program, we simply parse each piece of user input after it is obtained. The program appears in Figure 10.11. The reader is encouraged to go to the web site and experiment with both versions of this program.

NOTE
In Figure 10.9, we wanted numeric input from the user (an age), but didn't parse that input into a number. In that case, we got away with it since the program still worked. However, if we were to rewrite that program now, we would parse the user input. In fact, you should get in the habit of always parsing any input that is to be numeric. Sometimes you can get away without parsing, but if you always parse numeric input, you never have to worry. Don't get carried away, though. If the user is to enter a name as in Figure 10.8, just leave that input in the form of a string. You would have no luck trying to parse a string like "Bubba" into a number.

10.11 STATEMENTS AND PUNCTUATION

We have covered most of the actual programming concepts that are to be introduced in this lesson. But we have not talked much about the actual **syntax** of JavaScript. The syntax of a programming language refers to how the various symbols must be used (semicolons, quotes, periods, etc.) and to the structure of the statements themselves. The top-down logic for the programs we have written so far is not difficult to understand. Indeed, you will find that devising the logic for the homework programs presented at the end of this lesson is not overly difficult. However, when you sit down to write your first program, the syntax may appear mind-boggling. If even one semicolon or period is missing or out of place, the program will not work as intended or will not work at all. An explanation of some of the reasons behind the various syntax issues will certainly help things make more sense.

A JavaScript statement is a specific instruction that the computer is to follow. A semicolon tells the JavaScript interpreter that you are terminating the instruction. For example,

```
var x x=3;
```

would confuse the interpreter, causing neither statement to be carried out. In contrast,

```
var x; x=3;
```

provides two distinct instructions to the computer. We put both of these statements on the same line for illustrative purposes. But in practice, you should keep statements on separate lines for your own benefit. If you don't, as the programs you write get longer, you will have a jumbled mess. Even the program of Figure 10.11 would be pretty difficult for the human reader if the statements were not kept on different lines.

If you can't talk a statement through as a complete sentence, it is probably not a statement. For example, the three statements we have used so far, together with their English equivalents, are

> var x; (Set up an empty variable named x.)
>
> x=55; (Put the number 55 into x.)
>
> x=x+5; (Evaluate x+5 and put the result into x.)

The subject of each sentence is an understood "You", as in "You (the computer) do this for me." In contrast, the following are not statements:

> x;
>
> x+6;

Suppose the variable x contains the number 5. Then an instruction like "x;" is no more than telling the computer to

> 5;

which is meaningless. (On the street, you might have luck telling someone to "give me 5", but if you just go up to someone and say "Hey buddy, 5" you will no doubt get a strange reaction.) Similarly, the line x+6 is meaningless. To add 6 to the variable x would require

> x=x+6;

Some of the statements we have used make use of parentheses (). Now, you can use parentheses much as you would in a calculator to group arithmetic operations. For example, the expression $(1+2)*3$ is different from $1+2*3$, which uses the natural precedence of multiplication over addition. However, when you see parentheses on the end of a word in JavaScript, you are likely dealing with a **function.** Examples so far are *document.write()*, *prompt()*, and *parseFloat()*. Whether you noticed or not, we have already slipped the term function into the previous sections at various places when we referred to these "words" with parentheses. Think of a function as a built-in JavaScript utility that you can call upon to do something for you. The purpose of the parentheses is so that you can send information to the function. For example, the *document.write()* function needs the information that you wish to be written to the HTML document. The information you send to a function is called the **argument** of the function. The *document.write()* function takes a string as its argument and stands alone as a statement:

> document.write("hello");

Functions like *document.write()* that can stand alone as statements are called **procedure functions;** they carry out some procedure for you.

The *prompt()* and *parseFloat()* functions can't stand alone as statements. They are called **value functions** because they return a value when called upon. The *parseFloat()* function takes a string as its argument and returns the numeric equivalent of the string. For example,

> parseFloat("123");

is *not* a JavaScript statement because, upon returning its value, it is equivalent to

> 123;

which is not an instruction to the computer. The *prompt()* function is also a value function. It takes two strings separated by a comma (one for the instructions and one for initial content of the text entry field) as its arguments and returns what the user has entered. So the line of code

```
prompt("Enter your favorite animal name.", "");
```

is equivalent to

```
"wildebeest";
```

which is *not* a statement. (Of course, this presumes that the user entered "wildebeest".) You can see from the example programs in this lesson that, when we called upon a value function, the returned value was always assigned to a variable for storage. At this point in our exploration of JavaScript, there is no other alternative since value functions can't stand alone as statements.

10.12 ERRORS

By an **error** in a JavaScript program we mean something that will cause the program not to work as planned or not to work at all. Errors come in three flavors: **syntax errors, logic errors,** and **user errors.** A syntax error arises when you don't type in the JavaScript code correctly. Good examples include forgetting a quote symbol:

```
document.write("hello there);
```

forgetting to supply the required number of arguments for a function:

```
birthday=prompt("Please enter your birthday.");
```

or forgetting to terminate a statement with a semicolon. Another common syntax error involves cases. For example, trying to call the *parsefloat()* function will not work since the function's name is *parseFloat()*. Also recall that variable names are case-sensitive.

If you load a program that contains syntax errors into your browser, it simply may not work. For example, a prompt box might fail to appear, or text may not be written to the HTML document where it is supposed to be. Often, a syntax error will cause absolutely nothing to happen when you load the program into the browser. Finding syntax errors sometimes can be brutal. Sometimes it takes longer to **debug** (fix errors in) a program than to write it in the first place. But such is the nature of programming. Some browsers have features that help by pointing out JavaScript syntax errors, but this is inconsistent among browser types and versions. See the website for further information.

Logic errors involve writing JavaScript code in which the top-down logic does not accomplish what it is supposed to. Until we write more complicated programs, examples are hard to come by, but a simple example is an incorrect calculation such as trying to compute the average of two numbers with the statement

```
avg=50+100/2;
```

which results in *avg* containing the number 100, rather than the desired 75, since no grouping parentheses were supplied. A key to avoiding logic errors is carefully planning out the top-down logic of a program before you even sit down at the computer to write the program. That way, the logic is in place and all you have to worry about is the syntax. A common wise saying goes as follows: "The sooner you sit down at the computer, the longer it will take you to write the program." This statement might seem a bit convoluted, but it often holds true. A careful plan makes the actual code writing less cumbersome.

The third type of error, user errors, involves the user entering the wrong type of information. In time, we will learn some verification techniques to help alleviate this problem. But in the meantime, there is simply nothing that can be done to prevent such errors. For an example, refer back to the dog age program of Figure 10.9. Suppose some wise guy loads that program into a browser and enters his name, rather than his age, into the prompt window. The result would be that a string of text, "inglebert" for example, is stored in the variable *age*.

NOTE

The fact that the variable is named *age* has little significance to the computer. The descriptive variable name is for the benefit of the programmer. All the computer knows is that it has set up a variable and its name is *age*. That is, the computer has no clue that you intend to have a number entered into the variable, or that the number is to correspond to a person's age. Descriptive variable names are only for humans. It is crucial to remember that the computer never interprets your intentions, it just follows instructions!

With the text string "inglebert" stored in *age*, the dog age calculation becomes

```
dogage="inglebert"*7;
```

which is meaningless. Actually, what happens in this case is that the variable *dogage* is assigned the value NaN (Not a Number). So Inglebert would get the output message

You may be inglebert years old but, if you were a dog, you would be NaN years old!

The value NaN, which is technically neither a number nor a string, is JavaScript's default when it doesn't know what literal type is being assigned to a variable. This is a better alternative than causing an error. Note that trying to *parseFloat()* a string that is inherently a non-number also results in NaN. The following causes *x* to contain NaN:

```
x=parseFloat("oops");
```

10.13 FLEXIBILITY

The logical top-down flow of programming is somewhat flexible. In other words, there is usually more than one way to write a program. We demonstrate this with a program somewhat more complicated than we have seen thus far. The user is to enter a name and then a phone number. The user will then be prompted to order some quantity of XL t-shirts at $20 apiece. Similarly, the user will then be prompted to buy some large shirts at $17 apiece and some medium shirts at $14 apiece. The program will then figure the total bill, including 6% sales tax. The user's order will then be summarized as output.

OK, that's five prompt boxes, one for each of the name and phone number, and one for each of the three t-shirt sizes. Then some calculations are in order, followed by some output. The required logic is not unlike the previous programs of this section, but we choose to organize the order of the statements a little differently from those of Figure 10.11, for example. Our top-down logic is as follows.

-declare all variables (name, phone, xlarge, large, medium, subtotal, tax, total)

-prompt for the user input

-parse the numeric input (only the numeric input)

-calculate the subtotal: subtotal=(20*xlarge)+(17*large)+(14*medium)

-calculate the tax: tax=subtotal*.06

-calculate the total: total=subtotal+tax

-output the results

Figures 10.12 and 10.13 show the JavaScript code for this program and the output of that code.

Due to the length of the program, the window has been scrolled down in Figure 10.12. Not all of the HTML tags are visible. Compared to the previous examples, this is a long program that might appear intimidating. But, given the top-down logic, the code is easily derived. With some copying and pasting, it wasn't overly cumbersome to write.

To show that there is flexibility when designing the logic for a given program, we offer a second version of the logic for the Knuckles' Shirt Shop program.

-declare a variable for the name (name)

-prompt the user for the name

-declare a variable for the phone number (phone)

-prompt the user for the phone number

-declare a variable for the number of extra large (xlarge)

-prompt the user for the number of extra large

-parse xlarge into a number

-declare a variable for the number of large (large)

-prompt the user for the number of large

-parse large into a number

-declare a variable for the number of medium (medium)

-prompt the user for the number of medium

-parse large into a number

-calculate the subtotal: subtotal=(20*xlarge)+(17*large)+(14*medium)

-calculate the tax: tax=subtotal*.06

-calculate the total: total=subtotal+tax

-output the results

At first, the logic prior to the calculations appears substantially different from the first version. However, it accomplishes the same tasks; namely, it declares the necessary variables, initializes the variables with the user's input, and parses into numbers those variables

```
<HTML>
<HEAD>
<SCRIPT LANGUAGE=JavaScript><!--
var name;
var phone;
var xlarge;
var large;
var medium;
var subtotal;
var tax;
var total;

name=prompt("Please enter your name.","");
phone=prompt("Please enter your phone number.","");
xlarge=prompt("How many x-large t-shirts would you like to buy?
They are $20 each.","");
large=prompt("How many large t-shirts would you like to buy? They
are $17 each.","");
medium=prompt("How many medium t-shirts would you like to buy?
They are $14 each.","");

xlarge=parseFloat(xlarge);
large=parseFloat(large);
medium=parseFloat(medium);

subtotal=(20*xlarge)+(17*large)+(  *medium);
tax=subtotal*.06;
total=subtotal+tax;

document.write("Thank you for choosing Knuckles' shirt shop.
Here is a summary of your order.</P>");
document.write(name);
document.write("<BR>");
document.write(phone);
document.write("<P>");
document.write(xlarge);
document.write(" x-large at $20 apiece<BR>");
document.write(large);
document.write(" large at $17 apiece<BR>");
document.write(medium);
document.write(" medium at $14 apiece<P>");
document.write("Subtotal: $");
document.write(subtotal);
document.write("<BR>6% Tax: $");
document.write(tax);
document.write("<BR>Total: $");
document.write(total);
//--></SCRIPT>
</HEAD>
```

FIGURE 10.12   The JavaScript code for the t-shirt program.

that will be used in the calculations. This approach is much like the one used in Figure 10.11 where each variable is dealt with separately. In contrast, the first version declares all the variables, then initializes them with user input, and finally parses the necessary ones. You should take time and convince yourself that the two versions of the logic are equivalent.

So, if both versions produce the same results, which way is preferable? The answer is that most programmers prefer the first version, the version whose code appears in

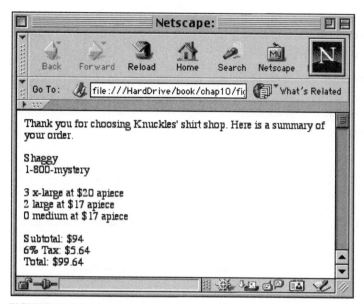

FIGURE 10.13 The output generated by Figure 10.12 with some user input.

Figure 10.12. It is customary to declare all variables at the top of a program. That way, it is easy to tell at a glance which variables are to be used in the program. Otherwise variable declarations are scattered throughout the body of the program and errors are more difficult to detect. You certainly don't have to declare variables right before you use them. Once declared at the top, you can initialize a variable any time you like.

But don't get carried away with the inherent flexibility afforded you when designing the logic of a program. It is certainly possible to design a program using faulty logic. For example, it makes no sense to try to parse the number of large shirts into a number before the user has entered the desired number of large shirts or to try to do the calculations before the necessary input has been obtained from the user. For another example, you can't reverse the order of the first two steps in the calculations

-calculate the tax: tax=subtotal*.06

-calculate the subtotal: subtotal=(20*xlarge)+(17*large)+(14*medium)

since that would attempt to use the value stored in *subtotal* to calculate the tax, but before *subtotal* has been initialized with a value.

NOTE

It is crucial to note that some of the statements in Figure 10.12 are long enough to have wrapped around in the window of our HTML editor. That causes no problem. But the key is that they wrapped around automatically, we didn't hit return on the keyboard to go to a new line. If you hit return in the middle of a JavaScript statement, you will effectively cut the statement in half, often causing an error to occur when you run the program. Hit return only after you have finished a statement.

10.14 SUMMARY

Key Terms

variable	syntax error	assignment	parse
integer	debug	procedure function	function
concatenate	string literal	logic error	value function
argument	floating point	numeric literal	user error

Any JavaScript code that appears in a web page must be included as content of the HTML <SCRIPT>...</SCRIPT> container element. Moreover, the language must be specified by the LANGUAGE attribute of the SCRIPT element. It is recommended that you use the <!--   //--> construct so that any JavaScript code in the HEAD section is hidden from the HTML interpreter. Thus, to save typing, it is advisable to keep a template file around that contains

<SCRIPT LANGUAGE="JavaScript"><!--

//--></SCRIPT>

in the HEAD section.

JavaScript code consists of statements, which are instructions for the computer to follow. Statements are used to declare variables, assign values to variables, and to send output back to the user. When a variable is declared, an empty, named storage location is set up inside the computer. Values are assigned to (stored in) variables using the assignment operator, =, which does not assert equality. The expression on the right of the assignment operator is first evaluated, and then the result is placed into the variable on the left of the assignment operator. The values that can be stored in variables are called literals, two varieties of which are numbers and strings. Strings are defined with quotation marks. Basically, computers pass information around in the form of strings, but need a distinct numeric format for doing calculations. The numeric variety of literal has two flavors: floating-point (with decimals) and integers (whole numbers). If decimal places are not required to represent the number, JavaScript defaults to the integer format.

One way to store information in a variable is by direct assignment, x=5 for example. Another way is to assign the result of a calculation to the variable. A third way is to acquire the information from the user using the *prompt()* function. But the *prompt()* function always returns the user's input as a string. So, if numeric information is sought from the user, you should always use the *parseFloat()* function to convert it into numeric format. In general, parsing a string means extracting information from a string, usually by chopping it into smaller pieces. However, for our present purposes, we just extract numeric information from a string. Concatenation uses the + sign to join two or more strings together. In a general sense, it is the opposite of parsing a string into smaller pieces.

Variables are essential for storing information, but we can make use of some JavaScript functions to aid in acquiring, converting, and outputting information. There are always brackets () after a function's name that are used to enclose the argument (or arguments) of the function. The argument of a function is the information you are sending to the function so that it can do its job. The *document.write()* function takes a string as its argument and causes that string to be written to the HTML document. Since it causes a procedure to be carried out, it is called a procedure function. Such a procedure function can stand alone as a JavaScript statement. The *prompt()* function takes two strings (separated by a comma) as arguments and returns the user's input. The *parseFloat()* function takes a string as its argument and returns the numeric equivalent of the string. Since these two functions return a value, they are called value functions. Value functions can't stand alone as JavaScript statements.

When confronted with the prospect of writing a program to accomplish some task, it is important first to construct the top-down logic for the program. JavaScript statements are interpreted from the top down. The top-down logic is thus the sequence of statements that you wish the computer to execute. Careful planning can help you avoid logic errors. Logic errors basically amount to giving the computer a list of instructions that don't accomplish the requisite task. Also, having a good plan before you sit down at the computer allows you to focus on writing the actual code. Writing JavaScript code is very nitpicky—you have to follow the syntax exactly. Syntax means all of the necessary formatting and punctuation. If even one " or . is missing, the program is likely not to work at all. The act of working errors out of a program is called debugging. Errors in programs are inevitable, even for highly skilled professional programmers.

10.15 REVIEW QUESTIONS

1. Name two reasons that it is advisable to use `<!--        //-->` to hide JavaScript from the HTML interpreter.

2. Give a simple algebraic example showing that the assignment operator can't be interpreted as an assertion of equality.

3. Discuss the rules for naming variables. Why use descriptive variable names?

4. Discuss the order in which HTML and JavaScript are interpreted. In particular, how does this relate to the *document.write()* function?

5. Discuss the nature of JavaScript statements. Why can't value functions stand alone as statements (give examples)?

6. Describe a possible user error and demonstrate that the outcome involves a third variable type (other than numbers or strings).

7. Debug the following JavaScript code:

```
var cool_word;
cool_word="lurk"
Document.write("The cool word of
  the day is ");
Document.write("cool_word");
```

8. Debug the following JavaScript code:

```
Var num1;
num1="15";
num1=num1*"2"
```

9. Debug the following JavaScript code:

```
var user-name;
user-name=prompt("Please enter
  your name");
document.write(Hello);
document.write(user-name);
```

10. Deduce the *exact* output of the following JavaScript statements:

```
var x;
var y;
y=15;
x="20";
y=x;
y=y+y;
document.write(y);
```

11. Deduce the *exact* output of the following JavaScript statements:

```
var s;
var t;
s=1;
s=s-10;
t=11;
t=t+s;
s=s*(-1);
document.write(s);
document.write("<BR>");
document.write(t);
```

12. Deduce the *exact* output of the following JavaScript statements. (There is potential debugging here, but give the results of the statements as they are written.)

```
var name;
var age;
name="Bert";
age=25;
document.write(name);
document.write("is <B>");
document.write("age");
document.write("</B>years old.");
```

10.16 EXERCISES

GENERAL

1. Write a program that prompts the user for a temperature in Fahrenheit and outputs the temperature in Celsius. (The conversion is C=(5/9)*(F-32).)

2. Write a program that prompts the user for the diameter of a circle. The program should output both the area of the circle and the circumference of the circle. (If r is the radius, then the area is given by πr^2 and the circumference is given by $2\pi r$. Use 3.14 for π.)

3. Write a program that prompts the user for the length of a side of a square. The program should output both the area of the square and the length of the perimeter of the square.

4. Write a program that prompts the user for the length of a side of a cube. The program should output both the area of the cube and the surface area of the cube.

5. Write a program that calculates simple interest. The program should prompt the user for a dollar amount (principal), a time period (in years), and an annual interest rate. The program should output both the amount of earned interest and the total accumulation (principal+ interest). (Simple interest is calculated by $I = prt$ (interest=principal*rate* time). For example, $100 invested for five years at 7.7% earns 100*.077*5 dollars in interest.)

6. Write a program that prompts the user for the scores (from 0 to 100) on three exams. The program should output the average of the three exam scores.

7. Make a version of the t-shirt program of Figure 10.12 that displays more information as output. Before you output the subtotal, tax, and total for all of the shirts, output the individual order totals (before tax) for each of the three sizes of shirts.

8. Write a program that simulates a pizza order. The program should prompt the user for a name and address. It should prompt the user for the desired number of pizzas (base price of $15 apiece). It should then prompt the user to enter the desired number of toppings ($1.50 apiece). Note that all of the pizzas will use this number of toppings. You should calculate the base total for the pizzas, the total of all the toppings, and the subtotal (pizzas + toppings). You should then calculate some sales tax and a total bill. The output should be well organized. Option: organize the output in an HTML table.

9. The first prompt box should ask for a name. The second prompt box should contain a personalized message asking the user how many years are left until retirement. A third personalized message should ask the user for the amount of his or her current savings. The program should echo back the user input and calculate the amount that the savings will grow to by retirement, using 8% simple interest (see Exercise 5). By "personalized message," we mean that the user's name should appear in the instructions in the second two prompt boxes. Hint: If x is a string variable, it can be concatenated in with the argument of the *prompt()* function. See Section 11.3.

10.17 PROJECT THREADS

Any exercises you do for this lesson should be referenced in your homework page following the guidelines outlined in Section 9.10.

MAKING DECISIONS

ESSON 10 provides the background necessary to use variables to store and process information. But one feature that was lacking was any type of decision-making process. The programs of Lesson 10 were able only to obtain input and do simple calculations. But most programming applications require some type of decision to be made based upon the user input: if the user enters something, the program should cause something to happen but, if he or she enters something else, it should cause something else to happen. Before charging straight into JavaScript's decision-making structures, though, some more programming fundamentals are in order.

11.1 BOOLEAN VARIABLES

So far in our exploration of JavaScript, variables can contain two types of literals, numbers and strings. Well, there is a third type, NaN, we have seen that is used when the result of a calculation doesn't make sense to the computer. Another literal type is the **Boolean literal,** which is named after the 19th-century British logician George Boole, who formalized many of the rules of symbolic logic. Unlike numbers and strings, which have an infinite number of potential values, Boolean literals take only two values,

true
false

So, for example,

```
var x;
x=false;
```

is valid, even though the value stored in *x* is neither a number nor a string. It's clearly not a number, but you may be thinking this is equivalent to x="false". It's not, however. The string "false" is just a meaningless character string as far as the computer is concerned.

The utility of Boolean variables comes in to play when we consider Boolean expressions. A **Boolean expression** evaluates to either true or false. The first type of Boolean expressions we consider make use of what we term as comparison operators. Although all of the symbols may not seem familiar, you have been using the actual comparison operations since you were a child. Often, these comparison operations are used to compare numbers, but they can be used to compare strings.

Operator	Operation
<	Less than
<=	Less than or equal to
>	Greater than
>=	Greater than or equal to
==	Equals
!=	Not equal to

Consider the following variable assignments. Assume that the variables have previously been declared. In fact, we will use numerous variables throughout this section without declaring them in an effort to make the examples more streamlined. When writing actual programs, you should always declare variables before using them.

```
x=(1<2);
y=(3.14>3.14);
z=(3.14>=3.14);
```

These assignments cause the variables x and z to contain true and the variable y to contain false. In each case, the expression on the right is a Boolean expression. You can see that these expressions are fundamentally different from those like (4.14−3.14) that result in a number, rather than a Boolean true or false. Note that Boolean expressions can also be more complicated. The statement

```
x=((8-3)>((17+3)/2));
```

causes x to contain false. In such cases, the grouping parentheses are very important because it's not clear how to evaluate $8 - 3 > 17 + 3/2$, or even if that makes sense.

Having discussed at length in Lesson 10 that the variable assignment symbol = does not assert equality, we merely point out that an assertion of equality uses the double ==. Rather than going into further discussion contrasting assignment with equality, we present some examples. In time, you will become accustomed to using a double equals sign for equality.

```
x=(1==2);
y=(3.14!=3.14);
z=((18/3)==(5+1));
```

The preceding statements cause the variables x and y to contain false and the variable z to contain true. It does look a bit funny at first to use three equal signs in one JavaScript statement. But, if you first focus on the expression and then assign the result to the variable, it's not so bad. Such statements (especially the third one) probably seem pointless, but the comparison operations are very useful in programming. Suppose that the user is prompted to enter a number into the variable *num*. Then the following code causes the variable *empty* to contain true if the user doesn't enter anything, or false if the user enters something into the prompt box:

$$empty=(num=="\ ");$$

So equality comparison can be used to test strings as well as numbers. The preceding statement simply checks to see if what the user enters is the empty string " ", in which case the user has left the text field of the prompt box blank.

You can also have a little fun with logic and use a variable *not_empty* in the opposite manner:

$$not\_empty=(x!="\ ");$$

If the user enters something, *not_empty* is true, otherwise it's false. You just can't beat fun with logic!

Checking to see if a string is empty is easy, but checking to see if two strings are equal is not so easy. For strings to be equal, they have to match letter for letter and case for case. If you prompt the user to enter a choice, medium or large pizzas, for example, checking the input is difficult. Examine the following Boolean assignment:

```
size="Large";
is_large=(size=="large");
```

Even though the strings match letter for letter, the variable *is_large* is false because the "l" is lowercase in one string and uppercase in the other.

In addition to comparison operations, we also have logical operations at our disposal. They are shown in the following table. These are fundamentally different in that they compare Boolean values rather than numbers.

Operator	Operation performed
&&	AND: true only if both values are true
||	OR: false only if both values are false
!	NOT: negates the value

Most people think that the use of "and", "or", and "not" is trivial. Perhaps in everyday speech they are, but not as much as people think. In fact, a first course in symbolic logic spends a significant amount of time dealing with these logical operators. The following truth tables give all of the logical combinations of "and" and "or".

Expression	Resulting value	Expression	Resulting value
true&&true	true	true||true	true
false&&true	false	false||true	true
true&&false	false	true||false	true
false&&false	false	false||false	false

Remember, "and" is true only if both operands are true, and "or" is false only if both operands are false. If you stop and think about this, it makes sense. The use of "not" is more straightforward. For example, the following statements cause x to contain true and y to contain false.

$$x=!(1==2);$$
$$y=!(1==1);$$

These operators are often used to provide the logical outcome of combinations of Boolean expressions. For example,

$$x=15;$$
$$small\_positive=((x>=0)\&\&(x<=25));$$

causes *small_positive* to contain true, since the value in x causes both conditions to be true. In this way, a variable such as x can be checked to see if certain conditions are met. If x had not been a small positive number (between 0 and 25, inclusive), the *small_positive* variable would contain false.

11.2 THE "if" STATEMENT: MAKING DECISIONS

Boolean variables are not overly useful by themselves unless you like to sit around on Saturday night and play with logic. However, when used with another JavaScript structure, programming gains the advantage of being able to make decisions. The basic structure in JavaScript that provides the ability to take different courses of action based upon some criterion is the "if ... then" statement.

The logic of these structures is used by humans in everyday life without much thought. For instance, before going out on a given day a person might abide by the statement: "If the forecast calls for rain, then take an umbrella." The "if" part specifies a condition to be checked (will it rain?), and the "then" part specifies a course of action to pursue only when the "if" part is true. When the "if" part is false, the "then" part is disregarded.

In JavaScript, the "if... then" structure omits the "then"

```
if (Boolean expression) {
    statement;
}
```

but the logic is essentially the same. If the Boolean expression is true, the statement is executed. If the Boolean expression is false, the statement is completely ignored by the computer and is not executed. The omission of the word "then" carries no significance; the logic is the same and there is one less word to type!

This structure can be extended to include any number of statements:

```
if (Boolean expression) {
    statement;
    ⋮
    statement;
}
```

In this case, *all* of the statements included between the brackets will be executed if the Boolean expression is true, otherwise they will *all* be ignored. Note that, in the above two "if" structures, the statement(s) bound to the structure are indented. This is not required by JavaScript, but will be helpful when we read and try to understand longer and longer programs. Also, the placement of the brackets may seem odd, but is a standard programming practice that lends itself to readability and error detection. The structure

if (Boolean expression) {statement; statement;}

is perfectly valid. The two statements are still bound to the "if" clause, but this is not the desirable way to format the code.

For a very simple example demonstrating the capabilities of the "if" statement, we will prompt the user for a number corresponding to the score on an exam. The program will decide if the user passed the exam. If the exam score is 60 or greater, the user passed. Otherwise, the user failed. With the new "if" statement, the top-down logic of the program is as follows:

-declare a variable for the score (score)

-prompt for (and parse) the score

-if (score>=60)

output a passing comment

-if (score<60)

output a failing comment

Let's run through the program as if we were the computer. We set up an empty variable named *score.* We prompt the user for information. He or she enters 50, we assign that to *score,* and then parse "50" into 50. We check the Boolean expression of the first "if". It is false, so we do nothing. We check the second "if" statement. The Boolean expression is true, so we execute the statements belonging to that "if". That's really all there is to it. The complete program appears in Figure 11.1.

```
<HTML>
<HEAD>
<SCRIPT LANGUAGE=JavaScript><!--
var score;
score=prompt("Please enter an exam score.","");
score=parseFloat(score);

if (score>=60) {
    document.write(score);
    document.write(" is a passing score.");
}
if (score<60) {
    document.write(score);
    document.write(" is a failing score.");
}
//--></SCRIPT>
</HEAD>
<BODY>
</BODY>
</HTML>
```

FIGURE 11.1 A simple program that makes a decision based on user input.

```
<HEAD>
<SCRIPT LANGUAGE=JavaScript><!--
var score;
var result;

score=prompt("Please enter an exam score.","");
score=parseFloat(score);

if (score>=60) {
    result="passing";
}
if (score<60) {
    result="failing";
}
document.write(score);
document.write(" is a ");
document.write(result);
document.write("  score.");
//--></SCRIPT>
</HEAD>
```

FIGURE 11.2 A version of the exam score program that uses a variable to store the outcome of the decision made by the "if" statements.

The use of "if" statements brings with it more clever ways to use variables. To illustrate this, we provide a second version of this program. Rather than generating potential output with each of the "if" statements, we use a second variable to store the decision made by the "if" statements. That is, we create a variable named *result* and store one of the two strings "passing" or "failing", depending upon the score the user enters. We then use the contents of *result* in a consolidated group of output statements. The logic of this version is quite similar to the above, so we go right ahead and display the actual program in Figure 11.2. This goes further toward illustrating that there is often more than one way to write a program. Both programs produce exactly the same results. However, the use of variables to store decision results is often preferable. In fact, this is a technique we will use on a regular basis.

NOTE An important note regarding syntax is in order at this point. We have preached that JavaScript statements should be terminated with semicolons. However, structures like the "if" statement are recognized by the JavaScript interpreter. It knows to terminate an "if" statement after the ending }. Thus, there is no need to use a semicolon to mark the end of an "if" statement. This makes perfect sense. When you are making up your own statements, JavaScript has no clue when to terminate one of your instructions unless you use the semicolon to mark the end of it. But since the "if" statement is part of its built-in structures, it knows what to do.

For a more involved example using "if" statements, let's write an interactive program which calculates the amount of take-home pay based on $25 per hour for the first 40 hours worked and time and a half for overtime hours. The program should prompt the user for the amount of hours worked in a given week, output a pay breakdown, and output the total pay. The top-down logic for the program is as follows:

-declare all variables (hours,reghours,regpay,overtime,otpay,total)

-prompt for (and parse) the hours worked (hours)

-if (hours<=40)
    reghours=hours
    overtime=0

-if (hours>40)
    reghours=40
    overtime=hours-40

-calculate regular pay (regpay=reghours*25)

-calculate overtime pay (otpay=overtime*25*1.5)

-calculate the total (total=regpay+otpay)

-output the results

```
<HEAD>
<SCRIPT LANGUAGE=JavaScript><!--
var hours;
var reghours;
var regpay;
var overtime;
var otpay;
var total;

hours=prompt("Enter the number of hours you worked this week.","");
hours=parseFloat(hours);

if(hours<=40) {
    reghours=hours;
    overtime=0;
}
if(hours>40) {
    reghours=40;
    overtime=hours-40;
}

regpay=reghours*25;
otpay=overtime*25*1.5;
total=regpay+otpay;

document.write("Your pay breakdown is as follows:<BR>");
document.write(reghours);
document.write(" regular hours: $");
document.write(regpay);
document.write("<BR>");
document.write(overtime);
document.write(" overtime hours: $");
document.write(otpay);
document.write("<BR>Total pay: $");
document.write(total);
//--></SCRIPT>
</HEAD>
```

FIGURE 11.3 An overtime pay program that makes a decision based on user input.

The "if" statements are used to determine the regular hours and overtime hours in each of the two possible cases. If the user worked less than 40 hours, the regular hours and overtime hours are set accordingly. If the user worked more than 40 hours, they are set accordingly. Note that it is not possible for both of the "if" clauses to be true. Hence, it is certain that only one set of the hours assignments will be executed. Remember, if an "if" criterion is false, the statements that are bound to it are completely skipped over by the JavaScript interpreter. The complete program is shown in Figure 11.3 and, in Figure 11.4,

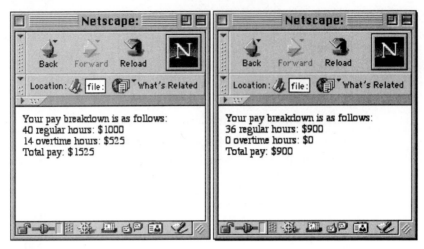

FIGURE 11.4 Output demonstrating the two distinct courses of action that the program can take.

output has been generated showing each of the two possible courses of action that the program can take.

11.3 A CONCATENATION SHORTCUT

To make life (at least your programming existence) a little easier, we digress for a moment. We considered introducing this shortcut in Lesson 10, but one can only digest (and understand what one digests) detailed programming syntax in small bytes (pun intended). In the overtime pay program of Section 11.2 above, the sheer number of *document.write()* functions necessary to output the results might seem excessive, perhaps not so much so from just reading the program, but actually generating the code is another matter.

The key to eliminate this annoyance is to remember that *document.write()* is a function that takes a string as its argument. Moreover, long strings can be made from shorter strings using concatenation. So, for example

```
reghours+"regular hours:$"+regpay+"<BR>"
```

is just one long string. Consequently, the statement

```
document.write(reghours+"regular hours:$"+regpay+"<BR>");
```

is perfectly valid. But wait a minute. The variable contents are numbers rather than strings. Remember from Section 10.9 that when we tried to average two user-inputted string-numbers without parsing them into actual numbers, the computer concatenated them, rather than adding them. In fact, any time *at least one* string is present, concatenation is going to occur rather than strict addition. For example,

$$"2"+10+55+123+84$$

would be concatenated into the string

"2105512384"

Here the first component is a string. With this in mind, the *document.write()* statements at the end of Figure 11.3, can be condensed into

```
document.write("Your pay breakdown is as follows:<BR>");
document.write(reghours+ " regular hours: $"+regpay+"<BR>");
document.write(overtime+ " overtime hours: $"+otpay);
document.write("<BR>Total pay: $"+total);
```

Of course, we could have condensed this into one long statement, but there is no point in getting carried away. In fact, long statements such as these are often mind-boggling to debug. If one quotation mark is missing, it can cause the whole program not to work. So use this shortcut judiciously, as we have done above.

> **NOTE**
> If one of your *document.write()* statements is long enough to wrap around in the window of your editor, let it do so automatically. Don't hit return in the middle of a statement. We hate to reiterate (see the note at the end of Section 10.12), but such an error is extremely difficult to detect.

11.4   THE "if ... else" STRUCTURE

The addition of "else" to the "if" cause essentially provides a default for when the "if" condition is not true. Going back to the human example, consider the statement "if the forecast calls for rain, then take an umbrella, else take sunglasses." The logic is essentially the same; however, the "else" part simply provides an alternate course of action for when the "if" part is false—a default, if you will. In terms of ordinary speech, the word "otherwise" would perhaps be chosen to replace "else". But, in this context the two words carry the same meaning.

In JavaScript, the "if ... then ... else" structure (actually just "if ... else") has the structure

```
if (Boolean Expression) {
    statement;
}
else {
    statement;
}
```

If the Boolean expression is true, the first statement is executed. If the Boolean expression is false, the second statement is executed. It is *never* the case that both statements are executed.

The "if . . . else" structure can also be used with groups of statements:

```
if (Boolean expression) {
    statement;
    ⋮
    statement;
}
else {
    statement;
    ⋮
    statement;
}
```

In the event that the Boolean expression is false, the entire first group of statements is skipped and the entire second group is executed.

In practice, the "if . . . else" statement can function just like two "if" statements. For example, we can rewrite the overtime pay program of Figure 11.3 using the "if . . . else" statement. Leaving the rest of the program the same, we simply write

```
if(hours<=40) {
    reghours=hours;
    overtime=0;
}
else{
    reghours=40;
    overtime=hours-40;
}
```

and the only apparent difference is that there is only one Boolean condition that the computer has to check. So the "if . . . else" statement is slightly more efficient in that respect. However, there is one subtle major difference. Suppose in the "if . . . else" version that the user enters bad input, like the string "oops", which is certainly not a number. Oddly enough, the Boolean expression ("oops"<=40) is false. You might say, "of course it's false," but in reality the expression makes no sense, and technically, that's different from being false. But in JavaScript, if it's not true, it's false, regardless of whether or not it makes sense. So, in the "if . . . else" version of the program, the "else" would actually be invoked upon bad user input. That's not to say that the program would do what it's supposed to. Given the bad user input, the output of the program would contain several instances of NaN (recall the discussion at the end of Section 10.11).

So, with respect to the overtime pay program, the above subtlety really makes no difference. With bad input, the program simply won't work as planned. But in a new setting we can actually exploit this advantage of the "if . . . else" statement. We wish to write an interactive pizza-ordering program that first asks users if they want medium ($10) or large

($15) pizzas. Based upon the input, they are then asked either how many medium or how many large pizzas they would like to order. In other words, the second prompt box should reflect the choice made in the first prompt box. The program will then calculate the subtotal, sales tax, and total bill.

The first prompt box will ask the user to enter a 1 if medium pizzas are desired or a 2 if large pizzas are desired. Utilizing the default capabilities of the "if ... else" statement, we set up the program so that if users enter anything but a 1, they get large pizzas by default. (We have a better profit margin on large pizzas!)

> if (size=="1")
>> give 'em medium pizzas
> else
>> give 'em large pizzas

That way, even if they enter gibberish into the prompt box, (size="1") is false, and they get large pizzas. The next thing to figure out is how to get the second prompt box to reflect the choice they made in the first prompt box. The first inclination is simply to do the following.

> if (size=="1")
>> prompt for medium pizzas
> else
>> prompt for large pizzas

That way, each prompt box can have the appropriate message. However, it is unnecessary to use two different *prompt()* functions. Recalling that the first argument of the *prompt()* function is a string, we employ the concatenation shortcut introduced in Section 11.3. The top-down logic for the program becomes

> -declare variables (size,type,price,num,subtotal,tax,total)
>
> -prompt for size (size)
>
> -if (size=="1")
>> type="medium"
>> price=10
>
> -else
>> type= "large"
>> price=15
>
> -prompt for (and parse) the number of pizzas, using *type* in the message (num)
>
> -calculate the subtotal, tax, and total
>
> -output the results

So based upon the user's first choice, we have both the price information stored for use in the calculations, and the pizza type stored for use in the second prompt box. The actual program appears in Figure 11.5. It is worth noting that we didn't parse the

```
<HEAD>
<SCRIPT LANGUAGE=JavaScript><!--
var size;
var type;
var price;
var num;
var subtotal;
var tax;
var total;

size=prompt("Please enter 1 if you would like to order medium pizzas
at $10 apiece or enter 2 if you would like to order large pizzas at
$15 apiece","");

if (size=="1"){
    type="medium";
    price=10;
}
else{
    type="large";
    price=15;
}
num=prompt("How many "+type+" pizzas would you like to order?","");
num=parseFloat(num);

subtotal=num*price;
tax=.06*subtotal;
total=subtotal +tax;

document.write("Order summary:<BR>"+num+" "+type+" pizzas at
$"+price+" each: $"+subtotal);
document.write("<BR>6% sales tax: $"+tax);
document.write("<BR>The total for your order: $"+total);
//--></SCRIPT>
</HEAD>
```

FIGURE 11.5 An interactive pizza order program in which information from the first prompt box is used as information in the second prompt box.

output of the first prompt box into a number, since we checked its value in string form. Also notice how the pizza type information is concatenated in with the argument of the second *prompt()* function, and how the output statements have been consolidated using concatenation.

The output of this program is typical, so we don't picture it. However, the most interesting feature of this program (other than the "if . . . else" usage) is how the first input affects the directions on the second prompt box. The reader is encouraged to go to the web site and play with this program. Notice especially how you get large pizzas even if you enter gibberish into the first prompt box. However, entering bad information into the second prompt box will still cause some NaN output.

As a final note on this program, it would have been tempting to just let the user type "medium" or "large" into the first prompt box. However, as we noted near the end of Section 11.1, checking strings for equality is very exacting. So, even if the user were to enter "Medium", "MEDIUM", or "   medium   " (extra spaces), the "if" part would be false, causing the program to default to large pizzas. The use of 0 and 1 was a better choice.

11.5 BASIC INPUT VERIFICATION

While the default capabilities of the "if...else" statement provided a measure of user error protection in the above pizza program, it is clear that this is not a viable way to verify user input. Indeed, even if we had used such a structure in the overtime pay program, bad user input would still result in several NaNs in the output. To aid in input verification, we will employ two new JavaScript functions.

First, the *alert()* function takes a string as its argument, and causes a small alert box to appear. The *alert()* function is a procedure function since it doesn't return a value. Thus, it stands alone as a statement. The following statement

```
alert("C'mon, buddy, enter the correct information.");
```

causes an alert box to appear. Obviously, the message on the alert box is given by the string you send to the *alert()* function. The execution of the JavaScript program does not resume until the user has hit the "OK" button. (I'm not sure what the guy on the left of the alert box is saying, but I don't think I would like my mother to hear it!)

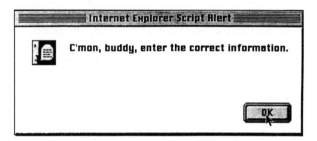

The second function we will make use of is the *isNaN()* function (is Not a Number). It is a value function which takes a string argument and returns a Boolean value. It returns true if the string you send it is not a number, and it returns false if the string you send it actually is a number. Well, technically no strings are numbers. What we mean here is that the function returns true if the string is not parsable into a number. (No way is the spell checker going to let "parsable" go, but when you write computer science textbooks, you get to make up new words.) The following examples should adequately clarify this point.

```
x=isNaN("22");
y=isNaN("2a");
```

In the above cases, the variable *x* would be assigned the value false, and the variable *y* would be assigned the value true.

To see how we would use these two functions to check user input, we return the overtime pay program of Figure 11.1. We wish to check for two things:

1. Make sure the user enters a number.
2. Make sure the user enters a number between 0 and 168 (there are only 168 hours in a week. If they can work that many hours, we'll pay 'em.).

Recall that the user enters the number of hours worked into the variable *hours*. To check the first condition, we can check the expression

isNaN(hours)

If it's a true Boolean expression, the user *didn't* enter a number. To check the second condition, we simply check the expression

(hours<0) || (168<hours)

If it's a true Boolean expression, then *hours* is *not* in the proper range.

With this in mind, the input verification takes on the following top-down logic

-obtain the input, *don't* try to parse it (hours)

-if (isNaN(hours) **or** ((hours<0) || (168<hours))

   alert the user that he or she entered an improper value

   reprompt for the input (hours)

-now parse hours

Let's talk this through. Get the input, if it's NaN **or** it's not in the right range, then give an alert box and prompt for the input a second time. Remember, or (||) gives false only if both of the conditions are false. So, if either of the conditions is true, the condition for the "if" statement is true and the alert and reprompt occur. Otherwise, the entire "if" statement is never executed.

Suitable JavaScript code for this is provided in Figure 11.6. We have included this code in with the overtime pay program so that you can see its place. However, we have not shown the whole program. The rest appears exactly as in Figure 11.3. The reader is encouraged to play with this program on the web site to get a feel for how it works.

```
<SCRIPT LANGUAGE=JavaScript><!--
var hours;
var reghours;
var regpay;
var overtime;
var otpay;
var total;

hours=prompt("Enter the number of hours you worked this week.","");

if (isNaN(hours) || ((hours<0) || (168<hours))){
   alert("Make sure you enter a number between 0 and 168");
   hours=prompt("Re-enter your hours.","");
}
hours=parseFloat(hours);

if(hours<=40) {
   reghours=hours;
   overtime=0;
}
if(hours>40) {
   reghours=40;
   overtime=hours-40;
```

FIGURE 11.6 Verifying that the user enters a number that is in the proper range.

A shortcoming of this verification technique comes into play if the user is obstinate and enters bad input twice in a row. After all, we are only checking the input once. If the program has to resort to executing the second prompt statement, there is no second line of defense. One could always put several copies the verification structure back to back with increasingly threatening messages, but that is not the desired strategy. We will have to be content with this for now. However, later in this book we will present a method that will verify user input indefinitely. In other words, the user could keep putting bad input all day, and would get nowhere.

11.6 WRITING PROGRAMS

At this point we have learned enough to write meaningful programs, ones that do more than simply write information to the browser window. At first, it seems simple to organize the concepts we have learned into a series of statements designed to accomplish some task. However, writing a program involves much more than just sitting down and typing. In most cases, a substantial bit of problem solving is required to write a program that not only does what it is supposed to do, but also is organized and efficient.

In the context of writing JavaScript programs, problem solving can be loosely summed up in three steps:

1. Thoroughly understand the problem at hand.
2. Devise a viable solution.
3. Implement the solution in the form of JavaScript code.

While this might seem a no-brainer, we emphasize that the first two steps are as important as the third. We have already mentioned the adage that "the sooner you start typing, the longer it will take you to write the program." However, most beginning programmers tend to discount this wisdom. The end product being a JavaScript program, the tendency is to hurry over the first two steps and just start typing. We have emphasized the top-down logic approach, and for good reason. Without proper planning, numerous hours can be spent typing aimlessly.

11.7 AN ADVANCED EXAMPLE (OPTIONAL)

We end this lesson on decision making in JavaScript with a somewhat more complicated example. The following are the guidelines for withholding federal taxes from paychecks as outlined in the 1998 Circular E, published by the Internal Revenue Service (IRS). (Through a little searching, such information is available to the public online!) Note that these guidelines don't determine how much in federal taxes you will owe at the end of the year, but how much is withheld from each paycheck. Note also that this is merely withholding for federal taxes, not state taxes, Social Security, etc. The guidelines are formulated for all of the common payroll periods, but we include only the common ones.

First, a flat amount from your gross earnings is exempted from tax for each dependent you claim on your W-4 form:

Payroll period	One withholding allowance
Weekly	51.92
Biweekly	103.85
Monthly	225.00

For example, if you claim two dependents and you are paid every two weeks, 2*103.85 = $207.70 of each paycheck is exempted from taxes. The following table for withholding taxes from each check applies to your gross earnings **after** your withholding allowances have been subtracted.

	Single		Married	
	Earning range	Percent withheld	Earning range	Percent withheld
Weekly	0–51	0%	0–124	0%
	51–517	15%	124–899	15%
	517–1105	28%	899–1855	28%
	1105–2493	31%	1855–3084	31%
	2493–5385	36%	3084–5439	36%
	5385→	39.6%	5439→	39.6%
Biweekly	0–102	0%	0–248	0%
	102–1035	15%	248–1798	15%
	1035–2210	28%	1798–3710	28%
	2210–4987	31%	3710–6167	31%
	4987–10769	36%	6167–10879	36%
	10769→	39.6%	10879→	39.6%
Monthly	0–221	0%	0–538	0%
	221–2242	15%	538–3896	15%
	2242–4788	28%	3896–8038	28%
	4788–10804	31%	8038–13363	31%
	10804–23333	36%	13363–23571	36%
	23333→	39.6%	23571→	39.6%

The thing to note is that a flat percentage is not withheld based upon your income. The more you earn, the higher your withholding percentage is. Let's run through a sample case to see how this works. Suppose you are single, claim one dependent, and get paid monthly in the amount of $5225. Since you claim one dependent, according to the first table above, you get a withholding exemption of 1*225 = $225. Your adjusted monthly income is then $5000. The actual withholding is then based on the second table using this adjusted income. Now, $5000 falls in the 31% range, but they do not simply withhold 31% of your adjusted earnings. They withhold 15% of the money you earn in the range from 221 to 2242, 28% of the money you earn in the range from 2242 to 4788, and 31% of the money you earn over 4788. So in this case the amount of withholding would be.

$$.15*(2242-221)+.28*(4788-2242)+.31*(5000-4788)$$

which totals $1081.75. So the calculation for your withholding is not overly complicated. The result is, however, a bit depressing!

The objective is to write a program that prompts users for their yearly salary, the number of dependents they have claimed, and how often they get paid. For simplicity, we will provide only the biweekly (every two weeks) and monthly options. Also, for simplicity, we will assume that the user is married for this example. The program will then calculate how much will be withheld from each paycheck.

The inputted yearly salary will go into a variable *salary* and the number of dependents into a variable *dependents*. This is simply numeric input. We will forgo formal verification of the user input, and leave that as an exercise. The major decision that has to be made is which type of pay period the user has entered. We will have the user enter 2 for biweekly or 1 for monthly into a variable *pay_period*. The basic top-down logic for the program is as follows.

-define variables(salary, dependents, pay_period, wage, adjwage, ouch) (may need more)

-prompt for user input

-if (pay_period== "1"){

   calculate monthly salary (wage)

   calculate adjusted wage(deduct dependent allowance) (adjwage)

   calculate federal withholding (ouch)

}

-if (pay_period== "2"){

   calculate biweekly salary (wage)

   calculate adjusted wage(deduct dependent allowance) (adjwage)

   calculate federal withholding (ouch)

}

-output the results

With this plan, which is not overly complicated, we must determine the nature of the calculations. So this plan does not cover all of the details, just the major logic of the program. With this in place, we can focus on the calculations. The monthly/biweekly wage and the dependent allowance calculations are straightforward and can be done on the fly. Calculating the withholding is, however, a good bit more complicated. In each case (monthly/biweekly) the procedure is essentially the same, only the numbers are different. There is not one right way to do this, but the following is straightforward:

if (15% range)

   calculate tax

if (28% range)

   calculate tax

$\vdots$

if (39.6% range)

   calculate tax

So, the calculate-federal-withholding part will have the above structure in each case. With such a structure predetermined, the only things left to figure out are the calculate-tax steps. These require some thought since the withholding is not a flat percentage. For an example, for a wage in the 36% range for monthly pay, a suitable calculation is

$$\text{ouch} = .15*(3896 - 538) + .28*(8038 - 3896) + 31*(13363 - 8038)$$
$$+ .36*(\text{wage} - 13363);$$

The above approach is in general a good way to figure out how to write a complicated program. First figure out the main logic—what fundamental decisions have to be made. With that in place, it is much easier to focus on the actual calculations. With a good plan for the structure of the program and the difficult calculations figured out, the actual program shown in Figure 11.7 is not too formidable to produce. The reader is encouraged to go to the web site and play with this program.

For someone not accustomed to programming, this program might seem very complicated due to the number of large calculations. However, having the logic of what that program was to do prior to writing it was more than half the battle. Sitting down at the keyboard without a detailed plan for this program would have been a time-consuming mistake.

There was one feature of the program that didn't become apparent until it was time to output the results. There needed to be some way to include in the output the type of payment period which was being considered. We simply declared a variable *period_type* and set its value accordingly in each case. Note its use in the *document.write( )* statement. Even armed with the logic of a program, you sometimes still have to "tweak" it a little.

The next example is a modification of the federal withholding program of Figure 11.7. This new version uses even more variables than the previous version. To save some space, we mention here that there is an allowable way to define several variables with one line of code. For example, the four variable declarations

```
var dependents;
var pay_period;
var wage;
var adjwage;
```

can be condensed into one line of code

```
var dependents, pay_period, wage, adjwage;
```

In practice, this shortcut is straightforward to use, so we say no more about it.

The goal of the modified version of the previous program is to allow yet another option. In addition to the other information that the user enters, the user will be prompted to determine whether withholding should be calculated for a married person or single person. Withholding for a single person amounts to no more than using a different set of cutoff values. These values are given in the above table to the right of the cutoff values for married withholding.

```
<HEAD>
<SCRIPT LANGUAGE=JavaScript><!--
var salary;
var dependents;
var pay_period;
var wage;
var adjwage;
var ouch;
var period_type;

salary=prompt("Please enter your yearly salary.","");
dependents=prompt("Please enter the number of dependents claimed on your W-4 form.","");
pay_period=prompt("Enter a 1 if you get paid monthly, or a 2 if you get paid biweekly.","");

salary=parseFloat(salary);
dependents=parseFloat(dependents);

if (pay_period=="1") {
   wage=salary/12;
   adjwage=wage-(dependents*225);

   if ((adjwage>538)&&(adjwage<=3896)){
      ouch=.15*(adjwage-538);
   }
   if ((adjwage>3896)&&(adjwage<=8038)){
      ouch=.15*(3896-538)+.28*(adjwage-3896);
   }
   if ((adjwage>8038)&&(adjwage<=13363)){
      ouch=.15*(3896-538)+.28*(8038-3896)+.31*(adjwage-8038);
   }
   if ((adjwage>13363)&&(adjwage<=23571)){
      ouch=.15*(3896-538)+.28*(8038-3896)+.31*(13363-8038)+.36*(adjwage-13363);
   }
   if (adjwage>23571){
      ouch=15*(3896-538)+.28*(8038-3896)+.31*(13363-8038)+.36*(13363-8038)+.396*(adjwage-23571);
   }
    period_type="monthly";
}

if (pay_period=="2") {
   wage=salary/26;adjwage=wage-(dependents*103.80);

   if ((adjwage>248)&&(adjwage<=1798)){
      ouch=.15*(adjwage-248);
   }
   if ((adjwage>1798)&&(adjwage<=3710)){
      ouch=.15*(1798-248)+.28*(adjwage-1798);
   }
   if ((adjwage>3710)&&(adjwage<=6167)){
      ouch=.15*(1798-248)+.28*(3710-1798)+.31*(adjwage-3710);
   }
   if ((adjwage>6167)&&(adjwage<=10879)){
      ouch=.15*(1798-248)+.28*(3710-1798)+.31*(6167-3710)+.36*(adjwage-6167);
   }
   if (adjwage>10879){
      ouch=15*(1798-248)+.28*(3710-1798)+.31*(6167-3710)+.36*(108796167)+.396*(adjwage-10879);
   }
   period_type="biweekly";
}
document.write("A married person earning $"+salary+" per year has a "+period_type+" gross
paycheck of $"+wage+".  With "+dependents+" dependents claimed, $"+ouch+" is withheld from each
paycheck for federal taxes alone!");
//--></SCRIPT>
</HEAD>
```

FIGURE 11.7 An interactive program that calculates withholding for federal taxes.

The first inclination is to structure the program just like the last one, but include four decision components instead of two:

> if (single and monthly)
>> do the calculations as before
>
> if (married and monthly)
>> do the calculations as before
>
> if (single and biweekly)
>> do the calculations as before
>
> if (married and biweekly)
>> do the calculations as before

This is a perfectly viable solution but would make for a long, cumbersome program. Indeed, each of the four calculations sections is itself a series of five "if" statements, each containing cumbersome calculations. That would make for a program roughly twice as long as the previous version. There is nothing wrong with that but, rather than simply using brute force, a bit of clever programming can make for a shorter and even more versatile program.

We note that the series of five "if ... then" statements required in each of the four calculations is exactly the same, except that the cutoff values for the withholding percentages vary among the four cases. Let's set up a variable for each cutoff point. The variables *cut0, cut15, cut28, cut31,* and *cut36* represent the cutoff points for the 0%, 15%, 28%, 31%, and 36% withholding levels, respectively. Then, for example for a salary falling into the 36% range, the calculation

```
if ((adjwage>cut31)&&(adjwage<=cut36))
    tax=.15*(cut15-cut0)+.28*(cut28-cut15)+.31*(cut31-cut28)
        +.36*(adjwage-cut31);
```

suffices for all four cases. The cutoff values simply have to be preset for each case. Since we have already gone through the acquisition of the user input, we omit this from the top-down logic for this version. In addition to the previous information, we will prompt users for whether they want single(1) or married(2) withholding. The basic logic becomes

-if (monthly)
> calculate monthly salary (wage)
>
> calculate adjusted wage(deduct dependent allowance) (adjwage)
>
> if (single)
>> set cutoff values (cut0, cut15, cut28, cut31, cut36)
>
> if (married)
>> set cutoff values (cut0, cut15, cut28, cut31, cut36)

(*continued on page 234.*)

```
<HEAD>
<SCRIPT LANGUAGE=JavaScript><!--
var salary, dependents, pay_period, withhold_type;
var wage, adjwage, ouch, period_type,withhold_status;
var cut0, cut15, cut28, cut31, cut36;

salary=prompt("Please enter your yearly salary.","");
dependents=prompt("Please enter the number of dependents claimed on your W-4 form.","");
pay_period=prompt("Enter a 1 if you get paid monthly, or a 2 if you get paid biweekly.","");
withhold_type=prompt("Enter a 1 for single, or a 2 for married withholding.","");

salary=parseFloat(salary);
dependents=parseFloat(dependents);

if (pay_period=="1") {
   wage=salary/12;
   adjwage=wage-(dependents*225);

   if (withhold_type="1"){
      cut0=221;cut15=2242;cut28=4788;cut31=10804;cut36=23333;
      withhold_status="single";
   }
   if (withhold_type="2"){
      cut0=538;cut15=3896;cut28=8038;cut31=13363;cut36=23571;
      withhold_status="married";
   }
   period_type="monthly";
}

if (pay_period=="2") {
   wage=salary/26;
   adjwage=wage-(dependents*103.80);

   if (withhold_type="1"){
      cut0=102;cut15=1035;cut28=2210;cut31=4987;cut36=10769;
      withhold_status="single";
   }
   if (withhold_type="2"){
      cut0=248;cut15=1798;cut28=3710;cut31=6167;cut36=10879;
      withhold_status="married";
   }
   period_type="biweekly";
}

if ((adjwage>cut0)&&(adjwage<=cut15)){
   ouch=.15*(adjwage-cut0);
}
if ((adjwage>cut15)&&(adjwage<=cut28)){
   ouch=.15*(cut15-cut0)+.28*(adjwage-cut15);
}
if ((adjwage>cut28)&&(adjwage<=cut31)){
   ouch=.15*(cut15-cut0)+.28*(cut28-cut15)+.31*(adjwage-cut28);
}
if ((adjwage>cut31)&&(adjwage<=cut36)){
   ouch=.15*(cut15-cut0)+.28*(cut28-cut15)+.31*(cut31-cut28)+.36*(adjwage-cut31);
}
if (adjwage>cut36){
   ouch=.15*(cut15-cut0)+.28*(cut28-cut15)+.31*(cut31-cut28)+.36*(cut36-
cut31)+.396*(adjwage-cut36);
}

document.write("A married person earning $"+salary+" per year has a "+period_type+" gross
paycheck of $"+wage+".  With "+dependents+" dependents claimed and withholding at the
"+withhold_status+ " rate, $"+ouch+" is withheld from each paycheck for federal taxes
alone!");
//--></SCRIPT>
</HEAD>
```

FIGURE 11.8 A more versatile version of the federal withholding program.

-if (biweekly)

    calculate biweekly salary (wage)

        calculate adjusted wage(deduct dependent allowance) (adjwage)

        if (single)

        set cutoff values (cut0, cut15, cut28, cut31, cut36)

    if (married)

        set cutoff values (cut0, cut15, cut28, cut31, cut36)

-calculate federal withholding

Then, with all the cutoff and withholding values predetermined, the calculation for federal with holding consists of five "if" statements, one for each withholding percentage. The complete program is shown in Figure 11.8. Again, we had to tweak the program a bit. We added another variable *withhold_status* to store the type of withholding that the user chooses. That way the output can include a textual description of the user's choice.

There are still several improvements that could be made to this program. We haven't included the weekly payroll option. Moreover, the program is highly vulnerable to user error. These improvements are left as exercises.

11.8 SUMMARY

Key Terms

Boolean literals   logical operation   Boolean expression   comparison operation

Boolean literals are needed to facilitate decision making in programming. Boolean variables make use of only two values, true and false. Thus, they are fundamentally different from either numeric or string literals. Boolean expressions evaluate to either true or false. The first type of Boolean expression makes use of comparison operations. Comparison operations are used to check or compare numbers or strings. Both of the comparison expressions using the equality comparison ==

$$(3.01==3)$$
$$(\text{"Yikes"}==\text{"yikes"})$$

evaluate to false. In particular, strings must match letter-for-letter and case-for-case to be equal.

The logical operations, AND(&&), OR(||), and NOT(!), are used not to compare numbers or strings, but to compare other Boolean expressions. You have been using these in speech since you were able to talk, but their interpretation is not as trivial as you may think. (We believe the review questions will convince you of this!) Given two Boolean expressions, AND is true *only* if both expressions are true; OR is false *only* if both expressions are false. Both of the following logical expressions are false:

$$(5>6) \,||\, (\text{"x"}==\text{"X"})$$
$$!(2*2*2==8)$$

The use of grouping parentheses () becomes very important in such compound expressions. While it is always fun to play with comparison and logical statements, their utility becomes apparent when used with the "if" and "if . . . else" statements. The "if" statement can provide for any number of different courses of action. Rather than formally defining it as we did in this lesson, we give the gist of what it accomplishes.

-if(condition to check)

    do something

-if(another condition to check)

    do something different

    ⋮

-if(yet another condition to check)

    yet another course of action

The conditions to be checked are Boolean expressions, the truth of which may depend on user input. The different courses of action are groups of (or single) JavaScript statements that are bound to the "if" statement with grouping brackets {}. If the condition of an "if" statement is false, all statements bound to the "if" are completely skipped over by the computer.

The "if . . . else" statement provides for two distinct courses of action. The "else" can be thought of as a default course of action:

-if(condition to check)

    do something

-else

    alternate course of action

Since the "if" and "if. . .else" statements are self-contained and recognizable by JavaScript, you can't terminate them with a semicolon. However, the statements bound to these structures that you define should still be terminated with a semicolon.

To avoid using a bunch of *document.write( )* statements to give output, several short strings can be concatenated as the argument. This tactic also can be used to send information for instructions in a prompt box. But be careful, since concatenating several strings together as the argument of a function gets a little syntactically demanding. Even one missing " or + will foul things up.

The "if" statement can be used to verify user input. A very useful function to aid in this is the *isNaN()* function, which takes a string argument and returns either true or false. For example, *isNaN("3")* is false and *isNaN("x")* is true. When verifying to see if input is numeric, it may also be desirable to check the input to see if it makes sense. If you request that users enter their age, it is reasonable to make sure that the age is in the range from 0 to 125, for example. The logic for verification is as follows:

-prompt

-if (input is bad)

    give alert

    reprompt

-parse (if necessary)

The "give alert" instruction involves the *alert()* function. It does not return a value and, thus, stands alone as a statement. It takes a string argument and gives that string as the message on the alert box. The program will not resume until the user hits OK on the alert box.

As a final note, you should never underestimate the importance of carefully planning out the logic of your programs. You are begging for a headache if you sit down at the computer to code a program without a good plan.

11.9 REVIEW QUESTIONS

1. Determine the value of each of the variables *a–e*.

```
a=((5<=5)&&((3*2)>=6));
b=(!(6*7==41)||(3==(2+2)));
c=(isNaN("2")&&true);
d=(isNaN("the")||false);
e=(("and"=="and")
    &&(!("good"=="evil")));
```

2. Determine the value of each of the variables *a–c*.

```
x="11";
y="ok";
a=((isNaN(x)==true)||(x<=0));
b=(isNaN(x)&&(x>0));
c=(isNaN(y)||(x<0)||(x>20));
```

3. Give an example where an "if … else" statement can be used in such a way that if user input is bad, the program resorts to a default behavior and still works. Discuss how the Boolean expression is used in this case.

4. The user has entered input into the variable *x*. Write an "if" statement whose Boolean expression is true if *x* is not a number or is a negative number.

5. The user has entered input into the variable *x*. Write an "if" statement whose Boolean expression is true if *x* is not a number, or if *x* is not in the range from 1 to 10.

6. Discuss a limitation to the verification method discussed in this lesson.

7. Find two logical errors in the following verification code:

```
x=prompt("Please enter a positive
    number.","");
if (isNaN(x)&&(x<0)){
    alert("I'll give you one more chance
```

```
    to enter a positive number.");
}
x=prompt("Please enter a positive
    number.","");
x=parseFloat(x);
```

8. The user is to enter a positive number. Write verification code for this input. The message in the alert box should use the actual user input as part of its message. For example, if the user enters −2, then the alert window should say "Please try again. −2 is not positive."

9. Find four syntax errors in the following code:

```
x=2;
y=3;
if(x<=y)
    document.write(I told you so);
}
if(y=x){
    document.write(I told you so)
};
```

10. Determine the output of the following code:

```
x=1;
y=2;
z=3;
if(x>=1){
    x=x+2;
    y=y+1;
}
else{
    z=11;
}
```

```
if(x!=y){
    x=5;
    y=5;
}
document.write(x+"<BR>"+y
    +"<BR>"+z+"<BR>");
```

11. Determine the output of the following code:

```
x=1;
y=2;
z=3;
t=true;
x=x+1;
if(x==z){
```

```
    t=false;
    y=y-1;
}
else{
    z=10;
    t=(y==x);
}
y=15;
if(t){
    x=y+y;
    t=y;
}
document.write(x+"<BR>"+y+"<BR>"
    +z+"<BR>"+t+"<BR>");
```

11.10 EXERCISES

1. Write a program that prompts for two test scores from 0 to 100, finds the average, and assigns a failing or passing grade. Passing is 60%. Option: verify the input.

2. Write a program that prompts for two test scores and then prompts for two quiz scores. The scores should be in the range from 0 to 100. The program calculates the quiz avarage and test average, and should assign a passing or failing grade using the better of the two averages. Passing is 60%. Option: verify the input.

3. Write a program that prompts for the user's name and age. The program should tell the user how many years he/she has left until retirement or how many years he/she has been retired. Retirement age is 65. Option: verify the age input. Reasonable ages: 0 to 125.

4. Write a program that prompts the user for a temperature in Fahrenheit. The program should convert the temperature into Celsius (see problem 10.15.1). If the temperature is above freezing (freezing is 32°F and 0°C), the user should be informed how many degrees above freezing the temperature is in both Fahrenheit and Celsius. If the temperature is below freezing, the user should be informed how many degrees below freezing the temperature is in both Fahrenheit and Celsius. Option: verify the input. Reasonable temperatures: $-100°$ to $200°$.

5. Write a program that asks how many wildebeest you would like to purchase for your herd. The first 100 you buy cost $1000 apiece. Any beyond 100 you buy are only $800 apiece. The program should output a purchase breakdown and should figure in the universal wildebeest tax. The first 100 are taxed at 8%, and any over that are taxed at 5%. Option: verify the input.

6. The user should be prompted as to whether they would like to convert Celsius to Fahrenheit or Fahrenheit to Celsius. Set up the program so that, if the user enters bad input, the program defaults to converting Fahrenheit to Celsius. Depending on the first input, the user should be prompted to enter either a Fahrenheit or Celsius temperature. The message of the second prompt box should reflect the type of conversion the user chose in the first prompt box. The output should reflect both the type of conversion and the result. The Celsius-to-Fahrenheit conversion is $F = (9/5)*C + 32$. See problem 10.15.1 for the other conversion formula. Option: verify the temperature input. Reasonable temperatures: $-100°$ to $200°$.

7. Redo the overtime program of Figure 11.3. The problem works in the same way: you still get overtime for any hours over 40, but for any hours over 60 you earn double time. Verify the input for this problem.

8. Social Security tax (FICA) is withheld at an approximate rate of 7.75% on the first $48,000 of your annual salary. If you work for two employers and they are each withholding FICA, you could end up having too much withheld (e.g., if you make $30,000 on each job you are taxed on $60,000). Assume the user is working for two employers. Prompt for the total yearly earnings from each job. Calculate the over-payment (if any). Option: Use appropriate verification.

9. (optional). Redo the withholding program of Figure 11.8. Do either (or both) of the following options: (a) Add in the weekly pay period option; (b) Verify all input.

11.11   PROJECT THREADS

Any exercises you do for this lesson should be referenced in your homework page following the guidelines in Section 9.10.

OBJECTS

ARE **WE** ready to use JavaScript to process HTML forms? Well, no, but almost! We have one last hurdle to jump. We have seen how variables store user input and how we can retrieve that information from the variables as needed for processing. If user input from HTML forms were stored into variables as we know them at this point, we would be ready to go. But information from HTML forms is stored in objects, so we must learn about those. That is not to say that we will depart from the use of variables. On the contrary, objects and variables are tied together in an inextricable way.

In this lesson, we explore the fundamental way that variables are bound to objects. But before we examine programming objects, a short excursion into the nature of objects in the real world is in order. You will see that many of the concepts pertaining to real-world objects carry over to programming objects.

12.1 THE NATURE OF OBJECTS

Webster's *Unabridged Dictionary* defines the noun *object as* "anything visible or tangible, a material product or substance." According to the semantics of the everyday use of the word object, an object is basically any tangible "something"—a person, a car, a baseball, an atom. In contrast, intangible things such as fear, joy, and laziness are not considered objects. On a superficial level, objects have names. A name is merely a reference to an object, it doesn't define the intrinsic nature of the object. For example, consider what Americans term a soccer ball. In most parts of the world, it's called a football.

It's clear then that the properties of the ball itself define its essence, rather than its name. Properties of a soccer ball include its color, shape, and weight. Going one step further, it's the values of these properties that really make it what it is. So you see that there are variables inherently associated with an object. To describe a given ball using the "variable notion," you might say *ball.color* = *"blue"*, *ball.shape* = *"round"*, and *ball.weight* = *1* (pound, that is). What's with all of the periods? Well, that's as good of a notation as any to indicate that the properties are tied to the ball. If we were merely to say *color=* *"blue"*, the meaning that the property and its value belong to the ball is lost. In this way, it is a natural notion that several variables be associated with a given physical object. Moreover, the values of an object's variables (properties) carry the defining information about the object.

Going beyond the physical properties of an object are its behaviors, that is, certain actions that can be forced upon an object. For example, a car can be driven and a baseball can be thrown. These behaviors are not interchangeable between the two objects; we generally don't drive baseballs or throw cars (unless Superman is around). The behaviors associated with an object are as important as its properties when assessing an object. While the aesthetically motivated person might point out the numerous visible properties of an object, the pragmatist might inquire to what usefulness the object can be put. To fully understand the nature of an object, both its properties and behaviors are required. While it is quite easy to tie in an object's properties with programming variables, it is not practical at this point to try to tie in the notion of object behaviors with programming. Rather, after some exploration of programming objects, we will revisit the behavior issue.

12.2 JAVASCRIPT OBJECTS

Building on the notion that it is natural to associate several variables with a real object, we introduce a programming object as an association of one or more variables. These variables are "bound" to the object and the values stored in these variables define the state of the object.

We begin by defining a very simple object. The statement

```
var car = new Object();
```

creates a new object whose name is *car*. The use of "var" indicates that we have declared a new variable named *car*. Well, technically we have, just a new kind of variable. But, more on that later. The expression on the right calls the **constructor function** *Object()* to create *car* as a new object.

At this point, we have merely created a generic object named *car,* but have not endowed it with any properties. As discussed in Section 12.1, it is necessary for an object to have properties to carry information that make the object what it is. A real-life car has many properties—make, model, engine size, year, etc. Likewise, in JavaScript, such properties may be assigned to the object *car*. For simplicity, we assign two properties to the new *car* object that represent the interior color and exterior color of the car. The assignments are as follows.

```
car.extcolor="blue";
car.intcolor="gray";
```

The name of the desired property is simply appended to the object name following a period. The property *extcolor* is a variable and is assigned the string literal "blue". Likewise, the property *intcolor* is a variable and is assigned the string literal "gray". Basically, all we are dealing with here is a data structure. We have two variables, *intcolor* and *extcolor,* bound to the *car* object. The two variables can be used as you would any other variables. The key is that you can use the variables only by referencing them as properties of *car*. For example, the statement

```
car.extcolor="white";
```

would change the contents of the *car.extcolor* variable to the string "white". However, if we were to try to retrieve the contents of *car.extcolor* without using the object reference

```
document.write(extcolor);                    (OOPS!)
```

we would get an error stating that *extcolor* is not defined. The computer simply does not recognize an object property unless the property is bound to its object.

In general, an object can contain as many properties as are required to embody the object with information essential to it. The definition of an object and its properties takes the general form

```
var my_object = new Object();

my_object.property1= someValue;
my_object.property2= someValue;
    ⋮
my_object.propertyN= someValue;
```

where the *N* properties of the object are assigned various literal values. At any time after an object is defined, a new property may be added simply by assigning it a value. For example, at a point further in the program, a new property can be added with a statement like

```
my_object.yetAnotherProperty = someValue;
```

It is, however, advisable to keep an object's definition together as a package to avoid possible confusion.

> **NOTE**
> The constructor function "Object()" doesn't require any parameters. In other words, you don't have to send it any information for it to do its job. All it does is set you up with a generic object, one with no properties. You can then define properties as above. It is important to note that it is customary for such constructor functions begin with a capital letter. The following object declarations are not valid:
>
> ```
> var pizza=new object();            (OOPS!)
> var hamburger=newObject();         (OOPS!)
> ```
>
> The constructor Object() must be capitalized, and must follow "new" after a space; "new" is always in lower case.

12.3 OBJECTS AND PRIMITIVES

We have mentioned that an object is a new type of variable. Given the existence of objects, ordinary variables are often called **primitives.** In turn, those types of literals that can be stored in primitives are often called **primitive types.** In JavaScript, the primary primitive types are number, string, and Boolean.

The difference between primitives and objects begins with the purposes of their names. Recall the analogy between a variable and a named box within the computer in which to store and retrieve information. Picture a box with the name of the variable in ink on the side of the box. The name and box are inextricable.

An object is very different. Think of an object as a big box with a lock. Inside the big box are smaller boxes, each one a property of the object. The actual information is contained in the smaller boxes. That is, the smaller boxes are the primitive variables that are the object's properties. An object's name is merely a reference to the object. Think of

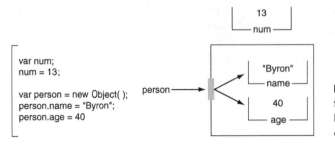

FIGURE 12.1 The fundamental difference between primitives and objects.

the name of an object as the key to the big box. You can't get at the properties of the object until you get inside.

Figure 12.1 serves to illustrate this point. In that figure, we define a primitive variable and an object with two properties. The primitive variable *num* is no different from the variables we have been dealing with all along. When its name is called, its contents are retrieved. On the other hand, *person* is an object. Its name does not retrieve information. Rather, the object's name allows access to its properties. Without referring to *person.name* and *person.age,* the variables *name* and *age* are inaccessible. On a fundamental level, an object is simply a group of related primitive variables bound together.

12.4 A SIMPLE PROGRAM USING OBJECTS

In order to see objects at work, we rewrite the pizza order program of Figure 11.5. That way you can focus more on the usage of objects, rather than the logic of a new program. Recall that the program was to ask users if they want medium ($10) or large ($15) pizzas. Based upon the input, they are then either asked how many medium or how many large pizzas they would like to order. In other words, the second prompt box should reflect the choice made in the first prompt box. The program will then calculate the subtotal, sales tax, and total bill.

There are basically two distinct objects that make sense for this program, a *pizza* object and a *bill* object. Refer back to the variable declarations in Figure 11.5. All the variables describe a property or component of one of these two objects except the variable *num*. It doesn't refer to a property of a particular pizza, nor does it refer to one of the bill components. So, we'll just leave *num* as a primitive. We'll bind all of the other variables to objects.

Using objects, the logic of the program really does not change, only the way the information is stored. The top-down logic for the program is provided below, and the actual program appears in Figure 12.2.

-declare the primitive (num)

-declare two objects (pizza and bill)

-prompt for size (pizza.size)

-if (pizza.size=="1")

   pizza .type="medium";

   pizza .price=10;

-else

   pizza .type="large";

   pizza .price=15;

-prompt for (and parse) the number of pizzas (num)

-calculate bill.subtotal, bill.tax, and bill.total

-output the results

```
<HEAD>
<SCRIPT LANGUAGE=JavaScript><!--
var num;

var pizza=new Object();
var bill=new Object();

pizza.size=prompt("Please enter 1 if you would like to order medium
pizzas at $10 apiece or enter 2 if you would like to order large pizzas
at $15 apiece","");

if (pizza.size=="1"){
   pizza.type="medium";
   pizza.price=10;
}
else{
   pizza.type="large";
   pizza.price=15;
}
num=prompt("How many "+pizza.type+" pizzas would you like to order?","");
num=parseFloat(num);

bill.subtotal=num*pizza.price;
bill.tax=.06*bill.subtotal;
bill.total=bill.subtotal +bill.tax;

document.write("Order summary:<BR>"+num+" "+pizza.type+" pizzas at
$"+pizza.price+" each: $"+bill.subtotal);
document.write("<BR>6% sales tax: $"+bill.tax);
document.write("<BR>The total for your order: $"+bill.total);
//--></SCRIPT>
</HEAD>
<BODY>
```

FIGURE 12.2 A pizza program in which most of the information is stored in properties of objects.

You can see that this program works in exactly the same way as the version in Figure 11.5. The only difference is that three of the variables are bound to the *pizza* object and three of the variables are bound to the *bill* object. Rather than declaring all the variables at the top as we did in Figure 11.5, we declare the primitive *num* and the two objects at the top. Then, when variables are needed in the program, we define them on the fly as properties of the objects. This actually makes the program harder to read. Indeed, other than providing exposure to object notation and the concept of objects in general, there is no point to using objects in this program at all. This program does, however, show you that objects are easy to comprehend and that, once you provide a reference using the object's name, the primitive variables bound to the object serve as ordinary variables.

12.5 COMPOUND OBJECTS

The objects we have created thus far all have primitives as properties. The utility of objects, however, goes far beyond simply building objects with primitive properties. Consider, for example, a *person* object with three properties, *name, age,* and *career*. However, for the sake of example, we wish *name* and *career* also to be objects, each with two properties. The *name* object is to have *first* and *last* properties and the *career* object is to have two properties, *occupation* and *experience*. The *age* property of the *person* object is to be primitive. Let's see how this works:

```
var person=new Object();
person.age=31;

person.name=new Object();
person.name.first="Bryan";
person.name.last="Moore";

person.career=new Object();
person.career.occupation="musician";
person.career.experience=12;
```

First, the *person* object is declared. It is given the primitive property *age,* into which the value 31 is stored. Next, the *name* property is declared as a new object, rather than a primitive. So *person.name* is now an object. As such, it needs primitive properties into which to store information. Accordingly, *person.name* is given two primitive properties. As you can see from their declarations, it requires full reference to both **parent** objects to store values in the primitives *person.name.first* and *person.name.last*. The declaration of the *person.career* object and its properties follows in similar fashion.

Aha, we slipped in the term "parent." Without the boldface, you might not have noticed. With these compound object structures, a natural **object hierarchy** is formed. The object to which a property belongs is called the parent of that property. Figure 12.3 illustrates the hierarchy of the person object as constructed above. (The way we have pictured the object hierarchy has nothing to do with actual JavaScript coding. It merely serves as a pictorial description of the compound object structure.)

It should be clear from the diagram that the *person* object is a parent of both the *name* and *career* objects. But the object hierarchy is not useful without primitive properties in which to store information. The primitive properties of each of the three objects are listed in square brackets following the object's name. The object hierarchy shows the reference required to access the primitives. For example, the full reference *person.name.career* is required to get the career information from the primitive. Indeed, this is in full evidence in the declarations prior to Figure 12.3.

This can be taken further. Objects can be nested indefinitely (within reason, of course). Figure 12.4 shows a hierarchy containing eight different objects, each with some properties.

person [age]

      ├──── **name** [first, last]

      └──── **career** [occupation, experience]   **FIGURE 12.3** The hierarchy of the *person* object.

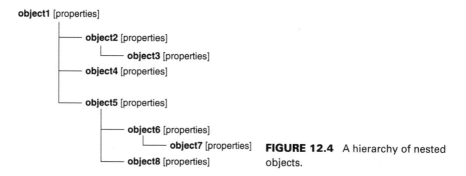

object1 [properties]

    object2 [properties]

        object3 [properties]

    object4 [properties]

    object5 [properties]

        object6 [properties]

          object7 [properties]

        object8 [properties]

FIGURE 12.4 A hierarchy of nested objects.

Here *object1* is the parent of all the other objects. The properties of an object fairly far down in the hierarchy must be accessed by referencing all of its parents. For example,

```
object1.object2.object3.property
```

would access a property of *object3*. Similarly,

```
object1.object5.object6.object7.property
```

would access a property of *object7*, the object furthest down in the hierarchy.

The construction of such an elaborate nesting of user-defined objects would rarely, if ever, be necessary in a JavaScript programming situation. But understanding the concept behind this is crucial in what is to follow.

> **NOTE**
>
> It is important to sum up the moral of this section. You need primitive variables to store information. Sometimes it is desirable to bind these primitives to objects. Sometimes, when several different groups of primitives are desired, it is necessary to bind the different groups of primitives into an object hierarchy. Whatever the case, there are variables that contain information at the ends of the hierarchy branches. To access this information, you may have to reference several object names.

12.6 THE OBJECT MODEL FOR THE BROWSER WINDOW

It would be counterproductive to contrive an example similar to that of Figure 12.2 that uses a larger, compound object structure. But you might be surprised to know that one exists naturally when you load a web page into a browser window. The window is an object, the HTML document it contains is a object, and most of the components comprising the HTML document are objects. A partial object hierarchy for this environment is pictured in Figure 12.5. The complete object hierarchy is quite large, so we mostly stick to objects that we will utilize in subsequent lessons.

As soon as a web page loads into a browser window, this hierarchy of objects is created automatically. The *window* object is the parent of this structure. It has some primitive properties that store information about the window. We have listed two of them. The *window.closed* primitive is Boolean and contains the value false, since the window is not closed. The *window.location* primitive contains a string containing the URL of the HTML

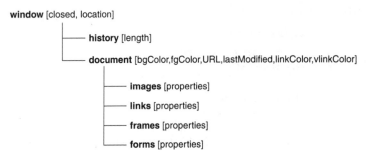

FIGURE 12.5 A partial browser window object hierarchy.

document displayed in the window. There are a few more primitive variables bound to the *window* object that contain information about the window, but it is not instructive at this point to go through all of them. It is simply natural for the existence of variables that contain information about the state of the open window.

Other information about the browser window is organized into objects. For example, the *window.history* object binds together several primitives that contain information about the documents that have previously been loaded into the window. The bad news is that the only property of the *window.history* object that both Netscape and Explorer currently support is *window.history.length*. This primitive contains a number corresponding to the number of documents that have previously been in the window. For example, if you have pulled up five web pages in your surfing endeavors, *window.history.length* contains the number 5.

The above properties of *window* are not overly useful in practice, but they do serve to illustrate how various information about the browser window is stored. We will focus much of our attention on the *window.document* object. The document loaded into the browser window is a tangible object. As such, it has properties that contain information about the state of the document. You can see several of the common ones listed in Figure 12.5. When a web page is loaded, the HTML markup instructions assign values to most of these properties (bgColor,fgColor,linkColor,vlinkColor). Other properties (URL, lastModified) contain the URL corresponding to where the document came from and the date on which the document was last modified.

Most of the things marked up into the web page are tangible objects in their own right. Images, links, frames, and forms, to name just a few, each have their own properties. We have not listed these properties because we will study most of these objects individually later. Besides, many of the properties are again objects, which would make the object diagram in Figure 12.5 quite large. The main goal of the next few lessons is to explore the *forms* object so that we can write interactive programs using HTML forms, rather than prompt boxes. In the meantime, we provide some examples to make you more comfortable with this object hierarchy.

NOTE Since the window is the parent of this whole environment, you don't always have to refer to the *window* object to access its properties. When an HTML document is loaded into a browser window, that window is the document's home, so to speak. Any JavaScript code in that document is inherently associated with that window. For example, *history.length* is sufficient to access the length of the window's history, and *document.bgColor* is sufficient to access the background color of the web page that the window contains. You can use the window reference if you wish, but it is not necessary to do so.

Further to emphasize this point, suppose you have two windows open, say *window1* and *window2*. It would then be necessary to use *window1.document.bgColor* to make it clear to which window you are referring. Mostly, we will be dealing with only one window, and we may refer directly to its properties without full reference to the *window* object. No ambiguity arises in this case.

12.7 USING WINDOW AND DOCUMENT PROPERTIES

The past few sections contain a lot of new concepts and terminology. They may seem mind-boggling, but it is surprisingly easy to access and change properties of the window and document objects. The first example, shown in Figure 12.6, simply retrieves some window and document properties and writes them to the HTML document. The results appear in Figure 12.7.

We have simply instructed that the contents of various properties be written to the web page so that we can examine their contents. So you can see that, with JavaScript, we can access various pieces of information about the document from the document's object properties. The program in Figure 12.6 is rather like a partial autobiography of the document. Through the *document.write()* method, we have forced the document to display vital information about itself. (Good thing there is no *document.secrets* property!)

The *document.bgColor* and *document.fgColor* (text color) properties have been written in both the head and body sections to illustrate a point. In the head section, the Boolean *closed* property of the *window* object contains false, as you would expect. The next two lines write the *document.bgColor* and *document.fgColor* properties. Since the attributes of the BODY tag specify that the text of the web page should be blue and the background

```
<HTML>
<HEAD>
<TITLE>Document Properties</TITLE>

<SCRIPT LANGUAGE=JavaScript><!--
document.write(closed);
document.write("<BR>"+ document.bgColor),
document.write("<BR>"+document.fgColor);
document.write("<BR>"+document.lastModified);
//--></SCRIPT>

</HEAD>
<BODY TEXT="#0000FF" BGCOLOR="#FFFFCC">
Blue text on a yellow background.<BR>

<SCRIPT LANGUAGE=JavaScript><!--
document.write("<BR>"+ document.bgColor);
document.write("<BR>"+document.fgColor);
//--></SCRIPT>

</BODY>
</HTML>
```

FIGURE 12.6 Writing the contents of some window and document properties.

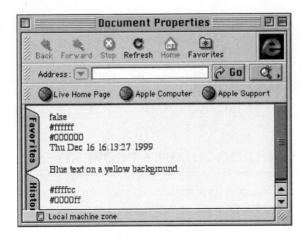

FIGURE 12.7 The rendering of the web page of Figure 12.6.

color should be yellow, it may be surprising that the default colors of a white background and black text are contained in these two properties. But remember that the HEAD section is read before the BODY section. Before the BODY tag is read by the browser, the *document.bgColor* and *document.fgColor* properties still contain the default colors for the page. Finally, the *document.lastModified* property has yielded the date on which the author last changed the HTML file of Figure 12.6.

When the *document.bgColor* and *document.fgColor* properties are rewritten in the BODY section, they have been updated. They now contain the colors specified by the HTML attributes in the BODY tag. This serves to illustrate an important concept. HTML markup instructions specify many of the properties of a web page. In order to facilitate interactive programming to support web pages, the browser creates the object structure as depicted in Figure 12.5. As the page is being loaded, the browser puts values in the object properties as it determines them. By the time the page is completely loaded, the object properties are in place for JavaScript to access. But, before the page is fully loaded, some of the document's properties as specified by the HTML markup instructions are not yet set in place.

NOTE

Figure 12.7 shows the *document.lastModified* property in the Explorer browser. In Netscape, this property is unreliable, often giving a strange date. In fact, many Netscape browsers on Macintosh computers give the date Nov. 10, 1929. (We are assuming that the fact that this date is in the middle of the great stock market crash of 1929 is merely a coincidence.) Some PC browsers have also given strange dates. Given that this document property is inconsistent among browsers, we recommend that you not use it in your web pages. In fact, when you see a web page that indicates when it was last updated, the author has most likely just added the date manually.

We have used this property only to bring up a good point. The **document object model (DOM)** varies from browser to browser. The fact that *document.lastModified* doesn't work consistently in Netscape is not necessarily a Netscape shortcoming. Netscape has several document properties that don't work on Explorer. The two browsers simply have different DOMs. Since it is desirable for client-side programming languages like JavaScript to be able to access and control a document's properties in a predictable way, a world consortium has called for a standardization of the DOM. We hope that, in the not so distant future, all browsers will have consistent DOMs.

```
<HTML>
<HEAD>
</HEAD>
<BODY>
Thanks for your support.

<SCRIPT LANGUAGE=JavaScript><!--
var x;
var y;

x=prompt("Enter 1 for red or 2 for a black background","");
y=prompt("Enter 1 for yellow or 2 for white text","");

if(x=="1"){
    document.bgColor="#ff0000";
}
else {
    document.bgColor="#000000";
}

if(y=="1"){
    document.fgColor="#ffff00";
}
else {
    document.fgColor="#ffffff";
}
//--></SCRIPT>

</BODY>
</HTML>
```

FIGURE 12.8 A program that lets the user set the *document.bgColor* and *document.fgColor* properties.

The program of Figure 12.6 serves to illustrate that the browser dynamically updates the document's properties as the page is being loaded. Once the document is fully rendered by the browser, many of the document's properties can't be changed by JavaScript. That is to say, once the web page is fully visible, browsers won't allow further changes to some aspects of the web page's appearance. You can, however, use JavaScript to set certain properties as the page loads. The next example allows the user to choose between background and text colors as the page is being loaded.

Users are prompted as to whether they would like a red or black background, and then as to whether they would like yellow or white text. The program then sets the colors appropriately. The program appears in Figure 12.8. We have put the script in the body section so that it will override any instructions from the body tag. The reader is encouraged to play with this program on the web site.

12.8 OBJECT METHODS

In Section 12.1, we mentioned that not only do the physical properties of an object define its essence, but the behaviors of an object govern its usefulness. The behaviors associated with programming objects are called methods. A **method** is a function that the object can use to accomplish various tasks. As luck would have it, we have been using several methods for some time. We have been calling them functions, which they are. Methods are special kinds of functions, functions that belong to objects.

We have made extensive use of the *document.write()* method. The function *write()* is simply a function attached to the *document* object. What does it do? It writes strings to the HTML document. Given the object notation, the use of the period in *document.write()* could be cause for confusion. Properties of objects store information about the object. Methods are functions that carry out a task for the object. Hence, objects have properties and behaviors.

Without such behaviors, an object would be no more than a data structure like the *person* object pictured in Figure 12.3. The values stored in the properties of that data structure define the state of the object. Object methods are defined so that you can change the state of the object by calling the method. A suitable method to change the state to the *person* object might be *growOlder()*. The call to *person.growOlder()* would cause the person to become one year older. That is, the method would augment the *person.age* property by 1. Defining our own methods is beyond the scope of this book. However, we take full advantage of existing JavaScript methods like *document.write(),* a function that can be used to change the state of the *document* object.

12.9 METHODS OF THE WINDOW OBJECT

Two methods of the window object that we have used are *prompt()* and *alert()*. Full reference to these methods can be given by *window.prompt()* and *window.alert()* but, given the Note at the end of Section 12.6, full reference of this sort is not required. It makes sense that these methods belong to the *window* object since the methods cause other windows to appear. These methods simply allow the parent window to open subsidiary windows, collect information or give an alert, as the case may be. Keeping in line with terminology, *alert()* is a procedure method and *prompt()* is a value method.

Another useful method of the *window* object is *confirm()*. The method takes one parameter, a string. It works very similarly to the *alert()* method in that the string you send to the method appears as a message on a new window. Such a window is shown in Figure 12.9. You can see the statement using *confirm()* in Figure 12.10, which shows a web

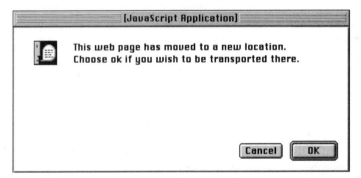

FIGURE 12.9 A window created by the *confirm()* method of the *window* object.

```
<HTML>
<HEAD>
<SCRIPT LANGUAGE=JavaScript><!--
var transfer;
transfer=window.confirm("This web page
   has moved to a new location.
   Choose ok if you wish to be
   transported there.");

if(transfer){
    window.location="newpage.html";
}
else{
   window.history.go(-1);
}
//--></SCRIPT>
</HEAD>
<BODY>
</BODY>
</HTML>
```

FIGURE 12.10 A document using the *confirm()* method to ask the user to make a decision.

page using the method. When the page is first loaded, users get a message asking if they would like to go to the new address of the page.

You can see that the variable *transfer* is declared into which the results of the call to *confirm()* are stored. Rather than returning a string like the *alert()* method, *confirm()* returns a Boolean value, true if the user hits "ok" or false if "cancel" is chosen. (The *alert()* method only has one button.) In Figure 12.10, the variable *transfer* is assigned the Boolean equivalent of the user's decision. Here is the top-down logic for the program:

-store decision from *confirm()* in transfer

-if(transfer is true)

  send user to new page

-else

  send user back from whence they came

Sending users to a new page is easy. You just assign the new URL to the *location* property of the *window* object. This causes the web page at the new URL to be automatically loaded into the browser. Of course, in the spirit of this example, you would most likely be sending the user to a different web server address. However, we have placed the new page in the same directory as the page of Figure 12.10, so the file name is sufficient.

In the else clause, where the user is to be sent back to the previous page that was loaded into their browser, we have used the *go()* method of the *history object*. As mentioned in Section 12.6, the *history* object keeps track of all the previous web pages that have been pulled up during that surfing session. Its *go()* method just causes the window to pull up one of the previous pages. In other words, the effect of *go(–1)* is like hitting the back button on the browser. The effect of *go(–2)* is like hitting the back button twice, and so forth. In this example, we have merely sent users back to the page they were viewing before they happened on the transfer page of Figure 12.10.

```
<HTML>
<HEAD>
<SCRIPT LANGUAGE=JavaScript><!--
window.open("secondpage.html","newWin","width=300,height=300");
//--></SCRIPT>
</HEAD>
<BODY>
</BODY>
</HTML>
```

FIGURE 12.11 The *open()* method of the *window* object causes a secondary window to be opened.

Another useful method of the window object is *open(),* which can take several parameters. This method simply opens a new window. A very brief script using this method is shown in Figure 12.11. When the page is loaded, a new secondary window is created. The new window has dimensions 300 × 300 (in pixels) and contains the web page generated by the HTML document "secondpage.html". You will have to visit the web site to see this script in action.

Causing unsolicited windows to pop up in such a fashion is not necessarily a good practice. In fact, it can be quite annoying. Commercial sites that allow you to put your web site on their server for free (or for a small fee) sometimes use such secondary windows for advertisement. When you pull up one of the pages that they are hosting, a small advertisement for their services pops up in a new window. Of course, you can close the window, but it is still annoying.

We present ways to use this method more constructively later in this book. In the meantime, we offer some explanation about the various parameters it can take. The first parameter is merely the URL of the page that is to be shown in the window. This can be an absolute URL, or simply a file path as in Figure 12.11. The second parameter is a name for the new window. This is something that must be present, but we shall not make further use of it. The third parameter is actually a group of instructions. An *open()* method that uses several instructions in addition to the ones in Figure 12.11 is shown below. The instructions specifying the window dimensions are straightforward. You are asked to explore the others as a review exercise. Note that all of the additional instructions are included in one set of quotation marks.

```
window.open("file.html","name","width=300,height=300,
    toolbar=yes,location=yes,scrollbars=yes,resizeable=yes");
```

NOTE In the example in this section, we have used the full object reference to emphasize that the methods do, in fact, belong to the *window* object. Once again, we could simply write *open("file.html","name")* for example.

12.10 THE *MATH* OBJECT

There are a few objects that are not part of the window-document-etc. object hierarchy. They are just lurking, waiting for a time when they can be useful. One such object is the

Math object. It has several useful properties that contain common mathematical constants. Two such properties are *Math.E* and *Math.PI*. Here E=2.718. . . is the base for the natural logarithm, and PI=3.145. . . is the ratio of any circle's circumference to its diameter. One can always just type in the decimal as we have done above, but these constants carry 16 decimal places of accuracy. When used in a calculation, reference to the *Math* object must be provided. For example,

```
area=radius*radius*Math.PI;
```

causes *area* to contain the area of a circle whose radius is stored in the variable *radius*.

We will scarcely have need to use such constants in this book, but the *Math* object has several methods that are quite useful. We present three below. The rest, as well as some more properties, are listed in Appendix B. The methods are all return methods.

```
x=Math.round(3.14);
y=Math.pow(2,5);
z=Math.random();
```

Math.round() takes one parameter and returns that number rounded off to the nearest whole number in the usual way. So *x* would contain 3. *Math.pow()* takes two parameters and returns the first raised to the power of the second parameter. So *y* contains 2 to the 5th power, or 32. *Math.random()* takes no parameters and returns a randomly chosen number in the range from 0 to 1. The author just used the method, and it caused *z* to contain .5202123682676099.

12.11 SUMMARY

Key Terms

object	document object	object hierarchy	property
primitive	constructor function	method	window object

In the simplest case, an object name binds together one or more primitive variables. The constructor function *Object()* creates a new object with no properties:

```
var house=new Object();
```

To add primitive properties, you simply define them using a period. It is important not to reuse the *var* declaration at this point. The object is already declared, and just needs properties.

```
house.price=150000;
house.location="1 Elm St.";
```

Of course, you can also assign user input to object properties using a prompt box. Once defined, you can use the object's properties just like normal primitive variables. In this way, several related primitives can be bound to one object. But you must refer to the object name in order to access the properties.

Object properties do not have to be primitive. You can create properties as new objects:

```
house.kitchen=new Object();
house.garage=new Object();
```

Then properties can be assigned to the compound objects:

```
house.kitchen.floor="tile"
house.kitchen.cabinets=15;
house.garage.cars=2;
house.garage.heated=true;
```

In this way, a type of data structure can be created. Such a structure is called an object hierarchy. An extensive object hierarchy is created automatically by a web browser when it opens a window and loads a web page. The main parent of this hierarchy is the *window* object. It has a few primitive properties that contain information about the window, but most of the properties bound to the *window* object are also objects. The one we are most concerned with is the *window.document* object, which refers to the HTML document that the window displays. Since the *window* object is the parent of the objects associated with the window, no ambiguity arises if you omit the *window* reference when you refer to its properties. For example, the document object can be referred to directly as the *document* object.

The *document* object has several primitive properties that contain information about the document. As a web page loads, values are assigned to these properties based upon the HTML markup instructions. These properties can also be assigned values by JavaScript as the page loads. The document has many properties that are objects in their own right. Web page components like images and forms are objects, and are properties of the document. These objects will be discussed in detail later in this text.

At any given time, the values stored in the properties of an object reflect the current state of the object. To give life to an object, a function can be associated with it. Such functions are called methods. The *prompt()* and *alert()* functions are actually methods of the *window* object, and could be called by full reference, *window.prompt()* and *window.alert()*. Moreover, *write()* is a method of the *document* object, but it must be called using full reference *document.write()*.

There is some discrepancy among browsers regarding the properties the *document* object has. The hierarchy of document objects created by a given browser is often referred to as the Document Object Model (DOM). The future will, we hope, see uniformity of the DOM across all web browsers.

We now have some new methods of the window object at our disposal. The *confirm()* method takes a string argument and returns a Boolean value corresponding to the user's decision. The *open()* method can take several parameters, and causes a new window to appear. We have also used a method *history.go()* of the *history* object. It takes one parameter, a negative whole number, and causes the browser to load a previously visited web page into the window. Finally, the *Math* object has some properties that carry useful constants, and some methods that can perform mathematical calculations. The *Math* object is not a property of any other object, and must always be capitalized.

12.12 REVIEW QUESTIONS

1. Discuss the fundamental difference between the name of a primitive variable and the name of an object.

2. Using Figure 12.4, refer to a property of object6. Refer to a property of object8.

3. Think of some physical object in the world, and construct a 3-deep object hierarchy similar to that of Figure 12.4. List at least two primitive properties at the end of each branch. Your primitive properties should include an example of each of the three primary primitive type literals.

4. The values stored in the same *Color* properties are written twice in Figure 12.7. Explain why two different sets of values arise from the same properties.

5. Why is it not advisable at this point to use the *document.lastModified* property in your web pages? Describe why this might be more reliable in the future.

6. Given that *alert()* and *prompt()* are methods of the *window* object, why is it permissible for us to call upon them without reference to the *window* object?

7. In the program of Figure 12.8, what happens if the user provides bad input (not a 1 or 2)?

8. Write a short program that displays the contents of the *location* property of the *window* object. Load in into your browser. What type of URL do you see? Why?

9. Near to the end of Section 12.9, several options are provided that can be sent as parameters to the *open()* method. Experiment with each one and find out their purposes.

10. Find three errors in the following code:

```
var rock=New Object;
rock="heavy";
```

11. Find three errors in the following code:

```
var computer=new Object();
var computer.memory=new Object();
computer.memory.ram=128;
computer.memory.hardDrive="10 gig";
computer.memory.hardDrive.full=false;

document.write("You have "+memory.ram+"
  of random access memory");
```

12.13 EXERCISES

1. Rewrite Exercise 11.10.1 using a *test* object with three properties, one for each test and one for the average.

2. Rewrite Exercise 11.10.2 using a *test* object with three properties, one for each test and one for the test average, and using a *quiz* object with three properties, one for each quiz and one for the quiz average. Use a primitive to store the better of the two averages and any other information you may need to store.

3. Write an interactive program that allows the user to choose the text color, background color, and link colors for the web page. To get good visual results, you will need to put some text and a couple of links in the web page.

4. Use the *confirm()* method to give users an option regarding which type of page loads. If they choose "OK", a simple borderless table page (or frames page) loads. Otherwise, a simple page with no table layout loads. (Do not cause a new window to appear.)

5. Put an image that functions as a link in a web page, perhaps a simple icon. Use that image link to cause a new window to appear. The page displayed in the new window should contain a brief message. Hint: the HREF attribute of the anchor element should not contain a URL but can contain a JavaScript statement as follows: HREF="javascript:statement;". In this way, clicking the link executes the statement following the colon.

6. Use the *confirm()* method to ask users whether they would like to view the web page in a new window. If so, open a new window for the page and close the original window. Otherwise, display the page in the original window. Just make a simple page with a brief message for display. Hint: There is a *close()* method of the *window* object that takes no parameters and closes the window in which it is called. Note: Some browsers will ask you if you are sure you want to close the window.

7. Use the *confirm()* method to ask users whether they would like to go back to the first page that they viewed in the browser window. If so, use the length property and *go()* method of the history object to send them back. Otherwise, some simple page should load. (Do not cause a new window to appear.)

12.14 PROJECT THREADS

Any exercises you do for this lesson should be referenced in your homework page following the guidelines in Section 9.10.

INTRODUCTION TO PROCESSING HTML FORMS

━━━▌**T IS** time to move on to using HTML forms to acquire user input. If you recall Section 9.1, which introduced the various HTML form elements, it should be clear that HTML forms provide a much more versatile means of obtaining user input than does the *prompt()* function. But this added versatility comes at a price. HTML forms are objects, and that adds an extra degree of difficulty. But with the notion of objects firmly in place, the transition is not overly difficult. It would, however, be a good idea to reread Section 9.1 so that the various form elements and their purposes are fresh in your mind. In this lesson, we focus on text fields, text areas, and generic buttons.

13.1 USER EVENTS

Refer back to Figure 9.1 of Section 9.1. This figure shows an HTML form loaded into a browser and waiting for something to happen. That is, the form is waiting for the user to interact with the form in some way. An **event** occurs when the user makes a change to one of the form elements. In that form, the particular event with the most significance is when the user clicks the "process order" button. Upon the event of the button click, JavaScript must jump into action to process the information from the form. This is the notion of event-driven programming. When certain user events occur, JavaScript must first detect the event, and then must do something about it.

Event detection is accomplished by **event handlers.** Let's consider the event of the user clicking a button. Since the actual button is created with HTML, it makes sense that the event handler to detect the button click is a special attribute of the HTML button element. The following button is endowed with the *onclick* event handler:

```
          Click Me
<FORM>
 <INPUT TYPE=button VALUE="Click Me" onclick="changecolor()">
</FORM>
```

When the user clicks the button, the *onclick* event handler is automatically activated. The value of this event handler is the call to a JavaScript function named *changecolor()*. So here

```
<HTML>
<HEAD>

<SCRIPT LANGUAGE=JavaScript><!--
function changecolor(){
    document.bgColor="#ff0000";
}
//--></SCRIPT>

</HEAD>
<BODY>

<FORM>
    <INPUT TYPE=button VALUE="Click Me" onclick="changecolor()">
</FORM>

</BODY>
</HTML>
```

FIGURE 13.1 This HTML document creates a button. When the button is clicked, the background color of the web page is changed to red.

is what happens. The user clicks the button; the onclick event handler detects the event and makes a call to the function *changecolor()*. The HTML and JavaScript used to implement this button in a web page are shown in Figure 13.1. The only thing visible on the web page is the button. When the button is clicked, the background color of the web page is changed to red. You should try it out on the web site.

You can see that the function called by the event handler is defined in the HEAD section of the document. All this function does is set the *bgColor* property of the *document* object to red. Since this is the first function we have created, some explanation is in order.

The functions we have been using in the previous lessons are built-in JavaScript functions (actually methods, since they are all associated with objects). When you need something done like *write()* to the document, *parceFloat()* a string, or *prompt()* the user for input, you call these methods. But now, we must define our own functions to call when an event handler is activated. There are simply no built-in functions to handle all of our form-processing needs. Function definitions take the following general form:

```
function name(){
    statement;
    ⋮
    statement;
}
```

The JavaScript statements inside the function are what make it accomplish the task for which it is defined. Once defined, you can call upon the function by name, just like the built-in functions. Since there is no object association with such self-defined functions, no object reference is required to call the function. In our present situation, we are letting the onclick event handler call the function.

So, in general, our strategy for handling user events is summed up in Figure 13.2. What happens when the button is clicked? That depends on the JavaScript instructions comprising

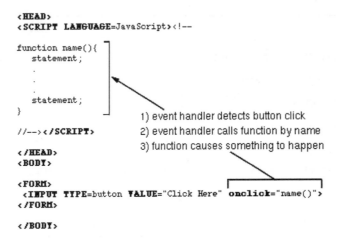

```
<HEAD>
<SCRIPT LANGUAGE=JavaScript><!--

function name(){
    statement;
    .
    .
    .
    statement;
}

//--></SCRIPT>

</HEAD>
<BODY>

<FORM>
 <INPUT TYPE=button VALUE="Click Here" onclick="name()">
</FORM>

</BODY>
```

1) event handler detects button click
2) event handler calls function by name
3) function causes something to happen

FIGURE 13.2 The strategy for handling user events.

the function. Maybe the function does something simple like change the background color of the web page, as in Figure 13.1. But maybe the function contains elaborate instructions, like those that would be necessary to process the pizza form of Figure 9.1.

NOTE Changing the background color of the web page by clicking a form button is fundamentally different from changing the background using a prompt box. In the example in Figure 12.8, the input from the prompt box was assigned to the document's properties as the web page was loading. With an HTML form, the page is completely loaded and the event handler is basically sitting there waiting for something to happen. In this case, the browser has already assigned "final" values to the properties of the document object.

Currently, not all browsers allow many of these properties to be changed after the web page is completely loaded. In fact, *document.bgColor* is the only property regarding the document's colors that can be changed in all browsers after the page has been loaded. In other words, some browsers won't allow the text color to be changed when the user clicks a button. If all browsers in the future adhere more closely to the recommended DOM, languages like JavaScript will be able to dynamically update more aspects of the document's appearance than is now possible.

13.2 THE *FORM* OBJECT

After the last note, you may be concerned that JavaScript has only limited control of the document after the page has been loaded. Consider the HTML form shown in Figure 13.3a. In Figure 13.3b, we have supplied the HTML file that generates the web page. The purpose of the form is simple: the user is to enter his or her first name into the text field. Upon clicking the message button, the user will get a personalized message in the text area at the bottom of the form. A reset button has also been supplied.

OK, so the user enters a first name into the text field. That name has to be stored into a variable. How is that accomplished? Well, it is stored into a property of an object. What object, you might say? To answer that question, one must get at the nature of the HTML form object.

FIGURE 13a An HTML form that generates a personalized message when the button is clicked.

```
<HTML>
<HEAD>
<SCRIPT LANGUAGE=JavaScript><!--
function giveMessage(){
document.messageform.reply.value=document.messageform.fname.value+
", have a nice day!";
}
//--></SCRIPT>
</HEAD>
<BODY BGCOLOR="#FFFFCC">
<FORM NAME=messageform>
   Please enter your first name:
   <INPUT TYPE=text NAME=fname VALUE="" SIZE=10><BR>
   <INPUT TYPE=button NAME=Button VALUE="Click here for a personal
      message." onclick="giveMessage()"><BR>
   <INPUT TYPE=reset VALUE="Reset Form"><BR>
   <TEXTAREA NAME=reply ROWS=3 COLS=27 WRAP=virtual></TEXTAREA>
</FORM>
</BODY>
</HTML>
```

FIGURE 13b The entire document containing the form of Figure 13.3a.

A form is a property of the document that contains it. But the form is also an object. Among its properties are the form elements comprising the form. These are also objects. Finally, the properties of the form's elements are primitives that contain the actual data associated with the form. Access to the form's properties is granted by the name of the form as supplied by the NAME attribute of the FORM tag. Similarly, access to the properties of the specific form elements is granted by the NAME attributes of the respective form elements. At the ends of the branches of this object hierarchy are primitive *value* properties that store information.

This all sounds quite complicated, but when diagrammed as an object hierarchy, the structure becomes apparent. With the names supplied in Figure 13.3b, the object hierarchy for the form is pictured in Figure 13.4. The buttons are also object properties of *messageform,* but we do not list them in the diagram. In fact, the buttons were not even given names in Figure 13.3b. There was no point in doing so, as we do not intend to access any of their properties. The only purpose of the buttons is to activate event handlers. The text field and text area handle all of the data.

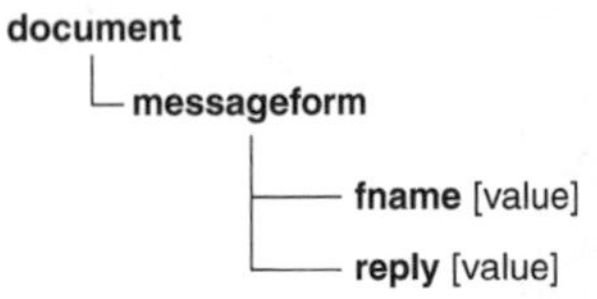

document
    └─ messageform
            ├─ **fname** [value]
            └─ **reply** [value]

FIGURE 13.4 A partial object hierarchy for the form of Figure 13.3.

The value of *document messageform.fname.value* is initially set by the VALUE attribute of the HTML tag for the text field when the page loads. It is initially an empty string, since we wanted the text field for the name to be empty when the page loads. The value of *document.messageform.reply.value* is initially set by the contents of the <TEXTAREA> ...</TEXTAREA> container element. We have left this value initially empty as well.

When the user enters a name, it is stored into the primitive *document.messageform. fname.value.* All we need to do is take this value, concatenate some message onto it, and assign the results to *document.messageform.reply.value.* The onclick event handler is set to call a function named *giveMessage().* In Figure 13.3b, this function is defined in the HEAD section of the document.

Aside from the cumbersome object notation, the function is very simple. It concatenates a short message onto the name that the user enters and assigns the whole string to the text area.

13.3   USING LOCAL VARIABLES IN FUNCTIONS

The form in Figure 13.5 contains two text fields into which the user is to enter two numbers. Then two buttons are presented. Clicking one causes the two numbers to be added, and clicking the other results in the product of the two numbers. The result is displayed in a text area. The first thing to note is that each of the buttons calls a different function. This is straightforward. One function adds the two numbers, and the other function multiplies the two numbers. The complete HTML file is shown in Figure 13.6.

FIGURE 13.5 An HTML form that gives the option of adding or multiplying two numbers.

```
<HTML>
<HEAD>
<SCRIPT LANGUAGE=JavaScript><!--
function plus(){
    var n1;
    var n2;
    n1=document.addmult.num1.value;
    n2=document.addmult.num2.value;

    n1=parseFloat(n1);
    n2=parseFloat(n2);

    document.addmult.result.value=n1+n2;
}
function times(){
    var n1;
    var n2;
    n1=document.addmult.num1.value;
    n2=document.addmult.num2.value;

    n1=parseFloat(n1);
    n2=parseFloat(n2);

    document.addmult.result.value=n1*n2;
}
//--></SCRIPT>
</HEAD>
<BODY BGCOLOR="#FFFFCC">
<FORM name=addmult>
    Enter a number in each field:
    <INPUT TYPE=text NAME=num1 VALUE="" SIZE=5>
    <INPUT TYPE=text NAME=num2 VALUE="" SIZE=5><BR>
    <INPUT TYPE=button NAME=Button VALUE="+" onclick="plus()">
    <INPUT TYPE=button NAME=Button VALUE="*" onclick="times()"><BR>
    <INPUT TYPE=reset VALUE="Reset Form"><BR>
    <TEXTAREA NAME=result ROWS=3 COLS=27 WRAP=virtual></TEXTAREA>
</FORM>
</BODY>
</HTML>
```

FIGURE 13.6 The complete document for the addition/multiplication form.

An object diagram showing only those form elements whose values we need is provided below.

```
document
    └─ addmult
            ├─ num1[value]
            ├─ num2[value]
            └─ result[value]
```

We first concentrate on the *plus()* function. Form values from text fields are *always* stored as strings, just as values from prompt boxes. So we are going to have to parse the values into numbers before adding them. Otherwise they will be concatenated. But this is not as simple as it may seem. In previous lessons, when we prompted for input, we put that input into a variable and then parsed that variable into a number. No problem. Suppose we try to parse the value of the first text field into an number:

```
document.addmult.num1.value=parseFloat(document.addmult.num1.value);
```

The statement is written correctly, but it does not work as planned. Not only are data stored in form *value* properties as strings, but *value* properties are incapable of holding numbers. In other words, you can't even assign a number to a form's value property as we attempted to do above. As soon as you try, the computer changes it back into a string.

The alternative is to store the two numbers from the form into local variables inside the function. The top-down logic of the *plus()* function in Figure 13.6 is

-store the text field values into new variables (n1,n2)

-parse *n1* and *n2*

-assign their sum to the value of the text area

While the two variables *n1* and *n2* are absolutely necessary if the form values are to be parsed into numbers, their use offers another advantage. Once the form values are stored into *n1* and *n2,* you can manipulate the data using the concise variable names, rather than having to refer to the long object references time after time. The functions in Figure 13.6 would not be as easily read if the full object references were carried through all of the statements. A few extra lines of code are required to declare the new variables, but that's OK. It's still better than carrying full object reference through the function.

The function *mult()* for the multiplication button is similar. The only difference between the two functions is that the last line of *mult()* involves multiplication rather than addition. The order in which they are defined is unimportant: we could switch the order in which the functions appear, and the form would work equally well.

We have slipped in another term, local variable, without any explanation. So a brief explanation is in order. The term **local variable** refers to variables that are declared inside a function and are used to process information only within that function. In Figure 13.6, each of the functions make use of their own local variables. It may seem a logical error on our part to formally declare the variables *n1* and *n2* twice, once in the *plus()* function and once in the *mult()* function. After all, a variable should only be declared once. After that, you are free to store information in and retrieve information from the variable as needed.

But, being declared inside functions, these local variables only exist during the function call. Let's go through the process. The page with the form is loaded. The user enters numbers into the two text fields and clicks the * button. The *mult()* function is called and the local variables *n1* and *n2* spring into action. They help process the form data. When the *mult()* function is done and the product of the two numbers is written to the text area, the two local variables are erased from the computer's memory.

Now the user clicks the + button. The *plus()* function is called and the local variables within that function spring into action. Once the function has done its thing, they are gone. The user could keep clicking the buttons all day. Each time one of the functions is called, the local variables within that function are declared and used only while that function is active. Then they are gone. In contrast, the values of the form elements are **global:** they exist the whole time the page is loaded and, at any given time, they reflect the current state of the form object. When the user is between button clicks and no function is in action, the local function variables simply don't exist.

Further to emphasize the limited existence of local function variables, we provide a simple example. The form appears in Figure 13.7. Rather than showing the whole HTML document, we have provided the JavaScript support for the form. The purpose of the form is evident from the textual instructions on the form itself. The name of the form is *clickform*

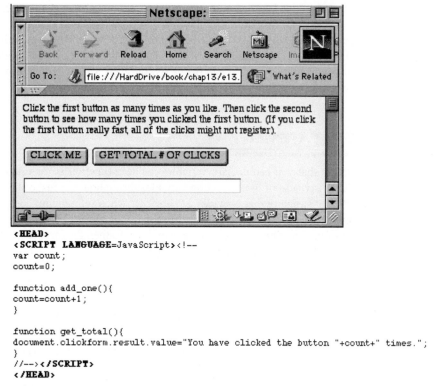

```
<HEAD>
<SCRIPT LANGUAGE=JavaScript><!--
var count;
count=0;

function add_one(){
count=count+1;
}

function get_total(){
document.clickform.result.value="You have clicked the button "+count+" times.";
}
//--></SCRIPT>
</HEAD>
```

FIGURE 13.7   A form that tallies the number of times the first button is clicked.

and the name of the text field is *result*. The function that the first button calls is named *add_one()* and the function that the second button calls is named *get_total()*. Notice that all the *add_one()* function does is add one to the *count* variable. The interesting feature of this variable is that it is not defined in the function. Rather, it is defined outside of both functions. When the page first loads, this variable is set up and initialized to 0. Each time the user clicks the first button, the *add_one()* function augments *count* by one. Finally, when the user clicks the second button, the contents of count are written to the text field with a message.

Let's look at the alternative. Suppose we had defined *count* as a local variable inside the *add_one().* function. When the user clicks the first button, *count* would be declared, initialized to 0 and bumped up to 1. After the function call, *count* would be erased from the computer's memory. The next time the user clicks the first button, the same thing would happen. The variable *count* would briefly contain 1, and then would be gone. In fact, the user could keep clicking the button all day, and *count* would only briefly exist each time. But that's not the worst problem. When the user finally clicks the button to receive the total number of clicks, the *get_total()* function would find no variable named *count* when it tried to write the total click count. Since the *add_one()* function would be dormant at that time, *count* would simply not exist.

When a document is loaded, all of the global variables are set up and given values. That is, the form's *value* properties and variables not defined in functions are given values. These variables contain information pertaining to the current state of the document. The functions and their local variables are merely "on call". When something like a user event happens, a function is called into action. This function call can change a global variable like *count* or one of a form's *value* properties. Any local function variables, like *n1* and *n2* of in Figure 13.6, aid the function in performing its task while the function is active, but don't carry information about the global state of the document. The local variables lie undefined until the next function call when they exist only for a brief moment in time, to help the function update the state of the document.

13.4   THE *WITH* STATEMENT

The notion that you can declare variables inside a function is important. In fact, we will make extensive use of local function variables throughout the rest of this text. But there is a JavaScript structure that provides a "shortcut" when referencing compound objects. We first rewrite the *times()* function using this notation, and then provide an explanation. In this version of the function, we use no local variables. Rather, the form properties are processed directly, without the help of temporary variables.

```
function times(){
  with(document.addmult){
    num1.value=parseFloat(num1.value);
    num2.value=parseFloat(num2.value);
    result.value=num1.value*num2.value;
  }
}
```

You can probably deduce how the statement works. The with statement specifies an object reference, in this case reference to the HTML form, *document.addmult*. With this reference specified, you can directly refer to its properties, in this case, the form elements. So, in general, the with statement takes the form

```
with (object) {
  refer directly to properties of object
}
```

But note that this referencing privilege applies only to statements within the friendly confines of the brackets {} that enclose the body of the with statement. It is also important to note that the object whose properties you reference can be compound. Indeed, that was the case in the *times()* function just above.

13.5   ORGANIZING FORMS WITH HTML TABLES

HTML forms can be made to appear much more organized when the form elements are contained in a borderless HTML table. This requires you to learn no new concepts. You were organizing whole web pages with borderless tables in Lesson 7. With the help of a good HTML editor, it requires very little extra work to put your form elements into a table.

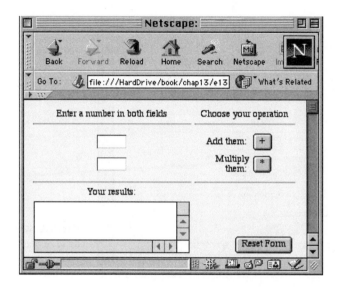

FIGURE 13.8 Form elements organized with a borderless HTML table.

You can put the FORM tags inside the TABLE tags

<TABLE><FORM>....</FORM></TABLE>

or vice versa:

<FORM><TABLE>....</TABLE></FORM>

Either way, the TABLE element won't interfere with your form. A tabular version of the adding and multiplication form of Figure 13.5 appears in Figure 13.8. We're not even claiming that this version is aesthetically superior. But it does serve to illustrate the point.

13.6 VERIFICATION OF TEXT INPUT

Verification of user input in HTML forms is really no different from the verification techniques we learned in Lesson 11. In fact, you could easily provide verification for the add/multiply example of Figure 13.5. You would want to verify that the user has entered numbers. This is left as an exercise.

To illustrate JavaScript's utility in form verification we provide a form that is to submit the user's name, address, and e-mail address to a guestbook database. The form is shown in Figure 13.9. It has been organized with a borderless table.

Recall Section 9.2 where we discussed the client-server model. Any permanent guestbook database would need to be kept on the web server. The purpose of the HTML form of Figure 13.9 is to acquire the information, verify it to some extent, and then send it to the server for permanent storage. Since the specifics of submitting form data to the web server are not discussed until Lesson 18, we will have to be content with a verification procedure for the form's data. The text area at the bottom of the form will simply echo the user's input and indicate that it has been submitted to the guestbook.

FIGURE 13.9 A form to acquire user information and submit it to a server-side database.

We have not supplied the HTML code for the form, but you should have the idea by now. We do, however, provide a partial object diagram for the form so that you can easily see the reference names for the form object and those elements whose values we will use.

```
document
    └─ infoform
            ├── fullname[value]
            ├── address[value]
            ├── email[value]
            └── display[value]
```

The verification we wish to accomplish is simply to make sure that no fields have been left blank. If one or more of the fields is blank, the user will be alerted. Otherwise, the user will see a summary of the information and an indication that it has been submitted. The function called by the onclick event handler of the submit button contains the following top-down logic:

-if (one or more fields are blank)

    alert the user

-else

    summarize the information in the text area

    (submit the form data to the server)

Of course, for this example, we are not going to submit the information to the server as the second line of the "else" clause indicates. We have included that only to give you the full flavor of this example. The complete code for the function is given below. You should experiment with this program on the web site. As long as least one field is empty, no matter how many times the user hits the submit button, the alert keeps popping up.

```
<HEAD>
<SCRIPT LANGUAGE=JavaScript><!--
function verify(){
 with(document.infoform){
   if((fullname.value=="")||(address.value=="")||(email.value=="")){
     alert("You have left one or more fields blank.  Please supply the
     necessary information, and  re-submit the form.");
   }
   else {
    display.value="The following information has been added to our
    guestbook:\r" +fullname.value+"\r"+ address.value +"\r" +email.value;
   }
 }
}
//--></SCRIPT>
</HEAD>
```

NOTE

There is a strange symbol used three times when assigning the long string to *display.value*. The symbol \r causes a carriage return in the text area. You can't use a <BR> tag to cause a line break in the text area. That is an HTML tag and is only used to write HTML instructions to the HTML document.

The text area is an object embedded in the web page. It displays character strings, rather than HTML. Markup instructions are useless in a text area. Rather, the \r return symbol causes the string to return to the next line.

13.7 AN ADVANCED EXAMPLE (OPTIONAL)

We end this lesson with a more complicated example that plays a guessing game with the user. The rules of the game are shown above the form in Figure 13.10. So that we don't have to display the HTML code for the form, a partial object diagram is given below.

document
  └── **guessform**
        ├── **guess**[value]
        └── **status**[value]

The name of the function that the button calls is *check()*. We need to set about writing this function. The first task at hand is to generate a random whole number in the range from 1 to 10. Recall from Section 12.10 that the *Math.random()* method returns a random floating-point number in the range 0 to 1. So getting a random whole number in the range from 1 to 10 is going to take a bit of work. The first inclination is to use 10 "if" statements.

```
r=Math.random();
if((0<=r)&&(r<.1){
  num=1;
}
if(.1<=r)&&(r<.2){
  num=2;
}
  ⋮
```

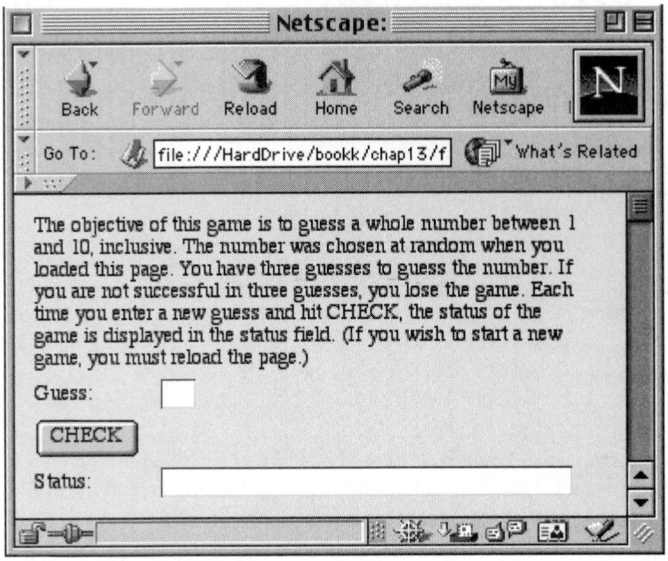

FIGURE 13.10 An interactive guessing game.

Then the variable *num* would contain the desired random number (i.e., if *r* is in [0, .1) set num=1, if *r* is in [.1, .2) set num=2, etc.). However, there is a much more concise way to accomplish the same thing. We first multiply r by 10:

$$r=r*10;$$

getting a random floating-point number in the range from 0 to 10. We could then use *Math.round()* to obtain the appropriate whole number. But this would not quite work. For starters, only the numbers in the range (9.5, 10) would round off to 10, whereas numbers in the range (8.5, 9.5) would round off to 9. The numbers 1 through 8 would be obtained in a fashion similar to 9. So 10 would be less likely to come up than the numbers 1 through 9. Another problem is that the range (0, .5) would round off to 0, which is not one of the desired numbers. To get around this, we multiply by 10 and add 1/2:

$$r=(r*10)+.5;$$

Then *r* is a random floating-point number in the range (.5, 10.5), giving each of the whole numbers 1–10 an equal chance of occurring after we round. Putting all of these ideas into one statement

$$r=Math.round((10*Math.random()+.5));$$

causes *r* to contain a random whole number in the range from 1 to 10.

OK, so we can get the random number. Now on to the logic of the problem. We wish to set up the function so that the user can't keep playing after the three guesses are used. A suitable top-down logic for the *check()* function is the following:

```
function check(){
if (still_playing)
    total_guesses=total_guesses+1
    if (user wins)
        give winning message
        still_playing=false
    else
        if(total_guesses==3)
            give losing message
            still_playing=false
        else
            tell them how many guesses are left
else
        alert the user that game is over
}
```

The logic goes like this. *still_playing* is a Boolean variable. The first decision to be made: is the game over? If *still_playing* is false, the user gets an alert. This is to prevent the user from keeping on playing after the game is over. If *still_playing* is true, we add one to *total_guesses*. Then another decision is to be made: has the user won? If so, a winning message is given and *still_playing* is set to false. If the user has not won, yet another decision has to be made: has the user lost? If *total_guesses* has reached 3, give a losing message and set *still_playing* to false. Otherwise, tell the user the number did not match, and say how many guesses are left.

If in that process *still_playing* is set to false, any further attempts to click the button (call the function) will result in an alert that the game is over. The only other alternative is that the user has guesses left, and *still_playing* remains true through the whole process. In this case, the user clicks the button (calls the function) with a new guess. The *total_guesses* variable is increased by 1 again, and the decisions are made. Eventually, *total_guesses* will get to 3 or the user will get the right number.

With this logic in mind, examine the entire function in Figure 13.11. You should play with this program on the web site to get a better feel for how it works.

The first glaring difference between this program and most of the previous programs in this lesson is that the variables are actually declared before the function. This is crucial. Remember, if variables are defined in a function they are created when the function is called and wiped out when the function is done. Playing the guessing game will, in general, involve several function calls. In this program, the contents of the variables must survive the function calls. There would be no other way to keep track of the total guesses that have been made and whether or not the game is over. Moreover, you certainly don't want to generate a new winning number each time the user guesses.

The three variables declared outside of the function are set up and initialized as soon as the page loads. They exist in the global setting. Upon each guess (function call), they are updated by the function. In this way, they can keep track of the status of the game. They simply could not have been defined as local variables inside the function.

```
<HTML>
<HEAD>
<SCRIPT LANGUAGE=JavaScript><!--
var winning_number;
var total_guesses;
var still_playing;

winning_number=Math.round((10*Math.random()+.5));
total_guesses=0;
still_playing=true;

function check(){
    with(document.guessform){
      if(still_playing){
        total_guesses=total_guesses+1;
          if (guess.value==winning_number){
              status.value="You have won in "+total_guesses+" guesses";
              still_playing=false;
          }
          else{
              if(total_guesses>=3){
                  status.value="You have lost the game";
                  still_playing=false;
              }
              else{
                  status.value="Incorrect. You have "+(3-total_guesses)+" guesses left.";
              }
          }
      }
      else{
        alert("C'mon, buddy, the game is over.  Reload the page to play again.");
      }
    }
}
//--></SCRIPT>
</HEAD>
```

FIGURE 13.11   The supporting JavaScript for the number-guessing form of Figure 13.10.

13.8   SUMMARY

Key Terms

event	event handler	text field
value property	text area	button
reset button	local variables	global variables

When an HTML form is loaded into a browser, it is basically sitting there waiting for a user event. The only event covered in this lesson is the act of the user clicking a button in a form. When such an event occurs, the *onclick* event handler detects it and calls a JavaScript function. The *onclick* event handler is given as an attribute of the form button that it is monitoring. The JavaScript function it calls is defined in the head section of the HTML document.

Although a button click can be used to change the background color of the document, the other physical appearance attributes of the document object are not subject to change in this way (at least at the present time), since the web page is fully loaded by the time a user clicks a form button. However, the values of form elements can be accessed and updated after the page is fully loaded.

An HTML form is an object and is a property of the document object. The form elements defined in a given form are also objects and are properties of that form. Finally, the values of the form elements are primitives. For text fields and text areas, these values contain the text appearing within that form element. Not only is information stored in value properties of forms as strings, but you can't even change that value property to numeric format. Value properties are simply incapable of holding numbers. When you must have numeric data from a form (for example, so that addition is not confused with concatenation), you can create local variables within the function to store the data temporarily. Variables can be declared and used inside a function as usual. However, local variables exist only during the function call to help the function do its job.

With the text field, the initial contents of its *value* property is set by the VALUE attribute of the INPUT tag that defines the field. However, with the text area, the initial contents of its *value* property is set by the contents of the <TEXTAREA>. . . </TEXTAREA> container element. To refer to these value properties with JavaScript, you must provide full object reference. This reference takes the form

document.formname.elementname.value

The names are set by the NAME attributes of the form and form element.

> **N O T E** So there is a lot going on here. Let's get some perspective. On the HTML side, you define the form, the name of the form, the names of the form elements, and the initial values of the form elements. The event handler is also defined as part of the HTML. On the JavaScript side, you define the function that the event handler calls, access the needed form element values, and can supply output as the *value* of a form element.

If there is more than one button in an HTML form, their event handlers can call different functions to perform different tasks. If more than one function is used, they must be defined separately and have different names. However, the order in which they appear in the HEAD section is unimportant.

A good way to avoid using full object reference is to use the "with" statement. You specify the desired object reference in the with statement, and you can directly access the object properties. When dealing with HTML forms, it is convenient to specify reference to *document.formname*. Then you can refer directly to the form elements inside the body of the "with" statement. Note that you still have to reference the name of a form element before you can access its *value* property.

Verification of form input is similar the verification techniques we learned in Lesson 11. When the button is clicked, the function checks the validity of the form's data. But in the case with forms, you do not have to reprompt for input. If the input is deficient, the user is alerted and is simply returned to the form to try again.

13.9 REVIEW QUESTIONS

1. Describe what happens when a form button is clicked in terms of the sequence of things that occur.

2. The reset button causes the form to be reset, yet it has no event handler. Speculate on how it works. (This was not addressed in this lesson. See answers in Appendix D.)

3. What would happen if you try to have a form button change the *document.fgColor* property?

4. Why did we not parse the form value in the form of Figure 13.3, but did so in the form of Figure 13.5?

5. When you have two different buttons in a form that are to accomplish two different tasks, how does the event handling work?

6. Suppose the user has entered a number into a text field of a form. What type of literal would the following statement cause to be stored in the value property of that text field? Why?

```
document.formname.fieldname.value=
    parseFloat (document.formname.
    fieldname.value);
```

7. For the form of Figure 13.7, why is the count variable not declared within the *add_one()* function? Discuss what would happen if it were.

8. Find three errors in the following code (assume that the rest of the document is present):

```
function process{
  with(document.formname){
  value=3;
}
<INPUT TYPE=button NAME=Button
VALUE="CLICK ME" onclick=process>
```

13.10 EXERCISES

1. Make a form with five buttons. Each button should cause the background of the web page to change to a different color.

2. Make a version of the background color program of Figure 13.1 so that, if the button is clicked a second time, the background changes back to its original color. Subsequent button clicks cause the background to change back and forth between the two colors.

3. Make a form that requests the user to enter a hexadecimal color into a text field and then click a button. When the button is clicked, the background changes to that color.

4. Make a version of the form of Figure 13.3 in which the user is alerted if the text field is left blank or contains a number rather than a name.

5. Make a version of the form of Figure 13.3 that has three buttons. One gives a positive comment, one gives a neutral comment, and the other gives an insult.

6. Add features to the addition/multiplication form of Figure 13.5 so that a complete message appears in each case. For example: "The sum of 1 and 1 is 2." or "The product of 3 and 4 is 12." Option: verify that the user has entered numbers.

7. Make a version of the addition/multiplication form of Figure 13.5 that includes subtraction and division. If division is clicked, the program should verify that the divisor is not 0. Option: also verify that the user has entered numbers into both fields.

8. Make a version of the button-clicking program of Figure 13.7 that has three different click-me buttons. It should have three text fields, one to give the number of clicks for each of the buttons. Moreover, the form doesn't have a button that gives the total number of clicks. Rather, each time one of the "click-me" buttons is clicked, the appropriate text field is immediately updated.

9. The swami program: Make a program that asks the user to enter a name. The user then gets one of seven fortunes upon clicking the button (only one button in this program besides a reset button). For example, "Raul, I see great things in your future." Each time the button is clicked, a new message is chosen at random. Hint: if you didn't read Section 13.7, you can find out there how to generate random numbers appropriately.

Note: Exercises 10–13 are modifications of the number-guessing game of Figure 13.11.

10. Verify the user's guesses. First check to see if a number in the proper range was entered (don't permit a guess of 11, for example.) Then round off the user's guess to remove any decimal places (don't permit a guess of 5.5, for example).

11. Add two more small text fields, one for each of the first two guesses. After the first guess, that guess appears in one of the fields. After the second guess, that guess appears in the second text field. That way the user can keep track of the previous guesses. Option: alert the user if he or she enters one of their previous guesses.

12. Modify the program so that there are 15 possible numbers and the user gets four guesses.

13. Modify the program so that there are 25 possible numbers and the user gets five guesses. There should be another text field. After each guess, the user is told whether the guess was hot (within 3), warmer (within 5), warm (within 7), or cold.

13.11 PROJECT THREADS

Any exercises you do for this lesson should be referenced in your homework page following the guidelines in Section 9.10.

OPTIONS IN HTML FORMS

WITH TEXT fields and text areas, you can use forms to obtain textual user input. However, checkboxes, radio buttons, and pull-down menus add the capability for the user to make choices in forms. It is a good idea to go back to Section 9.1 and refresh your memory on the basic nature of these three types of form elements. The strategy for dealing with them is the same: when the user clicks a button, an event handler calls a JavaScript function, and the function processes the information from the form.

As always, it is important to go to the web site and play with the example programs of this lesson. As the interactive capabilities of the examples increase, it is harder to get a complete feel for the program without testing all of the possible input possibilities for yourself.

14.1 THE CHECKBOX

A checkbox is fundamentally different from text input fields in that it provides an on-off capability, rather than being subject to a wide variety of user inputs. Such an on-off capability suggests a Boolean variable and, in fact, that's how a checkbox works. The *checkbox* object has a Boolean property. If the checkbox is chosen, the property contains true, otherwise it contains false. The property is aptly named *checked*. With the full object reference, this property is accessed with

document.formname.checkboxname.checked

and is either true or false depending upon the state of the checkbox.

To get the feel for this, it's best to proceed with an example. The form in Figure 14.1 simulates an online shopping cart. Each time the update-cart button is clicked, a summary of the selected items is displayed. Figure 14.2 contains the code for the document. Only the code for the HTML form and JavaScript function is provided. The rest of the document has been omitted to save space.

The function that the "Update Cart" button calls is worthy of explanation. We have used the with statement to shorten the object references, but that is old hat. After that, the top-down logic for the function goes as follows:

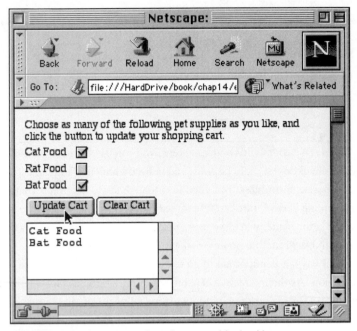

FIGURE 14.1 A pet store shopping cart with checkboxes.

```
<SCRIPT LANGUAGE=JavaScript><!--
function update(){
    with (document.storeform){
        var contents;
        contents="";
        if (item1.checked==true){
            contents=contents+"Cat Food\r";
        }
        if (item2.checked==true){
            contents=contents+"Rat Food\r";
        }
        if (item3.checked==true){
            contents=contents+"Bat Food\r";
        }
        if (contents==""){
        contents="Your cart is empty.";
        }
        display.value=contents;
    }
}
//--></SCRIPT>

<FORM name=storeform>
    <INPUT TYPE=checkbox NAME=item1>
    <INPUT TYPE=checkbox NAME=item2>
    <INPUT TYPE=checkbox NAME=item3>
    <INPUT TYPE=button VALUE="Update Cart" onclick="update()">
    <INPUT TYPE=reset VALUE="Clear Cart">
    <TEXTAREA NAME=display ROWS=4 COLS=18 WRAP=virtual>Happy Shopping!</TEXTAREA>
</FORM>
```

FIGURE 14.2 The essential code for the form in Figure 14.1.

-declare *contents* and start with an empty cart (contents="")

-if (item1 is selected)
    add cat food to *contents*

-if (item2 is selected)
    add rat food to *contents*

-if (item3 is selected)
    add bat food to *contents*

-if (cart is still empty)
    assign a suitable message to *contents*

-assign *contents* to text area

The logic of the function is pretty clear. Start with an empty string variable, and then test each checkbox. If it is checked, append that item onto the *contents* variable. If none of the items have been selected, *contents* remains empty and a message to that effect is assigned to *contents*. After that, you assign contents to the display area.

It is crucial that the *contents* variable be updated if a box has been selected, rather than simply reassigning it a value. For example, if the "if" statement for item2 contained only

```
contents="Rat Food";
```

any previous contents of the variable would be erased if the statement were executed. So, if both cat food and rat food had been chosen, the string "Rat Food" would actually replace "Cat Food", and there would be no mention of cat food in the shopping cart display. The assignment that augments *contents* while preserving any previous information it contains is of the form

```
contents=contents+"Rat Food\r";
```

where the carriage return will cause any subsequent additions to the cart to begin on the next line.

It is also worthy of note that the *contents* variable is a local function variable. Since the entire shopping cart display is re-evaluated each time the cart is updated, the value of *contents* need not survive the function call. Its value ends up being stored as the value of the display and is preserved as part of the current state of the form. When the function is called upon again, *contents* is recreated to help tally the current checkbox selections, and its legacy is left in the display area.

NOTE
There is an HTML attribute that will cause a checkbox to be checked when the page first loads. The attribute is named simply CHECKED. This attribute takes no value. If you include it in the definition of a checkbox

```
<INPUT TYPE=checkbox NAME=item CHECKED>
```

the checkbox is initially checked. Moreover, it can still be unchecked as usual. The radio button, which we discuss shortly, also uses this attribute.

14.2 USING HIDDEN VALUES FOR CHECKBOXES

Of course, the shopping-cart example of the previous section leaves a good bit to be desired. For starters, there was no mention of prices for the items. Second, a total should be given that reflects the sum of the prices of the selected items. Finally, it couldn't hurt to include a count of the number of items the user has selected.

To deal with the item prices, we employ the *value* property of a checkbox. Now, the value properties of text areas, text fields, and the buttons we have used contain information that is marked physically on the object in the web page. There is certainly no room to mark up "click me" on a checkbox, for example. That leaves the value property free to carry hidden information about the checkbox.

To illustrate this, we offer the better version of the above shopping cart. Since we will use the same form, you can refer back to Figure 14.1. As far as the HTML code for the form goes, the only difference is the addition of VALUE attributes for the checkboxes that contain the prices of the items. The new code for the input buttons is:

```
<INPUT TYPE=checkbox NAME=item1 VALUE=15>
<INPUT TYPE=checkbox NAME=item2 VALUE=12>
<INPUT TYPE=checkbox NAME=item3 VALUE=17>
```

To emphasize that two primitive properties of each of the checkbox objects are going to be used, an object diagram for the form is given in Figure 14.3. Figure 14.4 shows the JavaScript function for the improved shopping cart.

document
└─ **storeform**
   ├── **item1** [checked,value]
   ├── **item2** [checked,value]
   ├── **item3** [checked,value]
   └── **display** [value]

FIGURE 14.3 An object diagram for the improved shopping cart. Two properties of each checkbox are listed.

Other than the extra counting going on for the total price and the total number of selected items, the only substantial difference is in the need for local variables to store the hidden values from the checkboxes. Since these values are to be added and since value properties of HTML forms are incapable of containing numbers, we store these values into local variables before parsing them. The top-down logic for the function is as follows:

-declare the variables (contents, total_price,total_items, i1,i2,i3;)

-initialize the counters(contents="", total_price=0, total_items=0)

-transfer (and parse) the checkbox values to i1,i2, and i3

-if(item1 is checked)
    add item1 and its price to the cart
    add the price to the total
    increment the items counter by 1

-same process for the other two items

-assign the results to the display area

```
<SCRIPT LANGUAGE=JavaScript><!--
function update(){
   with (document.storeform){
      var contents, total_price,total_items,i1,i2,i3;

      contents="";
      total_price=0;
      total_items=0;

      i1=parseFloat(item1.value);
      i2=parseFloat(item2.value);
      i3=parseFloat(item3.value);

      if (item1.checked){
         contents="item1: $"+i1+"\r";
         total_price=total_price+i1;
         total_items=total_items+1;
      }
      if (item2.checked){
         contents=contents+"item2: $"+i2+"\r";
         total_price=total_price+i2;
         total_items=total_items+1;
      }
      if (item3.checked){
         contents=contents+"item3: $"+i3+"\r";
         total_price=total_price+i3;
         total_items=total_items+1;
      }

      display.value="Number of Items selected: "+ total_items +
         "\r"+ contents + "_____\rTOTAL BILL: $" + total_price;
   }
}
//--></SCRIPT>
```

FIGURE 14.4 The JavaScript function for the improved shopping cart.

There are two aspects of the function worthy of comment. First of all, the "if" statements test the truth value of (*item.checked*). The first shopping cart example tests the truth value of (*item.checked==true*). The two methods are equivalent. We have done it both ways for contrast. Second, the results are stored in the value of the display window in a rather elaborate way. A typical cart display is shown below. You should examine the display assignment and understand how it works.

```
Number of items selected: 2
item1: $15
item3: $17

_____
TOTAL BILL: $32
```

N O T E Real shopping-cart forms you find on the web have "check-out" buttons. While JavaScript provides a handy way to update a cart on the client, actually processing an order requires that the shopping results be sent to the web server. That is typically what the check-out button does. This might amount to simply writing the shopping results to a data file that can be printed out later. However, it might involve some more elaborate processing back on the web server.

14.3   RADIO BUTTONS AND THE *ELEMENTS[]* ARRAY

In Section 9.1, we indicated that radio buttons basically work like checkboxes, but provide an additional feature: a group of radio buttons can be configured so that only one of them can be selected. For example, Figure 14.5 shows a group of three radio buttons configured in such a way that only one of them can be selected at a given time.

You can see that the three radio each have the same name, *card*. In this case, the computer simply will not allow more than one of them to be selected. For example, if you were to select the Discover button in Figure 14.5, the computer would automatically cause the Visa button to become unselected. However, if the buttons had each been given different names, they would work just like checkboxes.

Choose payment type:
Visa ● Discover ○ Master Card ○

```
<FORM name=payform>
  Choose payment type:<BR>
  Visa <INPUT TYPE=radio NAME=card>
  Discover <INPUT TYPE=radio NAME=card>
  Master Card <INPUT TYPE=radio NAME=card>
</FORM>
```

FIGURE 14.5   When a group of radio buttons each have the same name, only one of them can be selected at a given time.

OK, then, how are we to determine which one of the radio buttons has been selected? With all three of the buttons sharing the same name, the reference

document.payform.card.checked

is ambiguous. Using the name of the radio element for reference no longer provides a unique access to the *checked* property of each radio button. So, in terms of using JavaScript to determine which button is checked, the buttons have lost their identity.

Fortunately, the DOM has a feature that provides an alternate way to reference HTML form elements. This is through the use of arrays. An **array** is an object that indexes a group of variables, which can be primitives or objects. Being an object, an array must serve to bind together a group of variables, just as we learned in Lesson 12. But it's the indexing capabilities of an array that distinguish it from an ordinary object.

Suppose a group of variables has some inherent ordering. For example, suppose four numbers are to be stored in a sequence of variables, and these variables are to be bound together as an object. It would be natural to define the object as follows:

```
var numbers=new Object();
numbers.num1=3.14;
numbers.num2=10.1;
numbers.num3=4.33;
numbers.num4=7.45;
```

The object simply binds together the four variables. The numbering of the object's properties serves to index them. A more concise indexing scheme for the object would be just to use numbers for the properties:

```
numbers.1=3.14;

numbers.2=10.1;

numbers.3=4.33;

numbers.4=7.45;
```

But numbers are not legal variable names, so the above is not viable. However, an array object has a built-in way to index variables. Using the built-in indexing capabilities of an array, we redefine the above object:

```
var numbers=new Array();
numbers[1]=3.14;
numbers[2]=10.1;
numbers[3]=4.33;
numbers[4]=7.45;
```

With the constructor function *Array()*, *numbers[ ]* is declared as an array rather than a generic object. Then, properties of the *numbers[ ]* array are assigned to different index values. The value in the [ ] brackets is called an **index.** The array *numbers* is an object whose properties are indexed.

Back to the situation at hand. We have a group of form elements for which we need a reference. Fortunately, when a form is loaded into a browser, an *elements[ ]* array is automatically created to index the elements in that form. In other words, you don't have to define this array as we did the *numbers[ ]* array above. The elements are indexed by the *elements[ ]* array in the same order that they are defined in the form. So, rather than having to refer to form elements by name, we use the elements array.

The indexing of the form's elements starts at 0, unlike the above examples in which the indexing starts at 1. Figure 14.6 shows a partial hierarchy for the document object and a form within that document. Rather than indexing primitives like the *numbers* array above, the *elements[ ]* array indexes objects, namely all of a form's elements.

So, to access the value property of the first form element, you provide the reference

document.formname.elements[0].value

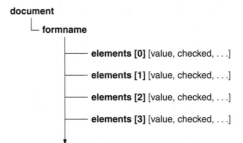

FIGURE 14.6 An object hierarchy for a form. The *elements[]* array, rather than the elements' names, is used to refer the form's elements.

That's all there is to it. Going back to the form of Figure 14.5, to see if the third checkbox is selected, the statement

if(document.payform.elements[2].checked){

    do something. . .

}

references the Master Card button without using its name.

N O T E   We have used radio buttons as a motivating need for the *elements[]* array. However, this array indexes *all* of the elements in a form, not just radio buttons. So, in practice, you can reference a property of any form element without using names. You can even use the with statement:

with(document.formname){

    refer directly to *elements[]* array

}

Perhaps the hardest part to get used to is indexing the elements starting with 0, rather than 1. But you will become accustomed to that over time.

14.4   USING RADIO BUTTONS AND THE *ELEMENTS[]* ARRAY

So that you can see the *elements[]* array in action, we offer another version of an online shopping cart for a pet store. Figure 14.7 shows a form with six radio buttons. The form has been formatted with a borderless HTML table, but we supply only the essential code for the form itself.

Conceptually, this example presents nothing different from the previous examples of this lesson, except for the grouping capabilities of the radio buttons and the need for the *elements[]* array. Here is how the form is to work. You can select either cat food, rat food, or both. These radio buttons function no differently than checkboxes. However, the two options for each type of food are grouped. That is, only one of the dry/moist options can be selected, and only one of the pellets/ground options can be selected. If the user selects one of the types of food, cat or rat, but fails to select the option for that type of food, the program defaults to the more expensive option (good for business). This is evidenced by the presence of ground-up rat food in the cart in Figure 14.7, even though that option has not been selected.

To set it up so that only one cat-food option can be selected, both options for cat food have been given the name *c*. Similarly, both options for rat food have been given the name *r*. Since we are going to use exclusively the *elements[]* array in this example, the names of the other radio buttons don't matter, as long the names don't match up with one of the two groups.

There are nine distinct elements in the form, so an *elements[]* array is automatically created with index values going from 0 to 8. The object diagram below shows only those form elements whose properties we shall use. For the six radio buttons, we will use only the checked property. We could use hidden values for the radio buttons, but we leave that as an exercise. You can see that the index of the *elements[]* array jumps from 5 to 8 when we skip over the "update cart" and "clear form" buttons. Of course, the 6 and 7 positions in the array exist, but since we don't need to use any properties of those elements, we have omitted them from the object diagram.

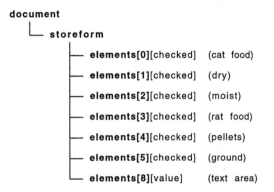

document
   └── **storeform**
         ├── **elements[0]**[checked]   (cat food)
         ├── **elements[1]**[checked]   (dry)
         ├── **elements[2]**[checked]   (moist)
         ├── **elements[3]**[checked]   (rat food)
         ├── **elements[4]**[checked]   (pellets)
         ├── **elements[5]**[checked]   (ground)
         └── **elements[8]**[value]   (text area)

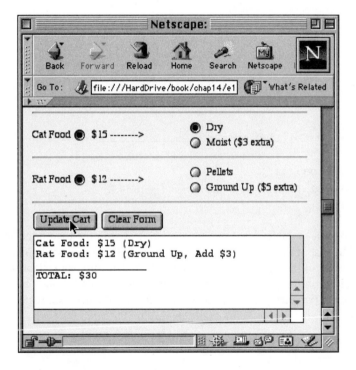

```
<FORM name=storeform>
Cat Food <INPUT TYPE=radio NAME=cat> $15 -------->
         <INPUT TYPE=radio NAME=c> Dry
         <INPUT TYPE=radio NAME=c> Moist ($3 extra)
Rat Food <INPUT TYPE=radio NAME=rat> $12 -------->
         <INPUT TYPE=radio NAME=r> Pellets
         <INPUT TYPE=radio NAME=r> Ground Up ($5 extra
         <INPUT TYPE=button VALUE="Update Cart" onclick="update()">
         <INPUT TYPE=reset VALUE="Clear Form">
         <TEXTAREA ROWS=6 COLS=40 WRAP=virtual></TEXTAREA>
</FORM>
```

FIGURE 14.7 A form that uses radio buttons to group options so that only one of the group can be selected.

```
<SCRIPT LANGUAGE=JavaScript><!--
function update(){
    with(document.storeform){
        var total;
        var contents;

        total=0;
        contents="";
        if(elements[0].checked){
            total=total+15;
            contents=contents+"Cat Food: $15 ";
            if(elements[1].checked){
                contents=contents+"(Dry)\r"
            }
            else{
                total=total+3;
                contents=contents+"(Moist, Add $3)\r";
            }
        }
        if(elements[3].checked){
            total=total+12;
            contents=contents+"Rat Food: $12 ";
            if(elements[4].checked){
                contents=contents+"(Pellets)\r";
            }
            else{
                total=total+3;
                contents=contents+"(Ground Up, Add $3)\r";
            }
        }
        elements[8].value= contents +"_____\rTOTAL: $"+total;
    }
}
//--></SCRIPT>
```

FIGURE 14.8 The function for the form of Figure 14.7.

We use variables *total* and *contents* to deal with the total price and contents of the cart. The rest of the function is straight-forward. The top-down logic appears below, and the code for the function appears in Figure 14.8. The only appreciable difference between the logic this example and the previous examples of this lesson is the use of nested "if" statements. For example, if cat food is not chosen, the decision regarding the type of cat food is never made.

-declare local variables (total, contents)

-if(catfood is checked)
   add 15 to total
   update cart contents
   if(dry is checked)
     update contents
  else
     update contents and total (give 'em moist)

-similar decision process for rat food

-assign results to cart display

14.5   THE PULL-DOWN MENU

In all of the other form objects we have used, their properties have been primitives. Value properties are strings and checked properties are Boolean. However, a pull-down menu is a more complex object. Figure 14.9 shows a pull-down menu with five options. The user chooses a color from the pull-down menu and clicks the button, and the background color of the web page changes accordingly. We will get to the function behind this shortly. In the meantime, we focus on the menu object itself.

```
<FORM name=colorform>
   <SELECT NAME=colormenu>
      <OPTION VALUE="#777777">flint
      <OPTION VALUE="#7465DC">violet dusk
      <OPTION VALUE="#2F8B20">clover
      <OPTION VALUE="#DA456B">carnation
      <OPTION VALUE="#FFCCCC">subtle pink
   </SELECT>
   <INPUT TYPE=button VALUE="Update Color" onclick="change()">
</FORM>
```

FIGURE 14.9 A pull-down menu with five options.

The menu object has a property that is also an object. The *options[]* array is a property of the menu object, and serves to index all of the menu's options. Like the *elements[]* array, the *options[]* array begins indexing all of the options of the menu, starting with the index of 0. A full object hierarchy for the form of Figure 14.9 is given in Figure 14.10. Although we will not need to access any properties of the button, we have included the button in the object diagram. Since the button has no name, we refer to it as *elements[1]* since it is the second form element. However, since we have given the menu the name *colormenu,* we refer to it by name, rather than by *elements[0].*

The first thing to note from the diagram is that, even though the menu has several options, it still counts as only one form element. Hence, the button is the second form element, *elements[1].* The *options[]* array indexes the menu's options as properties of the menu object itself, rather than as properties of the form. Each menu option has two properties that we will use.

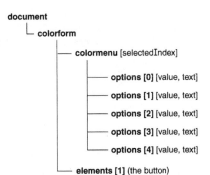

FIGURE 14.10 The object hierarchy for the form of Figure 14.9.

The *value* property carries hidden information about each option. For example,

> document.colorform.colormenu.options[2].value

contains the string "#2F8B20", a hexadecimal color representation. The *text* property contains the actual text appearing on the menu. So

> document.colorform.colormenu.options[2].text

contains the string "clover".

Aside from its *options[]* array property, the menu also has a primitive property, *selectedIndex*. (The I in index is upper-case.) This property contains the index of the currently selected option and is used to determine the option that the user has chosen. In Figure 14.9, the first menu item is selected, so

> document.colorform.colormenu.selectedIndex

contains 0. If the user were to select "carnation" on the menu, then the value of the *selectedIndex* property would be automatically changed to contain 3; The position in the *options[]* array that is currently selected is the value of *selectedIndex*.

With this in mind, the strategy for making use of the user's menu choice is

-determine the index of the currently selected option

-access the corresponding position of the menu's *options[]* array

So suitable code to access the hexadecimal color corresponding to the user's selection is

```
var i;
var color;

i=document.colorform.colormenu.selectedIndex;
color=document.colorform.colormenu.options[i].value
```

which causes the variable *color* to contain the value of the currently selected option. With this code in mind, we can refine the above strategy to:

-store the selected index in a variable *i*

-use a property of the ith position in the *options[]* array

With this strategy to assign the chosen background color to the *bgColor* property of the document, the function to support the form of Figure 14.9 is shown in Figure 14.11. Rather than using a *color* variable as in the above code, we have assigned the selected color straight to *document.bgColor*.

This same color-picking program could be written using five radio buttons grouped together with the same name so that only one of them could be selected. But that would have made the function contain substantially more code. You would have to include an "if" statement that checks each radio button to see if it is checked. That's five "if" statements.

```
<SCRIPT LANGUAGE=JavaScript><!--
function change(){
    var i=document.colorform.colormenu.selectedIndex;
    document.bgColor=document.colorform.colormenu.options[i].value;
}
//--></SCRIPT>
```

FIGURE 14.11 The function that sets the page background for the form in Figure 14.9.

NOTE	In general, a pull-down menu works just like a group of radio buttons, each with the same name. Either way, there is a list of options, and the user can only pick one. But there are two serious advantages of the pull-down menu. First, you can include a large list of options, and very little space is taken up in the web page since only one menu item is visible untill you open the menu. Second, the *selectedIndex* property tells you exactly which option is chosen. With a bunch of radio buttons, you have to check each one.

To wrap up this section, we present an example that makes use of two pull-down menu's. The form is shown in Figure 14.12. The values of the options in the first menu correspond to the base prices of cars, and the values of the options in the second menu correspond to sales tax percentages for states. (The tax rates and car prices are not necessarily accurate.)

Now for the function. When the button is clicked, we are going to have to determine the currently selected index of each menu. For this purpose, we employ two variables *i*

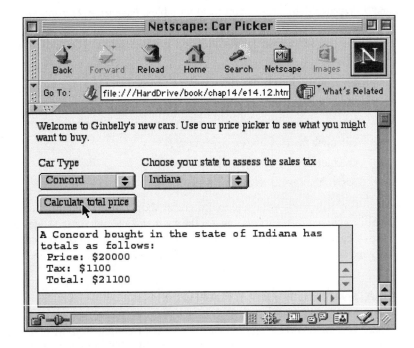

```
<FORM name=carform>
    <SELECT NAME=car>
        <OPTION VALUE=23000>Camry
        <OPTION VALUE=20000>Concord
        <OPTION VALUE=30000>Rivera
        <OPTION VALUE=22000>Camaro
    </SELECT>
    <SELECT NAME=state>
        <OPTION VALUE=".065">Illinois
        <OPTION VALUE=".055">Indiana
        <OPTION VALUE=".05">Wisconsin
    </SELECT>
    <INPUT TYPE=button VALUE="Calculate total price" onclick="calc()">
    <TEXTAREA NAME=display ROWS=5 COLS=45 WRAP=virtual></TEXTAREA>
</FORM>
```

FIGURE 14.12 A form with two pull-down menus.

```
<SCRIPT LANGUAGE=JavaScript><!--
function calc(){
   with (document.carform){
      var i,j,baseprice,taxrate,tax,total;

      i=car.selectedIndex;
      j=state.selectedIndex;

      baseprice=parseFloat(car.options[i].value);
      taxrate=parseFloat(state.options[j].value);
      tax=baseprice*taxrate;
      total=baseprice+tax;

      display.value="A "+car.options[i].text+" bought in the state of "
      +state.options[j].text+" has totals as follows:\r Price:$"
      +baseprice+"\r Tax: $"+tax+"\r Total: $"+total;
   }
}
//--></SCRIPT>
```

FIGURE 14.13 The function to process the form of Figure 14.12.

and *j*. We also define four extra local variables, *baseprice, taxrate, tax,* and *total,* to help with the calculation.

The top-down logic of the function is given below. The actual function is given in Figure 14.13.

-declare local variables (i,j,baseprice,taxrate,tax,total)

-store selected options indices in i and j

-store (and parse) the car price and tax rate (baseprice,taxrate)

-calculate tax (tax=baseprice*taxrate)

-calculate total (total=baseprice+tax)

-assign the results to display area

The main thing you have to be careful about when writing the code is that there are two different *options[ ]* arrays, one for the car menu and one for the state menu. The selected index *i* contains only the selected index of the car menu, and the selected index *j* contains only the selected index of the car menu. They are not interchangeable.

14.6 THE *ONCHANGE* EVENT HANDLER

There is another event handler that is useful in conjunction with the pull-down menu. *onchange* can be placed as an attribute of the SELECT element that creates the pull-down menu. This event handler detects a menu selection change by the user, and can call a JavaScript function just like *onclick*. For example, the color-changing form of Figure 14.9 doesn't even require a button, if causing a change to the menu calls the function. You would simply place *onchange* in the start tag for the menu:

<SELECT NAME=colormenu onchange="change()">

You could then completely eliminate the button. Or, if you wish, you could leave the button. It's OK for two different event handlers to call the same function. Only one of the event handlers can be activated at a given instant. You would have to have two different mouse cursors on the screen to cause a change in the menu and click the button at the same time.

A version of that form with no button is available on the web site for you to play with. A version of the car form of Figure 14.12 with no button is also available on the web site. Each menu has an *onchange* event handler that calls the *calc()* function.

NOTE In some browsers, the onchange event handler also works for checkboxes and radio buttons. In particular, however, it does not work with checkboxes and radio buttons in some Netscape versions. There is no reason to avoid using it for this reason, but you would not want do do away with the button. In the case that a browser doesn't recognize it, the user could still click the button as usual.

14.7 VERIFICATION OF USER CHOICES

There are not as many issues surrounding verification of choices as there are surrounding verification of text input. With text input, you might wish to check that the user actually entered something, entered a number, or entered a number in the proper range, for example. With a collection of checkbox or radio options, you might simply check to make sure that the user made a choice. That is, if all of a collection is unchecked, you might wish to alert the user to make a choice of some sort.

Such a verification would have the logic

-if((first is not checked)&&(second is not checked)&&. . .&&(last in not checked))

   alert the user

-else

   process the form

So, if none of the items is checked, the user gets an alert window and the form is not processed. It is also possible that you don't care whether none of the collection is selected. In that case, no verification is necessary.

A pull-down menu might require no verification. In all of the menus of the examples in Section 14.5 above, it is not possible for no choice to be made. In other words, a menu option is always visible, hence selected. Some menus are configured so that the first menu option is not one of the choices, but an instruction. For example, the menu for the background color picker of Figure 14.9 could have been set up as follows:

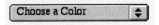

Once the menu is opened, the color options are present. It is reasonably common to find menus set up in this manner. In this case verification would be simple:

   -if (the selected index is 0)

      alert the user

   -else

      process form

14.8   AN ADVANCED EXAMPLE (OPTIONAL)

This example generates random numbers in various ranges. The form is pictured in Figure 14.14. The functionality of the form is described on the form itself, but it is unlikely that you will get a complete feel for it without testing it out on the web site. In particular, there are several verification features provided. You should try to violate the form in several possible ways. That way, it will be easier to understand the programming behind the form.

Since we will use the *elements[]* array to reference the form's elements, the names of the elements are inconsequential. Notice that we haven't even supplied names for most of the elements. Also, the only hidden values can be seen in the definition of the pull-down

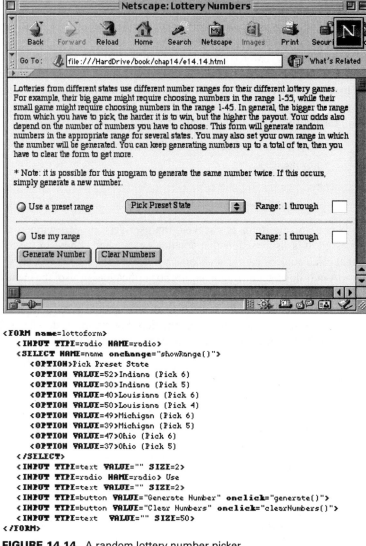

```
<FORM name=lottoform>
   <INPUT TYPE=radio NAME=radio>
   <SELECT NAME=name onchange="showRange()">
      <OPTION>Pick Preset State
      <OPTION VALUE=52>Indiana (Pick 6)
      <OPTION VALUE=30>Indiana (Pick 5)
      <OPTION VALUE=40>Louisiana (Pick 6)
      <OPTION VALUE=50>Louisiana (Pick 4)
      <OPTION VALUE=49>Michigan (Pick 6)
      <OPTION VALUE=39>Michigan (Pick 5)
      <OPTION VALUE=47>Ohio (Pick 6)
      <OPTION VALUE=37>Ohio (Pick 5)
   </SELECT>
   <INPUT TYPE=text VALUE="" SIZE=2>
   <INPUT TYPE=radio NAME=radio> Use
   <INPUT TYPE=text VALUE="" SIZE=2>
   <INPUT TYPE=button VALUE="Generate Number" onclick="generate()">
   <INPUT TYPE=button VALUE="Clear Numbers" onclick="clearNumbers()">
   <INPUT TYPE=text  VALUE="" SIZE=50>
</FORM>
```

FIGURE 14.14 A random lottery number picker.

menu. The two radio buttons are not to be both selected at once, so they have been given the same name. So the form is not overly complicated. It does get a little confusing when you have to keep track of all the different form elements by their positions in the *elements[ ]* array. A good way to keep the indexing straight is to make a quick sketch of the form on scrap paper and, next to each form element, write down its index (starting with 0, of course).

Now let's get to the functions. First, notice that we have included the *onchange* event handler in the pull-down menu. Each time the current selection is changed, the range of numbers for that lottery is instantly displayed in the text area to the right of the menu. All that amounts to is assigning the hidden value from the currently selected menu option to the value property of the text area. You can see from the source code in Figure 14.15 that the function *showRange()* called by the event handler of the menu does just that.

Since some information needs to survive several button clicks, global variables have been set up to store the number of random numbers that have been generated, the range in which the numbers are being generated, and the string of numbers that have previously been generated. These variables will exist between function calls. The "clear numbers" button calls the *clearNumbers()* function, which resets two of these variables. This function also clears the value property of the text area that displays the numbers.

Now down to the nitty-gritty. The "generate number" button calls the *generate()* function. Given all of the verification built into this function, it gets a bit complicated. The top-down logic of the function is provided below.

-extract the selected menu index (l)

-if(neither radio button is selected or ten numbers have been generated)

   alert the user

-else

  if(first radio selected)

    if(no state picked from menu)

      alert the user

    else

      set the range

      call the findNumber() function

  else

    if(users range is NaN or is too small or too big)

      alert the user

    else

      set the range

      call the findNumber() function

Notice that this function is mostly about verifying the form. If neither option is chosen or 10 numbers have already been generated, the user is alerted. Otherwise, see if the first option has been selected. If it has, make sure a state has been selected. If so, then set the range appropriately and call a function to find the number. (We will talk about this function shortly.) The process is similar if the user has chosen the second radio button. The user's range is verified. If it passes, the range is set and a function is called to find that number.

```
<SCRIPT LANGUAGE=JavaScript><!--
var count;
var previous;
var range;

count=0;
previous="";
range=0;

function findNumber(){
     count=count+1;
     rnum=Math.round((range*Math.random()+.5));
     previous=previous+rnum+" ";
     document.lottoform.elements[7].value=previous;
}
function clearNumbers(){
   count=0;
   previous="";
   document.lottoform.elements[7].value="";

}
function showRange(){
   with(document.lottoform){
   var i;
   i=elements[1].selectedIndex;
   elements[2].value=elements[1].options[i].value;
   }
}
function generate(){
   with(document.lottoform){
     var i;
     i=elements[1].selectedIndex;
     if(((!elements[0].checked)&&(!elements[3].checked))||(count==10)){
          alert(" Either you have not chosen whether you want to use a predefined range or
          your own range, or you have already generated 10 numbers.  Clear the numbers and
          start over.");
     }
     else{
        if(elements[0].checked){
          if(i==0){
            alert("You have chosen to use a preset state, but have not chosen a state.");
          }
          else{
            range=elements[1].options[i].value;
            findNumber();
          }
        }
        else{
          if(isNaN(elements[4].value)||(elements[4].value<2)||(elements[4].value>99.5)){
            alert("You have chosen to enter your own range, but have left the field blank or have
            not entered a number in the range from 2 to 99.");
          }
          else{
            range=elements[4].value;
            findNumber();
          }
        }
     }
   }
}
//--></SCRIPT>
```

FIGURE 14.15 The JavaScript to support the form of Figure 14.14.

So there are only two scenarios in which a number is to be generated. One could do the whole number-generation process in each case, but that would be redundant. Instead, we define a new function to do this. Then all we have to do is call the function in each case. Prior to this example, we have called our own functions only from event handlers. But calling your own function in the above manner is perfectly acceptable. The top-down logic for the function *findNumber()* that actually finds the number is given below. Remember that the appropriate range is set just before this function is called. All the function has to do is use the preset range to generate a random number in that range. (Generating a random number in a certain range was discussed in detail in Section 13.7.)

-add one to the counter

-generate a random number based on the range

-append this number to the string that contains the previously generated numbers

-assign the updated string of numbers to the display field

14.9 SUMMARY

Key Terms

checked property	array	array index
elements array	menu option	options array
selectedIndex property	text property	onchange

Checkboxes and radio buttons provide for user choices in HTML forms. In a group of checkboxes, any or all of them can be selected. However, if each radio button in a group has the same name, only one of that group can be selected. If radio buttons have different names, they work just as checkboxes do. Aside from the grouping capabilities, checkboxes and radio buttons work the same way. You can check to see if a given checkbox or radio button has been selected by using the *checked* property. The *checked* property is a Boolean variable that contains true if the button has been selected or false if the button has not been selected. The typical strategy for using this property is to use an "if" statement to cause something to happen only if *checked* is true: that is, if the option has been chosen by the user, react accordingly. Both checkboxes and radio buttons have a *value* property that can carry hidden information. Unlike text areas and fields, this value is not visible in the web page, but is used to carry hidden information for processing purposes. The *value* property is always a string.

The grouping capabilities of radio buttons necessitate the use of an array. Since some groups of radio buttons need to use the same name, their names are no longer sufficient individual references for them. Arrays are objects and therefore bind groups of variables together. But rather than referring to the properties of an array by names, they are referred to by an index value. This basically serves to provide a numbering scheme for variables that are bound together. Such a numbering scheme is ideal for numbering the elements of form.

When a web page is first loaded by a browser, an *elements[]* array is automatically created. Starting at 0, all of the elements in a form are indexed by this array. *elements[0]* refers to the first of the form's elements, *elements[1]* refers to the second of the form's elements, and so forth. This array indexes all of the form's elements, not just the radio buttons. A specific array index is used to refer to the a form element, making the element's name unnecessary when referencing the element. To access a property of the fifth of a form's elements, the object reference

document.formname.elements[4].property

is sufficient.

Pull-down menus provide for a group of options, only one of which can be selected. The options themselves are indexed by the *options[]* array. This array is a property of the menu. The menu itself only counts as one form element. The *options[]* array indexes the menu's options starting from 0.

Each option can carry a hidden value as well as the text that appears on the menu for each option. The value is stored in the *value* property and the text is stored in the *text* property. In order to access one of these properties, you can refer directly to the option's position in the *options[]* array.

For example,

document.formname.menuname.options[3].value

refers to the hidden value of the fourth option in the menu.

While direct reference in this manner is fine, you really need to refer directly to the particular option that the user has selected. The *selectedIndex* property of the menu contains the index of the currently selected option. *selectedIndex* is a property of the menu itself, rather than of a menu option. A suitable strategy for acessing a property of the currently selected option is as follows:

-store the selected index in a variable *i*

-use a property of the ith position in the *options[]* array

There is an event handler that can be used with a pull-down menu to call a function when the currently selected option is changed. The *onchange* event handler is defined as an attribute of the SELECT tag of the menu and calls a function in the same manner as *onclick*. This event handler also works with checkboxes and radio buttons, but not in all browsers.

14.10 REVIEW QUESTIONS

1. A form is named *formx*. Refer directly to the value property of the ninth element in the form.

2. A form is named *formx,* and a pull-down menu is the fourth element of the form. Refer directly to the *value* property of the third option of the menu.

3. In the pet-food example of Figure 14.2, what would typical output consist of if all of the statements like `contents=contents+"Rat Food\r"`; were replaced with more concise statements like `contents="Rat Food \r";`?

4. How can you cause a checkbox or radio button already to be chosen when the page loads?

5. Why does the reset button cause "Happy Shopping" to appear in the shopping cart in the example of Figure 14.2?

6. Explain the term "hidden values" as it pertains to the HTML form elements we studied in this Lesson. Contrast with *value* properties from the form elements studied in Lesson 13.

7. Explain in terms of programming logic how the program of Figure 14.7 defaults to the more expensive option, even if no options are selected (for example, if cat food is selected but neither of the cat-food options is selected).

8. Compare and/or contrast the functionality of radio buttons vs. pull-down menus.

9. Sketch a complete object hierarchy for the form of Figure 14.12. Use the *elements[]* array for all form elements.

10. The following code is attempting to access the user's selection in a pull-down menu. Find two errors.

```
k=document.formname.menuname.selectedindex;
price=document.formname.options[k].value;
```

11. Describe a strategy for verifying that the user has checked at least one checkbox.

14.11 EXERCISES

1. Make a form with four radio buttons corresponding to different types of credit cards. Only one of the buttons can be selected. When a button is clicked, the user is given a message in a text area that says something like "thank you for paying with ???."

2. Make a form with two pull-down menus and two text fields. One menu should contain the names of 10 U.S. states. When a state is selected, the capital city of that state should instantly appear in a text field. The other menu should contain the names of 10 countries. When a country is selected, the capital city of that country should instantly appear in the other text field.

3. Make a version of the example of Figure 14.2 that has four buttons and uses the *elements[]* array to reference all of the form's elements.

4. Rewrite the example of Figure 14.4 without using hidden value attributes. The program should give *exactly* the same output.

5. Make a version of the example of Figure 14.4 that has five options. The program should give a subtotal, some sales tax, and a total. Each of these quantities (subtotal, tax, and total) should be displayed in its own text field. The shopping cart should contain only a list of the chosen items.

6. Create a form that contains four radio buttons, only one of which can be selected. The form should contain a generic button that causes the background color to change based upon the user's choice. If the button is clicked but no color selection has been made, the user should be alerted as to the futility of the attempt.

7. Make a form for an online pizza shop. The form should have two options for the size of the pizza, only one of which can be selected. It should have three options for toppings, any of which can be selected. You can make up your own prices. The toppings are the same price regardless of the size of the pizza. The program should give a summary of the order in a text area when a button is clicked. A total price should be given. (No sales tax is necessary.) Option: Verify that at least one topping has been selected.

8. Work Exercise 7 above with the following additions. The form should have two pull-down menus, one for method of payment (check, Visa, etc.) and one for three different sales tax rates. (The pizza shop is near to the border of three states and must assess different tax rates.) The order should be summarized in a text area, but the subtotal, tax, and total should be given in their own text fields. Option: Verify that at least one topping has been selected.

9. Make a form for an online music shop. You will be selling only three titles, and can use your favorite CDs for the titles. Each title should have a checkbox used for selecting that title. Moreover, each title should have two options (CD, DVD), only one of which can be selected. If the user selects an option without selecting the title, nothing happens. If the user selects a title but fails to select an option, the program defaults to the more expensive option, DVDs. You can make your own prices, but DVDs should be more expensive. An order summary should be provided in a text area and an order total should be given in a separate text field. No sales tax is required for this problem.

10. Work Exercise 9 above with the following additions. The form should have a counter that counts up the total number of selections made by the user. The form should have a pull-down menu with shipping options (mail, two-day air, and overnight) with varying prices. The chosen shipping price should be multiplied by the number of selections made to determine shipping costs. No sales tax is required, but the subtotal, shipping, and total should be provided in separate text fields. The order should be summarized in a text area as usual.

*Exercises 11–12 are modifications of the lottery-number generator of Figure 14.14.

11. An alert is given if the button is clicked but neither of the two options has been selected or ten numbers have already been generated. Modify the program so that two different alerts are given to cover these cases.

12. Modify the program so that duplicate numbers cannot be generated. For simplicity, this version should generate only four lottery numbers before having to be reset. Hint: Store numbers already generated into global variables.

13. Make a new version of the program that provides four radio buttons, only one of which can be clicked. Each button is for a different range, say 1–30, 1–35, 1–40, and 1–45. When a "generate" button is clicked, a number in the appropriate range should be generated. The user should be alerted if none of the ranges are selected or if six numbers have been already been generated.

14. Work Exercise 13 above with the following additions. A pull-down menu should be provided that gives users three choices (4, 5, or 6) for how many numbers they would like to generate. After they have generated that many numbers, the program should alert them that they should start over. They should also be alerted if they click the "generate" button when no range has been chosen. Option: Make the program so that no duplicate numbers can be generated (see the hint for Exercise 12).

14.12 PROJECT THREADS

Any exercises you do for this lesson should be referenced in your homework page following the guidelines in Section 9.10.

LOOPS FOR REPETITION

WE **HAVE** been making decisions with the *if* statement for several lessons. The computer quickly evaluates the Boolean expression and takes the appropriate course of action. It then moves on to the next statement in the program. The *if* statement lacks the capability to make the computer do something repetitively. When several radio buttons or checkboxes need to be tested in repetition to see if they have been checked, we have had to resort to using one *if* statement for each option.

A structure called a **loop** can be used to help when such repetition is required. In this lesson, we will focus on two different loop structures, the *for* loop and the *while* loop. To illustrate the power of these structures, we begin discussion of each type of loop with some technical explanation. With that in place, we apply loops to processing HTML forms and to indefinite verification of prompted input. This lesson concludes with some optional material that further illustrates the power of loops when they are nested.

15.1 THE *FOR* LOOP

In order to show the fundamental nature of the *for* loop, we begin by creating a program that writes the numbers 1 through 1000 to the web page. Of course, we could make a painfully long *document.write()* statement, but we'll pass on that. You might be surprised to find out that only two short lines of JavaScript code are required. Such is the power of looping in programming. The required JavaScript code and the output are both shown in Figure 15.1.

In Figure 15.1, only the last ten or so of the resulting 1000 numbers are visible in the browser window, but they are all there. You can see that the body of the *for* statement consists of only one line of code, a *document.write()* statement that writes the contents of the variable *i* followed by a line break. Somehow, the *for* statement has executed this one line of code 1000 times, each time with a different value of *i*. Let's see how that happened.

The *for* statement is controlled by the variable *i*, which is called the **loop index.** Here is the sequence of events that caused the looping effect:

1. The loop index *i* is initialized to 1.
2. The Boolean condition $i <= 1000$ is checked and found to be true.
3. The Boolean statement being true, the *document.write()* statement is executed.

4. The assignment statement $i = i + 1$ causes the loop index i to be reassigned the value 2.

5. Steps (2)–(4) are repeated in order until the Boolean condition in step (2) is found to be false, at which time the loop is terminated.

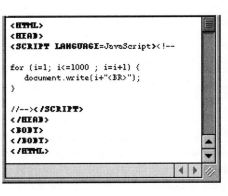

FIGURE 15.1 A program that writes the first 1000 whole numbers.

The above *for* statement has three components. The first one sets the loop index to 1. The second sets the upper limit for the loop index, in this case 1000. The third component serves to increase the index by 1 on each pass of the loop. Step (5) basically says that the loop is to keep executing the statement in its body until the loop index has become large enough that the Boolean condition is no longer true.

To further clarify step (5), it is worthwhile to go through the last executions of the loop. After many passes of the loop, the index i contains number 999 and 999 has just been written. Then i is increased to 1000. The Boolean expression ($i <= 1000$) is still true, so the *document.write()* statement executes, and 1000 is written. Then i is increased to 1001. The Boolean expression ($i <= 1000$) is now false. Rather than executing the *document.write()* statement one last time, the loop terminates immediately.

The Boolean condition in the *for* statement is commonly called the **loop condition.** The "life" of the loop is entirely dependent upon truth value of this condition.

In general, the *for* statement has the following form:

```
for (initialize index; loop condition; increment index) {
  statement;
  :
  statement;
}
```

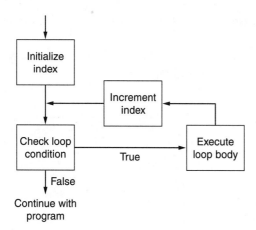

FIGURE 15.2 A graphic depiction of the execution of a *for* loop. In the top-down flow of a program, a loop serves to halt the flow for a while. The JavaScript interpreter does not move on to any further statements in the program until the loop has completely run its course. In the meantime, the statements in the body of the loop are executed over and over again.

All of the statements in the body of the *for* are executed time and time again until the loop condition fails to be true, at which time the computer passes over the body of the *for* statement and continues with the program. Figure 15.2 shows a graphic illustration of the structure of a *for* loop. The path of execution followed by the computer is indicated with arrows.

The term loop aptly describes what is occurring. Webster defines the transitive verb "loop" as "to wrap around one or more times; as to loop the wire around the post." The wire fence analogy is pretty good; the wire can't be continued past a post until it is looped around it sufficiently many times, much as a program can't continue until any loop encountered executes sufficiently many times.

There is a good measure of flexibility in the way the loop index is incremented. For example,

```
for (i=1; i<=100; i=i+2) {
  document.write(i+"<BR>");
}
```

would write all of the odd numbers less than 100. The loop starts with $i=1$ as before, but on each pass through the loop, i is incremented by 2. This results in the numbers 1, 3, 5, ..., 99 being written. On the last pass through the loop, i contains 99, and that number is written. It is then increased to 101, which causes the loop to terminate.

There is flexibility in initializing the loop index and setting the loop condition. For example,

```
for (i=0; i<12; i=i+3) {
  document.write(i+"<BR>");
}
```

would write the numbers 0, 3, 6, and 9. The number 12 would not be written since, on the last pass when i is increased to 12, the loop condition becomes false.

Loops can even run "backwards." For example, the loop

```
for (i=20; i>=10; i=i-2) {
  document.write(i+"<BR>");
}
```

starts with $i=20$. On each pass of the loop, the index is decreased by 2. This loop writes the numbers 20, 18, 16, 14, 12, and 10 to the browser. On the last pass i contains 10 and that number is written. Then i is changed to 8, which causes the loop to terminate.

NOTE

A word of caution is definitely in order. With just a couple of lines of code, it is possible to make the computer do thousands, millions, or even billions of calculations. As fast as computers now are, they still have their limitations. To illustrate this, consider a loop that does nothing:

```
for(i=1; i<1000000; i=i+1) {
}
```

Even though there are no statements in the body of the loop, the computer still executes the loop one million times. On a 400-megahertz computer, that takes in the neighborhood of 20 seconds. In other words, when the computer encounters the above loop, the top-down flow of the program is halted for 20 seconds while the computer goes through the loop one million times. Up the loop to 10 million calculations, and the time required is over four minutes. Add a couple more zeros, and the program will be halted for several hours. Some browsers actually have warning windows that pop up when you load such a loop. The window might say something like, "Are you sure you want to do this? Would you like the program to be aborted now?"

Worse yet is the dreaded infinite loop, one that will run forever. The loop condition in the loop

```
for(x=1; x>0; x=x+1) {
}
```

is always true and, therefore, the loop will never terminate. Although one would never intentionally include an infinite loop in a program, a slight programming error can cause one to occur. Fortunately, some browsers have built in warnings which allow for termination of such loops. Some don't. (When the author was testing an infinite loop on various browsers and platforms, he managed to crash the computer a couple of times while trying to force the browser to quit.) In the old days of programming (before JavaScript and the WWW were even a thought), an infinite loop would quite often crash the computer, making it necessary to restart it.

15.2 COUNTERS IN LOOPS

We wish to write a program that writes the sum and product of the first 15 numbers. The basic idea is the same, but rather than writing the value of the index each time through the loop, we must add its value to a running sum and multiply it by a running product. The top-down logic is as follows:

-initialize *sum* to 0

-initialize *product* to 1

-for(i=1 to 15)

    sum=sum+i

    product=product*i

-write *sum* and *product*

Before the loop, the *sum* and *product* variables are set to 0 and 1, respectively. Then the loop goes through index values from 1 to 15. On each pass through the loop, the *sum* and *product* variables are increased according to the current value of the loop index. Finally, after the loop has run its course, the final values of the *sum* and *product* are given as output. The necessary JavaScript code and the output are shown in Figure 15.3.

```
<SCRIPT LANGUAGE=JavaScript><!--
var sum,product;

sum=0;
product=1;

for (i=1; i<=15 ; i=i+1) {
   sum=sum+i;
   product=product*i;
}
document.write(sum+"<BR>");
document.write(product+"<BR>");

//--></SCRIPT>
```

output

```
120
1307674368000
```

FIGURE 15.3 A loop that calculates the sum and product of the first 15 whole numbers.

The first time through the loop, 1 is added to *sum* and *product* is multiplied by 1. The second time through the loop, 2 is added to *sum* and *product* is multiplied by 2. This progression continues until the last pass of the loop adds 15 to *sum* and multiplies *product* by 15. Only after the loop has completely run its course, and the two variables contain the final results, are their contents written.

It is important to note the positions of the statements in Figure 15.3. In particular, only the counters are in the body of the loop. You certainly <u>don't</u> want to initialize the counters in the loop body as in the incorrect version below.

```
for (i=1; i<=15; i=i+1) {
   sum=0;
   product=1;
   sum=sum+i;
   product=product*i;
}
```

On each pass of the this loop, the counters would be reset to their original values before being updated by the current loop index value. So the above version of the loop would result in *sum* and *product* both containing the value 15 after the loop had run its course. Being reset each time through the loop, the counters would lose their cumulative effect.

If the *document.write()* statements had been put in the body of the loop, the contents of *sum* and *product* would be written on each pass of the loop. There is nothing wrong with that, but we wished to write only the final results.

You may have been surprised in the output shown in Figure 15.3 that the product of the first 15 whole numbers is over 1 trillion. The number that was calculated is 15!, called 15 factorial. You have no doubt seen the factorial button, !, on a calculator. It just serves to multiply a number by all whole numbers smaller than itself. For example, 5! is 5*4*3*2*1, which is 120. You can see from the calculation of 15! in Figure 15.3 that factorials get big quickly. This is a bit beside the point of this section, but we will use the factorial again in Lesson 17.

Counters are used so frequently that many programming languages have some built-in shortcuts. JavaScript is no different. The shortcuts are in the form of special assignment operators, which we list in the table below. Of course, the variable names, x and y, are only for demonstration. These assignment shortcuts work with any choice of variable names. Their use is easily demonstrated. The loop index in Figure 15.3 could have been written as

```
for (i=1; i<=15; i++)
```

and the loop counters could have been written as

```
sum+=i;
product*=i;
```

We mention this because you may see these "shortcut" operators in use in other JavaScripts you might find on the web. In that case, you will know what they are. However, for the beginning programmer, their use just adds more confusing technical detail. We will not use them throughout the rest of the book.

Shortcut	Its effect
$x++$	$x = x + 1$
$x--$	$x = x - 1$
$x+ = y$	$x = x + y$
$x- = y$	$x = x - y$
$x* = y$	$x = x * y$
$x/ = y$	$x = x/y$

15.3 USING LOOPS TO PROCESS FORMS

In Lesson 14, all of the forms had only a few checkboxes or radio buttons. Determining whether each option was selected required a separate *if* statement: if the first option is selected, do something; if the second option is selected, do something, and so forth. Imagine if there were 10 or 15 options to check in a form: there would need to be 10 or 15 separate *if* statements.

But now that we have the *for* loop to handle repetition, we can implement a new strategy. Suppose that a form has 10 checkboxes as its first 10 elements. Then these checkboxes would occupy positions 0 through 9 in the *elements[]* array. Using a loop for repetition, we can check all of them as follows:

```
for (i=0; i<=9; i=i+1) {
  if (elements[i].checked) {
    do something
  }
}
```

On the first pass of the loop, when *i* is 0, the first checkbox (elements[0].checked) is tested by the *if* statement. On the second pass of the loop, when *i* is 1, the second checkbox (elements[1].checked) is tested by the *if* statement. Finally, on the last pass of the loop, when *i* is 9, the tenth checkbox (elements[9].checked) is tested by the *if* statement. In this way, one *if* statement is used to check all of the checkboxes. The loop serves to cycle through all ten index positions in the *elements[]* array. The current loop index is used as the current index in the *elements[]* array. Of course, the "do something" depends upon what the form is to accomplish.

Now, let's apply this strategy to a specific form. The form shown in Figure 15.4 is for a pizza order. There are 10 toppings, any of which can be selected. The base price for the pizza is $10, and each topping chosen adds $1.50 to the price. Upon the button click, the

```
<FORM name=pizzaform>
   <INPUT TYPE=checkbox NAME=Pepperoni>
      .
      .
      .
   <INPUT TYPE=checkbox NAME=Olives>

   <INPUT TYPE=button VALUE="Calculate Order" onclick="calc()">
   <INPUT TYPE=reset VALUE="Reset Form">

     <TEXTAREA NAME=name ROWS=5 COLS=50 WRAP=virtual></TEXTAREA>
</FORM>
```

FIGURE 15.4 A pizza form with 10 checkboxes.

```
<SCRIPT LANGUAGE=JavaScript><!--
function calc(){
   var toppings,topping_total,total;

   toppings="";
   topping_total=0;

   with (document.pizzaform){
      for(i=0 ; i<=9 ;i=i+1){
         if(elements[i].checked){
            toppings=toppings+elements[i].name+"  ";
            topping_total=topping_total+1.5;
         }
      }
      total=10+topping_total;
      elements[12].value=toppings+"\r_____\r Total of
         toppings: $"+topping_total+"\r Total Price: $"+total;
   }
}

//--></SCRIPT>
```

FIGURE 15.5 The function to process the form of Figure 15.4.

order is summarized in the text area. In the HTML code for the form, we omit all but the first and last checkboxes since they are all basically the same.

Not only will we use a loop to cycle through all of the checkboxes, but we will use counters in the loop to keep track of the chosen toppings and the total cost of the chosen toppings. In principle, these counters function in the same way as those discussed in Section 15.2 above. The counter for the names of the chosen toppings is *toppings,* and the counter for the prices of the toppings is *topping_total.* With these counter names, the top-down logic of the *calc()* function is given below:

-declare the variables

-initialize counters (toppings="", topping_total=0;

-for(i=0; i<=9; i=i+1)

  if(elements[i] is checked)

    augment the *toppings* string with topping name

    add 1.50 to *topping_total*

-calculate total (total=10 + topping_total)

-assign results to display area

The loop cycles through the *elements[]* array indices of each checkbox. If a given checkbox has been selected, its name is appended onto the string counter for the topping names, and $1.50 is added to the counter for the total topping costs. After the loop has run its course, we add the resulting topping total to the $10 base price of the pizza. Finally, the results are assigned to the display area. The actual function appears in Figure 15.5. There are many possible variations of this program, several of which are given as exercises.

NOTE A distinguishing feature of the pizza example in Figures 14.4 and 14.5 is that we used the *name* properties of the checkboxes to carry information used in processing the form. In all previous examples we used the *value* property to carry hidden information about a checkbox. Not only is a form element's name used for object reference, but it can be used as property of the element. When you use the *elements[]* array to refer to the form elements, the *name* is free for other use. You can carry hidden information about the form element in both the *name* and *value* properties. Use of the *value* property in conjunction with the *name* property to carry hidden information is left as an exercise.

We now present an example of a different flavor that uses the *for* loop. Loops are very useful any time repetition is needed, not just when you need to cycle through several checkboxes. In this example we construct a lottery form that generates random numbers. In order to generate these random numbers, we employ the *Math.random()* method mentioned in Section 12.10. This method returns a random floating-point number in the range [0, 1]. Any decimal in that range can come up (except irrational numbers, but that is definitely not a story for this book). For a lottery number it is desirable to generate a *whole* number in the range from 1 to 40, for example. A JavaScript expression that accomplishes this is

$$\text{Math.round}((40*\text{Math.random}())+.5)$$

which yields one of the whole numbers 1–40, with equal probability. We discussed this statement in detail in the optional Section 13.7. If you wish to understand this expression (and who wouldn't?), refer to the first couple pages of that section. Otherwise, just be content that it generates a whole number in the given range. Moreover, the range is flexible. The expression

$$\text{Math.round}((25*\text{Math.random}())+.5)$$

gives a randomly generated whole number in the range from 1 to 25.

The form that requires such a random number generator is given in Figure 15.6. Since there are numerous options for each pull-down menu, we have only shown the HTML source code for some of the options. The purpose of the form should be apparent from the form itself. The first thing we have to do is to extract the user's selections from the two pull-down menus. The strategy for that is familiar. The information we need from each menu actually appears on the menu. So we used no *value* properties when we defined the menu items. Rather, we extract the *text* property of the user's selection from each menu. The range the user selects is stored in a variable named *range*. The expression used to generate a random whole number in the appropriate range is then

$$\text{Math.round}((\mathbf{range}*\text{Math.random}())+.5)$$

according to the above discussion.

The amount of numbers the user wants to generate we store in a variable named *number*. In order to generate that many numbers, we use *number* as the upper limit for our loop index:

for (x=1; x<=**number**; x=x+1)
 generate random number
 update display window

That way, the user's choice actually controls how many times the loop executes and, therefore, how many random numbers are generated.

One feature of the form that it not apparent from the form itself is that we wish to alert users if they fail to make a choice from either menu. You can see from the source

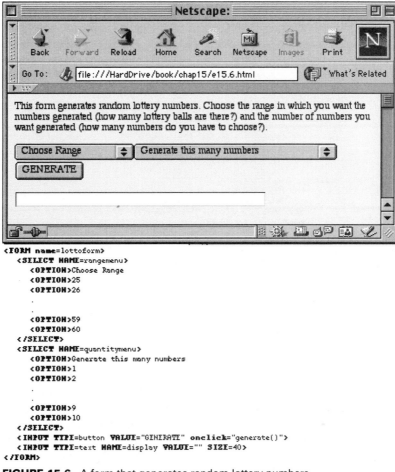

```
<FORM name=lottoform>
  <SELECT NAME=rangemenu>
    <OPTION>Choose Range
    <OPTION>25
    <OPTION>26
      .
      .
    <OPTION>59
    <OPTION>60
  </SELECT>
  <SELECT NAME=quantitymenu>
    <OPTION>Generate this many numbers
    <OPTION>1
    <OPTION>2
      .
      .
    <OPTION>9
    <OPTION>10
  </SELECT>
  <INPUT TYPE=button VALUE="GENERATE" onclick="generate()">
  <INPUT TYPE=text NAME=display VALUE="" SIZE=40>
</FORM>
```

FIGURE 15.6 A form that generates random lottery numbers.

code for the form that, when each menu first appears, the menu shows an instruction rather than one of the real options. With that in mind, the top-down logic for the function is given below.

-declare variables

-store selected option index of each menu (i, j)

-if (either menu is still at option 0)

   give an alert

-else

   store text for each of the selected options (range, number)

   set display string to empty (display.value="")

   for (x=1; x<=number; x=x+1)

     generate random number (rnumber)

     update display.value

```
<SCRIPT LANGUAGE=JavaScript><!--
function generate(){
   var i,j,range,number, rnumber ;

   with(document.lottoform){

      i=rangemenu.selectedIndex;
      j=quantitymenu.selectedIndex;

      if((i==0)||(j==0)){
         alert("Please make a range selection and choose the amount of numbers you wish to be
         generated before clicking the button.");
      }
      else{
         range=parseFloat(rangemenu.options[i].text);
         number=parseFloat(quantitymenu.options[j].text);

         display.value="";

         for (x=1 ; x<=number ;x=x+1){
            rnumber=Math.round((range*Math.random())+.5);
            display.value=display.value+rnumber+" ";
         }
      }
   }
}

//--></SCRIPT>
```

FIGURE 15.7   The function for the form in Figure 15.6.

The actual function appears in Figure 15.7. Perhaps the only feature requiring further explanation is the statement

$$display.value="";$$

appearing in the function. When the user clicks the "generate" button, several numbers will appear in the display field. Suppose the user then chooses to generate a new set of numbers. If the display field were not reset to the empty string before the new numbers were generated, the newly generated numbers would be added onto the string of old numbers. We simply wished to clear out any previously generated numbers from the display field before generating some new numbers.

If you play with this form for any length of time, you will notice that it often generates redundant numbers. In other words, the function has no built-in mechanism with which it checks a newly generated number against any previously generated numbers. This feature is quite difficult to implement, so we leave that as an optional section at the end of this lesson.

15.4 THE *WHILE* LOOP

The *for* loop is at its most useful when it is known in advance how many times the loop must execute. The previous examples in this lesson have used the *for* loop to write the first 1000 numbers, to cycle through 10 checkboxes, and to generate some number of random numbers. In each case the number of times the loop was to execute was predetermined. You may not be thinking the number of times the random number generating loop was to execute was predetermined, since that depended on the user's choice. But as far as the loop

```
<SCRIPT LANGUAGE=JavaScript><!--
var sum;
var i;

sum=0;
i=1;

while (sum <= 25000) {
    sum=sum+i;
    i=i+1;
}

document.write("It is necessary to add together the first
"+(i-1)+" numbers to reach a sum exceeding 25,000.  The
sum of these first "+(i-1)+" numbers is "+sum+".");
//--></SCRIPT>
```

> It is necessary to add together the first 224 numbers to reach a sum exceeding 25,000. The sum of these first 224 numbers is 25,200.

FIGURE 15.8 A program that uses the *while* loop. The output is provided.

was concerned, it was predetermined. By the time it was the loop's turn to do its thing, the variable *number* told it exactly how many times to execute.

However, the *for* loop is not equipped to handle certain situations. We saw in Figure 15.3 that the first 15 numbers add up to 120. We told the loop to execute exactly 15 times. But how about this problem: Starting with 1, how many consecutive numbers must we add until the total exceeds 25000? The problem asks us not to perform a task a fixed number of times, but to keep performing a task until a condition is met. The ideal structure for this is the *while* loop. We implement a solution to the above problem in Figure 15.8, explain how it works, and then present the general structure of the *while* loop.

This program uses two counters. The i counter starts at 1 and goes, one by one, through the positive numbers, and the *sum* counter adds the current value of i to its running total each time the loop executes. The loop continues until the running sum exceeds 25,000. That is when the Boolean expression that controls the loop becomes false. Note that the counters are not part of the actual declaration of the *while* statement. The steps of the execution of the loop are:

1. The Boolean expression is checked.
2. If it is true, the body of the loop executes.
3. Repeat (1) and (2) until the Boolean expression becomes false, at which time the loop is terminated.

It might seem strange that the *document.write()* statement uses *sum* as the final total but uses the value of $(i-1)$ to represent the number of numbers required to reach the final sum. However, a simple walk through the last pass of the loop sheds light on the reason behind this apparent discrepancy.

On the last pass of the loop, i is added to *sum*. Since this is to be the last pass, this addition causes *sum* to be greater than 25,000. The next statement in the loop body causes i to be increased by 1. The next would-be attempt through the loop finds the loop condition false. At this time, the loop is terminated, and the computer passes on to the next order of business, the *document.write()* statement. At this point *sum* contains the correct total, namely the first total exceeding 25,000. But, prior to checking the Boolean condition, the value of i was increased by 1. Now, the loop condition fails, and this final value of i is never added to *sum*. In other words, the previous value of i is the one that caused the sum to exceed 25,000.

The fact that there is no built-in counter for the *while* loop makes the positioning of your counters very important. For example, suppose we reverse the order of the statements in the loop, leaving the rest the same:

```
sum=0;
i=1;
while (sum<=25000) {
  i=i+1;
  sum=sum+i;
}
```

At first glance, this would seem to make no difference. But look again. Since the initializations of the counters have been left the same, *i* still starts at 1. But, before it is added to *sum,* it is increased to 2. So this version does not work correctly. We end up by adding $2 + 3 + 4 + \dots$, rather than the desired $1 + 2 + 3 + \dots$. A few similar examples are given as review questions. You just can't beat fun with counters!

In general, the *while* loop has the structure

```
while (Boolean condition) {
  statement;
    ⋮
  statement;
}
```

The computer keeps executing the body of the *while* loop as long as the Boolean expression is true. In contrast to the *for* loop, its flow of execution is according to the diagram in Figure 15.9.

The absence of a built-in counter is an immediate striking difference between the *while* loop and the *for* loop. Although in many applications the *while* loop is used in conjunction with a counter of some sort, one is not required. Most of the same conditions and restrictions that apply to the *for* loop also apply to the *while* loop. For example, if the controlling Boolean expression is *always* true, an infinite loop results.

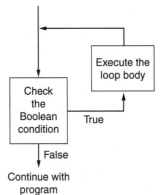

FIGURE 15.9 A graphic depiction of the execution of the *while* loop. As with the *for* loop, the top-down flow of the program halts until the loop has run its course. This loop has no built-in counter. The Boolean loop condition might not even depend directly on a counter.

There is little else worthy of comment in regard to the *while* loop since, in terms of the concept of looping, it is not overly different from the *for* loop. It merely has no built-in counter. In fact, in many situations either of the two loops would work equally well. For example, the loop of Figure 15.1:

```
for (var i=1; i<=100; i=i+1)
    document.write(i+"<BR>");
```

produces exactly the same results when reformulated as a *while* loop:

```
var i=1;
while(i<=100){
    document.write(i+"<BR>");
    i=i+1;
}
```

although the *for* loop is more compact in its structure. Again, several such comparisons are left as review questions.

15.5 INDEFINITE VERIFICATION OF PROMPT INPUT

The fact that the *while* loop keeps going until some condition is met makes it perfect for indefinite verification of user input for *prompt()* boxes. We have already seen that form input can be verified indefinitely. When the button is clicked, the function verifies

```
if(bad input)
    alert user
else
    process form
```

and the form is never processed until the input is good. Here the user supplies the repetition by clicking the button time after time. However, with prompted input, our only verification method has been

```
prompt
if(bad input)
    re-prompt
```

Now, we could just put five or 10 such *if* statements after the first *prompt()* and figure the user would acquiesce at some point and put in good information. An alternative is to keep the user entwined in a *while* loop until good input is supplied. In our example, we have set two secret passwords for our web page. Upon loading the page, the user is prompted for a password. If the user fails to enter a correct password, he or she is reprompted forever. When the user enters a correct password, the web page is allowed to load. The top-down logic for such a verification is:

-prompt for password (pass)

-assume it is incorrect (initialize correct=false)

```
while (not correct)
    if(pass fails to match one of the passwords)
        alert the user
        re-prompt
-else
    correct=true
```

We start out with the Boolean variable *correct* set to false. The *while* loop will keep going until *correct* is changed to true. Each time through the loop, if the password fails to match, the user is alerted and reprompted. Otherwise, *correct* is set to true. So the loop keeps going until the password matches. At that time, the loop condition becomes false and the loop terminates. If the password never matches, *correct* is never set to true and the loop never terminates. The actual JavaScript code for this program appears in Figure 15.10.

The first thing to note is that the two passwords are "buddy" and "pal". The page never loads unless one of those is exactly matched. Since the script is in the head section, the loop halts the progress of the web page right there. None of the body of the web page is yet visible. So this effectively keeps users from seeing the contents of the web page if they don't know the passwords. You will have to enter one of the correct passwords on the web site to see the web page that the passwords are protecting.

```
<HEAD>
<SCRIPT LANGUAGE=JavaScript><!--
var pass;
pass=prompt("Enter Your Password.","");

correct=false;

while(!correct){
    if((pass!="buddy")&&(pass!="pal")){
        alert("You have entered an incorrect password.");
        pass=prompt("Enter Your Password. Get it right this time.","");
    }
    else{
        correct=true;
    }
}
//--></SCRIPT>
</HEAD>
```

FIGURE 15.10   An indefinite password verification using the *while* loop.

NOTE   At first glance this appears to be a feeble attempt at protecting a page, since the passwords are in the source code. After all, once you have a web page loaded into your browser, you can view the source code. But, for that to happen, the page must be loaded. Since the above verification is in the head section, that never happens without a password, so the user can't view the source code and get the password.

We are not recommending that you protect your pages in this manner. In fact, it can serve to hang the browser in an infinite loop if the password is not known. In the browsers we checked, the only way out without a password is to force the browser to quit or to restart the computer. You could have fun and share a particular page only with your friends in this manner. However, if people without the password stumble upon the page, they are likely not going to be pleased with the results.

In order to keep passwords completely safe, they must be kept on the web server and accessed via CGI programs on the server. In that way, you can keep a database containing passwords, and the passwords are not transported to the browser with the web page.

15.6 NESTED LOOPS (OPTIONAL)

Dealing with one loop at a time is fairly straightforward. However, it is perfectly conceivable to include a loop inside the body of another loop. For example, consider the JavaScript code and its output in Figure 15.11.

Some explanation is in order. We'll refer to the loop with the *m* index as the "outer" loop and the one with the *n* index as the "inner" loop. The first time through the outer loop *m* contains the value of 10. The first thing encountered in the body of the outer loop is the inner loop. Executing the inner loop, the computer sets *n* to 1 and executes the *document.write()* statement, causing the value 10*1, namely 10, to be written followed by a space. The computer then increments *n* to 2, finds the inner loop condition still true, and writes the new product value of 10*2 followed by a space. Similarly, the inner loop writes the values 30, 40, and 50, each followed by a space. The inner loop now being completed, the computer passes to the next statement and writes the HTML <BR> tag. To finish the first pass of the outer loop, the index *m* is incremented to 11. The Boolean expression for the outer loop is still true, so it starts another pass. Again, the inner loop is the first order of business. The inner loop completely re-executes and causes *n* to range from 1 through 4. All the while *m* is still set at 11. So the numbers 11, 22, 33, 44, and 55 are written, each of course followed by a space. Now the HTML <BR> tag is written again and the outer loop starts over, this time with *m* containing 12. Similarly, except with *m* now equal to 12, the inner loop causes the values 12, 24, 36, 48, and 60 to be written. The process continues. The last time through the outer loop, with *m* equal to 20, the inner loop runs its course and causes the values of 20, 40, 60, 80, and 100 to be written. Finally *m* is incremented to 21, and the outer loop finally is exhausted.

To sum up that lengthy explanation, each time through the outer loop, the inner loop was executed to completion. Now, each time the inner loop ran its course entirely, the statement *document.write(m*n + " ")* was executed five times. But the inner loop was

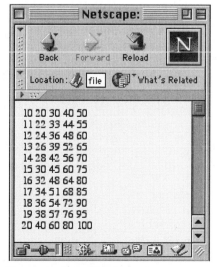

FIGURE 15.11 Nested *for* loops. The output is provided.

completely executed on each of the 10 passes through the outer loop. That makes for a total of 10*4 = 40 executions of the *document.write()* statement inside the inner loop.

Of course, nested *while* loops behave in the same fashion. In fact, *for* and *while* loops can be nested together, as the final example of this lesson attests. In general, given a nested loop structure composed of any combination of *for* and *while* loops, such as

```
outer loop (executes x times) {
    inner loop (excutes y times) {
        statement
    }
}
```

the statement in the body of the inner loop executes $x*y$ times. On each pass of the outer loop, the inner loop completely executes its y times. But the outer loop executes x times. That's a total of x times that the inner loop has run its complete course of y executions. Hence, there are $x*y$ executions of the statement in the body of the inner loop.

In effect, the program of Figure 15.11 created a tabular structure of rows and columns. Each execution of the outer loop created a new row, and that row was generated as the inner loop ran its course. This tabular structure suggests the feasibility of using nested loops to create HTML tables. For example, an educational site wishes to give a standard multiplication table using an HTML table for display.

A good alternative to making the table by hand is shown in Figure 15.12. Before the looping begins, the starting HTML TABLE tag is written. On the first pass of the outer loop,

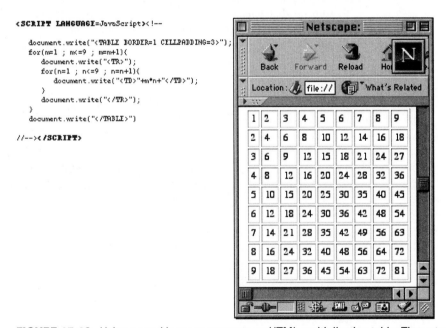

FIGURE 15.12 Using nested loops to generate an HTML multiplication table. The output is provided.

the <TR> tag is written, starting a new table row. Then the inner loop executes it nine times, each execution creating a new table cell containing the first nine multiples of $m=1$. When the inner loop is finished, the closing </TR> tag is written, thereby finishing the first row. Then the outer loop executes again, creating a new table row with $m=2$. The inner loop runs its course, writing the first nine multiples of $m=2$, each to a new table cell. Of course, this continues until, on the last pass of the outer loop, the first nine multiples of $m=9$ are written. Only after all the looping is finished is the closing table tag written.

An interesting variation on nested loops is when the number of times the inner loop executes depends upon how far the outer loop has progressed. Figure 15.13 contains such an example and its output.

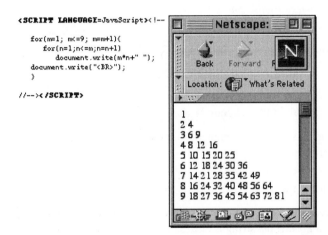

FIGURE 15.13 Nested loops in which the loop condition of the inner loop depends upon the loop index of the outer loop.

The loop condition for the inner loop is ($n<=m$), so the number of times it executes depends upon the state of m, the loop index of the outer loop. The first time through the outer loop $m=1$, so the inner loop executes only once. The second time through the outer loop $m=2$, so the inner loop executes twice. Finally, on the last pass through the outer loop, the inner loop executes nine times. You get what we term a "lower-left triangular" structure. Without much extra work, one can create an "upper-left triangular" version, but we leave that as an exercise.

15.7 AN EXAMPLE USING NESTED LOOPS (OPTIONAL)

To illustrate the use of nested loops to process HTML forms, we make a random-number lottery generator that extends the ideas of the example of Figure 15.6. In fact, this version uses the same HTML form. Rather than showing the form again, we refer you back to that figure. The function *generate()* that processed that form had no provision to guard against generating redundant numbers. This new version will not allow such redundancy. The user can select the range of numbers for the lottery and the amount of numbers to generate, and be assured that all of the numbers will be different.

The logic of the program is quite similar the version in Figure 15.6, except for checking the newly generated number against the previously generated numbers. The logic of the new version is:

> -declare variables
>
> -store selected option index of each menu (i, j)
>
> -if (either menu is still at option 0)
>> give an alert
>
> -else
>> store *text* for each of the selected options (range,number)
>> set display string to empty (display.value="")
>> for (x=1; x<=number; x=x+1)
>>> *already_used=true*
>>> *while (already_used)*
>>>> *generate random number (rnumber)*
>>>> *if (number is new)*
>>>>> *already_used=false*
>>> update display.value

The main structure of the program is still

> -if (user has not made a choice from one of the menus)
>> alert user
>
> -else
>> process the form

In the process-the-form part, we first have to determine the menu options the user has chosen. Then the display string is cleared of any previous numbers. The *for* loop now kicks in to generate the required *number* of random numbers. It executes *number* times, where *number* is the user's selection for the amount to generate. Each time the loop executes, a new random number is generated and appended to the end of the display string.

The program parts in italics above represent the new logic required to ensure that each new number generated is distinct from the previously generated numbers. That strategy can be summed up as follows. Assume the new number is bad, and keep looping with the *while* loop until a good number is generated. Each time through the *while* loop, generate a new number and check it against the previous numbers. If it is good, the Boolean variable is set to false, causing the loop to terminate. Otherwise, the *while* loop executes again, generating a new number and checking it.

But the key here is that this *while* loop runs its course for each execution of the *for* loop. It is worthwhile to break down this nesting to see what is occurring. Assume that the user has selected to generate 10 random numbers. That is, the *for* loop executes 10 times, once to generate each number. Below, we go through the 10 executions of the outer loop:

1. Generate first number: the *while* loop executes only once, since the first number is unique
2. Generate second number: the *while* loop keeps going until a number is generated different from first

3. Generate third number: the *while* loop keeps going until a number is generated different from first two

⋮

10. Generate tenth number: the *while* loop keeps going until a number is generated different from first nine

Broken down like that, it is somewhat easier to see what is going on. However, we have not given the details of checking a newly generated number against the previously generated numbers. In other words, details of the italicized part of the above logic need to be filled in.

For starters, we need some way to store the previously generated numbers. In Section 14.3, we briefly discussed how to define a new array. We construct one here to store the previously generated numbers:

```
var previous=new Array();
for(y=1; y<=10; y=y+1){
  previous[y]=0;
}
```

The name of the array is *previous[]*, and each of 10 index positions is initialized to contain the number 0. That is, *previous[]* binds together 10 indexed variables, each of which is set to contain 0. The above *for* statement is equivalent to

```
previous[1]=0;
previous[2]=0;
      ⋮
previous[10]=0;
```

With these preset storage positions, the details of the above italicized logic are:

```
for (x=1; x<=number; x=x+1)
  already_used=true;

  while(already_used)
    rnumber=Math.round((range*Math.random())+.5);
    match=false;
    for(z=1; z<=10; z=z+1)
      if(rnumber==previous[z])
        match=true;
    if(match==false)
      already_used=false;

  previous[x]=rnumber;
  display.value=display.value+rnumber+" ";
```

Generate a random number. Assume it doesn't match one of the previous numbers. The z-loop goes through all 10 positions of the *previous[]* array to see if there is a match. If there is, *match* is set to true. After the z-loop is done, we check to see if the *match* variable's false setting has survived. The only way *match* would have been changed to true is if the random number had matched one of the positions in the *previous[ ]* array. If the false setting has survived, we set *already_used to false,* thereby terminating the *while* loop. If the false setting has been changed because the random number had matched one of the previously generated ones, the *while* loop would execute again and test a new random number.

After the *while* loop is done, we are assured that *rnumber* contains a random number that is distinct from any previously generated ones. So, at this time, we add it to the previous array at the index *x* and update the display field. The first time through the *x*-loop puts the random number in *previous[1].* The second time through the *x*-loop puts the random number in *previous[2].* Finally, the last time through the *x*-loop puts the random number in *previous[number].* Any spots left unfilled in the *previous[ ]* array are still set to 0. Since the random numbers we are generating are all in the range from 1 to *range,* these unfilled spots can't cause a match to occur. Figure 15.14 gives the complete lottery-number function.

```
<SCRIPT LANGUAGE=JavaScript><!--
function generate(){
    var i,j,range,number, rnumber, already_used,match ;

    var previous=new Array();
    for(y=1 ; y<=10; y=y+1){
        previous[y]=0;
    }
    with(document.lottoform){
        i=rangemenu.selectedIndex;
        j=quantitymenu.selectedIndex;

        if((i==0)||(j==0)){
            alert("Please make a range selection and choose the amount of
            numbers you wish to be  generated before clicking the button.");
        }

    else{
        range=parseFloat(rangemenu.options[i].text);
        number=parseFloat(quantitymenu.options[j].text);

        display.value="";
        already_used=true;

        for (x=1 ; x<=number ;x=x+1){
            already_used=true;
            while(already_used){
                rnumber=Math.round((range*Math.random())+.5);
                match=false;
                for(z=1; z<=10; z=z+1){
                    if(rnumber==previous[z]){
                        match=true;
                    }
                }
                if(match==false){
                    already_used=false;
                }
            }
            previous[x]=rnumber;
            display.value=display.value+rnumber+" ";
        }
    }
  }
}

//--></SCRIPT>
```

FIGURE 15.14 The complete function to generate unique lottery numbers.

15.8 SUMMARY

Key Terms

loop   loop index   loop condition
infinite loop

Loops provide a means to tell the computer to do something repetitively. The *for* loop is ideal when something needs to be done a fixed number of times, such as testing 10 checkboxes or summing up 1000 numbers. The *while* loop is ideal when it is not known in advance how many times the loop must execute, such as looping until enough numbers are added to reach a certain total or looping until the user enters a correct password.

Since the *for* loop executes a fixed number of times, it has a built-in counter called the loop index. The loop keeps going until the counter violates the loop condition. The loop condition is the Boolean expression setting the condition that eventually terminates the loop when it becomes false. The *while* loop has no built-in counter, but it may be supplied with one. The loop condition for the *while* loop may have something to do with a supplied counter, or it may simply involve a Boolean variable that causes the loop to terminate when it becomes false for some reason.

When programming with loops, you must be careful not to make the program loop too many times. A loop requiring tens or hundreds of millions of executions can take even a fast computer several minutes or even hours to finish. It is even possible to have a loop in which the loop condition never becomes false. This is called an infinite loop. If you load an infinite loop into your browser, you may have to force your browser to quit. It is not uncommon for a computer to freeze up or even crash in that case.

15.9 REVIEW QUESTIONS

1. Determine the output of each *for* loop.

(a)
```
for(i=10; i<45; i=i+5){
   document.write(i+",");
}
```

(b)
```
for(i=25; i>=16; i=i-2){
   document.write(i+",");
}
```

(c)
```
for(i=0; i>=0; i=i+1){
   document.write(i+",");
}
```

(d)
```
for(i=0; i<0; i=i+1){
   document.write(i+",");
}
```

2. Determine the output of each *for* loop.

(a)
```
c=0;
for(x=1; x<=3; x=x+1){
   c=c+2*x;
}
document.write(c);
```

(b)
```
c=0
for(y=2; y<10; y=y+2){
   p=1;
   c=c+y;
   p=p*y;
}
document.write(c+","+p);
```

(c)
```
c=0;
for(i=1; i<=19; i=i+1){
   if(i==10){
      c=c+i;
   }
   else{
      c=c+1;
   }
}
document.write(c);
```

3. Determine the output of each *while* loop.

(a)
```
sum=0;
i=1;
```

```
while(sum<=17){
  sum=sum+2*i;
  i=i+1;
}
document.write(c+","+i);
```
(b)
```
sum=0;
i=1;
while(i<=17){
  i=i+1;
  sum=sum+2*i;
}
document.write(c+"," +i);
```
(c)
```
done=false;
c=2;
while(!done){
  c=c+2;
  if(c<10){
    c=c+1;
    document.write(c+",");
  }
  else{
    done=true;
  }
}
```

4. Rewrite the following as a *for* loop using the same loop condition:

```
i=1;
while(i<=10){
  i=i+1;
  sum=sum+i;
}
```

5. Rewrite the following as a *while* loop using the same loop condition:

```
for (x=100; x>0; x=x-10){
  total=total+x;
}
```

6. What happens in the password example of Figure 15.10 if the and (&&) is switched to or (||)?

7. What happens in the password example of Figure 15.10 if the user does not know the password?

8. In Figure 15.7, what would happen if the statement *display.value=" "* were removed from the program?

9. Write a JavaScript statement that generates a random whole number in the range from 1 to 100.

10. Find two errors in the following code:

```
for (i=1, i<10, i=i+1)
  sum=sum+i;
}
```

15.10 EXERCISES

1. A piece of paper is .005 inches thick. Write a program that finds out how many inches thick it would be if you folded it in half 35 times. Hint: Each time you fold it in half, it is twice as thick.

2. Make a form that asks the user to enter a number into a text field. The program then computes the factorial of that number. Option: Verify that the input is a number and that the number is in the range from 1 to 25. Also round off the number the user enters so that the program still works, even if a decimal is entered.

3. Make a version of the pizza form of Figure 15.4 that also keeps a running total of how many toppings are chosen. This total should also be included in the output.

4. Make a version of the pizza form of Figure 15.4 that assigns different prices to each of the toppings. The price of each topping should appear with that topping in the output. Otherwise, the program should work in the same way.

5. Make a version of the pizza form of Figure 15.4. This version should have two radio buttons, only one of which can be checked, for large ($13) and medium ($10) pizzas. The program should also assign different prices to each of the toppings. If large is chosen, the meat toppings (first row in form) cost twice as much each. The vegetable toppings (second row in form) are the same for large or small pizzas. You should keep separate running totals for each kind of topping. Both of these totals should appear as output. (We concede that anchovies are not vegetables.)

6. Do Exercise 15.2 with this option: instead of rounding off the user's input, include an extra verification step that alerts the user if a whole number has not been entered. Hint: Use a loop to check the input against all the whole numbers from 1 to 25.

7. Make a version of the lottery-picker program of Figure 15.6 that gives 10 radio buttons (only one of which can be chosen) for ranges of numbers, rather than using a menu. It should still have a menu for the amount of numbers to be chosen. Include no verification in this program.

8. Do Exercise 15.7 with verification: you should verify that the user has chosen a radio button and has made a menu selection.

9. In a lottery game in which a group of r balls is chosen from a total of n balls, with one ticket, your chances of matching all of them (winning the big payout) are

$$1 \text{ in} \frac{n!}{(n-r)! * r!}$$

For example, in a choose-5 game with 40 balls, your odds are

$$1 \text{ in} \frac{40!}{35! * 5!}$$

Write a program that finds the odds for a 52-balls, choose-6 game.

10. Make a version of the lottery-picker program of Figure 15.6 that has a text field displaying the odds of winning the grand payout for the game chosen by the user. See Exercise 15.9.

* The rest of the exercises refer to the optional sections.

11. Use nested loops to create 10 different 7×7 HTML tables. For simplicity, all cells of each of the tables need contain only a single character, say "x" or some other character.

12. Make an upper-left triangular multiplication table.

13. Make a version of the lower-left triangular table of Figure 15.13 in which each number appears in an HTML table. Note that some browsers will not render empty table cells. To avoid this, any empty table cells should contain a single character that is the same color as the web page, so that the cells will still appear empty.

14. Make a multiplication table in which only the first row and first column are TH cells, rather than TD cells.

15. Make a version of the lottery form of Figure 15.6 that uses 10 different text fields to display the lottery numbers.

15.11   PROJECT THREADS

Any exercises you do for this lesson should be referenced in your homework page following the guidelines in Section 9.10.

MORE ON ARRAYS

IN SECTION 14.3, we briefly introduced the necessary JavaScript code for defining new arrays. Since then, we have been using arrays that are automatically created when an HTML form is loaded into a browser. Of course we are referring to the *elements[]* array, which indexes a form's elements, and the *options[]* array, which indexes a pull-down menu's options. Each of these arrays is an simply an indexed group of objects. Rather than having to name each object, each of these arrays, through the array index, provides a natural ordering of the objects.

In this lesson, we concentrate on defining our own arrays for the purposes of indexing variables. At first, we will create arrays that serve to index groups of primitive variables. We will then create arrays to index groups of objects. Especially when combined with the power of looping, these self-defined arrays prove to be a valuable programming tool.

16.1 PARALLEL ARRAYS

Let's suppose that we are maintaining an online address directory so that old classmates can keep in touch. We will include a pull-down menu listing the names of classmates. We also wish to store their street addresses, states of residence, zip codes, phone numbers, and e-mail addresses. When a name is selected from the menu, the information for that person is displayed in several text fields. Such a form is shown in Figure 16.1.

That's five pieces of data in addition to the name. Now, the pull-down menu can carry only so much information in the *text* and *value* properties of its options. The names are to be visible on the menu itself, so the *text* property contains the names. We could store all of the rest of the information as a long string in the *value* property of each option, but then, when you retrieve that information for display, it would be just a long chunk of information that would be difficult to put into the various text fields.

In order to store all of the extra information, we define several arrays, each of which indexes one of the information types. We begin with the *address[]* array. First, a call to the *Array()* object constructor is made. Then addresses are assigned to different indices of the array:

```
var address=new Array();
address[1]="14 Schmo Lane";
address[2]="14 Schmart St.";
address[3]="14 Mell Ave.";
```

The rest of the array definitions are shown in Figure 16.2, which contains JavaScript code to process the form. There are two significant points to be made about the arrays. First, they are not defined within the function that is called by the *onchange* event handler when a change is made to the pull-down menu. These arrays contain permanent information used for the form. If they were defined locally within the function, they would be recreated each time the function is called. That is unnecessary. Rather, they are defined globally when the page first loads. Then, each time the function is called, the information from the arrays is accessed and used.

The second point to be made is that these arrays share a **parallel** relationship. That means that the information in the *i*th position in one array is related to the information in the *i*th positions of the other arrays. The notion of parallel arrays is illustrated graphically in Figure 16.3. You can see in Figure 16.2 that calling on the index 3, for example, in each of the different arrays serves to retrieve all the different information pieces for Pell Mell.

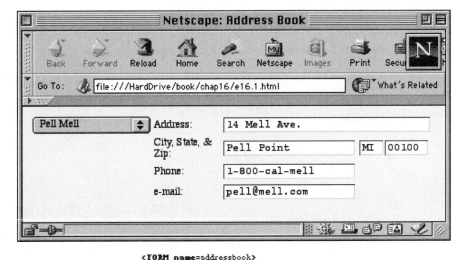

FIGURE 16.1 A form that displays information based upon a choice from a pull-down menu.

```
<SCRIPT LANGUAGE=JavaScript><!--
var address=new Array();
address[1]="14 Schmo Lane";
address[2]="14 Schmart St.";
address[3]="14 Mell Ave.";

var city=new Array();
city[1]="Fort Joe";
city[2]="Artville";
city[3]="Pell Point";

var state=new Array();
state[1]="WA";
state[2]="TN";
state[3]="MI";

var zip=new Array();
zip[1]="00001";
zip[2]="00010";
zip[3]="00100";

var phone=new Array();
phone[1]="1-800-cal-joey";
phone[2]="1-800-cal-arty";
phone[3]="1-800-cal-mell";

var email=new Array();
email[1]="joe@schmo.com";
email[2]="art@schmart.com";
email[3]="pell@mell.com";

function display(){
   with(document.addressbook){
      var i;
      i=elements[0].selectedIndex;

      if(i==0){
         for(x=1 ; x<=6 ; x=x+1){
            elements[x].value="";
         }
      }
      else{
         elements[1].value=address[i];
         elements[2].value=city[i];
         elements[3].value=state[i];
         elements[4].value=zip[i];
         elements[5].value=phone[i];
         elements[6].value=email[i];
      }
   }
}
//--></SCRIPT>
```

FIGURE 16.2 The JavaScript code for the address book form of Figure 16.1.

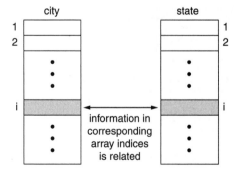

FIGURE 16.3 Parallel arrays organize related information. Related information in one or more parallel arrays share the same array index.

Now to the function in Figure 16.2. You can see from the form definition in Figure 16.1 that the first option in the menu is an instruction, rather than one of the names. That is, the 0 index of the menu's *options[]* array should produce blank information fields. When the page is first loaded, the HTML form attributes cause the information fields to be blank. But, after the user has looked at a few addresses, if the menu is set back to the instruction, the information fields need to be reset back to blank. With that in mind, the top-down logic for the function is as follows.

-extract the chosen index from the *options[]* array of the menu (i)

-if(the instruction in position 0 is selected)

    set all of the display fields to blank

-else

    assign the *i*th position of each self-defined array to the proper text field

After extracting the user's selection from the menu and storing it in the variable *i*, we see if the first menu item (the instruction) is selected. If so, we use a *for* loop to reset all of the text fields to the empty string. The text fields occupy positions 1 through 6 of the *elements[]* array. You can see in Figure 16.2 that the *for* loop does indeed loop through those positions of the *elements[]* array.

Otherwise, the user has chosen one of the names, in which case the *else* clause kicks in. Remember, *i* contains the index of the index choice of the user from the pull-down menu. So for example, if *i* is 2, then the second positions from all of the informational arrays are assigned to the proper text display fields of the form. That is where the parallel relationships among the arrays comes in to play. The information associated with the name in the *i*th index of the *options[]* array is stored in the *i*th positions of the informational arrays.

16.2 THE *ARRAY* OBJECT

On several occasions, we have stressed that arrays are objects. They have properties like any other object, but array properties are numbered, or indexed. The indices we have used have all been positive whole numbers, $0, 1, 2, \ldots$ But array properties can be numbered with any whole numbers, $\ldots, -2, -1, 0, 1, 2, \ldots$ For example, the array definition

```
var names=new Array();
names[-5]="Bernie";
names[-3]="Robbie";
names[-1]="Ben";
names[1]="Cris";
```

is perfectly valid. However, the numbers $-5, -3, -1, 1$ make for an unnatural indexing scheme. We choose to define as **standard arrays** those arrays whose properties are indexed starting with 0 and whose indices progress one by one through the positive whole numbers. So, for example, the *elements[]* and *options[]* arrays are standard arrays.

The reason for our choice of terminology has to do with the *length* property of array objects. Every array has this property, which simply gives the number of properties of the array. This property is accessed not by using the [] notation, as the indexed array properties are, but just by appending the *length* property onto the array name with standard object notation:

arrayname.length

But this property assumes the array is standard. For example, using this property to find the length of the *names[ ]* array defined above

```
x=names.length;
```

causes the variable *x* to contain the number 2. The length property saw that the highest array index was 1 and assumed that the array was standard, containing only the properties *names[0]* and *names[1]*.

When an empty array is declared,

```
var anarray=new Array();
```

the *length* property contains 0. Each time you add a property,

```
anarray[0]=3.14;
```

the *length* property is increased by 1. For example, the loop

```
for(i=0 ; i<=10 ; i=i+1){
    anarray[i]=Math.random();
}
```

causes *anarray.length* to contain the number 11, since there are 11 array properties indexed 0–10. Here each property 0–10 contains a randomly generated number. One could then use the *length* property to loop back through the array positions:

```
for(i=0 ; i<=(anarray.length-1) ; i=i+1){
    sum=sum+anarray[i];
}
```

causing all of the random numbers to be added. Note that the upper bound for the loop is (anarray.length-1) since the *length* of the array is 11, but we only wish to loop through the array index of 10. Having the zeroth index start off a standard array causes the *length* property to be one larger than the highest index. Another possibility for the previous loop condition is (i<anarray.length).

One might be tempted to fill a new array using the length property,

```
var somearray=new Array();
for(i=0; i<=(somearray.length-1) ; i=i+1){   (OOPS!)
    somearray[i]=Math.random();
}
```

but the loop never executes. When the new array is declared, its length is 0, causing (somearray.length-1) to be negative.

There is a way to predefine the length of an array: the *Array()* constructor can take a parameter. Declaring

```
var somearray=new Array(100);
```

sets up an array with 100 properties, indexed from 0 to 99. But you still have to define the contents of each property of the array. Even though the array is declared with 100 properties, they all contain the value null since they have been assigned no values. But, with *somearray.length* already containing 100, you can then use that property to fill the array with a loop, if you wish.

16.3   THE *IMAGE* OBJECT AND *IMAGES[]* ARRAY

When loaded into a browser, an image becomes an object with properties. Many of these properties' values are set by HTML attributes when the image is rendered. For example, an *image* object has properties *src, height, width, hspace,* and *vspace,* to name a few. That is natural since marked-up images are tangible objects with properties that define their state. Like the *document* object, most of whose properties can't be changed after the page is loaded, most of the properties of an image can't be updated after the page has been fully loaded. However, the *src* (source) property of an image can be changed after the page is loaded.

The *src* property of an image is initially set by the HTML SRC attribute, which gives the URL of the image to be displayed. But, even after the page is fully loaded, JavaScript can be used to give a new value to the *src* property of an image object. This value specifies the URL of a new image, and thus causes a new image to replace the original one in a web page.

When a web page with images is loaded by a browser, an *images[ ]* array is automatically created to index all of the images in the page. Like the other arrays that are automatically created, this array is standard, beginning with the 0 index. Images can be named just like HTML forms, but we will stick with the *images[ ]* array to reference the image objects in a web page. The partial object hierarchy for a web page with images is provided in Figure 16.4. The only property we have listed for each image is the *src* property, since that is the only one we can change with JavaScript. Note that *image* objects are properties of the document itself, unlike form elements, which are properties of the form, which is in turn a property of the document.

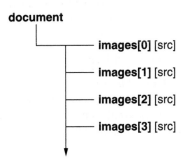

FIGURE 16.4 A partial object hierarchy for an HTML document with images.

```
<IMG SRC="left.gif" WIDTH=25 HEIGHT=25>
<FORM>
<INPUT TYPE=button VALUE="Left" onclick="left()">
<INPUT TYPE=button VALUE="Right" onclick="right()">
<INPUT TYPE=button VALUE="Up" onclick="up()">
<INPUT TYPE=button VALUE="Down" onclick="down()">
</FORM>
```

FIGURE 16.5 A web page that uses form buttons to change the *src* property of the *image* object after the page is fully loaded.

For a simple example, we create a web page with one image and four form buttons that change the source of the image. Each button changes the source of the image. The four images are shown below with their names, and the web page displaying the image and form buttons is shown in Figure 16.5.

left.gif   right.gif   up.gif   down.gif

You can see from the HTML code that marks up the image that, when the page loads, the left arrow, "left.gif", is the one displayed. Each of the buttons calls on a function that changes the *src* property of the *image* object. The JavaScript functions, which are in the HEAD section of the document as usual, are shown in Figure 16.6.

Since there is only one HTML IMG tag and hence only one image displayed in the web page, that image corresponds to the zeroth index of the *images[]* array. So the *src* property of the image is accessed with the object reference

document.images[0].src

Each function simply changes the source URL of the image object. Depending upon which button is clicked and consequently which function is called, the source of the image is changed to one of the other arrows. Note that all of the images are in the same directory as the HTML document, so the URLs of the images are just the file names.

```
<HEAD>
<SCRIPT LANGUAGE=JavaScript><!--
function left(){
    document.images[0].src="left.gif";
}
function right(){
    document.images[0].src="right.gif";
}
function up(){
    document.images[0].src="up.gif";
}
function down(){
    document.images[0].src="down.gif";
}
//--></SCRIPT>
</HEAD>
```

FIGURE 16.6 The functions that change the *src* property of the *image* object shown in Figure 16.5.

16.4 PRELOADING IMAGES INTO ARRAYS

Maybe you played with the web page of Figure 16.5 on the web site (as you should be doing with all of the examples). You may have noticed that there is something to be desired in that example. When the page is first loaded, the only image transported along with the web page and put in the browser's cache memory was "left.gif". (See Section 2.4 if you need a refresher on cache memory.) Then, when you hit one of the other buttons, "up" for example, the browser had to make a new connection to the web server to get the "up.gif" image file. No doubt this caused a pause of at least a second or two. Also, you may have noticed a message in the status bar of your browser indicating that a new connection to the server was being made. Before "up.gif" could be substituted as the new source for the image, it had to be transferred from the server into the cache. Likewise, clicking on the buttons for the other two images necessitates a new connection to the server.

> **N O T E**　If you didn't notice the extra server connections, but clicked all of the buttons, the images have already been transported to your cache. If you re-click the buttons, the browser will likely just retrieve them from the cache. If you wish to witness the new server connections again, you will have to go to the preferences in your browser, make it empty the cache, and try again. Or, if you are in a computer lab and don't have that privilege, go to a different computer to check it out.

The way to avoid extra server connections when *src* properties of images are updated after the page has loaded is to preload the images into an array. First, a new array has to be created:

```
var arrows=new Array();
```

Then, since each of the properties of this array is to be an image object, a call to the *Image()* object constructor is required for each image:

```
arrows[0]=new Image();
arrows[1]=new Image();
arrows[2]=new Image();
arrows[3]=new Image();
```

```
<HEAD>
<SCRIPT LANGUAGE=JavaScript><!--
var arrows=new Array();

for(i=0 ; i<=3 ; i=i+1){
  arrows[i]=new Image();
}
arrows[0].src="left.gif";
arrows[1].src="right.gif";
arrows[2].src="up.gif";
arrows[3].src="down.gif";

function left(){
   document.images[0].src=arrows[0].src;
}
function right(){
   document.images[0].src=arrows[1].src;
}
function up(){
   document.images[0].src=arrows[2].src;
}
function down(){
   document.images[0].src=arrows[3].src;
}
//--></SCRIPT>
</HEAD>
```

FIGURE 16.7 JavaScript code for the page of Figure 16.5 that preloads the images into an array of *image* objects.

Being created as new image objects, each of them has been endowed with a *src* property. We simply assign the URL of each of the images we wish to pre-load to one of the image objects:

$$arrows[0].src="left.gif";$$
$$arrows[1].src="right.gif";$$
$$arrows[2].src="up.gif";$$
$$arrows[3].src="down.gif";$$

The JavaScript code utilizing this strategy is shown in Figure 16.7. The first important point to be made is that the image array is not declared and loaded inside one of the functions. If that were the case, the images would not be transported to the cache until that function was called. It is important that they be loaded as global variables as soon as the web page loads.

One difference between the code in Figure 16.7 and the above discussion about preloading images is that a *for* loop has been used to set up all of the array properties as new *image* objects. You can see from the first way we did it above that the only thing varying in the four declarations is the array index. One should always be looking for ways to use loops when working with arrays.

Since the images are preloaded into the array, each function simply assigns the source of the appropriate array image to the source of the image in the web page. In this way, the preloaded images are substituted for the one in the web page as the buttons dictate.

16.5 THE *ONLOAD* EVENT HANDLER

In most browsers, you can't use JavaScript to set the *src* property of an image object before the HTML IMG tag has caused the object to be created. For example, consider the HTML document shown in Figure 16.8.

```
<HTML>
<HEAD>
<SCRIPT LANGUAGE=JavaScript><!--
var theimage=new Image();
theimage.src="img.gif";
document.images[0].src=theimage.src;
//--></SCRIPT>
</HEAD>
<BODY>
<IMG SRC="" WIDTH=25 HEIGHT=25>
</BODY>
</HTML>
```

FIGURE 16.8 An HTML document that attempts to set the source of an image with JavaScript before the browser has created the image object, in this case *images[0]*.

In the HEAD section, an image is preloaded into the image object *theimage*. Then, this image is assigned to *document.images[0].src*. The problem with this is that the browser has not yet set up the *images[ ]* array for the images marked up in the web page. Since no SRC has been specified by the HTML IMG tag, and the JavaScript statements have already been executed, the browser sets up *images[0],* but with no source. The HTML document of Figure 16.8 displays a blank 25×25 image location. Even if a SRC had been specified in the HTML IMG tag, the JavaScript preloaded image would not be substituted. In the examples of the previous section, the page is fully loaded before the buttons cause JavaScript to update the image source.

However, even without the use of form buttons, there is still a way to cause preloaded images in the head section to be displayed in the document. The HTML BODY tag can use the ***onload*** event handler. This event handler calls a JavaScript function just like other event handlers, but calls the function right before the page has finished loading. Figure 16.9 shows an HTML document that uses this event handler to accomplish what the document of Figure 16.8 fails to accomplish.

The *onload* event handler is timed so that all of the objects created by the HTML elements are in place, and accessible to JavaScript, before it calls the function. At first thought, this event handler is not like the others in that it does not seem to be sitting around waiting for the user to do something. However, loading a web page into a browser is an event caused by the user, whether by loading a page on the local computer or by clicking a link that causes a page to be loaded from a remote server.

```
<HTML>
<HEAD>
<SCRIPT LANGUAGE=JavaScript><!--
var theimage=new Image();
theimage.src="img.gif";

function getimage(){
document.images[0].src=theimage.src;
}
//--></SCRIPT>
</HEAD>
<BODY onload="getimage()">
<IMG SRC="" WIDTH=25 HEIGHT=25>
</BODY>
</HTML>
```

FIGURE 16.9 An HTML document that uses the *onload* event handler to mark up a preloaded image.

16.6 DISPLAYING A RANDOMLY SELECTED IMAGE

The first application we present that uses preloaded images is displaying a randomly selected image. Perhaps you have seen web pages in which a different image appears in a given location each time the page loads. One way to do this is to preload several images and use a randomly generated number to pick one of them. Since the image is chosen randomly by JavaScript in the head section of the document, we employ the *onload* event handler of the BODY tag to put the image in its place.

For this example, we choose randomly from among three advertisement images, "ad1.gif", "ad2.gif", and "ad3.gif". First, the images need to be preloaded into an array of image objects, say a standard array with indices 0–2. Next, a random number (0, 1, or 2) is generated. All that is left to do is for the function called by the *onload* event handler to put the image corresponding to the generated number into the *src* property of the image marked up by the HTML IMG tag. The HTML document that accomplishes this is shown in Figure 16.10.

The random numbers we have generated in previous examples have been in the range from 1 to some number. In this example, the range is 0 to 2. The statement that generates such a number uses a minus sign rather than a plus sign. The reader is invited to think about why that is.

NOTE
There is a disadvantage to including random images using an array of preloaded images. If you have 10 or 15 such images from which to choose, a significant time delay could result as all of the images preload into the cache. After all, only one of them is to be displayed. However, for a few small images this strategy should pose no problem.

```
<HTML>
<HEAD>
<SCRIPT LANGUAGE=JavaScript><!--
var ads=new Array();
for(x=0 ;x<=2;x=x+1){
    ads[x]=new Image();
}
var i;
i=Math.round(3*Math.random()-.5);

ads[0].src="ad1.gif";
ads[1].src="ad2.gif";
ads[2].src="ad3.gif";

function putin(){
   document.images[0].src=ads[i].src;
}
//--></SCRIPT>
</HEAD>

<BODY onload="putin()">
<IMG SRC="" WIDTH=206 HEIGHT=61>
</BODY>
</HTML>
```

FIGURE 16.10 A document that displays a randomly selected image.

There are a couple of ways to display a randomly chosen image without having to preload all of the possibilities. One such alternative is left as an exercise. Another alternative is to store all of the image URLs as primitive string variables:

```
var urls=new Array();
urls[0]="ad1.gif";
urls[1]="ad2.gif";
urls[2]="ad3.gif";
```

That does *not* cause the images to be preloaded into the cache. Then, you simply assign the appropriate URL to the *src* attribute of the image in the web page. At that time, a server connection is made for the image but, since the page is just loading, there will be no perceived delay. It will appear as if the image was marked up as normal with the HTML IMG tag.

16.7 CYCLING IMAGE DISPLAYS

The second example using preloaded images creates what is commonly termed a cycling banner. This involves two or more images that are to appear in sequence with a time delay. In other words, the page loads and an image appears. After a while, say 10 seconds, another image replaces it. After another 10 seconds, a third image replaces it. The process repeats in a cyclic fashion.

We have not yet seen a JavaScript mechanism with which we can control the flow of time in a web page, so we present that first and then move on to the cycling banner example. (Well, I guess we know how to freeze up the browser with an infinite loop, but that doesn't count.)

JavaScript has a function (actually a method of the *window* object) that causes another function to be called automatically at regular time intervals. For a quick example, Figure 16.11 shows the HEAD section of an HTML document that contains two simple JavaScript functions and two calls to the *setInterval()* function. (Capital I in Interval)

You see two very simple self-defined functions. One turns the background of the web page red when called, and the other turns it blue when called. The *setInterval()* function takes two arguments. The first is the name of a function and the second is a time in milliseconds (1/1000 of a second). The first use of *setInterval()* in Figure 16.11 specifies that the *redit()* function be called once every second. The second use of *setInterval()* function specifies that the *blueit()* function be called once every two seconds. Moreover, this function calling

```
<HEAD>
<SCRIPT LANGUAGE=JavaScript><!--
function redit(){
 document.bgColor="red";
}
function blueit(){
 document.bgColor="blue";
}
setInterval("redit()",1000);
setInterval("blueit()",2000);
//--></SCRIPT>
</HEAD>
```

FIGURE 16.11 Using the *setInterval()* function to call other functions at regular time intervals.

is repetitive: each of the color-changing functions will automatically be called indefinitely, at the specified time intervals. Not even the stop button on most browsers will stop the function calls from continuing.

If you check out the page generated by Figure 16.11 on the web site, you will quickly learn why that is not a particularly eye-pleasing use of the *setInterval()* function. However, it does provide a good mechanism with which to set the time interval for a cycling banner display.

In the cycling banner example, we use the same three advertisement images, "ad1.gif", "ad2.gif", and "ad3.gif". The source code for the whole web page is shown in Figure 16.12. We go through the steps that occur as the page loads.

First, the images are preloaded into an array of image objects. Next, a global variable named *current* is declared and set to contain a randomly generated number in the range from 0 to 2. This variable is to keep track of which image is currently on display. Since its contents must survive the function calls, the variable must be declared globally. So as to give no preference to any of the ads, the initially displayed ad is selected randomly.

The rest of the JavaScript code is comprised of two functions, so these are noted by the JavaScript interpreter but are not invoked. Thus all that has happened is that some images have been pre-loaded and a global variable has been set up. Clearly, nothing else can happen until one of the functions is called. As the page finishes loading, the *onload* event handler calls the *getfirst()* function. This function does two things. First, it sets the source

```
<HTML>
<HEAD>
<SCRIPT LANGUAGE=JavaScript><!--
var ads=new Array();

for(i=0 ;i<=2;i=i+1){
    ads[i]=new Image();
}

ads[0].src="ad1.gif";
ads[1].src="ad2.gif";
ads[2].src="ad3.gif";

var current;
current=Math.round(3*Math.random()-.5);

function rotate(){
    if(current<2){
        current=current+1;
    }
    else{
        current=0;
    }
    document.images[0].src=ads[current].src
}

function getfirst(){
    document.images[0].src=ads[current].src;
    setInterval("rotate()",2000);
}
//--></SCRIPT>
</HEAD>
<BODY onload="getfirst()">
<P><IMG SRC="" WIDTH=206 HEIGHT=61>
</BODY>
```

FIGURE 16.12 An HTML document that creates a cycling advertisement.

of the image in the web page to the randomly chosen index of the *ads[]* array. Second, it calls the *setInterval()* function that instructs the computer to call the *rotate()* function every two seconds henceforth.

The logic of the *rotate()* function is summarized as follows:

-if(not the last image)
   set *current* to the next image

-else
   set *current* back to the first image

-display the new *current* image

It simply adds one to the currently displayed index of the *ads[]* array, or sets the current index back to 0 if the last index of the array is currently on display. Since this function is going to be called every two seconds, the displayed ad is going to be cycled through the indices of the *ads[]* array. For example, if *current* is randomly set to 1 when the page first loads, the ads will cycle according to the array indices 1, 2, 0, 1, 2, 0, 1, 2, 0, 1, 2, . . . indefinitely.

16.8 SEARCHING ARRAYS (OPTIONAL)

The information used in the examples of this section was obtained from the NFL.com web site for the National Football League. In particular, information pertaining to the 1999 Pittsburgh Steelers roster is used. The first example uses three parallel arrays containing information about the players, *names[], heights[],* and *weights[]*. The information contained in each array should be apparent from the array names.

The purpose of the first example is to search the *heights[]* array for the tallest players on the roster and to search the *weights[]* array for the heaviest players. In order to make the example more interesting, we have added two fictitious players to the end of the roster. We do this so that the tallest and heaviest players on the team are not unique. In other words, when we search the arrays, we wish to find more than one tallest and heaviest player. Since each array has a length of 60, we provide only a partial definition of each array. The array declarations appear in Figure 16.13. Since the arrays are parallel, all the information for each player can be found using one index value. So, for example, the 58th index of each array contains information for Amos Zereoue. The heights are given in inches and the weights in pounds.

The HTML forms that will display the information from these arrays are pictured in Figure 16.14. There are two separate forms in the web page. The first, named *rosterform,* is on the left and contains over 60 text fields, more than enough to accommodate the Steelers roster. The second form, named *searchform,* is on the right. It contains two buttons and a text area. Since we use the *elements[]* array to access the form elements in this example, we have not supplied the HTML code for the form. Just remember there are two distinct forms whose names have been supplied above. Of course, you can view the source code for the whole document on the web site.

All that is left to do is to write the necessary functions. You can see in Figure 16.13 where they go in relation to the arrays that contain all of the information. As usual, the

```
<HEAD>
<SCRIPT LANGUAGE=JavaScript><!--
var names=new Array();
names[0]="Bettis, Jerome";
names[1]="Blackwell, Will";
names[2]="Brown,  Anthony";
.
.
names[58]="Zereoue, Amos";
names[59]="Tall,Johnny";
names[60]="McHeavy,Ian";

var heights=new Array();
heights[0]=71;
heights[1]=72;
heights[2]=77;
.
.
heights[58]=68;
heights[59]=79;
heights[60]=75;

var weights=new Array();
weights[0]=250;
weights[1]=190;
weights[2]=315;
.
.
weights[58]=202;
weights[59]=311;
weights[60]=322;

*Functions go here.*
//--></SCRIPT>
</HEAD>
<BODY onload="showroster()">
```

FIGURE 16.13 Three parallel arrays of information.

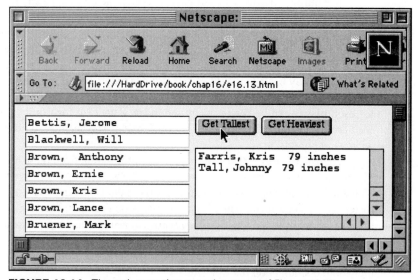

FIGURE 16.14 The web page that uses the arrays of Figure 16.13.

arrays are defined as global variables, outside of the functions. Also, notice in Figure 16.13 that the onload event handler in the BODY tag calls a function named *showroster()*. When the page loads, this function transfers the player names from the *names()* array into the text fields of the first form, *rosterform*. One loop serves to accomplish this:

```
for(i=1 ; i<names.length ; i=i+1)
    document.rosterform.elements[i].value=names[i]
```

Each index of the *names[]* array is assigned to the same index of the *elements[]* array of the form. Since both are standard arrays, the assignment is straightforward.

We chose to define a second form for the buttons and the text area since the first form has so many text fields. With a new FORM tag for the second form, *searchform,* it is clear that the text area can be accessed by *elements[2]* of that form. Certainly you could put all the form elements of Figure 16.14 into one form, but then you would have to count to find that the text area would be something like *elements[66]*. It was simply easier to use two forms.

Now for the functions that the buttons of the second form call. The first button calls a function named *searchtall()*. First a local variable

```
var temp_max;
temp_max=0;
```

is declared and set to 0. We then loop through the entire *heights[]* array, and each time a new temporary maximum height is found, that height is stored in *temp_max:*

```
for(i=0 ; i<heights.length ; i=i+1)
    if(heights[i]>temp_max)
        temp_max=heights[i];
```

Since *temp_max* has been preset to 0, on the first pass of the loop, *heights[0]* is stored in *temp_max*. On each subsequent pass of the loop, the new height is stored into *temp_max,* only if that height is larger than the previous value of *temp_max*. In other words, each time through the loop, if a new height is encountered that is larger than any of the previously encountered heights, *temp_max* is replaced by that height. So *temp_max* is updated each time a larger height is encountered, but left unchanged otherwise. In this way, after the loop has gone through the whole *heights[]* array, *temp_max* will be left holding the maximum height found in the array.

But we wish to do more than put this maximum height into the text area. The names of all the players sharing that height should be displayed. To find out which players share this maximum, we loop back through the *heights[]* array. Each time a height is found that matches *temp_max,* some information about that player is written to the text area:

```
for(i=0 ; i<heights.length ; i=i+1)
    if(heights[i]==temp_max)
        display info for player i
```

The entire *searchtall()* function is displayed in Figure 16.15. The only aspect of this function we have not covered is the statement that clears the text area of any previous contents. At this point, you should be accustomed to the necessity for that. The function that the button for the

```
*Arrays go here.*

function showroster(){
   for(i=0 ; i<names.length ;i=i+1){
      document.rosterform.elements[i].value=names[i];
   }
}
function searchtall(){
   with(document){

      var temp_max;
      temp_max=0;

      searchform.elements[2].value="";

      for(i=0 ; i<heights.length ; i=i+1){
         if(heights[i]>temp_max){
            temp_max=heights[i];
         }
      }
      for(i=0 ; i<heights.length ; i=i+1){
         if(heights[i]==temp_max){
            searchform.elements[2].value=searchform.elements[2].value+
            names[i]+"  "+heights[i]+" inches\r";
         }
      }
   }
}
```

FIGURE 16.15 The functions called by the *onload* event handler and the "get tallest" button in Figure 16.14.

heaviest calls is very similar, so we don't show both functions. However, the *showroster()* function that loads the players into the first form is shown.

The second example involving searching arrays uses the same three arrays as defined in Figure 16.13, but also uses a fourth array. This array, named *positions[],* contains the position played by each player. Of course, this array shares a parallel relationship with the other three. A partial definition for the *positions[]* array follows:

```
var positions=new Array();
positions[0]="RB";
positions[1]="WR";
positions[2]="T";
positions[3]="DE";
positions[4]="K";
positions[5]="DB";
   .
   .
positions[56]="RB";
positions[57]="QB";
positions[58]="RB";
```

The positions are given with the standard notation for football. The good news is that you don't have to understand what these symbols stand for. It suffices to realize that there are 12 different positions that subdivide the roster into 12 categories. The 12 different positions are shown in Figure 16.16, which shows the web page for this example. A position can be chosen, and with the button click, all players for that position are displayed.

This page uses the same *showroster()* function called by the *onload* event handler as shown in Figure 16.15. When the page is first loaded, the player names are displayed in the

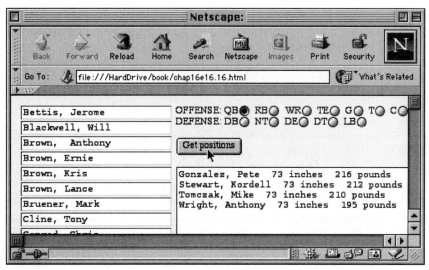

FIGURE 16.16   A web page that uses four parallel arrays to search for players according to position.

text fields of the first form. The second form, named *searchform* as in the previous example, contains the 12 radio buttons, the "get positions" button, and the text area. Once again, it is better just to make a new form so that we don't have to worry about all 60-some of the elements array positions for the text fields in the first form.

The function that the "get positions" button calls is named *search()*. First this function needs a local variable in which to store the chosen option from the radio buttons. We name this variable *search_string*. The *value* properties of the radio buttons contain the position abbreviations. So, to get the abbreviation of the players to be searched for, we loop through the radio buttons and get the contents of the *value* property of the chosen one. The position abbreviation corresponding to the chosen radio button is stored in *search_string:*

```
for(i=0 ; i<=11 ; i=i+1)
   if(searchform.elements[i].checked)
      search_string=searchform.elements[i].value;
```

All that is left to do is to is to loop through the *positions()* array and see which players' position matches the position stored in *search_string*. If a player matches, the information for that player is extracted from the other three arrays and assigned to the text area. Remember, for a given index in the *positions()* array, the rest of the information for that player is in the same index of the other arrays.

```
for(i=0 ; i<names.length ; i=i+1)
   if(positions[i]==search_string)
      assign info for that player to text area
```

The entire *search()* function is shown in Figure 16.17.

```
function search(){
  with(document){

    var search_string;
    search_string="";

    for(i=0 ; i<=11 ; i=i+1){
      if(searchform.elements[i].checked){
        search_string=searchform.elements[i].value;
      }
    }
    searchform.elements[13].value="";

    for(i=0 ; i<positions.length ; i=i+1){
      if(positions[i]==search_string){
        searchform.elements[13].value=searchform.elements[13].value+
          names[i]+"  "+heights[i]+" inches  "+weights[i]+
          " pounds\r";
      }
    }
  }
}
```

FIGURE 16.17 The function called by the "get position" button of Figure 16.16.

16.9 SUMMARY

Key Terms

parallel arrays standard arrays *length* property
image object *images[]* array *src* property
preloaded image *onload* event cycling image
setInterval()

Parallel arrays serve to organize groups of related information. When several arrays share a parallel relationship, the information in the *i*th index position of each array is related. For example, if the fifth index of a *names[]* array contains the desired name, then the fifth index of the other arrays contains information related to the name. In this way, one array can serve as a reference array and the rest of the parallel arrays can carry all of the related information behind the scenes.

In general, self-defined arrays are declared using the *Array()* object constructor. Once an array is declared by name, values can be added to different array indices by direct assignment. You can assign information to any index value that is a whole number, even negative. However, arrays that use index values 0, 1, 2, . . . are called standard arrays. Aside from an array object's indexed properties, all JavaScript arrays have a *length* property. This property is accessed using standard object notation:

arrayname.length

and contains a number corresponding to the length of the array. This property assumes that the array is standard. Thus, if the highest index of the array is 25, for example, the *length* property contains 26. The extra property corresponds to the zeroth index of the standard array.

When a web page is loaded into a browser, the browser not only marks up each image in the web page, but it creates an *image* object for each IMG tag it finds. These image objects are indexed by the *images[]* array. This array is a standard array (like the *elements[]* and *options[]* arrays), and is a property of the *document* object. Each *image* object has several properties corresponding to the physical characteristics of the image, but the only property that most browsers allow to be changed after the page is fully loaded is the *src* (source) property. So, for example, you can use a form button to change the source property of an image object and cause a new image to be rendered in the same space in the web page.

If several images are to be used to update the web page after it is fully loaded, it is advantageous to preload all of the images into a self-defined array of image objects. If the images are not preloaded, each time you try to use one of them to update the web page, a new connection to the server has to be made. The strategy for preloading images is as follows:

1. create a *new Array()*
2. define each index of the array as a *new Image()* object
3. assign the URL of an image to the *src* property of each image object.

A *for* loop is often useful when initializing several indices of an array as *image* objects.

Once images are preloaded into an array, they are sitting in the browser's cache waiting to be used. To update an image in a web page, you assign the *src* property of one of the preloaded images to the *src* property of the corresponding position of the *images[]* array. For example, to update the fifth image in a web page with the image in the zeroth position of the preloaded image array, you would use the following assignment:

```
document.images[4].src=preloaded[0].src;
```

The original image is immediately replaced with the preloaded image.

The *onload* event handler can be used in the BODY tag to call a function right as the page is finishing being loaded. One application of this event handler is to have it call a function that causes a preloaded image to appear in the web page right as the page loads. That way, you can randomly select from among several images to appear. Each time the page loads, a randomly chosen image appears in the same location.

When used in conjunction with the *setInterval()* function, preloaded images can create a cycling image display. Every few seconds, a different image is cycled into the display. The *setInterval()* function takes two arguments: the first is the name of a function and the second is a time given in milliseconds. The function is called repetitively at regular time intervals as specified by the time setting. In a cycling image display, the *setInterval()* function is used to repetitively call a function that changes the image in the display.

16.10   REVIEW QUESTIONS

1. Define two parallel standard arrays, each with four indices, that contain European countries and their corresponding capitals.

2. Declare an array and write a *for* loop to assign a random number in the range from 0 to 1 to indices 2, 4, 6, ..., 50 of the array. Use the *length* property of the array in the loop condition.

3. The following function is called from a form button and replaces the first image of the web page with another image. What is a distinct disadvantage to this type of assignment?

```
function replace(){
  document.images[0].src="newimg.gif";
}
```

4. Write the code necessary to preload one image and assign it to take the place of the third image in the web page. Assume a button calls a function named *replace()* to make the switch.

5. Suppose an IMG HTML tag in a page specifies SRC=" ", so that no image URL is given. How can you cause an image to appear in that spot anyway, without having the user click a form button?

6. When does the *onload* event handler activate?

7. How can you display a random image when a page loads without preloading all of the potential images?

8. Write a line of JavaScript code that causes the function *change()* to be called every 5.5 seconds.

9. Ten images are preloaded into a standard array for a cycling image display. The array index of the currently displayed image is stored in the global variable *current*. Write down an *if* statement that updates the variable *current* in such a way as to cycle through the images when the *if* statement is invoked repetitively.

10. Find two errors in the following code, which is to fill the *numbers[]* array with randomly selected numbers:

```
var numbers=new array();
for (i=1 , i<numbers.length , i=i+1){
  numbers[i]=Math.random();
}
```

11. Find two errors in the following code. All 10 indices of the <u>standard</u> array are to be filled with randomly selected numbers:

```
var numbers=new Array(10);
for (i=1 , i<=10 , i=i+1){
    numbers[i]=Math.random();
}
```

12. Find all errors in the following code. Three images are to be preloaded into the *images[]* array:

```
var images=new Array();
for (i=0 , i<=2 , i=i+1){
   images[i]=new Object();
}
images[0]="img1.gif";
images[1]="img2.gif";
images[2]="img3.gif";
```

16.11 EXERCISES

1. Make a version of the addresses example of Figure 16.1 in which the pull-down menu is defined *after* the other form elements.

2. Make a version of the addresses example of Figure 16.1 that has a checkbox. If the checkbox is checked, only the phone number and e-mail address of the selected person are displayed. If it is not checked, all of the information is shown as usual.

3. You will have to do a little research on the Internet for this exercise. For 10 U.S. states, find the date it became a state, its capital city, the mayor of the capital city, and the current governor of the state. Organize this information into parallel arrays. When a state is selected from a pull-down menu, the rest of that state's information is displayed in text fields. The first position of the pull-down menu should contain an instruction.

4. Make a version of the arrows page of Figure 16.5 that preloads the images and uses a pull-down menu to chose which image is currently displayed. You can get the images on the web site in the exercises for Lesson 16.

5. Make a version of the arrows page of Figure 16.5 that preloads the images and uses only one button. When that button is clicked, one of the arrows is randomly chosen for display. You can get the images on the web site in the exercises for Lesson 16.

6. Make a slide-show presentation using the three ad images in Figure 16.10. When the page first loads, the first ad should be displayed. There should be two buttons, "next" and "previous". When the "next" button is clicked, the next ad should be displayed. If "next" is clicked and the third ad is already displayed, the first ad should come up. The "previous" button should work similarly. You can get the images on the web site in the exercises for Lesson 16.

7. Do Exercise 16.6, except use the left and right arrow images instead of form buttons. The images should act as links. You can get the images on the web site in the exercises for Lesson 16. Hint: The HREF attribute of the anchor elements can call JavaScript functions. For example,

  <A HREF="javascript:somefunction()">.....</A>

calls the function when the link is clicked.

8. Make a version of the random-image display that does not preload the images. Don't use the method presented in Section 16.6. Rather, use the following hint: File names can be created with concatenation. For example,

```
    i=3;
    name="image"+ i +".gif";
```

causes the variable *name* to contain the string "image3.gif". You can get the images on the web site in the exercises for Lesson 16.

9. Make a version of the cycling image display of Section 16.7 that cycles the images randomly. Every few seconds, a randomly chosen image appears. You can get the images on the web site in the exercises for Lesson 16.

10. Make the following version of the cycling image display of Section 16.7. When the page loads, all three images are visible. Every few seconds, the images rotate in a cyclic fashion. In other words, the leftmost two images move one to the right, and the one on the right moves to the leftmost position. This is like a wraparound image display. You can get the images on the web site in the exercises for Lesson 16.

11. Make the following version of the cycling image display of Section 16.7. Suppose that "Moe's Tavern" has paid twice as much for the advertisement. Thus, that ad should be displayed twice as long as the others. You should accomplish this using only one call to *setInterval()* and without having to reload that image twice. That is, Moe's ad should stay put for the extra time, and not simply be replaced an

extra time. You can get the images on the web site in the exercises for Lesson 16.

The rest of the exercises refer to the optional section.

12. Make a version of the form of Figure 16.14 that also has buttons for the lightest (smallest in weight) and shortest players. One of those searches turns up only one player. Add another fictitious player so that at least two players show up for each search.

13. Make a version of the form of Figure 16.16 that searches for the tallest and heaviest by position, rather than listing all players for a selected position.

14. Do exercise 16.13, but include buttons for the lightest (smallest in weight) and shortest player(s) as well.

16.12   PROJECT THREADS

Any exercises you do for this lesson should be referenced in your homework page following the guidelines in Section 9.10.

MORE ON FUNCTIONS

WE ARE familiar with the concept of sending information to built-in JavaScript methods. The information we send to a method in the form of a parameter is necessary for the function to do its job. For example, how could the *alert()* method do its job if the string parameter was not used? There would be no way to instruct the method what text to display in the alert window. In other words, if the method used no parameter the resulting alert window would have to have some generic message like "Hey buddy, you goofed." Clearly that would not be conducive to using the method to provide customized alerts in a variety of settings. The fact that the string parameter sends information to the method makes the method versatile and reusable.

Now, methods are no more than functions bound to objects. So this is really an issue of sending information to functions. In this lesson, we apply the notion of sending information using parameters to self-defined functions. We have been making extensive use of self-defined functions for several lessons. But all of the functions we have defined to handle user events have used no parameters. Adding the information-passing capability of function parameters to our self-defined functions enables the functions to be used for much more than processing information as the result of a user event.

Recall that procedure functions don't return values, but cause something to happen. We have used several built-in JavaScript procedure methods, like *document.write()* and *window.open()*, that do something to affect the global environment. We have also used several value methods, like *Math.round()* and *confirm()*, that return values. Moreover, all of the above methods require information to be sent as parameters. We first discuss the use of parameters in self-defined procedure functions. (All of the self-defined functions we created in previous lessons have been procedure functions.) We then discuss how to create self-defined value functions that use parameters.

17.1 CALLING SELF-DEFINED PROCEDURE FUNCTIONS WITHOUT EVENT HANDLERS

There is a striking difference between the ways we have used built-in JavaScript functions and self-defined functions. The self-defined functions have been called into action by user

```
<HTML>
<HEAD>
<SCRIPT LANGUAGE=JavaScript><!--
function  hrule(){
  document.write("<P ALIGN=center>*************************");
}
//--></SCRIPT>
</HEAD>
<BODY BGCOLOR="#FFFFCC">
<CENTER><FONT SIZE="+2">101 Tips For College
Students</FONT></CENTER>

<SCRIPT LANGUAGE=JavaScript><!--
hrule();
document.write("<P ALIGN=center>#1 Study More.");
hrule()
document.write("<P ALIGN=center>#2 Party Less.");
hrule();
document.write("<P ALIGN=center>#3 Sleep More.");
hrule();
document.write("<P ALIGN=center>#4 Do Laundry More Often.");
hrule();
document.write("<P ALIGN=center>#5 Eat More Vegetables.");
//--></SCRIPT>
</BODY>
</HTML>
```

FIGURE 17.1 A document that makes repetitive use of a self-defined function.

events. In contrast, we have called built-in functions (methods) in JavaScript statements when their services were needed. Self-defined functions can also be used in that way. Consider the following function, which writes a centered string of 25 asterisks to the document:

```
function hrule(){
document.write("<P ALIGN=center>*************************</P>");
}
```

A call to the *hrule()* function creates a customized line break in the web page. This function would be useless if called as the result of a user event, but can be used to make a textual web page with several such customized horizontal line breaks. Figure 17.1 contains an HTML document that calls *hrule()* five times.

The *hrule()* function is defined in the head section and called several times in the body section. It is obviously a procedure function since it returns no value. Moreover, it stands by itself as a statement, something that value functions can't do. Each time a line break is desired, a call to the function is made. That's really all there is to it. You can define a function and, rather than requiring a user event to call the function, you call on it any time you require its services. The web page generated by the document of Figure 17.1 is shown in Figure 17.2.

We are certainly not suggesting that you should use JavaScript to generate a page such as this, but it does serve to illustrate that you can define functions and call them repetitively to accomplish certain tasks. We will also use two versions of this function in the next section to illustrate the use of parameters in self-defined functions. In reality, you would make the web page of Figure 17.2 without JavaScript, and would simply copy and paste the line break each time you wished to use it. Or you simply would use the HTML HR element.

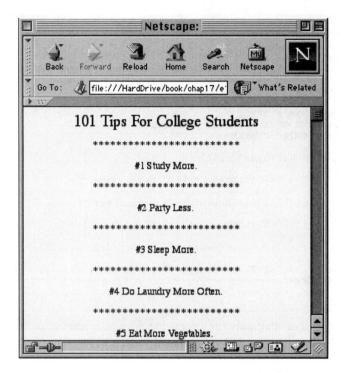

FIGURE 17.2 The rendering of the document of Figure 17.1.

17.2 USING PARAMETERS IN PROCEDURE FUNCTIONS

In this section, we make two versions of the *hrule()* function. The first uses one parameter and the second uses two parameters. In the first version, we wish to be able to tell the function how many characters wide the horizontal rule is to be. That is, by sending different values to the function, it will produce horizontal rules of different lengths. The definition of the function is given below. We name the function *hrule1():*

```
function hrule1(width){
    document.write("<P ALIGN=center>");
    for(i=1; i<=width; i=i+1){
      document.write("*");
    }
    document.write("</P>");
}
```

The main difference between this function and the ones defined in previous sections is the variable name *width* that appears in parentheses in the function definition. The variable *width* is the parameter that receives the value sent to the function. For example, the call

```
hrule1(30);
```

sends the number 30 to the function. This causes the variable *width* to contain 30. Function parameters act just as local function variables, except that the parameter is initialized by the function call. The parameter (variable) exists only during the function call, and is then erased from the computer's memory. But during the function call, we use the parameter as a local variable.

First a new centered paragraph is begun. Next, we loop from 1 to *width,* each time through the loop writing an asterisk. Finally, after the loop has run its course, we close the paragraph and terminate the function. So you see, each call to the function potentially sends a different value to the parameter *width*. Since the loop condition depends upon this parameter, horizontal rules of varying widths can be created with different function calls. All you have to do is to send different values to the function with different function calls.

The second version of the function, which we name *hrule2(),* uses two parameters. The first parameter controls the width of the rule, just as in *hrule1()*. The second parameter is used to set the keyboard character used to make the rule. The definition for *hrule2()* is:

```
function hrule2(width,str){
    document.write("<P ALIGN=center>");
    for(i=1; i<=width; i=i+1){
      document.write(str);
    }
    document.write("</P>");
}
```

The second parameter is defined in the function definition, following the first parameter and a comma. The function call

```
hrule2(15,"%");
```

causes *width* to contain 15 and *str* to contain the string "%". The function then works in the same way as the previous version except that, each time through the loop, the contents of *str* are written to the document. Thus, you control both the width and the character comprising the rule with each call you make to the function. Both versions of the function are defined and called in the document of Figure 17.3, and that document is rendered in Figure 17.4.

Perhaps the most important thing to note about calling functions with parameters is that you must supply the right number of parameters for each function, and in the correct order. For example, the following calls to the two functions are not appropriate:

```
hrule1(10,"!");                    (OOPS!)
hrule2(12);                        (OOPS!)
hrule2("Z",11);                    (OOPS!)
```

In the first case, *hrule1()* only has one parameter, so sending it two values makes no sense. Similarly, in the second case, it makes no sense to send only one value to *hrule2(),* since that function is set up to receive two parameters. Finally, in the third case, the order of the parameters has been violated. You must send values to function parameters in the same order in which the parameters are defined in the function definition. Otherwise, the values get stored in the wrong parameter. For example, in the call

```
hrule2("&",5);
```

the variable *width* would receive the value "&". Because of the way the function is defined, this would cause the loop to execute from 1 to "&", which makes no sense.

```
<HTML>
<HEAD>
<SCRIPT LANGUAGE=JavaScript><!--
function hrule1(width){
    document.write("<P ALIGN=center>");
      for(i=1 ;   i<=width ; i=i+1){
        document.write("*");
      }
    document.write("</P>");
}
function hrule2(width,str){
    document.write("<P ALIGN=center>");
      for(i=1 ;   i<=width ; i=i+1){
        document.write(str);
      }
    document.write("</P>");
}
//--></SCRIPT>
</HEAD>
<BODY BGCOLOR="#FFFFCC">
<P ALIGN=center>HRULES GALORE AND MORE

<SCRIPT LANGUAGE=JavaScript><!--
hrule1(10);
hrule1(15);
hrule2(15,"=");
hrule2(10,"x x");
//--></SCRIPT>
</BODY>
</HTML>
```

FIGURE 17.3 A document that defines two procedure functions with parameters and calls each function twice.

We wish to stress again that the parameters are used just like local function variables during the function call. Once the function terminates, they are gone. When the next call to the function is made, the parameters spring back into action to receive the new values. While the above examples do not use any local variables besides the function parameters, it is certainly appropriate to define other local variables that you might need in the function. We will see examples of this as this lesson progresses. In the meantime, Figure 17.5 depicts

FIGURE 17.4 The rendering of the document of Figure 17.3.

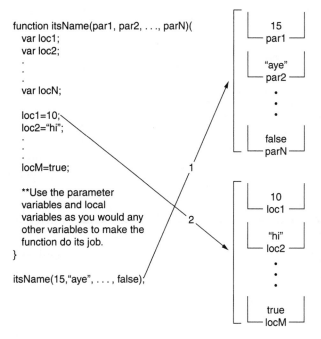

```
function itsName(par1, par2, . . ., parN)(
    var loc1;
    var loc2;
    .
    .
    .
    var locN;

    loc1=10;
    loc2="hi";
    .
    .
    locM=true;

    **Use the parameter
    variables and local
    variables as you would any
    other variables to make the
    function do its job.
}

itsName(15,"aye", . . . , false);
```

FIGURE 17.5 Functions can be declared with any number of parameters to receive information, and with any number of local variables needed to assist in processing that information. 1) The parameters are automatically declared upon the function call, and initialized with the values sent to the function. The values are stored in the parameters in the order in which they are sent in the function call. After that, they work just like local variables during the function call. 2) Any local variables needed in the function are declared and initialized.

a function with *N* parameters and *M* local variables. No matter how many parameters you need for the function to receive information or how many local variables you need to help you process that information, the theory is the same. Values are received and assigned to the parameters in order, and then any local variables are set up and initialized as usual. Also note in Figure 17.5 that, just like normal variables, function parameters can receive any of the three primitive-type literals.

17.3 OPENING NEW WINDOWS WITH FORM BUTTONS

The first application of using parameters in self-defined functions we present involves using generic HTML form buttons to call a function that opens a new window. The form appears in Figure 17.6 and contains four buttons. Each button is to cause a small map of a European country to appear in a new window.

Our first inclination is simply to define four functions, one for each button to call. However, with the use of parameters, we can define one function that does the job. Each button sends the URL of the corresponding country map to a parameter of the function. That parameter is then used to give the URL to the *open()* method of the window object. Figure 17.7 shows the HTML file that generates the page of Figure 17.6. In each case, the URL for the image file is just the name of the file, since the images are stored in the same directory as the document.

When a button is clicked, the image file name is sent to the *show()* function and stored in the parameter *map*. All that is left to do is call on the *open()* method. (See Section 12.9

FIGURE 17.6 A form with four buttons, each of which causes a small map of a European country to appear in a new window.

```
<HTML>
<HEAD>
<SCRIPT LANGUAGE=JavaScript><!--
function show(map) {
open(map,"newWin","width=367,height=393");
}
//--></SCRIPT>
</HEAD>
<BODY BGCOLOR="#FFFFCC">
Click one of the buttons to see a small map of
that country in a new window.
<FORM>
<INPUT TYPE=button VALUE="Belgium" onclick="show('belg.gif')">
<INPUT TYPE=button VALUE="Bulgaria" onclick="show('bulg.gif')">
<INPUT TYPE=button VALUE="Liechtenstein" onclick="show('liec.gif')">
<INPUT TYPE=button VALUE="Luxembourg" onclick="show('luxe.gif')">
</FORM>
</BODY>
</HTML>
```

FIGURE 17.7 The document that generates the page in Figure 17.6.

if you need a refresher on that method.) Rather than giving a specific image file as the first parameter of the *open()* method, we send the value stored in the parameter *map*. Since *map* contains an image file name unique to the particular button that was clicked, the appropriate image is displayed in a new window.

> **N O T E**
>
> There is a very subtle point to be made about sending string parameters to functions from event handlers. Since the value of the event handler is defined with quotation marks, using another set of quotation marks to define the string causes problems. For example,
>
> onclick="show("belg.gif")"   **(OOPS!)**
>
> would cause confusion about the correct value of the *onclick* event handler. Using nested quotes makes it appear that "show(" is the value for the event handler. As you can see in Figure 17.7, an alternative is to use single quotes. This causes no confusion on the correct value of onclick. If fact, any time you need to nest quotes, just use single quotes on the inside and you should be good to go.

17.4 IMAGE ROLLOVERS

Another practical application of using parameters in self-defined functions involves image rollovers. You have not doubt seen many examples of this while surfing the web. When a web page loads, an image will be present.

When you move your mouse cursor onto the image, it automatically changes to another image.

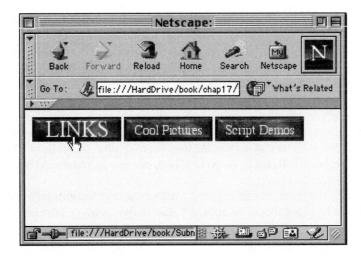

When you move your mouse cursor back off the image, it reverts to its original form. A page containing three such rollover images appears in Figure 17.8. The mouse has been moved onto the "Cool Links" image, causing it to change to "LINKS". Of course, to get a complete feel for this, you should play with the page on the web site.

The first thing you have to do is to find some suitable image pairs. You can find suitable images in GIF archives on the web or make them yourself with a graphic editor. The important thing is that the images come in pairs and that they are of the same size. You can't switch images in and out if they are not the same size. Any rollover images you need for the homework exercises are available for download on the web site.

OK, so how do the rollover images of Figure 17.8 work? For starters, there are three pairs of images:

links1.gif	pics1.gif	demos1.gif
links2.gif	pics2.gif	demos2.gif

Each pair creates one of the rollover images. It should be apparent from the names of the image files which pair is for which rollover. The first thing to do is to preload the images into arrays of *image* objects. (The technique for preloading images was discussed in

FIGURE 17.8 A web page with three rollover images.

```
<HTML>
<HEAD>
<SCRIPT LANGUAGE=JavaScript><!--
var first=new Array();
var second=new Array();

for(i=0;i<=2;i=i+1){
    first[i]=new Image();
}
for(i=0;i<=2;i=i+1){
    second[i]=new Image();
}
first[0].src="links1.gif";
first[1].src="pics1.gif";
first[2].src="demos1.gif";

second[0].src="links2.gif";
second[1].src="pics2.gif";
second[2].src="demos2.gif";

function change(which){
    document.images[which].src=second[which].src;
}
function changeback(which){
    document.images[which].src=first[which].src;
}
//--></SCRIPT>
</HEAD>
<BODY BGCOLOR="#FFFFCC">
<A HREF="links.html" onmouseover="change(0)" onmouseout="changeback(0)">
<IMG SRC="links1.gif" WIDTH=97 HEIGHT=26 BORDER=0>
</A>
<A HREF="pics.html" onmouseover="change(1)" onmouseout="changeback(1)">
<IMG SRC="pics1.gif" WIDTH=97 HEIGHT=26 BORDER=0>
</A>
<A HREF="demos.html" onmouseover="change(2)" onmouseout="changeback(2)">
<IMG SRC="demos1.gif" WIDTH=97 HEIGHT=26 BORDER=0>
</A>
</BODY>
</HTML>
```

FIGURE 17.9   The document that generates the web page of Figure 17.8.

Section 16.4.) In this case, we load the images for the original images into an array named *first[],* and the images that appear when the mouse moves onto the original images into an array named *second[ ].* Moreover, these arrays are parallel: the two images for each rollover share a common index value. The entire document that creates the image rollover appears in Figure 17.9. All the JavaScript code appearing prior to the two function definitions preloads the images.

Before discussing the functions that accomplish the rollovers, we need to get a handle on the HTML part of the document. When the page is first loaded, the original images are set by HTML IMG tags. Moreover, the images are set up as image links. The anchor element surrounding each IMG tag points to an HTML document. You should be quite familiar with image links at this point.

The event handlers that trigger the image rollovers are **onmouseover** and **onmouse-out.** Their purposes should be apparent. The former is triggered when the mouse moves over the image link and the latter is triggered when the mouse moves back off. As you can see in Figure 17.9, these event handlers are defined in the anchor elements, rather than the IMG elements. When the mouse moves onto an image the *change()* function is called. Let's see how that function works.

Since the *change()* function is to accomplish the image swap for all three image links, we have given it a parameter *which*. Each time the *change()* function is called, a number corresponding to the position of the image that triggered the call is sent to the function parameter. Since the three images are the only images in the web page and hence the first three, they occupy the indices 0, 1, and 2 of the *images[]* array. We have chosen to send these indices to the function as identification.

The parallel arrays containing the preloaded images were defined as standard arrays so that they are also parallel to the *images[]* array. Since the call to the *change()* function assigns to the parameter *which* the array index of the image that the mouse has passed over, all the function has to do is take the image in the *which* index of the *second[]* array and assign it to the *which* index of the *images[]* array. For example, if the mouse passes onto the first image, the call *change(0)* is made. That causes 0 to be assigned to the parameter *which*. The assignment statement in the function is then equivalent to

```
document.images[0].src=second[0].src
```

Thus, the image "links2.gif" replaces the original image "links1.gif".

A rollover is completed when the user passes the mouse back off one of the images. This causes the *changeback()* function to be called. That function works in a very similar fashion: its *which* parameter receives the index of the image that needs switching, and it assigns the *which* position of the *first[]* array to the *which* position of the *images[]* array. So the original image is put back into place and the rollover is complete.

N O T E Most often, rollover images are used as an eye-catching mechanism to support links in a web page. So, with the anchor element surrounding each image, it is natural to place the *onmouseover* and *onmouseout* event handlers in the anchor element rather than in the IMG element. Not all browsers will activate these event handlers if they are placed in the IMG element. Given the lack of uniform browser support for *onmouseover* and *onmouseout* in the IMG element, we do not recommend using these event handlers in that HTML element.

17.5 SELF-DEFINED VALUE FUNCTIONS

For starters, self-defined value functions can make use of parameters in the same way as procedure functions. There must be one parameter to receive each piece of information sent to the function, and the parameters must be defined in the proper order to receive the information. In fact, the overview of function parameters given in Figure 17.5 applies to value functions as well. So the issue of using parameters in value functions warrants no further discussion.

To see how value functions work, we define and discuss a simple one. The purpose of the value function below is easily explained: the number you send to the function is to be returned multiplied by 2.

```
function times2(num){
  num=num*2;
  return num;
}
```

The function parameter receives the number sent by the function call. Then the value contained in the parameter is doubled. Finally, the **return** statement terminates the function call. That's all there is to it. The value stored in *num* is returned by the function.

So, the function call

```
x=times2(50);
```

causes the variable *x* to contain the number 100. On the function call, 50 is sent to the parameter *num*. The value is then doubled to 100, and returned.

The call to this value function as a stand-alone statement

```
times2(10.5);                        (OOPS!)
```

is not viable since, after the function call, the statement becomes

```
21;
```

which is certainly not a statement telling the JavaScript interpreter to do something. In effect, the function call is completely replaced by the expression that follows the return statement. Using the terminology of the last sentence, the return statement can be followed by an expression, rather than merely a variable. Indeed, the following definition of *times2()* works equally well:

```
function times2(num){
  return (num*2);
}
```

We mentioned above that the return statement terminates the function. Prior to defining the *times2()* function above, all the self-defined functions we have constructed in this book have terminated precisely when the closing bracket of the function body was reached. But a value function is automatically terminated immediately when return statement is encountered. In fact, a value function can have more than one return statement. But won't that confuse the JavaScript interpreter as to which return statement should be used to return the function's value? Well, no, because only one of the return functions will ever be encountered. In the top-down flow of the function, when a return is encountered, the function call is over and the value specified by that return statement is returned. With the function call over at that point, there simply is no possibility for another return function to be executed.

To illustrate this, we define a function with three return statements:

```
function isItBig(num){
  if(num<1000){
    return false;
  }
  if(1000<num){
    return true;
  }
  return "maybe";
}
```

A number is sent to the function and the function returns a value based on the size of the number. For example, the call

```
result=isItBig(1001);
```

causes the variable *result* to contain true. In that case, the last statement in the function, the one that would return "maybe", is never executed since the function terminates as soon as it encounters a return statement. While the *isItBig()* function serves to illustrate a point, one would never construct a function that has the potential of returning a Boolean value or a string. In general, a given function should be able to return only one of the three types number, string, or Boolean.

For a practical example showing the utility of self-defined return functions, we first construct a function that returns the factorial of the number sent to it. (if you don't recall what the factorial of a number is, see the brief discussion in Section 15.2.) Such a value function is:

```
function factorial(num){
  var product;
  product=1;
  for(i=1; i<=num; i=i+1){
    product=product*i;
  }
  return product;
}
```

For example, if the call

```
x=factorial(5);
```

is made, the variable *x* will contain the value 120, since 5! = 120.

Next, we use this function to help calculate the odds for various lottery games. Consider a big state lottery game that chooses from among 40 numbered balls. They then draw five of them at random. In order to win the big prize, you have to match all five of the balls (in any order). The odds of winning the big prize in such a game are

$$1 \text{ in } \frac{40!}{35! * 5!}$$

FIGURE 17.10   A web page that calculates odds of winning the big prize for various lottery games.

where the calculation involves computing three factorials. In general, if a lottery game chooses from *n* numbered balls and chooses a group of *r* of them, the odds of matching all of them (winning the big payout) are given by

$$1 \text{ in } \frac{n!}{(n-r)! * r!}$$

Going back to the 40-choose-5 game above, you can see how the specific numbers for the three factorials arise.

The form for this example is shown in Figure 17.10. Since we will use the *elements[]* array to reference the form elements, we have not provided the HTML code for the form. The name of the form is *lottoform* and the function that the button calls is named *getodds()*. The results of a typical calculation are shown below Figure 17.10. You can see that the choices for the total number of balls and the number of balls drawn are stored in the *text* properties of the menu's options.

Without the use of the self-defined value function *factorial()*, the JavaScript code for this example would get somewhat messy. Aside from the other code, the odds calculation would require three different for loops, one to calculate each of the three factorials. However, with the self-defined value function, the logic of the program is straightforward. We have included a feature to alert users of they have not made a choice from each of the pull-down menus. Otherwise, the odds are calculated. The top-down logic for the *getodds()* function called by the button is

-declare variables (*i, j, n, r,* odds)

-store selected indices from the two pull-down menus(*i, j*)

-if (either is still in position 0)
   alert the user

-else

   store (and parse) the total number of balls and the number of balls drawn (*n, r*)
   calculate the odds by making three calls to the *factorial( )* function (odds)
   assign odds to text field

The actual JavaScript code is shown in Figure 17.11. First, the *factorial( )* function
is defined. Then, the *getodds( )* function is defined. When the "GET ODDS" button in the
form is clicked, that function is called to calculate the odds. Assuming the user has made
a choice in both menus, the number of balls in the game and the number of balls drawn
are stored in the variables *n* and *r*. In order to calculate the odds, the *factorial( )* function is
called three different times. Each time a different value is sent to the *factorial( )* parameter
num, and the factorial of that value is returned. So, rather than using three different loops

```
<HEAD>
<SCRIPT LANGUAGE=JavaScript><!--
function factorial(num){
   var product;
   product=1;
   for(i=1 ;  i<=num ; i=i+1){
      product=product*i;
   }
   return product;
}
function getodds(){
   with(document.lottoform){
      var i,j,n,r,odds;

      i=elements[0].selectedIndex;
      j=elements[1].selectedIndex;

      if((i==0)||(j==0)){
         alert("Please make a selection from both menus.");
      }
      else{
         n=parseFloat(elements[0].options[i].text);
         r=parseFloat(elements[1].options[j].text);

         odds=factorial(n)/(factorial(n-r)*factorial(r));

         elements[3].value=Math.round(odds);
      }
   }
}
//--></SCRIPT>
</HEAD>
```

FIGURE 17.11 The JavaScript functions that process the form of Figure 17.10.

to compute each of the three factorials, the same loop is used three times, once during each call of the *factorial()* function.

> **NOTE** When you create your own functions, it is advisable to define them before you call upon them. For example, in Figure 17.11 the *factorial()* function is defined above the *getodds()* function that calls upon it. In JavaScript this is not always crucial, but it is nonetheless a good programming practice.

17.6 USING BOOLEAN RETURN FUNCTIONS TO VERIFY FORM INPUT

For another practical application of value functions, we offer an example that uses several self-defined value functions to verify some form input. The form we verify is shown in Figure 17.12. Once again, we will use the *elements[]* array to reference the form elements, so the HTML code for the form is not provided. The name of the form is *infoform* and the function that the "Submit" button calls is named *check()*. The submit button is a generic button, that mimics the act of submitting the information from the form to a database on the server (see Lesson 18).

FIGURE 17.12 A form with three text fields that mimics submitting the form input to a database.

We give an alert message if any of the following occur:

1. the name field is empty or contains a number
2. the e-mail field is empty or contains a number
3. the zip code field is empty or doesn't contain a number

To proceed with this verification, we apply a modular approach using value functions that return Boolean values. We begin with the function *check()* that the button calls. The top-down logic is as follows:

-if(nameOK() *and* emailOK() *and* zipOK()) {

    submit input

-else

    give alert for bad info

The logic of the function is very simple: if all of the three input fields are OK, submit the information. Otherwise, alert the user. Of course, it can't be that simple. We actually haven't checked anything. The three functions *nameOK(), emailOK(),* and *zipOK()* in the "if" clause are to do that work. Each of the three functions checks the appropriate input field and returns true if the input for that field is OK or false if the input does not pass. If any (or all) of the three functions returns false, the "else" clause executes, causing an alert. The only way the expression (nameOK() && emailOK() && zipOK()) is true is when the three functions all return true. In that case each of the three input fields has passed the test and the "if" clause executes.

Now for the logic of the *nameOK()* function:

-if(field is empty *or* is a number)

    return false

-else

    return true

The *nameOK()* function simply checks to see if the field is empty or a number has been entered into the field. If so, the function returns false, indicating bad input. Otherwise, it returns true. The other two functions work similarly, so we do not supply their logic. All three of these functions appear in Figure 17.13, which contains the complete JavaScript code to support the form.

To sum up what we have termed a modular approach, the button calls the *check()* function. This function either gives an alert or allows the form to be submitted. Rather than tackling the details of the verification in the *check()* function, the details are left to other functions, one for each of the input fields. This serves to break up the verification into smaller pieces, each of which can be dealt with separately. Using functions to divide up the whole task into smaller pieces makes the code modular and more readable. Moreover, if you wish to add another field to the form, say for the person's age, all you need to do is to create a new function for that field and add that function to the condition of the "if" statement in the *check()* function.

```
<HEAD>
<SCRIPT LANGUAGE=JavaScript><!--
function nameOK(){
    with(document.infoform.elements[0]){
        if((value=="")|| !isNaN(value)){
            return false;
        }
        else{
            return true;
        }
    }
}
function emailOK(){
    with(document.infoform.elements[1]){
        if((value=="")){
            return false;
        }
        else{
            return true;
        }
    }
}
function zipOK(){
    with(document.infoform.elements[2]){
        if((value=="")|| isNaN(value)){
            return false;
        }
        else{
            return true;
        }
    }
}
function check(){
    if(nameOK()&& emailOK()&& zipOK()){
        with(document.infoform){
            elements[4].value="The following information has
            been submitted:\r\r"+elements[0].value+"\r"
            +elements[1].value+"\r"+elements[2].value;
        }
    }
    else{
        alert("You have entered bad information into one or
        more of the fields");
    }
}
//--></SCRIPT>
</HEAD>
```

FIGURE 17.13 The JavaScript code for the form of Figure 17.12.

17.7 THE *STRING* OBJECT AND VERIFICATION

The *String* object is very useful for verification of form input. When a string literal is stored in a variable, that variable is inherently a *String* object. As such, properties and methods of that object are available. The only property of a *String* object is *length*. For example,

```
str="Scooby";
x=str.length;
```

causes the variable x to contain the value 6, since the string "Scooby" is six characters in length. This property is particularly useful for verifying text input. For example, you might wish to verify that a zip code is five characters long.

Several methods of the *String* object are listed in Appendix B. Three we discuss here are the *charAt(), indexOf(),* and *lastIndexOf().* The characters comprising a string are indexed starting from 0. In this respect you can think of a string as a standard array of single characters. The *charAt()* method takes an index value as its argument and returns the character at that index as its value. For example, using the above variable *str* containing the string "Scooby",

```
x=str.charAt(0);
y=str.charAt(4);
```

causes x to contain "S" and y to contain "b". Note that the value is returned as a one-character string.

The *indexOf()* method takes a one-character string as its argument and returns the first index at which that character is found in the string:

```
x=str.indexOf("y");
y=str.indexOf("o");
```

causes x to contain 5 and y to contain 2. Note that an "o" is also present at index 3, but the method returned 2 since that is where the first "o" was found. It is possible that the given character is not found in the string. In that case, *indexOf()* returns a -1 as its value. For example, you might wish to verify that an e-mail address contains the "@" character:

-if(address.indexOf("@")==-1)

    there is no "@" in the address

-else

    the character is present in the address

The *lastIndexOf()* method works in a very similar fashion. It takes a one-character string as its argument and returns the last index at which that character is found in the string. Again using the *str* variable from above,

```
x=str.lastIndexOf("y");
y=str.lastindexOf("o");
```

causes x to contain 5 and y to contain 3. This method also returns a -1 if the character is not present in the string.

In practice, the above property and methods of string objects are quite easy to use. Just remember that, as with the standard array, the *length* property is one larger than the highest index value, since the indexing starts at 0. So, to count the number of periods in an e-mail address, for example, you would loop from 0 to one less than the *length* property:

```
count=0;
for(i=0; i<=(address.length-1); i=i+1){
   if(address.charAt(i)="."){
     count=count+1;
   }
}
```

Some easy verification techniques using the string object to strengthen the verification of the form in Figure 17.12 are given as exercises. Some more difficult techniques are presented in the optional section 17.8.

> **NOTE** All of these methods of the *String* object consist of compound words. After the first word of the method name, any subsequent words are capitalized. If you fail to capitalize these words, the methods will not work.

17.8 ADVANCED FORM VERIFICATION USING THE *STRING* OBJECT (OPTIONAL)

In this section, we use the *String* object to apply some advanced verification techniques to the input from the form of Figure 17.12. We wish to verify the following:

1. The name is at least four characters long and contains at least one blank space.
2. The e-mail address is at least five characters long, contains no blank spaces, contains exactly one "@" symbol, and contains at least one period.
3. The zip is at least five characters long and contains no blank spaces.

There are numerous other possibilities for the verification, but these are reasonable. You have to set some minimal standard. For example, assuming you want a full name (both first and last), there should be a blank space separating them. It's OK if there is more than one blank space, since a middle name could be present. A minimal standard for a full name might be "Ty X", which has four characters including the blank space.

A minimal e-mail standard might be x@y.z, which contains five characters, an "@", a period, and has no blank spaces. A zip code should be at least five characters long and have no spaces. Assuming you will allow a zip code of the form 12345-6789, it is OK to have more than five characters.

We proceed as in the example of Section 17.6 with the function that the button calls being minimal:

-if(nameOK() *and* emailOK() *and* zipOK()){
   submit input
-else
   give alert for bad info

We let a separate function do the dirty work for each of the three input fields. The alert is given only if one or more of the three functions returns true. Otherwise, the form is submitted. Now, each function is going to have to assess the number of characters in the input, but that is easy using the *length* property of *String* objects. The more difficult task is that each of the three functions are going to have to count the number of various characters, "@", ".", or " ". Before we tackle the *nameOK(), emailOK(),* and *zipOK()* functions, we set up one function to do all of the various character-counting chores. We call this function *numchar()* and send it two values as parameters: the string that is to be checked and the character that is to be counted in that string:

```
function numchar(str,thechar)){
  var count;
  count=0;
  for(i=0; i<=(str.length-1); i=i+1){
    if(str.charAt(i)==thechar){
      count=count+1;
    }
  }
  return count;
}
```

The function receives a string to be examined in the *str* parameter and the character to be counted in the parameter *thechar*. (*char* is a JavaScript reserved word.) A counter is set to 0 and then a loop goes through each character index of the string *str*. The *charAt()* each index is checked against *thechar*. If the character at that index of the string matches *thechar*, then 1 is added to the counter. After each character of the string has been checked, the counter contains the number of occurrences of *thechar*. That value is then returned by the function.

Armed with this function, we define the *emailOK()* function. We choose this function for discussion since is involves the most elaborate verification of the three. The functions for the other two input fields are shown in Figure 17.14, together with the rest of the JavaScript code.

```
function emailOK(){
  with(document.infoform.elements[1]){
    if((value.length<5)||(numchar(value," ")>0)||
    (numchar(value,"@")!=1)||(numchar(value,".")==0)){
    return false;
    }
    else{
      return true;
    }
  }
}
```

The function first gives reference straight to the *value* of the e-mail field using the *with* statement. Using the *value* property, there are four conditions that this function checks. If any of them are true, the e-mail input does not pass the test and the function

```
<HEAD>
<SCRIPT LANGUAGE=JavaScript><!--
function numchar(str,thechar){
    var count;
    count=0;
    for(i=0; i<(str.length-1) ; i=i+1){
        if(str.charAt(i)==thechar){
            count=count+1;
        }
    }
    return count;
}
function nameOK(){
    with(document.infoform.elements[0]){
        if((value.length<4)||(numchar(value," ")==0)){
            return false;
        }
        else{
            return true;
        }
    }
}
function emailOK(){
    with(document.infoform.elements[1]){
        if((value.length<5)||(numchar(value," ")>0)
         ||(numchar(value,"@")!=1)||(numchar(value,".")==0)){
            return false;
        }
        else{
            return true;
        }
    }
}
function zipOK(){
    with(document.infoform.elements[2]){
        if((value.length<5)||(numchar(value," ")>0)){
            return false;
        }
        else{
            return true;
        }
    }
}
function check(){
    if(nameOK()&& emailOK()&& zipOK()){
        with(document.infoform){
            elements[4].value="The following information has
            been submitted:\r\r"+elements[0].value+"\r"
            +elements[1].value+"\r"+elements[2].value;
        }
    }
    else{
    alert("You have entered bad information into one or more
     of the fields");
    }
}
//--></SCRIPT>
</HEAD>
```

FIGURE 17.14 Verification for the form of Figure 17.12 using the *String* object.

returns false. If (value.length<5), then the string is too short. If

$$(numchar(value," ")>0)$$

then the e-mail address contains a blank space. Note that we have sent both the value of the e-mail field and the blank space character to the *numchar()* function. The call

$$numchar(value," ")$$

returns the number of blank spaces in the value property of the e-mail field. Similarly, if

$$(\text{numchar}(\text{value},``@")!==1)$$

then the e-mail input does not have exactly one "@" symbol. Finally, if

$$(\text{numchar}(\text{value},``.")==0)$$

then the e-mail input has no period. Only if all four of these conditions are false does the *emailOK( )* function return true.

17.9 SUMMARY

Key Terms

parameter	image rollover	onmouseover
onmouseout	return statement	modular programs

A self-defined procedure function is called as a statement

```
functionName();
```

but a self-defined value function can't stand alone as a statement. A typical way to call a value function is to store the returned value into a variable:

```
x=functionName();
```

In other words, self-defined functions can be called in the same manner as built-in functions (methods).

Just as many built-in methods require that information be sent as a parameter, it is advantageous to send information to self-defined functions. A parameter must be declared for each piece of information that is to be sent to a function. Parameters are variables that are named within the parentheses following the function name when the function is defined. When the function is called, the information you send is automatically put into the parameter variables. After that, the parameters can be used just as local function variables.

One application of function parameters in procedure functions is to define one function that is called by several form buttons. For example, if each button is to open a different file in a new window, one function is sufficient. The event handler for each button simply passes a different file name to the function. This is often preferable to defining one function for each button.

Another application of parameters in procedure functions involves image rollovers, where an image changes when the mouse passes over the image, and changes back when the mouse passes back off the image. A good way to accomplish this is to preload the images for the rollovers into arrays of *image* objects that run parallel to the positions of the images in the *images[]* array. That way, only two functions are required to make the image changes. One function is called by the onmouseover event handler and replaces the original image with a second image. The other function is called by the onmouseout event handler and puts the original image back in place. Regardless of whether the mouse is passing onto an image or passing off an image, since all of the arrays are parallel, the only information the functions need to know is the array index of the particular image. Passing this index to a function parameter enables the rollovers to be accomplished by two functions, rather than special functions for each image rollover.

In order for a value function to return a value, it must be endowed with a return statement. The expression that follows the return statement is the value returned by the function. After a return statement is encountered, the call to the value function terminates and the appropriate value is returned. Self-defined value functions are not very useful without parameters. For example, one could make a function *factorial10()* that returns 10! = 3628800, but you might just as well type in that number each time you need it. However, when a number can be sent to the *factorial()* function as a parameter, that one function can be called over and over to compute many different factorials. It would not be surprising if such a function is added as a built-in method for the Math object in the future.

Self-defined functions also provide a good mechanism with which to write programs in a modular fashion. For example, form input is to be verified for submission to the web server upon the click of a form button. It is convenient to delegate the verification for each different input field to different functions. Suppose the button calls a function *check():*

```
function check()
  if(field1ok()   &&   field2ok()   &&...&&fieldNok())
    submit form
  else
    give alert
```

The verification checks for each input field are localized in one function. Such modularization creates more readable and more easily debugged programs. Each "chunk" of work is contained in a self-contained function definition.

The *String* object is quite useful for verification of form input. When a string is stored in a variable, that variable automatically has access to the *length* property and several methods. The *length* property contains the length of the string in terms of the number of characters comprising the string. The characters of a string are indexed like a standard array, starting with 0 for the first character. The *charAt()* method takes an index value as a parameter, and returns the character at that index. The *indexOf()* method takes a one-character string as an argument and returns the first index of the string at which that character appears. If the character is not found in the string, the method returns −1. The *lastIndexOf()* method works similarly, but returns the last index at which that character appears.

17.10 REVIEW QUESTIONS

1. Compare and contrast function parameters and local variables.

2. The function *hrule2()* of Section 17.2 is set up to take two parameters. But what is wrong with the call

```
hrule2("#", 25);
```

which sends it two pieces of information?

3. Write down a procedure function named *alt()* that takes two characters, one in each of two different parameters. The function writes each character to the document 25 times in an alternating fashion (e.g., ˆ&&&...). Make a call to this function without using a form button.

4. Write down a value function named *avg()* that takes two numeric parameters and returns the average of the two numbers. Make a call to this function without using a form button.

5. When sending a string to a function that is called by an event handler, what problem arises? How can you correct the problem?

6. In an image rollover, in which HTML element should you put the onmouseover and onmouseout event handlers? Why?

7. What happens if a return function contains several return statements?

8. The string "the wildebeest" is stored in the variable *astring*. What values are assigned to the following variables?

```
w=astring.length;
x=astring.charAt(3);
y=astring.indexOf("e");
z=astring.lastIndexOf("e");
```

9. Write a function named *ageOK()* that takes one parameter. That function should return true if the function is sent a number in the range 18–110. Otherwise, the function should return false.

10. Write a function named *emailOK()* that takes one parameter, a string. If that string is less than four characters long or has no "@" symbol, the function should return false. Otherwise, the function should return true.

17.11 EXERCISES

1. There is a built-in method of the *document* object that is called by *document.writeLn()*. It takes a string as an argument and writes the string to the document followed by a line break. (It works just like *document.write()* except that it also causes a line break.) However, this method does not work consistently on all browsers. Make your own procedure function named *writeLn()* that accomplishes the same thing. Use this function three times in a web page.

2. Make a version of the *hrule2()* function that takes an additional parameter. That is, the new version should have three parameters. The new parameter should be Boolean. If the value true is sent to this parameter, the function should center the rule. If false is sent to the parameter, the rule should not be centered. Use the function in a web page twice, once each way.

3. Make a web page with three buttons. Each button should show the name of a popular commercial web site. When that button is clicked, that web site is loaded into the same window. The key element of this exercise is that all three buttons should call the same function. In other words, one function suffices for all three buttons.

4. Make a version of the form of Figure 17.6 that uses a pull-down menu to let the user choose the country. Hint: you don't need to use parameters in the function for this problem.

5. Make a version of the form of Figure 17.6 in which each map is opened in its own window. That is, if all the buttons are clicked, there will be four new windows, one for each country. Hint: use a second parameter in the function and send a different window name with each different button.

6. Use the images supplied on the web site to create a rollover image for each of the countries of Figure 17.6. When the link for that country is clicked, a web page containing the map for that country should load into the same window. (No new windows are needed for this exercise.) Moreover, the page containing each map should have a form button that causes the original page containing the rollover images to reappear.

7. Make a web page that displays the blank image found on the web site. Below that blank image should appear an image link for each of the countries in Figure 17.6. Suitable images for these links are provided on the web site. When the mouse moves onto a link for a country, the blank image should be replaced by the image for that country. When the mouse moves back off the link, the original blank image should appear. This is rather like a slide-show presentation for the countries.

8. Make a version of the lottery-odds program that gives odds for winning not only the grand prize, but also the second prize and third prize. Suppose there are n total balls, and r of them are drawn to determine the winning numbers. You win the second prize if you match any $(r - 1)$ of them, and you win the third prize if you match any $(r - 2)$ of them. For example, in a 40-choose-5 game, the grand prize is matching all five selected balls, the second prize is matching any four of the selected balls, and the third prize is matching any three of the selected balls. The odds of matching $(r - 1)$ of the selected balls (second prize) are

$$r^*(n - r) \text{ in } \frac{n!}{(n - r)!^*r!}$$

and the odds of matching $(r - 2)$ of the selected balls (third prize) are

$$\frac{r!^*(n - r)!}{4^*(r - 2)!^*(n - r - 2)!} \text{ in } \frac{n!}{(n - r)!^*r!}$$

9. Alter the validation program of Figure 7.13 so that it includes either or both of the following features.

(a) A fourth input field should be added that requests an age from the user. You should verify three things for the age: that it is not left blank, that it is a number, and that the number is between 18 and 120.

(b) The alert message should give a specialized message about which tests that the input failed. Hint: set up a global variable named *message* in the first line of the SCRIPT section (i.e., don't define it as a local variable in one of the functions). Each time one of the tests fail in an "OK" function, simply add a short string onto the *message* variable. In the *check()* function, send the resulting message to the *alert()* function. For example,

```
alert("Your data had the following
      problems:"+message);
```

where *message* might contain

"-you left the e-mail field empty—you entered a number in the name field-"

for example. It is important that *message* be a global variable so that it can be updated or accessed from within any of the different function calls.

10. (May include any of the options from Exercise 9) Make a form similar to that of Figure 17.12 and add the following features to the verification program of Figure 7.13 using the *String* object. The name should be at least four characters long, the e-mail address should be at least five characters long and contain an "@" symbol, and the zip should be at least five characters long.

The following pertain to the optional section.

11. Make a form with one text field for an e-mail address. Add any (or all) of the following features to the verification of the e-mail field:

(a) It must have *exactly* one "@" symbol.

(b) The "@" symbol must not be the first or last character of the address.

(c) It must have at least one ".", but if it has more than one, no two periods can be consecutive ".." It can have no more than three periods. (We wish to allow x@y.a.b.c, but not x@a..b)

(d) The address can have no "." before the "@".

(e) A "." may not be the first or last character of the address.

12. Add any (or all) of the features outlined in Exercise 11 to strengthen the verification of the e-mail field in Figure 17.14.

13. Make a form similar to the following that requests information for a demographics survey:

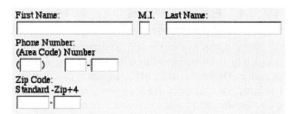

Add the following features to a JavaScript verification of the form. *Option*: Add an e-mail field and include some of the verifications of Exercise 11.

(a) Name fields:
(i) The first and last names must each be more than two characters, but no more than 20 characters. They must not be numbers.
(ii) The middle initial field may be left blank. But if it is filled in, it must be exactly one character, and not be a number.

(b) Phone number fields:
The first two fields must be exactly three characters, and the third field must be exactly four characters. All fields must be numbers.

(c) Zip code fields.
(i) The first field must contain exactly five characters and must be a number.
(ii) The second field may be empty. But if it is filled in, it must contain exactly four digits and be a number.

17.12 PROJECT THREADS

Any exercises you do for this lesson should be referenced in your homework page following the guidelines in Section 9.10.

JAVASCRIPT SECURITY AND SUBMITTING FORM DATA

THIS BEING the last lesson of our book (how time flies!), we wish to tie down some loose ends we have left dangling. In particular, the loose ends provide a setting for discussion about three HTML form elements that we have not yet covered: password fields, submit buttons, and hidden form elements. The material of this lesson provides the perfect setting for introduction to these last three form elements, as well as a fitting capstone for this book.

The first loose end involves security, namely password-protecting web pages. You have no doubt had to fill out user name and password fields in a web page before you were granted access to another page. The bad news is that JavaScript can only provide limited security. Remember, JavaScript is portable code—code that is transported to the client's browser with the web page. Thus, it is virtually impossible to provide complete password protection with JavaScript. All the user has to do is to view the source code for the page, and right there is the very JavaScript code that is intended to protect the page. Nonetheless, JavaScript can be used to provide a certain level of security, so we present several techniques. But keep in mind that any serious password protection has to be done back on the web server, with the help of a database and a CGI program. You will never catch (we hope) an online e-tailer using only JavaScript to protect sensitive information like passwords and credit card numbers.

The second loose end involves sending data back to the server for processing by CGI programs. Certainly, JavaScript's security weaknesses provide a natural motivation for this. We invite the reader to reread Section 9.2 for a refresher on some of the terminology surrounding the client-server model. (That's less an invitation, and more a strong suggestion.) The CGI programs we refer to in this lesson are written in Perl (Practical Extraction and Report Language). We will not show any Perl code in this lesson, but will send data to some Perl programs sitting on the server that serves up the web site for this book. At least you will get a feel for how JavaScript can be used to help in such transactions.

Finally, the material of this lesson is meant to be dependent only upon the JavaScript Lessons 9 through 14. In other words, you need not learn Lessons 15 through 17 in order to understand this material. However, an example from Lesson 15.5 provides a natural segue into the topic of security, so we mention that in the first paragraph of Section 18.1. If you have not learned Lesson 15, skipping that paragraph will cause no difficulty whatsoever. Also, there are some homework exercises that require knowledge from Lessons 15 through 17. But that is no problem, as there are ample exercises that are not dependent upon those lessons.

18.1 THE PASSWORD INPUT ELEMENT

In Section 15.5, the while loop was employed to provide password protection for a web page. The loop is in the head section of the page, and indefinitely rerequests that a password be entered into a text field as long as the user keeps entering an incorrect password. If the password is correct, the loop terminates and the page is loaded into the browser. Otherwise, the while loop runs indefinitely in the head section, causing the browser never to get past the head section in its effort to display the page. Thus, if the password is not known, the browser is effectively hung in an infinite loop, causing the user to force the browser to quit, or to restart the computer. While effective, you can easily see why that is not a desirable protection strategy. Indeed, that example was geared more towards demonstrating the *while* loop than towards providing a viable protection strategy for the page.

There is an HTML input element, TYPE="password", that we could have used in that example to collect the password, instead of the standard TYPE="text" input element. But rather than using a password field in such a browser-crashing attempt at password protection, we use one to provide a more standard type of protection. The user gets what we term an entry page that contains a verification form. Only if the user enters a valid user name and password is access to the protected web page granted. Such an entry page is shown in Figure 18.1. If the verification is successful, the user is transferred (see Section 12.9) to the protected page. Otherwise, the form is cleared and the user is asked to try again.

A password field in an HTML form is defined by

<INPUT TYPE="password">

and can make use of the NAME, VALUE, and SIZE attributes just as the standard TYPE= "text" text field. In terms of functionality, the password field is exactly like the standard text field except that whatever text the user enters is obscured. Figure 18.1 shows an entry page that requests a user name and a password. The user has entered "opensesame" into the password field. Although the form is organized with a borderless table, only the code for the HTML form is provided. As you can see, the button calls a JavaScript function named *verify()*. The logic for the function is given below.

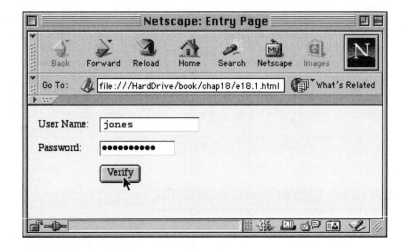

```
<FORM NAME=passform>
   User Name:<INPUT TYPE=text NAME=user VALUE="" SIZE=15>
   Password:<INPUT TYPE=password NAME=pass VALUE="" SIZE=15>
   <INPUT TYPE=button VALUE="Verify" onclick="verify()">
</FORM>
```

FIGURE 18.1 A typical entry page for a protected page. The user name is entered into a text field and the password into a password field.

-if (user name and password are correct)
   transfer the user to the protected page

-else
   alert the user
   clear the entry fields

For simplicity, we supply only one correct user name (jones) and password (opensesame). Of course, it would not be difficult to include several valid user name and password pairs, but we leave that as an exercise, along with some other variations. The JavaScript to support the form of Figure 18.1 is given in Figure 18.2.

```
<SCRIPT LANGUAGE=JavaScript><!--
function verify(){
   with(document.passform){
      if((user.value=="jones")&&(pass.value=="opensesame")){
         window.location="protectedpage.html";
      }
      else{
         alert("User Name or Password incorrect. Try again.");
         user.value="";
         pass.value="";
      }
   }
}
//--></SCRIPT>
```

FIGURE 18.2 The *verify()* function called by the form of Figure 18.1.

> **NOTE**
>
> A glaring weakness of this type of password protection is the fact that the user name and password are present in the head section of the web page, and thus are transported to the client's browser along with the page. All the user has to do is to select "view source" in one of the browser's pull-down menus to see the source code of the entry page. The user name and password are then easy prey. Moreover, the actual name of the protected page appears in the source code of the entry page. One merely would have to deduce the file path on the server to the file and make an http browser request straight for the file. (The file path can be deduced from the URL that loads the entry page, together with the relative URL in the location statement in the JavaScript function.) This strategy for protection will keep only the casual web surfer out of the protected page.

18.2 IMPORTING EXTERNAL SCRIPTS

In some cases, several web pages at a given web site might require the same JavaScript code. In these cases, an external script can be imported into the different pages using the SRC (source) attribute of the HTML SCRIPT element. The file containing the external JavaScript code should be appended with the file suffix ".js", and the value of the SRC attribute is simply the relative URL pointing to the external JavaScript file. To demonstrate this, we use an external script containing the same JavaScript as shown in Figure 18.2 to verify a password. Keep in mind that password protection is only one potential use of external scripts. Scripts can be imported for a variety of reasons and are especially useful when the same JavaScript code is to be used in more than one page.

Figure 18.3 shows the HEAD section of the document that creates the entry page of Figure 18.1. But in this version, the entire script is stored in an external script named "external.js". You can see in Figure 18.3 that "external.js" is no more than a plain text file, which can be created with "Simple Text" or "Notepad." The external text file with the Javascript code contains no SCRIPT tags. The statements in "external.js" are included within the SCRIPT element whose SRC attribute called the file, just as if they were part of that document. However, when the entry page is loaded into the user's browser, its source code contains only the name of the external JavaScript file, rather than its contents. The only evidence of JavaScript in the entry page is the empty SCRIPT element whose SRC attribute points to the actual file containing all of the JavaScript. In this way, neither the user name-password pair or the name of the protected file is present in the source code of the entry page.

> **NOTE**
>
> At first glance, it might appear that this is a very secure method of providing password protection for a web page. However, as in any attempt for security on the client, there are loopholes. The name of the external script is present in the source code of the entry page. The user can get the name of the external file, deduce the file path from the URL of the entry page, and make a browser request like
>
> http://www.uweb.edu/scripts/external.js
>
> in an attempt to pull up the external script itself. But since this file is not an HTML file, not all browsers will automatically load the script. However, a reasonably skilled surfer can alter a browser's helper applications (plugins) so that ".js" files are automatically opened by a text editor, for example.

```
┌─────────────────────────────────────────────────┐
│ □ ▤▤▤▤▤▤▤▤▤▤  external.js ▤▤▤▤▤▤▤▤▤  ▣ ▤│
├─────────────────────────────────────────────────┤
│ function verify(){                                │
│  with(document.passform){                         │
│   if((user.value=="jones")&&(pass.value=="opensesame")){ │
│    window.location="protectedpage.html";          │
│   }                                               │
│   else{                                           │
│    alert("User Name or Password incorrect. Try again."); │
│    user.value="";                                 │
│    pass.value="";                                 │
│   }                                               │
│  }                                             ▲  │
│ }                                              ▼  │
├─────────────────────────────────────────────────┤
│                                                ⟋  │
└─────────────────────────────────────────────────┘
```

```
┌─────────────────────────────────────────────────┐
│ <HTML>                                         ▤ │
│ <HEAD>                                            │
│                                                   │
│ <SCRIPT LANGUAGE=JavaScript SRC="external.js"><!-- │
│ //--></SCRIPT>                                    │
│                                                   │
│ </HEAD>                                           │
│ <BODY>                                            │
│ <FORM NAME=passform>                              │
│    User Name:<INPUT TYPE=text NAME=user VALUE="" SIZE=15><BR> │
│    Password:<INPUT TYPE=password NAME=pass VALUE="" SIZE=15><BR> │
│    <INPUT TYPE=button VALUE="Verify" onclick="verify()"> │
│ </FORM>                                           │
│ </BODY>                                        ▲ │
│ </HTML>                                        ▼ │
├─────────────────────────────────────────────────┤
│                                          ◄│►  ⟋  │
└─────────────────────────────────────────────────┘
```

FIGURE 18.3 The SRC (source) attribute of the SCRIPT element imports JavaScript code from an external text file.

> On some web servers, it may be possible to set up a directory for such password scripts that is accessible only via internal requests, and not from requests from external sources. That way, a page stored on the server can call the script for support, but no external source could steal the script. But there are numerous server types, not all of which can effectively accomplish this.

18.3 OTHER SECURITY TRICKS ON THE CLIENT

Other techniques have been employed to provide some measure of security on the client without having to rely on server-side database and CGI. Two of which we briefly mention here. A simple technique is to request a password from the user and store it into a JavaScript variable named *password*, for example. We then concatenate ".html" onto the password:

```
filename=password+".html";
```

Using the location property of the window object again, we transfer the user to the protected page:

```
window.location=filename;
```

For a quick runthrough this, suppose the password is "aardvark". When the user enters this word, it is stored in the *password* variable. The concatenation results in the variable *filename* containing the string "aardvark.html". Then the window location is set to that file. If the user enters an incorrect password, he or she simply gets a message from the server indicating the file can't be found—a nonexistent page. The user then would use the back button on the browser to go back to the entry page. Other modifications of this can be used, but those are left as exercises. One such modification is to concatenate both the user name and password to get the file path to the protected file, much as in the note below, but with access provided by an entry page.

> **N O T E**
>
> Note that the above technique is roughly equivalent to putting a file somewhere in your web site, but providing no links to the file. In that case, someone would have to know the exact name of the file and the path on the server to the file. For example, someone might have to know the exact URL
>
> http://www.uweb.edu/jones/aardvark.html
>
> in order to find the page. This is roughly equivalent to having jones as the user name and aardvark as the password. Only someone who knows the user name and password can find the page, since there are no links to it. Knowing the password name and user name would be equivalent to knowing the name of a directory on the server, and a file in that directory. Of course, such a technique assumes that you have used index files to hide all of your directories. Otherwise, a clever surfer can browse your directories and find any of your files.

One last technique involves encryption. In such a technique, the user name and passwords can be included into the source code for the entry page, but are encrypted into an unintelligible form. For example, the password can be converted into a number and then run through some complex mathematical equations. In this way, a word like "opensesame" can be converted into a number like 087345608273456. While the number would actually appear in the source code of the entry page, someone would have to find the inverse of the encryption process to obtain the password. If the encryption process is sufficiently complicated this could be a daunting task, even for a skilled mathematician. With such a strategy, it is also necessary to encrypt the name of the protected HTML file, since otherwise it would be visible in the "window.location" transfer statement. Of course, such encryption techniques are well beyond the scope of this book, but many such scripts can be found in free script libraries on the Internet. Several such libraries are referenced in the web site.

18.4 CGI PROGRAMS

We now shift gears a bit and discuss the rudiments of submitting form data to the web server. In case you missed our suggestion in the introduction to this lesson, we reiterate that you should reread Section 9.2 at this point to remind yourself of some of the terminology surrounding the notion of the client-server model. In light of the preceding sections of the current lesson, one compelling reason to send form data back to the server is to verify a password, but from a database which is secure on the server. Clearly, JavaScript is somewhat security-challenged. While this book can't explore the details of managing secure password files on a web server, the remaining sections do cover the basics of sending data to the server.

CGI programs are merely text files that contain lines of programming code (in our case Perl code), not too much unlike JavaScript code. In fact, Perl uses basically the same programming concepts you have learned with JavaScript in this book, although its syntax is significantly more complicated. In particular, a CGI program makes use of variables to store information. Now, a CGI program is sitting on the web server waiting for data from an HTML form. As part of the CGI standardization, there are special variables, called **environment variables,** into which your browser can put information from the HTML form. These environment variables are also accessible to the CGI program. That way, the CGI program can retrieve contents of the environment variables and process that information on the server. In this respect, the environment variables are rather like intermediate storage variables between the browser and web server. Figure 18.4 demonstrates this:

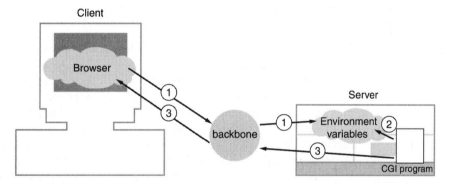

FIGURE 18.4 The environment variables are variables on the server into which a browser can store information. CGI programs get the information from these variables and process it.

1. The browser stores information into the environment variables. This information can include data from HTML forms.

2. The CGI program accesses the environment variables and processes the information they contain. This can include calculations and entering form data into a database on the server.

3. The CGI program sends the results back to the browser in the form of a new web page. This new page can contain information retrieved from the database.

Figure 18.5 provides a few concrete examples of the types of information that the browser puts into the environment variables, and the values passed to them by the browser. The sole purpose of this transaction was to send a user name and password to the web server. The user name and password were obtained from a form similar to that of Figure 8.1. The data from the form is contained in the QUERY_STRING variable. As you can see, along with the form data, the browser has transferred a good bit of other information to other

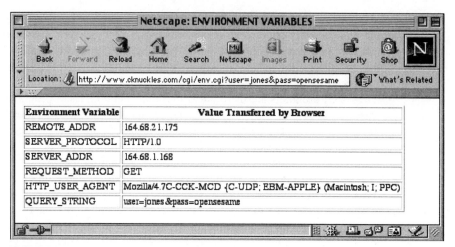

FIGURE 18.5 A table containing some environment variables. The values in the variables are the result of a transaction in which the author's browser sent a user name and password to the server, and a CGI program returned the variable names and their contents to the browser.

environment variables. Even the type of computer the author was using is evidenced just above the QUERY_STRING variable.

Since some of the values of these variables are determined by the browser on the remote host (your computer), you are encouraged to go to the web site and see what values your browser sends to these variables. Rather than just returning a few of the variables as in Figure 18.5, the version on the web site returns all of the variables and their contents.

On at least two occasions earlier in this book, we mentioned that sometimes a URL contains information other than just the protocol, server address, and file path. In fact, the note at the end of Section 9.2 gives such an example. We termed the information after the question mark of a URL a **query string.** In the browser's address window in Figure 18.5, the query string is in full evidence. That is, in fact, how a browser gets the form data to the QUERY_STRING environment variable. It simply tacks it onto the end of the URL that is sent to the server. The server parses the query string off the end of the URL and places it into the QUERY_STRING variable so that programs on the server can access its contents.

18.5 THE SUBMIT BUTTON

OK, so how do we transfer form data to the QUERY_STRING environment variable on the web server? Well, just get it onto the end of a URL in the form of a query string. So, it seems the real question is how to accomplish that. The HTML form element that accomplishes this is the Submit button. It is defined just like the other two types of buttons (generic and reset), but using TYPE="submit" in the INPUT element:

<INPUT TYPE="submit" VALUE="Click here to Submit Form">

As with the other buttons, the value of the VALUE attribute is what physically appears on the button in the web page. While a submit button can utilize the onclick event handler to call a JavaScript function like the other button types, one often uses its built-in event handler, which automatically calls the *submit( )* function when the user clicks the button. You don't have to define the built-in *submit( )* function, or even make any reference to it. The Submit button calls it for you and the *submit( )* function works behind the scenes.

The *submit( )* function causes the form's data to be attached to the end of a URL as a query string. But what URL? Determining that is the ACTION attribute of the FORM element as shown below:

<FORM ACTION="http://www.cknuckles.com/cgi/verify.cgi" METHOD="GET">

The value of the ACTION attribute is no more than a URL giving the location of the CGI program, in this case "verify.cgi". The CGI program is simply sitting on the web server account in a directory named "cgi". So the *submit( )* function takes the URL given by the ACTION attribute and tacks the form data onto the end of the URL in the form of the query string.

We choose the name "verify.cgi" for the CGI program, since the following example uses the program to verify a user name and password on the web server. But before we get to that example, one last explanation is in order. The METHOD="GET" attribute-value pair you see in the FORM tag specifies the method in which the form data is sent to the CGI program. Here, the GET method tells the *submit( )* function to send the form's data in the form of a query string. We use only the GET method in this lesson, but a note at the end of this section briefly explains a limitation of this and another alternative. However, don't confuse this GET with the get-type transaction used in ftp. This GET is completely different in concept.

CGI programs like "verify.cgi" typically check a database to see if the information is correct. If it is, the user goes to a protected web page. Otherwise, the user is asked to try again. The form and its defining HTML code are given in Figure 18.6. The form submit button has been clicked so that the GET method has caused the form's data to be appended to the URL.

The entire query string is not entirely visible in the address field of the browser due to its length, so we supply it:

?user=jones&pass=opensesame&Button=Submit+Form

That's the whole query string that is stored in the QUERY_STRING environment variable on the server. You can see that the name and value of each of the form's elements appears in the query string. For example, the name of the password field as defined in the form is "pass". So, in the query string, you see

pass=opensesame

which is the value that Jones entered into the obscured password field. Moreover, you can see that the name-value pairs for the three form elements are separated (delimited) by "&" symbols. That's part of the CGI specification, providing a standardized for transmission of data from HTML forms. It's the job of the actual CGI program to extract the data from the QUERY_STRING variable on the server and to "parse" the desired information out of it. We shall not concern ourselves with those details.

The rest of the transaction is simply stated. The user name and password are checked for validity against a secure database on the server side. Then the CGI program either

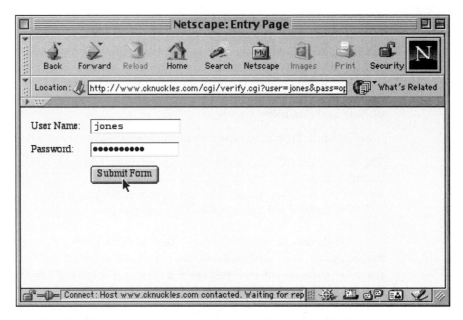

```
<FORM ACTION="http://www.cknuckles.com/cgi/verify.cgi" METHOD=GET>
    User Name:<INPUT TYPE=text NAME=user VALUE="" SIZE=15>
    Password: <INPUT TYPE=password NAME=pass VALUE="" SIZE=15>
    <INPUT TYPE=submit NAME=Submit VALUE="Submit Form">
</FORM>
```

FIGURE 18.6 The browser window immediately after the Submit button has been clicked. The GET method has caused the form data to be sent to the CGI program specified by the ACTION attribute. The form data is added onto the end of the URL in the form of a query string.

spits back the protected page, or tells the user access is denied. You should play with the program on the web site for this book. An interesting feature of this example is that no JavaScript is used to process the form. Rather, the built-in *submit()* function handles the form's submission to the server and the CGI program handles the rest.

NOTE | One limitation of the GET method is that the length of the query string is limited by most web servers. In fact, a common limitation is that a maximum of 256 characters can be appended onto a URL. There is another form-submission method that circumvents this problem, namely METHOD=POST. If this method is specified, the form data is sent to the CGI program in a more direct fashion, not using a query string and not limiting the amount of form data. The details of POST are well beyond the scope of this book, but you should at least be aware that GET and POST are the only two methods of form submission.

18.6 USING HIDDEN FORM ELEMENTS

Consider again the form of Figure 18.6, in which a user name and password were submitted to the server for verification. The query string that was sent to the server,

?user=jones&pass=opensesame&Button=Submit+Form

actually carried much more information than necessary. In fact, the query string contains three name-value pairs, one for each of the three form elements. You can see that the pairs "user=jones" and "pass=opensesame" each contain the name of one of the form's TYPE=text input elements, together with the value of the form element as entered by the user. But even the submit button is represented as a name-value pair. The pair "Button=Submit+Form" contains a generic name given to the button and the value of the button. Since the CGI program needs only the user name and password, we really need only send something like

?info=jones-opensesame

to the server.

The only type of HTML form element we have yet to discuss in this book can help us "clean up" the form data before sending it to the server. A form element defined by

<INPUT TYPE=hidden NAME=somename VALUE=somevalue>

is aptly termed a hidden form element. It is called hidden because it is not visible in the web page itself. That's right, if you put some of these in an HTML form, the browser will not mark them up at all. There will be no trace of them in the web page.

We can use such TYPE=hidden input elements to submit cleaned-up data to the web server. It is best to proceed with an example. Figure 18.7 shows the source code for a new version of the entry page we saw in Figure 18.6. The entry form, as it appears in the web

```
<HTML>
<HEAD><TITLE>Entry Page</TITLE>

<SCRIPT LANGUAGE=JavaScript><!--
function clean(){
   with(document){
      cleanform.info.value=rawform.user.value+"-"+rawform.pass.value;
      cleanform.submit();
   }
}
//--></SCRIPT>

</HEAD>
<BODY BGCOLOR="#FFFFCC">

<FORM name=rawform>
   User Name:<INPUT TYPE=text NAME=user VALUE="" SIZE=15>
   Password: <INPUT TYPE=password NAME=pass VALUE="" SIZE=15>
   <INPUT TYPE=button NAME=Button VALUE="Submit Form" onclick="clean()">
</FORM>

<FORM ACTION="http://www.cknuckles.com/cgi/verify2.cgi"
METHOD=GET name=cleanform>
   <INPUT TYPE=hidden NAME=info VALUE="">
</FORM>

</BODY>
</HTML>
```

FIGURE 18.7 The source code for a version of the entry page of Figure 18.6. This version uses JavaScript to clean up the data and a hidden form to submit the data to the server.

page, is no different from that of Figure 18.6. Again, we give only the HTML code for the actual form and omit the table used for formatting the page.

Unlike the entry form of Figure 18.6, this one uses JavaScript. But before getting to that, we first explain the forms. There are two of them. The first one is roughly the same as used in Figure 18.6. However, it uses a generic button rather than a submit button, and has no ACTION attribute to call a CGI program. The second form is not visible in the web page. Its only form element is a hidden field. As you can see, the hidden form does contain an ACTION attribute to call a CGI program named "verify2.cgi" using the GET (query string) method. Interestingly, though, it does not contain a submit button (otherwise it would not be hidden) to call the *submit()* function. Since this hidden form is the one with the ACTION attribute, it stands to reason that this is the form we will use to submit the data from the input form after it has been cleaned up. But since the hidden form has no submit button, how are we to do that?

As we saw in earlier lessons, HTML forms are objects. Of course, objects have methods, which are functions that belong to the object. As it turns out, the *submit()* function is a method of the form object. Suppose a form is named "formname" and has a submit button. We have indicated that clicking the submit button automatically calls a built-in *submit()* function. This is true, but the button actually calls

```
formname.submit();
```

since the *submit()* function is a method of the form. The key to submitting the hidden form is to make a call to its submit method. This does not have to be done using a submit button, but can be done using one line of JavaScript code.

With that in mind, let's go through the data-cleaning technique in Figure 18.7. First, the user enters the user name and password into the form named "rawform". When the submit button (actually a generic button) in that form is clicked, the JavaScript function *clean()* is called. First, this function takes the user name and password entered into the first form and stores them into the hidden input field of the second form. In that assignment statement, a "-" is inserted to put the data into the form

jones-opensesame

The second line of JavaScript in the function simply invokes the *submit()* method of the hidden form. The result is the query string

?info=jones-opensesame

is sent to the server on the end of the URL. This is still a name-value pair, where "info" is the name of the hidden form element and the value is the user's input. However, it is much less cumbersome than a long query string that contains name-value pairs for each of the three form elements of the data-entry form. The user does not perceive that the apparent submit button is actually a generic button that calls a function that submits a different, hidden form.

For another example, consider the form shown in Figure 18.8. The form contains five questions. For each question, a radio button is provided for each of the possible answers. Instead of giving the entire HTML code for the form, we give an outline that includes the main form and the hidden form used for submitting the data. There is no point in showing

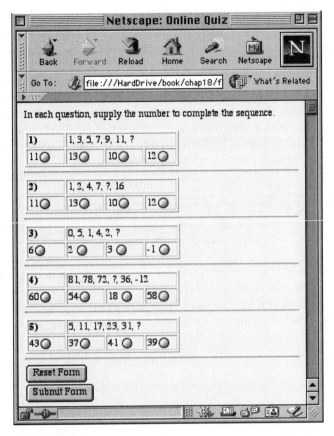

```
<FORM name=quizform>
     the 20 radio buttons go here
     <INPUT TYPE=reset VALUE="Reset Form"><BR>
     <INPUT TYPE=button VALUE="Submit Form" onclick="grade()">
</FORM>

<FORM ACTION="http://www.cknuckles.com/cgi/quiz.cgi" METHOD=GET
name=cleanform>
     <INPUT TYPE=hidden NAME=correct VALUE="">
</FORM>
```

FIGURE 18.8 An online quiz with five questions. When the quiz is submitted to the server, a results page is sent back telling how many right answers were given, the number of people who have previously taken the quiz, and the average of the scores of all these people.

the code for the 20 radio buttons. Since each group of radio buttons shares the same name (so only one of each group can be selected), we will have to refer to them using the *elements[]* array anyway.

When the questions are answered and the submit button is clicked, the form is submitted to a CGI program named "quiz.cgi" on the server. Then a results page is returned that contains the number of correct answers, the total number of people who have taken the quiz, and the average score. It is clear that the CGI program on the server will have to keep a database file containing scores of people who have previously taken the quiz. Otherwise, it would be impossible for it to return information based upon past quizzes to you. But once again, we won't concern ourselves with the actual CGI program, but with how to get the information from the form to the server.

There are 20 radio buttons in the form, four for each of the five questions. We could submit the whole form to the CGI program, but that would be 20 name-value pairs just for the radio buttons. That means the query string would be around 200 characters long, even if we choose two-letter names for each of the radio buttons. To eliminate this waste, we send only the correct number of responses to the CGI program. So rather than a 200-character query string, we send only a query string of the form

?correct=4

Once again, the input form appears to contain a submit button. But it is actually a generic button that calls a JavaScript function called *grade()*, which effectively grades the quiz. Figure 18.9 shows the JavaScript that cleans up the input form and submits the hidden form.

The function simply checks to see if each correct radio button is checked. If it is, 1 is added onto the running *correct* counter. Then the final total in the *correct* counter is stored into the hidden form element, and the hidden form is submitted to the server. From the name of the hidden form element, you can see that the query string will indeed be of the form

?correct=3

if the user had chosen three correct answers, for example.

```
<SCRIPT LANGUAGE=JavaScript><!--
function grade(){
   var correct=0;
   with(document){
      if(quizform.elements[0].checked){
         correct=correct+1;
      }
      if(quizform.elements[4].checked){
         correct=correct+1;
      }
      if(quizform.elements[8].checked){
         correct=correct+1;
      }
      if(quizform.elements[12].checked){
         correct=correct+1;
      }
      if(quizform.elements[16].checked){
         correct=correct+1;
      }
      cleanform.correct.value=correct;
      cleanform.submit();
   }
}
//--></SCRIPT>
```

FIGURE 18.9 The function *clean()* that is called to clean up the input form of Figure 18.8. This function stores the correct number of answers in the hidden input element and submits that form.

NOTE

We did not supply the correct answers is Figure 18.9. We have added 1 to the *correct* counter if the first choice for each question is checked, and those are not necessarily the correct answers. The radio buttons occupy array positions *elements[0]* through *elements[19]*. One would simply find the array positions of the correct answers and use those positions in the five "if" statements.

We hope that the reader will go to the web site and take the quiz. That way you can see the trimmed-down query string being sent to the server, and the results that the CGI program spits back. Also, you will see the cumulative average after many people have taken the quiz. That average is the result of a cumulative database on the server that the CGI program updates each time someone fills out the quiz and submits it. You just can't do any real data storage on the client.

One flaw you might notice in the previous example is that the correct answers appear in the source code. In the version on the web site, we have included the correct answers, but have used an external Script to import the *clean()* function so the answers don't appear in the source code. That's certainly not foolproof, as we mentioned earlier in this lesson, but it will keep most surfers from getting the correct answers. A more secure version of the quiz would be one in which the user's selection's were sent back to the server. You could send the five name-value pairs that the user selected. That's still better than sending the pairs for all 20 radio buttons. In that way, the answers are kept securely on the server and the CGI program checks them against the user's choices. We leave that as an exercise.

18.7 SUMMARY

Key Terms

password form element	external script	SRC attribute
environment variables	QUERY_STRING	of SCRIPT tag
submit button	*submit()* function	query string
METHOD=GET	hidden form element	ACTION

The TYPE=password input form element can be used to request a password from the user. It functions just like the TYPE=text input element except that the characters that the user enters are obscured. The security examples in this lesson involve collecting a user name and password from the user. If they are correct, the user is transferred to the protected web page.

A simple way to verify passwords is to check them in the HEAD section of the document using JavaScript. If the information is correct, the user is transferred to the protected page using the *window.location* property. A slightly more secure way to protect the page is to use an external script that contains the verification JavaScript. External scripts are imported using the SRC attribute of the SCRIPT element:

<SCRIPT LANGUAGE=JavaScript SRC="somescript.js"><!--

//--></SCRIPT>

The external script should not contain SCRIPT tags, but just the JavaScript code itself. While hiding a password-protection script is one use of external scripts, they are very useful in other situations. External scripts are especially useful when more than one page on a web site requires the same Javascript support. In that case, one copy of a script can be used in several web pages.

Other methods can be used to provide a measure of security on the client. One such method is to set up the password as the file name. You then transfer the user

```
window.location=password+".html";
```

to the page by concatenating the ".html" suffix onto the password. This method is fairly secure, since a hacker would need to know the password to find the file. However, it is cumbersome since a different file needs to be created for each password. Another security measure involves encrypting (scrambling) the password in a verification script. This is also fairly secure, but it requires some serious knowhow to accomplish.

Most password protection is accomplished using CGI programs on the web server. An entry page that contains a verification form is sent to the client. The input to the form is appended onto the end of a URL in the form of a query string, and sent back to the QUERY_STRING variable on the server. The CGI program can access the form data from the QUERY_STRING variable and use that data to check the user name and password against a secure database on the server. If the data is valid, the CGI program sends back the protected page.

While the details of CGI programs are beyond the scope of this book, we can use the TYPE= submit input form element to send form data to a pre-existing CGI program on the server. The CGI programs to which we refer in this book are written in Perl. The ACTION attribute of the FORM tag supplies the URL of the CGI program, and the METHOD=GET pair makes sure that the form data is sent back as a query string. The submit button calls a built in *submit()* function when clicked. This function automatically appends the query string onto the URL given by the ACTION attribute, and initiates the transaction with the server.

A query string is added to the end of a URL following a question mark. It consists of name-value pairs for each of the form's elements. By name-value pair, we mean the name of the form element together with its value. This value can be defined in the form definition or supplied by the user into an input element. The length of a query string is limited to 256 characters by many web servers. So a form with a lot of form elements or one in which the values are particularly long might not be viable for submission via query string.

One strategy that can be employed when a query string would be too long, or even just longer than it need be, is to use a hidden form element. A hidden form element is defined with the standard INPUT form element, but with TYPE=hidden. Hidden form elements are not marked up in the web page. A viewer would not even perceive that one was present without viewing the source code.

The strategy of "cleaning" form data using hidden form elements can be summarized as follows:

1. A hidden form, one which contains only hidden elements, is defined. This form is completely separate from the actual data entry form.

2. Rather than using a submit button, the data entry form uses a generic button disguised as a submit button. This generic button calls a JavaScript function.

3. The JavaScript function separates out the useful information from the data entry form and assigns it to the hidden input element in the hidden form.

4. The function then calls the submit method of the hidden form, causing only one name-value pair to be sent as the query string. This name-value pair consists of the name of the hidden form element and its value. Of course, its value is the cleaned-up data from the input form.

18.8   REVIEW QUESTIONS

1.   How is a TYPE=password input form element different from a TYPE=text input form element?

2.   Give two serious weaknesses to the method of password protection supplied in Figures 18.1 and 18.2.

3. What type of file should an external script be, and what file extension (suffix) should the file have?

4. Describe a security risk when an external script is used to conceal JavaScript written for password verification.

5. When password-protecting a web page on a web site, why is it important for the directories on the web site to contain index files?

6. In the example of Figures 18.1 and 18.2, what happens if the password is not correct? On the other hand, when using the strategy of using a password as part of the protected file's name, what happens if the password is not correct?

7. Explain the difference between QUERY_STRING and a query string.

8. Why do you not need to use the *onclick* event handler with a submit button?

9. Describe in detail the components of a query string, including the use of the "=" and "&" symbols.

10. When using a hidden form to submit cleaned up input data, why does the form not contain a submit button? Since it doesn't, how is it submitted to the server?

18.9 EXERCISES

1. Go to the web site for this book and pull up the page for Figure 18.5. Using the returned list of environment variables, deduce the IP address of the computer you are using.

2. Add any (or all) of the following features to the security example of Figures 18.1 and 18.2:

(a) Include three correct user name/password pairs.

(b) The alert given to the user upon an invalid user name or password should say whether the user name or password (or both) was unrecognizable. Only the fields that were incorrect should be cleared.

(c) Use the *toLowerCase()* method of the string object to convert the user name and password into all lower-case letters before checking them. That way, Jones would still match jones, for example. Hint: the following lines of code cause x to contain "scooby".

```
var x="SCOOBY";
x=x.toLowerCase(x);
```

3. Do Exercise 2, but use an external script.

4. (Requires Lessons 15 and 16) Use an external script that contains two parallel arrays, one with 10 user names and the other with 10 passwords. The external script should also contain a variable into which a string is stored corresponding to the name of the protected file. Thus, all of the sensitive material is stored in the external script. The rest of the JavaScript should be defined in the actual entry page. Use a loop to check the entered user name and password against the ones in the arrays. When it comes time to assign the protected page to *window.location,* just assign the variable containing the file name, leaving all of the sensitive information in the external script. Include option c of Exercise 2 in your design.

5. Make a protected web page using the trick of including the password as part of the protected file's name. Use option c of Exercise 2 to make case sensitivity not an issue. Also, include both the user name and the password in the protected file name, so that the user has to know both to find the file. Hint: keep your user name and password to three letters each. Some computers don't like long file names.

6. Make a form that requests a first name and last name using two different input fields. The page should contain a hidden form used for submitting the cleaned form data. The query string must be in the exact form

?names=first-last

or the CGI program will not work. You are to submit the query string to http://www.cknuckles.com/cgi/address.cgi. If the name exactly matches one found in the database, an address for that person will be returned. Otherwise, you will get a "sorry" message. There are three valid names in the data base: Danny Jones, Bryan Moore, and Steve Grodrian. Case sensitivity does not matter when searching the data base.

7. Make a secure version of the quiz of Figure 18.8 that submits the indices of the selected answers to a CGI program. You may copy the source code for the form from the web site so you don't have to type it all in. The selected indices must be submitted in a query string of the exact form

?chosen=3-7-11-15-19

or the CGI program won't work. The radio buttons are in positions 0-19 of the form's elements array. So, for example, the above query string would result if the user chooses the fourth option of each question. You are to submit the query string to http://www.cknuckles.com/cgi/quiz2.cgi.

8. On the web site under this question, you will find images for a pattern matching quiz with eight questions (the questions are pretty cool, too!). You are to make a viable online quiz using these patterns. There are two options for this problem:

(a) Take an approach like that of Figure 18.8, and submit a query string containing only the correct number of responses. The query string must be exactly like

?correct=4

You are to submit the quiz to http://www.cknuckles.com/cgi/pattern.cgi.

(b) (Requires Lesson 15) Take an approach like that of Exercise 7, and submit the indices of the users' choices. Since there are eight questions, each with six answers, there will be 48 radio buttons. Make sure that there are no other form elements defined before them so that they occupy positions 0–47 of the elements array. So if the user chooses the first answer from each question, the query string will be exactly like

?chosen=0-6-12-18-24-30-36-42

it should be submitted to http://www.cknuckles.com/cgi/pattern2.cgi.

18.10 PROJECT THREADS

Any exercises you do for this lesson should be referenced in your homework page following the guidelines in Section 9.10.

HTML QUICK REFERENCE

This appendix provides a quick reference for the HTML elements covered in this book. This list of elements is not exhaustive. In other words, we don't supply a list of all HTML elements, but just of the ones covered in this text. A full reference for all HTML elements can be found in *HTML 4.0 Sourcebook,* by Ian Graham (Wiley). The ones presented here are more than adequate for general web-page design.

`<A>...</A>` ANCHOR (Hypertext Link/Named Anchor)

NOTES   One of the attributes HREF or NAME must be present. When HREF is present, the content of the element is marked up as the underlined text of a hypertext link. When NAME is present, the element functions as an anchor in the page. In this case, content is not necessary.

Attributes	*Values*	*Default*
HREF	URL (relative, absolute, fragment)	–

Specifies HTML document or image file that the hypertext link is to load. Can point to a fragment identifier for named anchor.

NAME	name of anchor	–

Specifies name of page anchor. Typically the HREF atribute of a hypertext link points to this name as a fragment identifier.

TARGET	name of frame	–

Causes the HTML document or image file specified by the HREF attribute to be loaded into the specified frame name. If a frame of that name can't be found, a new window is created into which the document is loaded.

Event Handlers:
onmouseover
onmouseout
onclick

<AREA>...</AREA>

NOTES

Used only inside the MAP element. Defines an area of the MAP to be used in an image map. Depending on the value of the SHAPE specified, the COORDS attribute supplies the (x, y) coordinates necessary to define the SHAPE.

Attributes	*Values*	*Default*
COORDS	sequence of (x, y) coordinates	–

Specifies the center and radius of a circle, upper left and lower right corners of a rectangle, or the coordinates of the vertices of a polygon.

HREF	URL (relative, absolute, fragment)	–

Specifies the document or image to which the area is to link.

SHAPE	rect, circle, poly	–

Indicates whether the COORDS attribute should expect defining coordinates for a rectangle, circle, or polygon, respectively.

TARGET	name of frame	–

Not discussed explicitly in the text, but works just like the TARGET attribute of the anchor element.

<B>...</B>   BOLDFACE

NOTES

Causes textual contents to be marked in boldface.

<BLOCKQUOTE>...</BLOCKQUOTE>

NOTES

Causes the contents to be uniformly indented on both the left and right margins.

<BODY>...</BODY>

NOTES

Defines the body the HTML document. Should be absent only when FRAMESET tags are present.

Attributes	*Values*	*Default*
ALINK	color (named, hexadecimal)	browser-dependent

Specifies the color of active links, that is, links in the process of being clicked.

BACKGROUND	URL (usually relative)	–

Points to a background image that is to be tiled as the background of the web page. Overrides BGCOLOR.

BGCOLOR   color (named hexadecimal)   white or gray

Sets a background color for the page. Is suppressed by BACKGROUND.

LINK   color (named, hexadecimal)   browser-dependent

Sets the color for hypertext links that have not been visited.

TEXT   color (named, hexadecimal)   black

Sets the background color for text (except links) in the page. Is suppressed by FONT or use of style sheets.

VLINK   color (named, hexadecimal)   browser-dependent

Sets the color for hypertext links that have been visited.

Event Handlers:
onload
onunload

    LINE BREAK

NOTES   Causes subsequent markup to begin on the next line. Similar to hitting return in word processing.

<CENTER>...</CENTER>   (DEPRECIATED/May be deleted from future HTML versions.)

NOTES   Centers enclosed objects, text or otherwise. Earmarked to be replaced with style sheet use. Can also be accomplished using <P ALIGN=center>...</P>, although this causes a blank line after the centered object, rather than just a line break. (At the time this book was printed, the CENTER tag was used by virtually all HTML editors.)

<FORM>...</FORM>   FORM AREA

NOTES   All form elements must be defined within this element.

Attributes   *Values*   *Default*

ACTION   URL (relative, absolute)   –

Gives location of CGI program for submitting form data.

METHOD   GET, POST   –

Specifies the method used to transfer form data to the server. GET causes the form data to be appended to the end of the URL. The POST method is not used in this book.

NAME   character string   –

Specifies a name for the form for object reference.

<FRAMESET>...</FRAMESET>   FRAME REGIONS

NOTES

Sets the general structure for a framed HTML document. Replaces the BODY element. The actual content of the frames is determined by the FRAME element. Should contain a number of FRAME elements commensurate with the number of frames allocated by FRAMESET.

Attributes	*Values*	*Default*
BORDER	pixels	5

Specifies the border between frames.

BORDER COLOR	color (named, hexadecimal)	browser-dependent

Specifies the color of the border separating frames.

COLS	%, pixels, *	*

Sets the number of columns of the frameset. The * symbol means to allocate the remaining space to the column. Example: COLS="100,*,*" means the first column should be 100 pixels wide and the other two columns should evenly divide the remaining space.

ROWS	%, pixels, *	*

Sets the number of rows of the frameset. The * symbol means to allocate the remaining space to the row. Example: ROWS="100,*,*" means the first row should be 100 pixels wide and the other two rows should evenly divide the remaining space.

<FRAME>...</FRAME>   FRAME CONTENT

NOTES

Sets the content for each frame in a FRAMESET document. There should be exactly one FRAME element for each frame allocated by a FRAMESET element.

Attributes	*Values*	*Default*
MARGINHEIGHT	pixels	10

Specifies the amount of space above and below the frame's contents. Serves to pad the frame's contents from the top and bottom borders of the frame.

MARGINWIDTH	pixels	10

Specifies the amount of space to the left and right of the frame's contents. Serves to pad the frame's contents from the left and right borders of the frame.

NAME	name of frame	–

Specifies the name of a frame. Used for referencing a frame in order to TARGET a document to the frame using a hypertext link.

SCROLLING	yes, no, auto	auto

Determines whether or not a scrollbar should be provided for a frame. The default, auto, lets the browser decide based on need.

SRC   URL (usually relative)   –

Specifies the HTML document to be initially loaded into the frame. If no document is specified or the specified document can't be found, the frame is initially blank.

<FONT>...</FONT>   (DEPRECIATED/May be deleted from future HTML versions.)

NOTES   Used to control text properties. Destined to be replaced by style sheets. (At the time this book was printed, this tag was used by virtually all HTML editors.)

Attributes	*Values*	*Default*
COLOR	color (named, hexadecimal)	black

Sets the color of text.

FACE   named font family   browser-dependent

Sets the font type for text. The particular font must be present on the browser's computer or else it can't be rendered. If a font can't be found, the browser will resort to the default. Examples are Courier, Helvetica, Times, etc.

SIZE   absolute (1–7), relative (±1,2,3,..)   3 (usually)

Sets the size of enclosed text. The default of 3 is roughly equivalent to a 10–12 pt word-processing font. A relative value of +1, for example, makes the enclosed font one step above the default.

<H1>...</H1>   HEADINGS (H1–H6)

NOTES   The heading elements range from H1 to H6. Each one renders the enclosed text in boldface. The sizes range from quite large (H1) to quite small (H6). All heading elements cause a line break followed by a blank line.

<HEAD>...</HEAD>   HEAD SECTION OF DOCUMENT

NOTES   Defines the head section of the HTML document. This section provides information about the web page, rather than actual content for the page. It is recommended that the HEAD section contain the TITLE element. Otherwise, no other HTML elements discussed in this book are allowed inside the HEAD section. The exception is the SCRIPT element (see Lesson 9 or Appendix B).

<HR>   HORIZONTAL RULE

NOTES   Used to provide an aesthetically pleasing horizontal line break in the page.

Attributes	*Values*	*Default*
ALIGN	left, right, center	center

Aligns the rule horizontally on the page.

NOSHADE	–	shaded

Takes no value and causes the rule to be rendered in solid black, rather than multiple shades of gray. This serves to override the three-dimensional illusion accomplished by shading.

SIZE	pixels	2 pixels

Sets the thickness of the rule.

WIDTH	%, pixels	100%

Sets the width of the rule.

<HTML>...</HTML>

N O T E S Completely defines the HTML document. In other words, the HTML element tells the browser that its contents are HTML markup instructions.

<I>...</I> ITALIC

N O T E S Textual contents are displayed in italic face.

<IMG>...</IMG> IMAGE

N O T E S Used to embed images in a web page. The HEIGHT and WIDTH attributes should always be used, even if you don't intend to resize the image. Their use can help a web page with images load into a browser substantially more quickly. When used as an image map, the MAP element is required to define the regions for the image map.

Attributes	*Values*	*Default*
ALIGN	left, right, top, middle, bottom	bottom

The "left, right" values cause text to flow around the image. Otherwise, the image is put inline with the text. In that case, the default is that the text aligns with the bottom of the image. The other two values cause the text to align with the middle or top of the image.

ALT	brief description	–

The value of ALT provides a text alternative for (brief description of) the image in case a browser does not support images or has image viewing disabled for faster surfing.

BORDER	pixels	0

Provides a solid black border around the image.

HEIGHT   pixels   –

Tells the browser how many pixels to allocate for the image's height.

HSPACE   pixels   browser-dependent

Applies only when images are floated (ALIGN="left" or ALIGN="right"). In this case it provides padding to the left and right of the image so text doesn't flow right up against the image.

ISMAP   –   –

Informs the browser that the image is going to be used as an image map.

SRC   URL (usually relative)   –

Specifies the source of the image to be embedded. The value is usually a relative URL point to the image on the local web site.

USEMAP   name of map   –

The name of the map should be preceded by a # symbol. Used to specify the name of the MAP element used to define regions for an image map.

VSPACE   pixels   browser-dependent

Applies only when images are floated (ALIGN="left" or ALIGN="right"). In this case it provides padding above and below the image so text doesn't flow right up against the image.

WIDTH   pixels   –

Tells the browser how many pixels to allocate for the image's width.

\<INPUT TYPE=button\>   GENERIC BUTTON

NOTES   Must be defined within the HTML FORM element. Usually used with the *onclick* event handler to call a self-defined function to process the form.

Attributes	*Values*	*Default*
VALUE	character string	–

The character string provides the text on the button.

Event Handlers:
onclick

\<INPUT TYPE=checkbox\> CHECKBOX

NOTES   Must be defined within the HTML FORM element.

Attributes	*Values*	*Default*
CHECKED	–	not checked

When present, causes the checkbox to be selected when the page loads.

NAME	character string	–

Specifies a name for the checkbox for object reference. Can be omitted when you refer to the checkbox using the *elements[ ]* array.

VALUE	character string	–

The character string is not visible in the web page. Its value is assigned to the *value* property of the object.

Event Handlers:
onchange (somewhat unreliable)

\<INPUT TYPE=hidden\> HIDDEN FORM ELEMENT

N O T E S Must be defined within the HTML FORM element. This form element does not appear in the web page. It is used for storing extra information behind the scenes.

Attributes	*Values*	*Default*
NAME	character string	–

Specifies a name for the hidden element for object reference.

VALUE	character string	–

This attribute is used to store data in the hidden element.

\<INPUT TYPE=password\> PASSWORD FIELD

N O T E S Must be defined within the HTML FORM element. Works exactly like a text input field, except that the characters entered by the user are obscured.

Attributes	*Values*	*Default*
NAME	character string	–

Specifies a name for the password field for object reference.

SIZE	positive integer	30

Specifies the width, in characters, of the password field.

VALUE	character string	–

The character string provides the initial text shown in the field, and sets the initial value of the *value* property of the object.

\<INPUT TYPE=radio\>   RADIO BUTTON

N O T E S Must be defined within the HTML FORM element. If each radio button in a group has the same name, only one of that group can be selected. In this case, they must be referred to using the *elements[]* array.

Attributes	*Values*	*Default*
CHECKED	–	not checked

When present, causes the radio button to be selected when the page loads.

NAME	character string	–

Specifies a name for the radio button for object reference.

VALUE	character string	–

The character string is not visible in the web page. Its value is assigned to the *value* property of the object.

Event Handlers:
onchange   (somewhat unreliable)

\<INPUT TYPE=reset\>   RESET BUTTON

N O T E S Must be defined within the HTML FORM element. Causes all elements of the form that contains it to revert to their original state.

Attributes	*Values*	*Default*
VALUE	character string	–

The character string provides the text on the button.

Event Handlers:
Has built-in event handler. Automatically calls the *reset()* method of the *form* object.

\<INPUT TYPE=submit\>   SUBMIT BUTTON

N O T E S Must be defined within the HTML FORM element. Used to initiate the submission of form data to the server. Clicking this button is equivalent to manually calling the *formname.submit()* method.

Attributes	_Values_	_Default_
VALUE	character string	–

The character string provides the text on the button.

**Event Handlers:**
onclick

<INPUT TYPE=text>   TEXT FIELD

> **N O T E S**   Must be defined within the HTML FORM element. Used for obtaining short textual input from the user.

Attributes	_Values_	_Default_
NAME	character string	–

Specifies a name for the text field for object reference.

SIZE	positive integer	30

Specifies the width, in characters, of the text field.

VALUE	character string	–

The character string provides the initial text shown in the field, and sets the initial value of the _value_ property of the object.

<LI>...</LI>   LIST ITEM

> **N O T E S**   Only used inside the UL (unordered list) and OL (ordered list) elements to define individual items for the list. The LI element can take the TYPE attribute. However, this attribute is most often used in the UL and OL elements themselves, and takes different values in each case. See those elements for descriptions.

<LINK>...</LINK>   Relationship to other documents

> **N O T E S**   Used only in this text to specify an external style sheet. It should be used in the following form:

<LINK HREF="sheetname.css" REL="STYLESHEET" TYPE="text/css">

where the only thing you need to change is the name of (or relative URL to) the style sheet. This name is the value of the HREF attribute.

\<MAP>...\</MAP>

NOTES

Defines the map to be used in an image map. The AREA elements used inside the MAP element provide the bounding coordinates of regions that, in turn, define ares of an image. The image in question references the MAP by its name as specified in the NAME attribute.

Attributes	*Values*	*Default*
NAME	name of map	–

Defines the name of the map so an image can use the map. This name is referenced with the USEMAP attribute of the IMG element.

\<OL>...\</OL>   ORDERED LIST

NOTES

Defines an ordered list whose items are ordered with numbers, letters, or Roman numerals. The actual list items must be defined within the OL element using the LI (list item) element.

Attributes	*Values*	*Default*
TYPE	1, A, a, l, i	1

Defines whether the list is indexed with regular numerals (integers), upper-case letters, lower-case letters, upper-case Roman numerals, or lower-case Roman numerals, respectively.

START	integers	1

Defines the starting index for the list. In other words, you can start indexing the list items with other than the first character of the sequence. For example, when used with TYPE="i", START=6 will cause the indexing to begin with the Roman numeral "vi".

\<OPTION>   OPTION FOR PULL-DOWN MENU

NOTES

Must be defined within the HTML SELECT element. The text appearing after an OPTION tag and before the next OPTION tag is marked up as the text for that option on the menu. Since no NAME attribute is provided, the different option objects of a menu must be referenced with the *options[]* array. Each menu OPTION does not count as an individual form element.

Attributes	*Values*	*Default*
SELECTED	–	not selected

When present in one of the OPTION tags, that option is automatically selected when the page loads.

VALUE	character string	–

The character string is not visible in the web page. Its value is assigned to the *value* property of the object.

<P>...</P>   PARAGRAPH

N O T E S
Can be used as a noncontainer element <P> or container element <P>...</P>. When used as <P>, it creates a line break followed by a blank line. When used as a container element <P>...</P>, it is useful to use the ALIGN attribute.

Attributes	*Values*	*Default*
ALIGN	center, left, right, justify	left

The center value causes no justification. The left and right options cause only left and right justification, respectively. The justify option provides full justification. Only the newest browser versions support full justification.

<PRE>...</PRE>   PRE-FORMATTED TEXT

N O T E S
Preserves extra spacing so that the enclosed text adheres to its pre-markup state. Extra spacing within this element could be created using the space bar rather than tabs. Usually browsers don't exactly preserve the format, but come pretty close.

<SELECT>...<SELECT>   PULL-DOWN MENU

N O T E S
Must be defined within the HTML FORM element. Contains the OPTION tags that create the menu options. Even if several OPTIONS are included, the menu counts as only one form element.

Attributes	*Values*	*Default*
NAME	character string	–

Specifies a name for the menu for object reference.

SIZE	positive integer	1

Can be used to make more than one menu option visible.

Event Handlers:
onchange

<SPAN>...</SPAN>

N O T E S
A generic element useful for marking a span of text for application of a style sheet definition.

Attributes	*Values*	*Default*
CLASS	class name	–

This attribute can be used with virtually any HTML element to call upon a specific style class.

<STYLE>...</STYLE>

NOTES
Used in the HEAD section to define style rules. The browser knows that it should treat the contents of the STYLE element as style sheet definitions. This element is not necessary if style rules are imported from an external style sheet using the LINK element. Some properties that can be imposed to fine-tune HTML elements within the STYLE element include the following. The list is nowhere near exhaustive, but provides adequate flexibility for the beginner.

Property	_Values_	_Example_
color	named color, hexadecimal color	red, #FF0000
font-size	pt	14pt
font-family	named font	Times
text-align	left, right, center, justify	
text-indent	inches, centimeters	.5in, 3cm
line-height	integer	1, 2, 3, 4, . . .
margin-left	inches, centimeters, pixels	2in, 1cm, 72
-right	" "	" "
-top	" "	" "
-bottom	" "	" "

<TEXTAREA>...</TEXTAREA>   TEXT AREA

NOTES
Must be defined within the HTML FORM element. The contents of the TEXTAREA container element are displayed as the initial text shown in the text area. Also, these contents are assigned to the _value_ property of the object. Use "\r" in a string to force text to begin on a new line within a text area.

Attributes	_Values_	_Default_
COLS	positive integer	27

Specifies the width, in characters, of the text area.

NAME	character string	–

Specifies a name for the menu for object reference.

ROWS	positive integer	7

Specifies the height, in character rows, of the text area

<TITLE>...</TITLE>

NOTES
Used in the HEAD section to define a title for the web page. This is different from the actual name of the HTML document. The document's TITLE is usually displayed at the top of the browser.

<TABLE>...</TABLE>

N O T E S Defines an HTML table. Actually, the TR and TD elements must be used inside the TABLE element to define the actual table cells. The attributes of the TABLE element affect properties of the entire table, whereas attributes of TR and TD can be used to alter properties of individual table rows or cells, respectively.

Attributes	*Values*	*Default*
ALIGN	left, right, center	left

The "left, right" values cause text to flow around the table. This is useful for small tables used to support text. You would rarely use this attribute in a table used for a page layout. The center attribute is not supported in some version-3 and earlier browsers. If the browser doesn't support center, the default is used.

BACKGROUND	URL (usually relative)	–

Not mentioned in the text because you would most likely set a background image for a table cell on the TD level, especially if the table is for page layout. However, this can be used to set a background image for an entire table.

BGCOLOR	color (named, hexadecimal)	same as page

Provides a background color for the entire table.

BORDER	pixels	0

Specifies the thickness of the border around the table and between cells of the table. When made thick, a three-dimensional border is created.

CELLPADDING	pixels	1

Creates space within table cells to provide a cushion between the cell's contents and border.

CELLSPACING	pixels	2

Creates space between table cells.

HEIGHT	pixels, %	minimum

Specifies the height of the table as rendered in the page. The default is to make the table just high enough to accommodate the contents of the table.

WIDTH	pixels, %	minimum

Specifies the width of the table as rendered in the page. The default is to make the table just wide enough to accommodate the contents of the table.

<TD>...</TD>   TABLE DATA

N O T E S Used within the TR element to define actual cells of the table. Each TD element defines a column of the table.

Attributes	*Values*	*Default*
ALIGN	left, right, center	left

Specifies how the contents of a cell are aligned horizontally within that cell.

BACKGROUND	URL (usually relative)	–

Specifies a background image for the table cell. This is unreliable in some version-3 and older browsers.

BGCOLOR	color (named, hexadecimal)	same as page

Provides a background color for the table cell.

COLSPAN	positive integer (0, 1, 2, 3, ...)	0

Specifies how many columns a given table cell spans. Spans cells to the right of the cell in which it is used.

HEIGHT	pixels, %	minimum

Specifies the height of a table cell. If not used, the height of the cell is determined by the contents of the cell. The entire row is adjusted to be the height of the highest cell of the row.

ROWSPAN	positive integer (0, 1, 2, 3, ...)	0

Specifies how many rows a given table cell spans. Spans cells below the cell in which it is used.

VALIGN	bottom, middle, top	middle

Specifies how the contents of a cell are aligned vertically within that cell.

WIDTH	pixels, %	minimum

Specifies the width of a table cell. If not used, the width of the cell is determined by the contents of the cell. The entire column is adjusted to be the width of the widest cell of the row.

<TH>...</TH>   TABLE HEADING

NOTES   Works just like TD except that textual content is rendered in bold. Takes the same attributes as TD. See above.

<TR>...</TR>   TABLE ROW

NOTES   Used within the TABLE element to define rows of the table. The actual cells of the table are created within the TR element using the TD element. While the attributes below are sometimes useful, controlling table properties at the TD level provides more flexibility.

Attributes	*Values*	*Default*
ALIGN	left, right, center	left

Specifies how the contents of a cell are aligned horizontally within that cell. When used in TR, applies to all the cells within the table row.

BGCOLOR   color (named, hexadecimal)   same as page

Provides a background color for the entire table row.

VALIGN   bottom, middle, top   middle

Specifies how the contents of a cell are aligned vertically within that cell. When used in TR, applies to all the cells within the table row.

\<UL\>...\</UL\>   UNORDERED LIST

NOTES

Defines an unordered list whose items are market with bullet symbols. UL basically defines a bullet list. The actual list items must be defined within the UL element using the LI (list item) element.

Attributes	*Values*	*Default*
TYPE	circle, disc, square	disc

Defines the symbol used to mark the list items. A disc is a solid circle. The square is not solid.

JAVASCRIPT OBJECTS

This appendix provides a quick reference for JavaScript objects and reserved words. This list is not exhaustive, but sticks to a common subset of JavaScript/Jscript that nearly any browser supports.

Array

NOTES New arrays are created with the *Array()* constructor. The constructor may take a positive integer as a parameter to set the length of the array, but this is not required.

Properties

length The length of the array. This property assumes the array to be standard.

Methods

join(character) Returns a string that consists of all the array values fused together. The character separates the values in the new string.

reverse() Reverses the indexing in the array.

Date

NOTES New date objects are created with the *Date()* constructor. For example,

var d=new Date();

document.write ("The month day is "+ d.getDate());

Methods

getDate() Returns the day of the month (1–31).
getDay() Returns the day of the week (1–7).
getHours() Returns the hours (0–23).
getMonth() Returns the month (1–12).
getSeconds() Returns the seconds (0–59).
getYear() Returns the year.

document

NOTES This object is a property of the *window* object, and is created automatically when a page is loaded. The only property that can be consistently changed in most browsers after the document is fully loaded is *bgColor*.

Properties

alinkColor   Contains the color of active links.

bgColor   Contains the color of the background.

fgColor   Contains the color of the text.

Form   See Form Object.

Image   See Image Object.

lastModified   Contains the date the document was last changed. (Unreliable.)

alinkColor   Contains the color of unvisited links.

referrer   Contains the URL of the page whose link caused the current document to be loaded.

vlinkColor   Contains the color of visited links.

Methods

write(str)   Writes a string to the HTML document.

elements[] array

NOTES This object is a property of the *form* object that contains it. When the document loads, an *elements[]* array is created to index all of the form's elements. The *elements[]* array is standard.

Properties   The properties are according to the type of form element.

button   name
value

checkbox   checked
name
value

radio button   checked
name
value

reset   name
value

select   name
options[]- See options[] object.
selectedIndex
value

text field	name
	value
text area	name
	value

Form

N O T E S This object is a property of the *document* object. When the document loads, a *forms[]* array is created to index all of the document's form objects. The *forms[]* array is standard.

Properties

elements[]   See elements object.

Methods

submit()   Submits form to a CGI program.

reset()   Resets a forms elements to their original states.

Global

N O T E S This object is not a property of any object, nor does it have to be referenced to call its methods. You simply call the methods by name.

Methods

isNaN(num)   Returns true if the number is actually a number. Otherwise, it returns false. For example, 34z is not a number.

parseFloat(str)   Returns the string converted to a floating-point (decimal) number.

parseInt(str,num)   Returns the string converted to an integer represented in the base given by the second argument. It may be used without the second argument. In that case, it defaults to returning a base-10 integer.

history

N O T E S This object is a property of the *window* object.

Properties

length   Contains a number corresponding to the number of documents that have previously been loaded into the window.

Methods

back()   Causes the same effect as hitting the back button on your browser.

forward()   Causes the same effect as hitting the forward button on your browser.

go(-num)   Takes a negative integer as a parameter, and causes the window to display a document back in the window's history list.

Image

NOTES This object is a property of the document object. An *images[]* array is automatically created to index all of the images that have been marked up with the HTML IMG tag. A background image is not indexed. The only property that can be consistently changed in most browsers after the document is fully loaded is *src*. Also, to preload images, a new image object can be constructed with the *Image()* constructor.

Properties

border   Contains the image's border setting in pixels.

height   Contains the image's height in pixels.

hspace   Contains the image's horizontal padding setting in pixels.

name   Can be set with the NAME attribute of the HTML IMG tag. Can be declared when a new image is constructed with Image().

src   Contains the image's source URL.

vspace   Contains the image's vertical padding setting in pixels.

width   Contains the image's width in pixels.

Math

NOTES If you know enough about mathematics to use many of the properties and methods listed below, you will know what they do. A new Math object does not have to be created to call upon the properties or methods.

Properties

E   Contains base of natural log.

PI   Contains the ratio of any circle's circumference to its diameter.

Methods

abs(num)   Returns the absolute value of its argument.

acos(num)   Returns the arc cosine of its argument. The argument is in radians.

asin(num)   Returns the arc sine of its argument. The argument is in radians.

atan(num)   Returns the arc tangent of its argument. The argument is in radians.

ceil(num)   Returns the least integer greater than its argument.

cos(num)   Returns the cosine of its argument. The argument is in radians.

exp(num)   Returns e to the power of its argument.

floor(num)   Returns greatest integer less than its argument.

log(num)   Returns log base *e* of its argument.

max(num1,num2)   Returns the greater of its two arguments.

min(num1,num2)   Returns the lesser of its two arguments.

pow(base,exponent)   Returns its first argument raised to the power of its second argument.

random()   Returns a randomly generated number between 0 and 1. Takes no argument.

round(num)   Returns its argument rounded to the nearest integer.

sin(num)   Returns the sine of its argument. The argument is in radians.

sqrt(num)   Returns the square root of its argument.

tan(num)   Returns the tangent of its argument. The argument is in radians.

navigator

N O T E S   This object has properties containing information about the browser that has loaded the web page. It is created automatically by the browser. For example, document.write ("Aha, so you use "+ navigator.platform +" computers.");

Properties

appName   Contains the browser's name.

appVersion   Contains the browser's version number.

platform   Contains the platform on which the browser is running.

plugins[]   A standard array that indexes the browser's plugins.

options[] array

N O T E S   This object is a property of a SELECT menu. It is standard array that indexes all of a pull-down menu's options. Each option has the following properties.

Properties

index   Contains a number corresponding to the particular index position that the option holds in the options[] array.

text   Contains the text string that appears on the menu for that option.

value   Can carry a hidden value for the option.

String

N O T E S   This object is created automatically for each string. It is not a property of another object.

Properties

length   Contains a number corresponding to the length of the string in characters (blank spaces count).

Methods

charAt(index)   Returns the character in the string at the specified index.

charCodeAt(index)   Returns the ASCII number for the character in the string at the specified index.

fromCharCodeAt(num)   Returns the ASCII character corresponding to the number.

indexOf(character)   Returns the first index at which the character is found. Returns -1 if the character is not found.

lastIndexOf(character)   Returns the last index at which the character is found. Returns -1 if the character is not found.

split(character)   Returns an array of substrings. Breaks the string up into substrings delimited by the character.

substring(index)   Returns the substring starting from the given index.

toLowerCase()   Returns the string, all in lower case.

toUpperCase()   Returns the string, all in upper case.

window

NOTES   This object is the parent object of the *document* object. When referring to properties of this object, it is not necessary to use the *window* object reference.

Properties

closed   Contains a Boolean value corresponding to whether or not the window is open.

document   See document object.

history   See history object.

location   Contains the URL of the document currently displayed in the window. Can be changed to cause a new document to be displayed.

name   Contains the name of the document currently displayed in the window. The name property is set by the second argument of the *open()* method. It is useful when you need to refer to more than one open window.

Methods

alert(str)   Displays an alert window containing the string argument as text.

clearInterval(name)   Clears a *setInterval()* call. To use this, the *name=setInterval()* call is assigned to a variable name. To clear an interval timer, send the name to this method.

clearTimeout(name)   Clears a *setTimeout()* call. To use this, the *name=setTimeout()* call is assigned to a variable name. To clear the timeout, send the name to this method.

close() Closes the current window. If the name of another open window is sent as an argument, this method closes that window.

confirm(str) Displays a confirm window containing the string argument as text.

open(url,name,"options") Opens a new window containing the document at the given URL. When more than one window is open, the name can be used to call methods from other open windows. The available options are given in Section 12.9.

prompt(str,str) Opens a new prompt window and returns the user input in the form of a string. The first argument contains instructions to appear in the prompt window. The second argument contains the default input, and is often left as the empty string.

setInterval(function,time) Causes the function to be repetitively called at regular time intervals. The time is given in milliseconds.

setTimeout(function,time) Causes the function to be called once, after a time delay. The time is given in milliseconds.

Javascript Reserved Words

(In alphabetical order.) These words cannot be used as variable or function names.

abstract	Boolean	break	byte
case	catch	char	class
const	continue	default	delete
do	double	else	extends
false	final	finally	float
for	function	goto	if
implements	import	in	instanceof
int	interface	long	native
new	null	package	private
protected	public	reset	return
short	static	super	switch
synchronized	this	throw	throws
transient	true	try	typeof
var	void	while	with

HEXADECIMAL COLOR REPRESENTATIONS

The normal numbers we use every day are in base 10. For example, each of the digits in the number 2364 represents a power of 10. The breakdown is as follows:

2	3	6	4
10^3	10^2	10^1	10^0
1000	100	10	1

The number is then calculated by

$$(2 \times 1000) + (3 \times 100) + (6 \times 10) + (4 \times 1)$$

Of course, we don't think about base-10 numbers in this degree of detail since we all grew up using them. Number systems that use other bases work in the same way. Two common bases associated with computers are binary (base 2) and hexadecimal (base 16). Computers basically function in binary. However, a convenient way for computers to represent colors is in hexadecimal (hex). Fortunately, for color purposes, two-digit hex numbers are sufficient.

You may well know that binary numbers use only two digits, namely 0 and 1. As we all know, base-10 numbers use the 10 digits 0–9. Keeping with this logic, base-16 hex numbers require 16 digits. For 10 of these digits, it is convenient to use 0–9, but then six more digits are required. For this purpose, the first six letters of the alphabet are employed, namely A-F. So each digit of a hex number is one of the digits

$$0, 1, 2, 3, 4, 5, 6, 7, 8, 9, A, B, C, D, E, F$$

Moreover, each digit represents a power of 16. So, for example, the two-digit hex number 4C has the following breakdown.

4	C
16^1	16^0
16	1

Using the fact that C represents 12, the conversion into base 10 is accomplished by

$$(4 \times 16) + (C \times 1) = (4 \times 16) + (12 \times 1) = 76$$

The smallest two-digit hex number is 00 and the largest is FF. By similar calculations into base 10, 00 = 0 and FF = 255. So, using their base-10 conversions, two-digit hex numbers fall in the base-10 range of 0–255. That's 256 possible two-digit hex numbers. Another way to see this is that there are 16 possibilities for each digit, making the total possibilities for two digits $16 \times 16 = 256$.

There are three color components to a hexadecimal representation. Each component is a two-digit hex number. For example, #2C45F2 breaks down as follows.

#	2C	45	F2
	red	green	blue

For this reason, six-digit hex colors are also called RGB colors. With this in mind, we focus back on each individual color. None of a color is given by 00, and a full saturation of a color is given by FF. That makes sense given that these are the smallest and largest two-digit hex numbers, respectively. Some different values of the red component of an RGB color are given below.

hex	*base 10*	*amount of red*	
00	0	none	(black)
33	51	little	(very dark red, almost black)
66	102	some	(dark red)
99	153	more	(medium red)
CC	204	a lot	(medium bright red)
FF	255	full saturation	(bright red)

The descriptions (which we contrived) of the different red saturations sound like designations for ordering steak, but better terminology is hard to come by. If you remember that the absence of all color is black, the designations toward the low-saturation end make some sense.

Each of the other two color components (G and B) works similarly. They range from very dark shades at low saturations to very bright shades at high saturations. This should seem pretty clear, but when you put all three colors together to create an RGB color, it is a little less straightforward. For starters, #FFFFFF, a full saturation of each color, represents white. That might seem strange, but an easy way to remember this is the fact that sunlight (or white light) actually contains a full saturation of all colors. A prism easily demonstrates this.

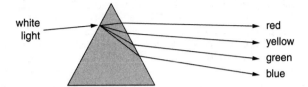

Black, the absence of all color, is given by the RGB number #000000. The intermediate RGB colors are somewhat tricky to predict, but as a general rule, the less saturation of each RGB component, the darker the color. That makes sense because, as you decrease the saturation of each color, you are getting closer to the state of the absence of color—black.

For simplicity in characterizing intermediate RGB colors, we stick to the web-safe colors. Web-safe colors use only the values 00, 33, 66, 99, CC, FF for each of the RGB components. Indeed, when we characterized red above, we used only the web-safe values. That's only six saturation levels for each component. So, figuring in six possibilities for each of R, G and B, that makes the number of web safe colors $6 \times 6 \times 6 = 216$. That pales in comparison to the total number of hexadecimal RGB colors, which is $256 \times 256 \times 256 = 16,777,216$.

Just to give some indications of how the RGB components combine to form intermediate colors, we supply some examples. However, note that these examples are for illustrative purposes only. In practice, you needn't learn how to predict RGB colors. There are several freeware RGB color pickers referenced in the web site. Nonetheless, these examples will help you understand the nature of RGB hex colors.

Equal saturations of each component give greys:

#333333	very dark grey, almost black
#666666	medium grey
#CCCCCC	light grey

If you step up one of the components just a little over the others, you get a subdued version of that color:

#336633	dark subtle green
#99CC99	light subtle green

If you step up one color a lot over the others, you get much brighter shades:

#33FF33	bright green
#99FF99	light bright green

Creating other familiar colors follows the familiar rules. For example, red and blue make purple:

#660066	medium purple
#FF00FF	bright purple

NOTES

You may be wondering why red, green, and blue are used for colors in computer monitors (and even TV screens), rather than the primary colors (red, yellow, and blue) you learned in grade school. While the RYB colors you learned in school are convenient for mixing paint and the like, RGB is more in tune with our eyes. The light receptors in our eyes, called cones, have three varieties. Each of the three varieties of cones has its peak sensitivity near to one of the wavelengths of red, green, or blue light. Thus, each component of an RGB color is roughly in tune with one of the cone types in our eyes. Simply put, RGB is more in tune with the way our eyes process light than RYB. But computer monitors and TV screens are not perfectly in tune with our eyes. The phosphors on the screen used to create RGB are not exactly in tune with the peak sensitivities of our RGB cones. In other words, you are never going to see the sunset on TV quite as you will in nature.

ANSWERS TO SELECTED REVIEW QUESTIONS

CHAPTER 10

10.15.7

   1. var cool_word;

   2. cool_word="lurk"

   3. Document.write("The cool word of the day is ");

   4. Document.write("cool_word");

There are four errors. The statement in line 2 should be terminated with a semicolon. Function names are case-sensitive. The capital Ds in lines 3 and 4 should be lower-case. Line 4 should be

document.write(cool_word);

otherwise the string "cool_word" would be written to the document rather than the contents of the variable *cool_word*.

10.15.8

   1. Var num1;

   2. num1="15";

   3. num1=num1*"2"

There are four errors. In line 1, var should not be capitalized. In lines 2 and 3, the values 15 and 2 are clearly intended for use in numerical calculations, and should not be given as strings with quotes. The statement in line 3 should be terminated with a semicolon.

10.15.9

   1. var user-name;

   2. user-name=prompt("Please enter your name");

   3. document.write(Hello);

   4. document.write(user-name);

There are three errors. The variable name *user-name* is not a valid variable name. It should be something like *user_name* or simply *name*. In line 2, the *prompt()* function requires two arguments. Line 3 should be

document.write("Hello ");

Otherwise the interpreter looks for a variable named *Hello,* and there is none.

10.13.10   The output is

2020

10.13.11   The output is

9
2

10.13.12   The output is

Bertis **age**years old.

11.9.1   Start from the inside out.

a=true&&true

a=true

b=!false||false

b=true||false

b=true

c=false&&true

c=false

d=true||false

d=true

e=true&&!false

e=true&&true

e=true

11.9.2   Start from the inside out.

a=(false==true)||false)

a=false||false

a=false

b=false&true

b=false

c=true||false||false

c=true

(Given a string of several ORs, the whole expression is true as long as at least one of the conditions is true. If you stop and think about that, it makes sense.)

11.9.4   One solution:

```
if((isNan(x)==true)||(x<0)){
give alert. . . reprompt
}
```

Another solution:

```
if((isNan(x))||(x<0)){
    give alert. . . reprompt
}
```

11.9.5   One solution:

```
if((isNan(x)==true)||(x<1)||(x>10)){
    give alert. . . reprompt
}
```

Another solution:

```
if((isNan(x))||(x<1)||(x>10)){
    give alert. . . reprompt
}
```

11.9.7   First, the "if" condition is wrong. It is *always* going to be false. The and (&&) should be changed to an or (||).

Second, the second prompt statement should be inside the "if" statement. The way it is written, the user will *always* be prompted a second time, even if correct information is entered initially.

11.9.8

```
num=prompt("Enter a positive number."," ");
if((isNan(x))||(x<0)){
    alert(num+" is not valid input, try again");
    num=prompt("Enter a positive number this time, pal."," ");
}
num=parseFloat(num);
```

11.9.9

1. x=2;
2. y=3;
3. if (x<=y)
4.   document.write(I told you so);
5. }
6. if (y==x) {
7.   document.write(I told you so)
8. };

In line 3, the *if* statement has no beginning {. The *document.write( )* statements have no quotes inside for the string. In line 7, the statement is not terminated with a semicolon. In line 8, the *if* statement should not be terminated with a semicolon.

11.9.10   The output is

$$3$$
$$3$$
$$3$$

11.9.11   The output is

$$30$$
$$15$$
$$10$$
$$15$$

12.10.3   This explanation is actually more detailed than the question requires. The hierarchy actually goes four deep. The primitive Boolean properties (and some probable values) are *animal.biped==false, animal.wildebeest.head.brain.large==false,* and *animal.wildebeest.legs.hooved==true*. The rest of the primitive properties are numeric in nature except *animal.wildebeest.head.eyes.color,* which would probably contain "brown". A suitable method for the wildebeest object might be *animal.wildebeest. crocLunch( ),* which would no doubt substantially alter the values stored in the *wildebeest* properties, drastically changing the state of the *wildebeest* object.

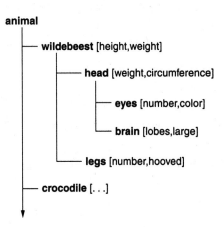

12.10.10   In line 1, New should not be capitalized. Also in line 1, the constructor Object should be *Object( )*. In line 2, "heavy" should not be assigned to the object. *rock* is an object not a primitive. What would be appropriate is rock.weight="heavy".

1. var rock=New Object;
2. rock="heavy";

12.10.11   In line 2, *computer.memory* is declared as a new object using *var*. Once the object computer is declared in line 1, it requires only

$$computer.memory=new\ Object();$$

to set up *memory* as an object property of *computer*. Line 2 would attempt to set up an entirely new object named *computer.memory,* which would be completely unassociated with the *computer* object, rather than one of its properties. In such a case, the name *computer.memory* would actually violate the rules for naming variables. *Computer_memory* would work, but this new object would have nothing to do with *computer*.

In line 5, you can't assign a property to *computer.memory.hardDrive*. You can see from line 4 that *hardDrive* is a primitive rather than an object. In line 6, the full object reference *computer.memory.ram* is required.

1. var computer=new Object();
2. var computer.memory=new Object();
3. computer.memory.ram=128;
4. computer.memory.hardDrive="10 gig";
5. computer.memory.hardDrive.full=false;
6. document.write("You have "+memory.ram+" of random access memory");

13.9.2   The reset button has a built-in event handler that clears the form. The function it calls is the *document.formname.reset()* method.

13.9.8   In lines 1 and 5, the function should be *process()*. In line 3, you have to supply reference to the form element as well: *elementname.value*. After line 4, there needs to be another } to end the function. The first } closes the *with* statement. Remember, the fact that the bracket in line 4 in not indented makes no difference to the computer.

1. function process{
2.   with(document.formname){
3.   value=3;
4. }
5. <INPUT TYPE=button NAME=Button VALUE="CLICK ME" onclick="process">

14.10.1   document.formx.elements[8].value

14.10.2   document.formx.elements[3].options[2].value

14.10.5   If the first option is not chosen, it doesn't matter if the second is chosen or not:

> if (cheap option is chosen)
>   give 'em cheap
> else
>   give 'em expensive

14.10.7

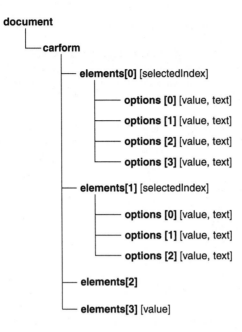

document
└── **carform**
    ├── **elements[0]** [selectedIndex]
    │   ├── **options [0]** [value, text]
    │   ├── **options [1]** [value, text]
    │   ├── **options [2]** [value, text]
    │   └── **options [3]** [value, text]
    ├── **elements[1]** [selectedIndex]
    │   ├── **options [0]** [value, text]
    │   ├── **options [1]** [value, text]
    │   └── **options [2]** [value, text]
    ├── **elements[2]**
    └── **elements[3]** [value]

14.10.10   In line 1, the *selectedIndex* property should have a capital I. The *options[]* array is a property of the menu, not a property of the form. The correct reference in line 2 is price=document. formname.menuname.options[k].value;

1. k=document.formname.menuname.selectedindex;

2. price=document.formname.options[k].value;

14.10.11

> if(none are selected)
>   alert user
> else
>   process form

15.9.1
a) 10, 15, 20, 25, 30, 35, 40
b) 25, 23, 21, 19, 17
c) Infinite loop—the loop condition never becomes false.
d) No output—the loop never executes since the loop condition is initially false. The computer would pass right over this loop.

15.9.2
a) 12
b) 20, 8
c) 28

15.9.3

   a) 18, 5

   b) 18, 4

   c) 5, 8

15.9.4   The first i value added to the sum is $i = 2$.

```
for (i=2  ;  i<=10  ;  i=i+1){
    sum=sum+i;
}
```

15.9.5   The first x value added to the total is $x = 100$.

```
x=100;
while (x>0){
    total=total+x;
    x=x-10;
}
```

Notice that the following does *not* do the same thing.

```
while (x>0){
    x=x-10;
    total=total+x;
}
```

15.9.10   Both errors are in the first line. The "for" statement uses semicolons, rather than commas. Also, the beginning bracket for the loop body has been omitted.

16.10.1   Since the arrays are to be standard, the indexing starts with 0.

```
var countries=new Array();
countries[0]="Germany";
countries[1]="France";
countries[2]="England";
countries[3]="Spain";

var capitals=new Array();
capitals[0]="Berlin";
capitals[1]="Paris";
capitals[2]="London";
capitals[3]="Madrid";
```

16.10.2   Since the length property is to be used in the loop condition, we must define the array length when we declare it. When defining the length of an array, the array is assumed to be standard. Declaring the array to be of length 51 creates indices 0–50. However, we fill only the even indices, starting with 2.

```
var numbers=new Array(51);
for(i=2 ; i<=(numbers.length-1) ; i=i+2){
    numbers[i]=Math.random();
}
```

Also, the loop condition (i<numbers.length) suffices.

16.10.4   There is no need to create an array to preload one image. We just create one *image* object:

```
var img=new image();
img.src="animage.gif";

function replace(){
    document.images[2].src=img.src;
}
```

16.10.8

```
setInterval("change()", 5500);
```

16.10.9   Since the array is standard, indices 0–9 are used:

```
if(current<9){
    current=current+1;
}
else{
    current=0;
}
```

16.10.10   In line 1, the array constructor should be *Array()*. In line 2, the property *numbers.length* contains 0, since the array has no properties. Hence, the loop never executes. One would have to specify *new Array(10),* for example.

1. var numbers=new array();
2. for (i=1 ; i<numbers.length ; i=i+1){
3.   numbers[i]=Math.random();
   }

16.10.11   Both errors are in line 2. *Array(10)* creates a standard array with indices 0–9. The loop starts with i=1, which fails to put a random number in *numbers[0]*. The loop ends with i=10, but the highest index of the array is only to be 9.

1. var numbers=new Array(10);
2. for (i=1 ; i<=10 ; i=i+1){
3.   numbers[i]=Math.random();
   }

16.10.12.   In line 3, each position in the *images[ ]* array should be a *new Image()*, rather than simply a new generic object. In lines 4–6, one must assign the image URL to the *src* properties of image objects. The following would store the image URLs as primitive strings, and would not preload the images.

1. var images=new Array();

2. for (i=0 ; i<=2 ; i=i+1){

3.   images[i]=new Object();
   }

4.   images[0]="img1.gif ";

5.   images[1]="img2.gif ";

6.   images[2]="img3.gif ";

17.10.3

```
function alt(char1,char2){
  for(i=1 ;  i<=25 ;  i=i+1){
     document.write(char1+char2)
  }
}
```

Call the function.

```
alt("#", "$");
```

17.10.4

```
function avg(num1,num2){
  var avg;
  avg=(num1+num2)/2;
  return avg;
}
```

Another possibility:

```
function avg(num1,num2){
  return ((num1+num2)/2);
}
```

Call the function:

```
x=avg (10, 15);
```

17.10.8   Remember, just as with standard arrays, the character indexing begins at 0.

w contains 14

x contains " "   a blank space string

y contains 2

w contains 11

17.10.9

```
function ageOK(num){
  if((isNaN(num)) || (num<18)||(num>110)){
    return false;
  }
  else{
    return true;
  }
}
```

17.10.10

```
function emailOK(str){
  if((str.length<4) || (str.indexOf("@")==-1)){
    return false;
  }
  else{
    return true;
  }
}
```

INDEX

~, 15
#, 70, 101, 104
.. /, 93
\r (carriage return in text area), 267

A tag (*see* anchor)
absolute link/URL, 90, 96, 115
ACTION attribute of FORM, 373
Active Server Pages (ASP), 183
ActiveX, 183
alert(), 225
alignment
  paragraph, 68
anchor, 88
  attributes of, 107
  HREF (links), 88
  named (bookmark), 100
animated GIF, 125
anonymous ftp, 30, 114
applet (JAVA), 182
application, 20
  ftp, 33
  HTML editor, 45, 136
  telnet, 41
  text editor (Notepad, Simple
    Text), 21, 45
argument of function, 204
arithmetic operations, 195
ARPANET, 3
array, 278
  index, 279
  length property, 322
  parallel, 318
  searching, 331
  standard, 321
ASCII, 21, 36, 124
assignment operator for variables,
  199
attributes
  for A element, 88, 100, 107
  for BODY element, 69, 85

for FONT element, 72, 85
for FRAME element, 161, 170
for FRAMESET element, 160,
  170
for HR element, 62, 84
for IMG element, 132
for P element, 68, 84
for TABLE element, 142, 154
for TD/TR elements, 144, 154
in general, 66
audio, 74
automatic (in ftp application), 124

B (bold) tag, 51
backbone, 2
background
  color of page, 70, 247
  color of table, 144
  color of table cell, 145
  image, 125, 145
bandwidth, 2
BLOCKQUOTE tag, 56
BODY tag, 47
  attributes of, 69, 85, 125
bookmark (*see* named anchor)
Boolean
  expression, 213
  literal, 213
  operator, 214
  return function, 354
BR tag, 50
browser
  version (current), 45
browser-safe colors, 70
button
  generic, 175, 184, 256
  reset, 175, 184, 259
  submit, 372

cable modem, 6
cables

conventional copper, 1
  fiber optic, 2
cache (browser cache), 27,
  117, 325
carriage return in text area (\r),
  267
cascading style sheet (*see* CSS)
case
  insensitive, 49
  sensitive, 11, 73, 95, 123, 196,
    205, 358
CGI, 178, 370
checkbox, 175, 184, 273
checked property
  of checkboxes, 273
  of radio buttons, 278
CLASS attribute (for CSS), 77
client, 178
  processing on, 178
client-server model, 178, 370
color
  background, 70
  browser-safe, 70
  hexadecimal (*see* appendix C), 70
  named, 70
  RGB (*see* appendix C), 70
  web-safe, 70
command line (for telnet), 42
comment symbols for HTML, 76,
  190
common gateway interface (*see*
  CGI)
compiled language, 180
concatenate, 198, 220
confirm(), 250
constructor function
  for array, 318
  for generic object, 240
  for image object, 325
container element (HTML), 49, 67
  nested, 49

counter, 276
  in for loop, 297
  in while loop, 305
CSS, 71, 76
  external style sheet, 81
  LINK element, 82
  style properties, 78, 86
cycling image display, 329

database, 178
debug, 205
declaring variable, 192
default,
  file (for directory), 39
  settings, 61
depreciated HTML element, 52
dimensions (of image), 112
directory
  root of domain, 13
  public, 31, 39
DNS, 12
DOM (Document Object Model), 246, 248, 258
document object, 246
document.write(), 186
domain, 12
  name, 11
  name server (DNS), 12
  suffix, 15
DSL, 6
download, 23, 33
  images (how to), 114

element (HTML), 49
  container, 49
  non-container, 52, 67
elements[] array, 279
e-mail (see mailto protocol)
encryption, 370
end tag, 49
ENIAC, 3
environment variables, 371
errors
  frames page not working, 171
  HTML syntax, 67
  images not working right, 132
  Javascript syntax, 203, 205
  link not working, 106
  logic error in JavaScript, 205

site works locally but not on server, 107
  user error in JavaScript, 205
event, 256
event handler, 256
  onchange, 286
  onclick, 256
  onload, 326
  onmouseover, 348
  onmouseout, 348
expression
  arithmetic, 199
  Boolean, 213
external
  scripts, 368
  style sheet, 81

factorial, 298, 351
Fetch, 33
file protocol, 9, 23, 47
file size, 113
file suffix, 21
freeware, 29
font
  face, 72
  size, 72
FONT tag, 71
  attributes of, 72, 85
fragment identifier, 101
frames
  nested, 165
  targeting, 163
FRAME element, 159
  attributes of, 161, 170
FRAMESET tag, 158
  attributes of, 160, 170
for loop, 294
FORM tag, 176
form elements, 175
  organized with HTML table, 264
form object, 246, 259
  value property, 259
ftp, 9, 28
  anonymous, 30, 114
  get, 35
  non-anonymous, 34
  put, 35
  to web server, 33, 43, 97
function, 204
  argument of, 204

parameters, 342, 349
procedure, 204, 340
return statement, 350
self-defined, 257, 340, 349
value, 204, 349

get (ftp transaction), 35
GET transaction with server, 373
GIF image, 111
  animated, 125
  transparent, 124
global variable, 262, 326
graphic (see image)
graphic editor, 112, 125

H1-H6 (heading) tags, 55
HEAD tag, 47
header element, 55
hexadecimal color (see appendix C), 70
hidden form elements, 374
hierarchical web site, 98
hierarchy
  object, 244
history object, 246
horizontal rule (see HR tag)
host (Internet), 6
HR (horizontal rule) tag, 53
  attributes of, 62, 85
HREF anchor, 89
HTML, 22, 46
  attributes, 62
  document structure, 46
  editor, 45, 136
  element, 49
  tag, 46
http, 9, 25
hypertext, 9
  markup language(HTML), 22, 46
  reference (HREF), 89
  transfer protocol (http), 9
hyperlink, 25

I (italic) tag, 51
if...else statement, 221
if statement, 216
image
  animated, 125
  background, 125

cycling display, 329
dimensions, 112
display randomly selected, 328
download (how to), 114
file, 112
GIF/JPEG, 112
links, 121
maps, 127
preloading, 325, 337, 347
rollovers, 347
size, 113, 116
thumbnail, 122
transparent, 124
Image() constructor function, 325
Images[] array, 323
image object, 323
IMG tag, 115
attributes of, 115, 132
import
script, 368
style sheet, 81
index
file, 39, 94
of array, 279
of loop, 294
infinite loop, 297, 308
initialize variable, 192
inner loop, 309
INPUT tag, 176, 184, 366, 375
Internet, 2
host, 6
service provider, 6
interpreted language, 180
interpreter (JavaScript), 189
InterNIC, 11
intranet, 4
IP address, 5
isNaN() function (is Not a Number),
225

J++, 183
JScript, 183
JAVA, 181
JPEG image, 111
justify text (left,right,full),
52, 69

length
property of array, 322
property of String object, 356

line break
in web page (*see* BR tag)
in text area (*see* carriage return)
linear web site, 98
LINK element, 82
link (*see* anchor), 25, 71
absolute, 90
active, 71
ftp, 29
image, 121
local, 92
mailto, 106
navigational, 92, 98
not working, 106
relative, 91
targeting to frame, 161
visited, 71, 89
literals
Boolean, 213
numeric, 196
string, 196
list
ordered, 139
unordered, 137
local
link, 92
network, 4
variable, 262, 343
logic
error in Javascript, 205
operator, 215
top-down, 193
log on, 41
loop, 294
condition, 295
counter, 297, 305
for loop, 294
index, 194
infinite, 297, 308
nested, 309
while loop, 304

Macintosh, 8, 20
mailto
protocol, 9, 105
link, 105
Math object, 252
methods (of objects), 249
modular programming approach,
355

named
address, 10
anchor (bookmark), 100
anchor in other documents, 104
color, 70
NaN (Not a Number), 206, 225
navigation bar, 149
navigational links, 92, 98
fixed, 168
pseudo-fixed, 168
nested
container elements, 49
frames, 165
lists, 137
loops, 309
quotes, 346
tables, 148
network, 5
news protocol, 9
non-anonymous ftp, 34
non-container element (HTML),
52, 67
Notepad, 21, 45
NSFNET, 3
number
literal, 196
floating-point, 197
integer, 197

Object() constructor function, 240
objects, 183
hierarchy, 244
in real life, 239
Javascript objects, 240
methods, 249
parent of, 244
properties, 240
object oriented programming, 183
OL tag, 139
onchange event handler, 286
onclick event handler, 256
onload event handler, 326
onmouseover event handler, 348
onmouseout event handler, 348
open() (window), 252, 345
operating system, 8, 20
LINUX, 8
Mac OS, 8, 20
Windows, 8, 20
UNIX, 8

operator
  arithmetic, 195
  Boolean, 214
  concatenation, 198, 220
  logical, 215
  shortcut for arithmetic, 299
  variable assignment, 199
options[] array of pull-down menu,
  283
ordered list, 139
outer loop, 309

P (paragraph) tag, 53
  attributes of, 68, 85
pagemark (*see* named anchor)
parallel array, 318
PC, 8, 20
packet, 7
parameter
  in self-defined procedure
    function, 342
parent window, 165
parse, 198, 200
parse Float(), 200
password, 308, 365
  form element, 366
PERL, 178, 365
pixel, 63, 113
platform, 20
  dependent, 20, 181
  independent, 21, 180
pop-up menu (*see* pull-down menu)
portable code, 178, 365
portability (of web site), 96
POST transaction with server, 374
PRE (pre-formatted text) tag, 56
preloading images, 325, 337, 347
primitive, 241
procedure function, 204
  self defined, 340
  self defined with parameters, 342
prompt(), 191, 307
protocol, 5
  file (local), 9, 23, 47
  file transfer (ftp), 9, 28, 33
  hypertext transfer (http), 9, 23
  mailto, 9, 105
  news, 9
  telnet, 9, 41
  TCP/IP, 5

WWW, 9
public directory (on server), 31,
  39
pull-down menu, 175, 184, 283
put (ftp transaction), 35

QUERY-STRING environment
  variable, 371
query string, 180, 198, 372
quotes nested, 346

radio button, 175, 184
random numbers (generating), 267,
  302, 328
randomly selected image display,
  328
raw data, 124
relative URL, 91, 96, 115
resolution, 64
return statement, 350
RGB color (*see* appendix C), 70
rollovers for images, 347
root directory (of domain), 13
router, 7, 12

scanner, 114
screen shot, 114
searching arrays, 331
security, 365
selectedIndex property of pull-down
  menu, 284
SCRIPT tag, 186
SELECT tag, 177, 184
self (frame), 164
self-defined functions
  procedure functions, 340
  using parameters, 342, 349
  value functions, 349
server, 2, 12
  accounts, 14, 33
  database on, 179
  processing on, 178
  submit data to, 373
service provider, 6, 31
setInterval() function, 329
shareware, 29
shortcut operators for arithmetic,
  299
Simple Text, 21, 45
spaces

in font names, 73
in HTML document, 48
in HTML tags, 67
SPAN tag, 77
spanning in tables, 149
src property of images[] array, 324
SRC (source attribute), 115, 159,
  368
standard array, 321
start tag, 49
statements (JavaScript), 203
status bar, 28, 89
string
  concatenate, 198, 220
  equality of, 215
  literal, 196
  object, 356
style sheet (*see* CSS)
STYLE tag, 76
submit button, 372
submit() method, 373
suffix
  domain, 15
  file, 21, 37, 46
  for image files, 111
syntax, 203
  error in JavaScript, 205

TABLE tag, 141
  attributes of, 142, 154
targeting links to frames, 163
TD tag (table data), 141
  attributes of, 142, 154
TR tag (table row), 141, 154
  attributes of, 142
tables, 141
  borderless for page layout, 146
  organizing forms with, 164
  spanning rows and columns, 1492
tag (HTML), 46
  end, 49
  start, 49
TCP/IP protocol, 5
telnet protocol, 9, 41
TEXTAREA tag, 177, 184, 259
text area, 175, 184, 259
text field, 175, 184, 259
text property of pull-down menu,
  183
thumbnail, 122

tilde (~), 15
tiling (of background image), 126
time control, 329
TITLE tag, 47
top-down logic, 193
transparent GIF, 124

UL tag, 138
Uniform Resource Locator (URL), 8
unordered list, 137
upload, 33, 43
URL, 8, 26
   absolute, 90, 96, 115
   case sensitive, 95
   in link, 89
   relative, 91, 96, 115
user error in JavaScript, 205
user name, 14

value function, 204, 349
   return statement, 350
value property
   of checkbox, 276
   of pull-down menu, 283

of radio button, 279
of text field and textarea, 260
variable, 191
   assignment, 199
   Boolean, 213
   declaring, 192
   global, 262, 326
   initializing, 192
   local, 262, 343
   numeric, 196
   primitive, 241
   rules for names, 195
   string, 196
verification
   JavaScript weaknesses, 367
   indefinite with while loop, 307
   of input from text field using
      alert(), 265
   of prompted input using alert(),
      225
   of selection in pull-down menu,
      287
   using Boolean return functions, 354
   using String object, 356

video, 174
virus, 28, 30

web-safe colors, 70
web site, 91
   hierarchal, 98
   linear, 98
   portability, 96
   works locally but not on server,
      107
ws_ftp le, 33
WWW, 7
   protocol, 9
while loop, 304
window
   object, 245, 345
   object methods, 250
   parent, 165
with statement, 264
World Wide Web, 7
wrap-around
   in JavaScript Statement,
     210, 221
   text in web page, 53